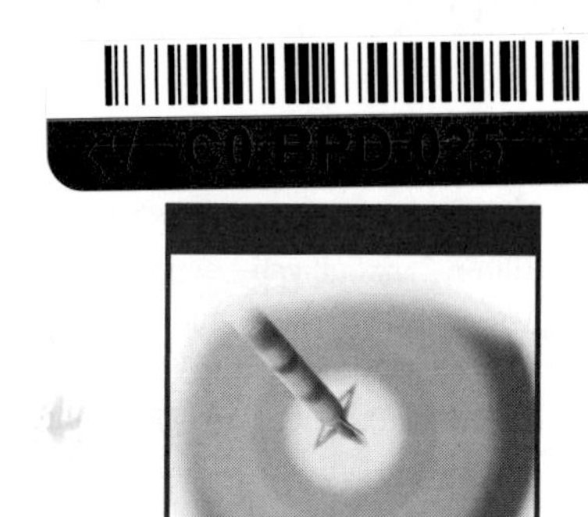

One-to-One Web Marketing, Second Edition:

Build a Relationship Marketing Strategy One Customer at a Time

Cliff Allen
Deborah Kania
Beth Yaeckel

With a Foreword by Christopher Locke

Wiley Computer Publishing

John Wiley & Sons, Inc.

NEW YORK • CHICHESTER • WEINHEIM • BRISBANE • SINGAPORE • TORONTO

Publisher: Robert Ipsen
Editor: Cary Sullivan
Assistant Editor: Christina Berry
Managing Editor: Marnie Wielage
Electronic Products, Associate Editor: Brian Snapp
Text Design & Composition: Pronto Design and Production, Inc.

This book is printed on acid-free paper.♾

Published by John Wiley & Sons, Inc.

Published simultaneously in Canada.

Library of Congress Cataloging-in-Publication Data:
Allen, Cliff, 1948-
One-to-One Web Marketing : build a relationship marketing strategy one customer at a time / Cliff Allen, Deborah Kania, Beth Yaeckel.—2nd ed
p. cm.
"Wiley computer publishing".
Previously published as: Internet world guide to one-to-one Web marketing. New York: Wiley Computer Pub., c1998.
Includes index.
ISBN 0-471-40400-4 (pbk. : alk. paper)
1. Internet marketing. 2. Market segmentation. 3. Web sites–Design. 4. Internet advertising. I. Kania, Deborah, 1963- II. Yaeckel, Beth. III. Allen, Cliff, 1948-Internet world guide to one-to-one Web marketing. IV. Title.

HF5415.1265 A419 2001
658.8'4—dc21 00-068488

Printed in the United States of America.

10 9 8 7 6 5 4 3 2 1

Contents

Foreword

Markets are becoming increasingly fragmented as the result of global competition. As more companies vie for niche market positions, they spin out a broader array of product and service offerings. The Web, with its relatively low barriers to entry, has accelerated this competition by orders of magnitude. The wide availability of online information resources has also made potential customers far more aware of their options than did broadcast media, as well as greatly raised their expectations.

Both increased choice and greater knowledge have made traditional advertising much less effective online than it was in previous media. Banner ads—an interesting novelty not many years ago—are largely ignored today unless they are closely linked to the interests of a specific Web audience. Unlike those of TV viewers, these interests can have an extremely narrow focus. On the Internet, people often gravitate toward sites that provide social interaction organized around highly specific concerns.

The first corporate efforts to capitalize on these network dynamics sought to use conventional demographic segmentation and targeting techniques that were first developed for offline advertising. However, such approaches do not port well to the Internet. First, they rely on historical customer behavior data, which is often missing or undeveloped online. Second, the new communities of interest now forming online are rarely segments that have broken off from larger pre-existing markets. Instead, they represent entirely new micromarkets that are emerging from the Web bottom-up.

Because these communities tend to be small—at least in their present germinal phase—they are also more intimate. Because they enable members to interact directly with one another via e-mail and discussion boards, people often know each other by name. Distinct personalities come to light. The group even begins to form consensus opinions and values. The medium of exchange in such communities is not money. It is conversation.

When companies that have been used to broadcast and direct marketing encounter such an audience, the mismatch is usually glaring. Corporations are nearly always more interested in dictating commands than in listening to the interests of their markets. They therefore continue to spew the same kind of humorless and homogenized key messages at Web communities that they've been broadcasting to television audiences for decades. Such marketing was always intrusive and annoying. Online, it is not only ineffective, it creates active hostility. Imagine someone trying to do an antiperspirant ad at an otherwise congenial cocktail party.

To connect with these new micromarkets, companies need to take an altogether different approach—not just tailoring information content and product presentation to the interests of specific groups, but also entering into the spirit and substance of their social exchange. Paradoxically, to market effectively on the Web, companies and the people who represent them are going to have to drop their obsessive focus on marketing—and join the conversation.

But that alone is not enough. The companies that will be most successful in working with networked micromarkets will be those that not only connect to these markets, but that also help connect the members of such markets to each other. Only by facilitating genuine community—and the kind of convivial discourse that sustains it—will companies win back the credibility that has become a non-negotiable prerequisite for conducting business online.

The importance of companies communicating directly with individuals is the essence of this book about one-to-one Web marketing.

Christopher Locke
Co-author, *The Cluetrain Manifesto*
Boulder, Colorado
November, 2000

Acknowledgments

Many people have played a role in advancing the concept of one-to-one Web marketing. Early marketing leaders such as Regis McKenna and Geoffrey Moore introduced many people to the need to develop relationships with customers. Don Peppers and Martha Rogers took the concept of relationships to the next level with the term *one-to-one marketing*.

In addition to being inspired by these leaders, friends and family have supported us with the love, support, encouragement, and patience that made this book possible. The individuals who deserve special recognition are Carolyn Allen, Chris Allen, and Jeff Anderson.

Introduction

The Web has brought tremendous change to the way companies market their products and services to individuals. But one thing that has not changed over the years is that individuals like to be treated as individuals.

Web marketers face many challenges in today's competitive environment, and one-to-one Web marketing can help overcome these challenges by helping you learn the needs of each person and providing the information they need to buy the products that meet those needs.

There are many benefits that result from applying one-to-one Web marketing techniques. Initially, marketers use one-to-one marketing to build relationships that bring Web visitors back over and over again. As Web traffic grows, marketers use one-to-one marketing again to generate repeat sales to loyal and profitable customers for the long-term.

We have designed this book to help you sort through the wide array of Web technologies that are available for building relationships. You will learn how to create a loyal user base and gain a competitive advantage by understanding—and meeting—the needs of individuals who come to your Web site or receive your e-mail messages.

You will learn how one-to-one Web marketing can make a dramatic difference in your success in using the Internet to create loyal customers.

Along the way, you'll see how others are successfully using one-to-one techniques. You'll see how a college uses personalization to touch the lives of prospective applicants and students. You'll see how an online travel company helps customers find the best values. And, you'll see how a content site uses data analysis techniques to learn about the needs of their audience.

Plus, we've included hundreds of Web resources, such as the top vendors and key information sources, to make it easier for you to get started applying one-to-one. In addition, the companion CD-ROM and Web site provide checklists, templates, and databases to help you begin applying one-to-one marketing after reading each chapter.

How This Book Is Organized

We've arranged the chapters in the order that will help a marketer take a Web site from initial relationship building to fully integrating one-to-one marketing across the entire enterprise.

For instance, if you are not yet using personalization, e-mail marketing, and targeted advertising, then you will want to explore the first few chapters. If your site already uses these techniques, then you will want to move quickly through the first few chapters and concentrate more on the chapters dealing with community, data mining, and customer relationship management.

Chapter 1: One-to-One Web Marketing Overview

In Chapter 1, we set the stage for one-to-one Web marketing. We discuss the principles forged by well-respected relationship marketing experts. Once you have absorbed these principles, the rest of the book shows you how to apply them to your Web site creation, enhancement, and marketing. One-to-one marketing is the future of marketing, and the Web is one of the best mediums to leverage all of the benefits, including fostering customer loyalty and staving off competition. One-to-one Web marketing will enable you to build relationships with your customers one at a time, for the long term.

Chapter 2: One-to-One Web Site Personalization

As the number of Web sites grows and the size of the average Web site becomes larger, you will want to consider enlisting one of the Web site personalization technologies. Early in the history of the Web, surfers visited sites and saw the same information every other Web surfer saw. Now there are many sites that create a different Web site experience for each user. With the integration of databases and the use of user tracking and profile information, Web sites can now provide personalized content. Chapter 2 shows you how personalized Web sites can make it easier for your customers to do business with you.

Chapter 3: One-to-One E-Mail

E-mail is the most prevalent activity on the Internet. In this chapter, we show you how to use e-mail to pull people back to your organization and your Web site on a regular basis. There are emerging technologies that allow you to send each customer his or her own personalized e-mail so you can build individual relationships with all of your users and customers. Chapter 3 shows you how to write effective e-mail messages and subject lines so that the e-mail will be useful instead of being mistaken for spam and deleted before being read by the recipient.

Chapter 4: One-to-One Web Advertising and Promotion

Online advertising has moved from simple Web banners to fully interactive online ad experiences. Web advertising and promotion can now be targeted to specific people, or even block advertising from being viewed by people who don't fit the target market. The online advertising future will allow TV commercial-like advertising, transactions within the advertisement itself, and bringing advertising to anyone, anywhere (for example, wireless devices such as cell phones and personal digital assistants [PDAs]). Chapter 4 discusses the many types of advertising and promotion that can be implemented on the Web. It also discusses the role of advertising networks and advertising management software in enabling targeted and one-to-one advertising.

Chapter 5: One-to-One Web Community

In Chapter 5, we discuss how online communities can provide a one-to-one experience for users. This chapter explores the history, emergence, and popularity of this Web phenomenon. Online communities were first used as a way for people to interact socially with others via the Internet. Now many companies are establishing online communities to allow customers to interact with other customers, and for customers to interact with company representatives. Users of Web sites with chat and discussion forums typically spend more time on these sites versus sites without these features. This chapter explores a few different online community models.

Chapter 6: One-to-One Web Data Analysis

Most Web managers have the ability to track user interaction with their Web site. There are many products and services available that help capture and report site activity. Chapter 6 explains the nuts and bolts of Web site traffic analysis. One key to providing one-to-one Web marketing is understanding what Web visitors need by using profiles and tracking data collected on the Web site. This chapter discusses concepts such as data mining and data warehousing, and explains how these techniques can be used to enhance your efforts to satisfy each customer according to his or her individual Web profile and activity.

Chapter 7: One-to-One Web CRM

As companies began to apply one-to-one Web marketing techniques to the rest of their organization, a new term was created to describe the process: Customer Relationship Management (CRM). CRM is a philosophy of centralizing the information a company has about an individual, and this chapter covers the integration of one-to-one Web marketing with other systems across the enterprise.

Chapter 8: One-to-One Web Collaboration

Chapter 8 provides an in-depth look into how to conduct presentations and conferencing over the Web. It familiarizes you with the multimedia communication and application standards and technologies as well as covers how to select the best Web conferencing technology for your marketing needs. It also discusses what types of presentations you can make to enhance your one-to-one Web marketing efforts. This chapter shows you how to use of the bandwidth limitations of today's Internet.

Chapter 9: One-to-One Web Privacy

What makes one-to-one Web marketing possible has caused a lot of uproar in the Web community. Chapter 9 discusses the issues surrounding online privacy from both the users' and marketers' perspectives. Personal information is what makes one-to-one marketing possible, but there is a delicate balance. In order to overcome this very real hurdle, this chapter provides you with ways to make your online audience more comfortable with Web personalization and other privacy-related concerns.

Chapter 10: The One-to-One Web Marketing Future

In this chapter, we mix a little serious business with a little fun. We discuss what is in store for one-to-one Web marketing and give you a sneak peek into some really leading-edge, Star Trek-like, one-to-one communications.

Who Will Find This Book Useful

If your Web site is an integral part of your overall strategy, then it must be treated strategically. Some of these technologies can be expensive to build and maintain, so you will want to have a clear objective of what you wish to accomplish before you begin. This book helps you identify how one-to-one Web marketing can work for many different Web business models: marketing communications, commerce, advertiser-supported services, and community.

This book is a useful resource if you are a marketing executive, marketing manager, business manager, direct marketer, new media manager, or interactive technology manager. If you focus on the *marketing side* of Web management, you will benefit from this combination of marketing strategy and Web technologies.

About the One-to-One Web Marketing Companion Web Site and CD-ROM

The world of one-to-one Web marketing is continually evolving, so we created a Web site that provides interactive tools, up-to-date news and information, and a database of vendors.

The 1to1Web.com site (www.1to1Web.com) has a wealth of information to help you in your quest to identify one-to-one Web technologies that best fit your objectives. The Web site also features an e-mail newsletter to keep you informed of happenings in the area of one-to-one Web marketing.

The CD-ROM included with this book contains a variety of interactive checklists, spreadsheets, bookmarks, and other marketing management tools. In addition, experts in several fields have provided a variety of detailed white papers.

Summary

One-to-one Web marketing has benefits for both Web visitors and Web marketers. It helps Web visitors make buying decisions more quickly, and it helps marketers learn more about how to meet the needs of the visitors who come to their Web site—which is the essence of one-to-one marketing.

We invite you to explore each chapter individually to see how you can start applying one-to-one marketing tools and techniques to achieve success for your Web site.

One-to-One Web Marketing Overview

"This is not a fad. The 'one-to-one future' is no longer the future. It's happening now."

Don Peppers and Martha Rogers, *The One to One Manager*

In 1991, we were inspired by the introduction of Regis McKenna's book, *Relationship Marketing* (Addison-Wesley, 1991). In his book, McKenna discussed the age of customer-centered and knowledge-based marketing. Then the marketing floodgates opened in 1993 with the best-selling book, *The One to One Future* written by Don Peppers and Martha Rogers (Doubleday, 1993). At that time, Peppers and Rogers discussed the combined future of marketing and technology and described one-to-one technologies of the future. They discussed the characteristics of one-to-one marketing using individually addressable technologies and mass customization. Even though their book was written before the existence of the World Wide Web, they described technologies that sounded very much like what we now know as the Web.

In this chapter, we provide an overview of relationship and one-to-one marketing concepts. We set the stage for putting these concepts into action in your Web development and marketing efforts. The most important thing to remember when thinking about and implementing these technologies is that technology by itself will not make you successful on the Web. It is the balance of your company's best practices and the creative implementation of the technologies that will make your site a success.

Time Flies When You're Having Fun

When we wrote the first edition of this book, the Web was embraced as a promising new medium. Well, the Web is here to stay. Wow, we got here quickly, yet we have a long way to go to realize the full potential the Web offers in terms of building customer relationships. Morgan Stanley's technology research report, *Advertising Report* (HarperBusiness, 1997), showed how long it would take for the Internet to reach 50 million users relative to other communications media:

Radio	38 years
TV	13 years
Cable	10 years
Internet	5 years (estimated)

The worldwide Internet user population now is more than 300 million and is expected to more than double by 2005. For both consumer and business industries, the Web is now a legitimate channel for communication and commerce.

In 1997, IDC predicted the Web population would grow from 50.2 million in 1997 to 174.5 million in 2001. The latest estimates show the Web population at more than 300 million in 2000.

According to Forrester Research, total U.S. e-commerce was $110 billion in 1999 and is expected to reach more than $1.3 trillion in 2003. Of the total e-commerce transactions in 2003, $110 billion will be business-to-consumer (B2C) transactions. In 2003, offline B2C transactions will be $7 trillion, and offline business-to-business (B2B) transactions will be about $13 trillion.

In 1998, there were more than 191,000 active B2C Web sites in operation according to ActivMedia. In 1999, there were more than 696,000.

As you can see, the Web is far ahead of the past predictions, and the Web is still growing at a rapid pace. While the Web has been growing, clever marketers are experimenting, creating new marketing models using the Web medium, and figuring how the Web fits into the overall marketing mix. Also, marketers are creating methods to tailor messages to target markets, market segments, and even each individual Web customer.

The State of Web Marketing

Previously, Web sites were something that marketers felt they should have. Today, marketers' Web sites are important to them as another way to reach customers. As sites cost more to develop, marketers are getting quite serious about making their markets aware that their sites are available. Web site addresses are everywhere—TV ads, magazine ads, sides of trucks, and billboards. Although they are still a small portion of media budgets, online advertising, online promotions, and e-mail marketing are growing in importance.

Since 1995, we authors have seen a maelstrom of new marketing ideas and models, from simple static Web pages to full-blown virtual retailing applications. In the first edition of this book, we focused on customization and personalization of Web pages and online advertising. At that time we also observed that a Web site was a standalone entity. Silent. Flat. Alone. Now, sites are more interactive and dynamic. We now see Web sites, call centers, retail stores, and other channels becoming integrated with one another to a greater degree than before. Now, a customer can actually connect with a human being through a Web site. Web personalization and database marketing are now just the very first steps in the new larger opportunity of customer relationship management (CRM) where the Web site will play an integral part.

Online advertising has also changed quite considerably since 1997. Forrester Research estimated that online advertising was $37 million in 1995. Between 1996 and 2004, U.S. online ad spending will experience an average annual growth rate of 65 percent, according to eMarketer. Although Web banner ads are still the predominant form of online advertising, now advertisers can create interactive multimedia online ads that can be full screen and can include audio and video. Some traditional marketing tactics have made their way online, including sweepstakes and coupons. Currently, e-mail advertising and marketing are hugely popular Web marketing activities. More than online advertising, e-mail marketing can go beyond segmented targeting to one-to-one targeting. Jupiter Communications estimates that commercial e-mail spending will grow from $164 million in 1999 to $7.3 billion in 2005.

The Internet is now moving beyond the PC. Although it is too soon to tell, some believe the number of wireless devices such as cell phones and personal digital assistants (PDAs) may overtake the number of PCs hooked up to the Internet. According to Ovum Research, mobile advertising will generate 20 percent of total Internet advertising revenues by 2005. Imagine getting a special personalized promotion for a new book by your favorite author sent to your Palm device? If we marketers believed that online customers have unprecedented control and choice over Internet advertising, then consumers with wireless devices will have even greater control over what advertising and promotional messages they receive on their cell phones and pagers.

What Is One-to-One Web Marketing?

Fundamentally, one-to-one Web marketing is the practice of tailoring messages, services, products, and promotions to an individual Web user. Don Peppers and Martha Rogers introduced this marketing technique when they wrote *The One to One Future* in 1993.

One-to-one marketing is not a new concept in the physical world. Nordstrom's, an upscale department store, has a personal shopping service that helps customers buy clothing that best suits their lifestyles, jobs, and personal tastes. Web sites, online stores, and online information services are taking cues from services like Nordstrom and are leveraging information technology to bring one-to-one services to the online masses.

To see what the future holds for marketing on the Web, let's review how one-to-one marketing is different from other types of marketing:

Mass marketing. One-to-all or one-to-many communications without specialization of message or medium.

Target marketing. One-to-many or one-to-few communications with specialization of message and medium for each identified segment of the whole market.

One-to-one marketing. One-to-few or one-to-one communications with individualized message and medium for each highly targeted market or individual customer.

There are many good marketing experts with significant ideas about marketing on the Web. For our book, we focused on relationship, one-to-one, and loyalty marketing ideas. We selected notable experts in each of these fields. We hope that we do justice to applying their great ideas to the Web. First, we will provide you with a condensed version of the key concepts.

Relationship Marketing

Regis McKenna wrote a definitive book, *Relationship Marketing* (Addison-Wesley, 1991), about the changes marketers needed to make to become more customer centered with their marketing efforts. Instead of simply producing and distributing goods and services in mass quantities with no choices in features, he discussed how marketers could find a segment of a market and dominate it through relationship marketing. This mindset could enable a company to create products that closely fit the needs of a particular customer set. In order to leverage relationship marketing, marketers needed to move from monologue to dialogue with customers. Here is the condensed version of some of the important principles from his book:

- Owning the market.
  - Define which whole pie (market segment) is yours and dominate it.
  - Develop products and services to serve that market specifically.
  - Define the standards in that market.
  - Deepen relationships with customers.
- Knowledge-based marketing.
  - Integrate the customer into the product and service design process to guarantee that the product is tailored to the customer's needs, desires, and strategies.
  - Generate niche thinking—use the company's knowledge of channels and markets to identify market segments that you can own.
  - Develop an infrastructure of suppliers, vendors, partners, and users that help sustain and support your edge in the market segment.
- Experience-based marketing.
  - Spend time with customers.
  - Monitor competitors.
  - Develop feedback analysis that turns information about markets and competition into product intelligence.
- Adaptive marketing.
  - Sensitivity—communications and feedback channels.
  - Flexibility—organizational structure and operational style that take advantage of the new opportunities feedback brings about.
  - Resiliency—learning from mistakes.

One-to-One Marketing by Peppers and Rogers

Don Peppers and Martha Rogers have written two books on the subject of one-to-one marketing. The books are full of thought-provoking concepts that can be applied to Web site creation and promotion programs. Following are some of the highlights from each of their groundbreaking books.

The One to One Future

The *One to One Future* was published in 1993, which was well into the high time of database marketing. It presented groundbreaking and earth-shattering concepts to marketers. Here are just a few of the book's key concepts that can be applied using the Web:

Share of the customer. Peppers and Rogers presented the idea of switching the marketer's mindset from share of the market to share of the customer. Instead of focusing solely on the higher investment of marketing to your entire marketplace in order to increase revenue, you want to focus as well on increasing the revenue of each customer—also known as increasing the share of each customer on a one-to-one basis. This idea has the benefit of increased profitability because it is cheaper to increase sales to existing customers than to acquire new customers. Another benefit is that during the process of increasing the share of each customer, you are building longer-term and loyal relationships with customers. In order to maximize the share of each customer, you will need to know what that customer thinks, which can be done only with one-to-one communication mechanisms.

Customer retention versus acquisition. Typically it costs five times more to acquire a new customer than it does to retain a customer. Most businesses experience a customer churn rate of about 25 percent annually. According to Peppers and Rogers, if you are able to reduce this by 5 percent, you could add as much as 100 percent to your bottom line. The idea is basic: Higher revenue at the same expense falls directly to the bottom line as higher profit.

Law of repeat purchases. The more successful you are in getting each customer to buy from you, the more you can increase your long-term profits. The more units you sell to a particular and valuable customer, the higher each unit's margin will be over time. The overhead associated with each purchase decreases when the cost of marketing to a loyal customer declines.

Customer dialogue. "In the one-to-one future, it won't be how much you know about all of your customers that's important, but how much you know about each of your customers." The way to apply this concept is to use interactive communications with your customers. Dialogue is two-way, not one-way. It is an exchange of ideas between two parties. Using two-way communications vehicles and feedback mechanisms enables you to learn more than you would through market research. Make it easy for customers to communicate with your organization. Act on what they say in order to build trusting and loyal relationships, which will translate into more sales and better profit margins.

Enterprise One to One

In 1997 Peppers and Rogers dealt the second blow to the marketing community with *Enterprise One to One.* This book revisited the one-to-one mantra with added excitement surrounding the limitless technological possibilities of the Web, interactivity, and the use of customer data. Here are the pertinent concepts from this book:

The new competitive rules. Customer-driven competition is synonymous with one-to-one marketing. With traditional marketing methods, this type of competition was cost prohibitive. Information technology, including Web technology, can raise the competitive playing field because it can track customers, enable interactive dialogue, and allow mass customization where products and services can be created to the specifications of an individual customer.

The learning relationship. The way to build the strongest link between you and your customers is to establish a learning relationship. To do this, follow these four steps:

1. Find out what your customer needs through interaction and feedback.
2. Meet these needs by customizing your product or service, and remember the specifications.
3. Continue interaction and feedback to learn more about the customer's individual needs.
4. Keep your customers satisfied so that you do not lose them to your competition.

Convenience and incentive. If you make it convenient for customers to give information about themselves, the better the opportunity you have to learn more about them, and the more they will do repeat business with you. In addition to important personal communications between your customers and company representatives in sales, marketing, and support, the Web and other interactive media can make it convenient for customers to share their thoughts with you. You can also provide an incentive to customers to enter into a learning relationship with your organization—free add-ons, free service, discounts, special memberships, and so forth.

Some rules for the (information) road. Now that you have the powerful one-to-one marketing tool of the Web, you will want to consider how to approach customers for their personal information. First, you don't want to ask for all of the information at once. A learning relationship should be conducted in the long term, especially because markets and customers rapidly change. Second, give the customer the choice of what information to provide. This establishes a relationship based on trust, which will widen the communications channel between you and your customer. Third, you want to make the customer's life better with the information you are collecting. You will want to create an equitable value exchange between the information you are collecting and the service you provide in return. Finally, you will want to establish a Privacy Bill of Rights. See Chapter 9, "One-to-One Web Privacy," on how to create privacy policies to increase your customers' confidence in the learning relationship.

One of the profound quotes to remember from the book is this: "If a firm is not in direct touch with its customers, then every single interaction is a priceless opportunity to learn more."

Building Loyalty through Marketing

On average, the marketing costs required to acquire a new customer are five to six times more than the marketing costs needed to get customers to reorder from a company. Thus, a company with a highly loyal customer base will be more profitable than a company that has a less loyal customer base where this company has to constantly acquire new customers at a higher cost to achieve revenue goals.

Frederick Reichheld is a leader of Bain & Company's (www.bain.com) Loyalty Practice and author of *The Loyalty Effect* (Harvard Business School Press, 1996). He has conducted extensive research to uncover the effect of increasing customer loyalty in various industries. In 1989 he published a study that showed that raising customer retention rates by 5 percentage points could increase the value of an average customer by 25 to 100 percent. Customer loyalty has two important effects on a company.

The first is the *customer volume effect*. If you can reduce customer attrition, you gain a larger growth in volume of existing customer revenue versus trying to make up lost volume from customer attrition by acquiring new customers. The second effect is the *profit-per-customer* effect. In many industries, companies actually lose money when they acquire new customers, and it takes several transactions over time to see profit materialize from these customers. If you lose mature customers, you actually lose the ability to recoup acquisition investment, break even, or receive profit. Loyal customers' spending tends to accelerate over time. The more a single customer orders over time, the more profit a company receives because each interaction generally requires less investment by the company than initial transactions. The goal is to increase repeat purchases by focusing on loyalty-building efforts to increase customer profitability.

Customer Relationship Management (CRM)

A new wave in the marketing industry is customer relationship management (CRM). According to Fredrick Newell in his book, *Loyalty.com* (McGraw-Hill, 2000), customer relationship management "is a process of modifying customer behavior over time and learning from every interaction, customizing customer treatment, and strengthening the bond between the customer and the company." Newell suggests that marketers must change their practice of company-centric database marketing to the practice of customer-centric CRM. With database marketing, marketers target customers so they can sell more at less cost. With CRM, marketers focus on what the customer wants rather than what the company wants to sell. The Web is a good platform for applying CRM because of its ability to cost effectively customize the Web experience, e-mail, and online promotions. CRM systems also allow companies to recognize specific customers across channels—phone, Web, e-mail, direct mail, retail point-of-sale (POS) systems, and so forth.

According to Newell, "The key to CRM is identifying what creates value for the customer and then delivering it." The primary way to deliver CRM is to capture information about a customer, not only what he or she bought, but also his or her behavior, feeling, and environment that affects his or her buying decisions. This data is managed in a way to enable the marketer to predict future purchases and buying behavior. But, would a marketer perform CRM on every customer? No, marketers can use CRM methods to identify the most profitable customer relationships. CRM also helps marketers optimize communications from the customer's point of view in order to maximize customer value (relevant to specific customer groups) and enhance customer loyalty among profitable customer segments. CRM is a long-term profit-building process, which can take many years and a considerable investment.

The Web: A Relationship-Building Platform

Jim McCann, the founder and president of 1-800-Flowers.com (www.1800flowers.com), wrote an article for *Upside* magazine in November 1997 entitled "Interactive Customer Service." In this article, he warned that computers are just tools that allow companies to provide interactivity, and they cannot motivate customers or nurture the bond that results in repeat business by themselves. In his words:

> Despite our name, 1-800-Flowers, we're in the "social expression" business, like the people who sell greeting cards and chocolates. Flowers are symbolic, timeless, not high tech. And yet we conduct 10 percent of our business online. We're using this new channel to reach a growing market segment that is embracing new technology and is motivated by convenience. But we've never lost sight of customer satisfaction, which we handle the old-fashion way: one-to-one.

Jim McCann and his company were pioneers on the Web, and their Web site is held as one of the standards among online retailers. His point is important to consider. The Web and one-to-one marketing technologies are only vehicles for building one-to-one relationships with your online customers. The magic of one-to-one marketing happens during the interaction with the customer. Your site should interact with the customer in a nurturing, two-way manner. In fact, there are some interactions that should never be left to the Web to handle, such as complex customer support issues. This is where human interaction will succeed. Your Web site should interact with customers in a very human-like way. Put your thinking caps on before you implement what can be very expensive technology. Think about why and how the system will be designed to facilitate relationship building. Be careful not to let the excitement of cool technology drive your one-to-one marketing strategy. The long-term goal of increasing company value (i.e., revenue and profits) is a key step in evaluating one-to-one opportunities. An equally important step is to understand how customers would value a one-to-one relationship with your company.

Marketers now have a tool they have been envisioning for many years—a tool that allows them to know their customer more intimately than before. Marketers no longer have to make uninformed decisions about their customers because of the two-way interaction and communication capabilities that the Web allows.

One-to-One Web Marketing Matrix

Currently, the Web does a better job of targeting segments or groups of customers than other media. Some online marketing techniques such as Web site and e-mail marketing enable true one-to-one marketing. For example, Amazon.com is one of the more experienced one-to-one Web sites that presents personalized recommendation on books, music, and other products. Amazon.com learns about individual customers from each and every transaction, and it also incorporates data from other customers with similar buying behavior and preferences. This allows Amazon.com to personalize the Web experience, resulting in over 70 percent repeat customer purchases.

The Web is continuing to make technology advances that allow marketers to further personalize the Web experience in real-time based on the customer's current site behavior, not just past behavior. This profiling capability will also help marketers predict future behavior. The CRM, or eCRM, movement allows marketers to take data from all media and channels the customer interacts with to build an ongoing relationship. Another major Web enhancement is the ability for customers to interact with real human beings behind the Web site with the use of "live help" technologies such as real-time text chat, Web telephony, and cobrowsing. We are also seeing the emergence of "virtual retailing" applications that use 3-D, Shockwave, Flash, and other virtual applications to make the Web experience highly interactive and personalized.

The purpose of this book is to show you technologies and techniques to increase the return on your Web site and marketing investments. In each chapter we present in-depth discussions of each of the one-to-one marketing applications that can be used on the Web. Depending on your budgets and objectives, you may use one technique, a combination of techniques, or all of them. Table 1.1 outlines the Web marketing technologies and how to apply each of them.

Embracing One-to-One Web Marketing Challenges

We have a long, one-to-one Web marketing future ahead of us. Now is the time to consider leveraging the potential of the Web to build relationships with customers and users. On the other hand, there are a couple of important obstacles that need to be removed before both you and your customer can truly benefit from one-to-one relationships. The three main hurdles are *expense*, *technology*, and *privacy*.

Expense

Historically, one-to-one sales, marketing, and service came at a premium. Personal shoppers and other personalized services were limited to people

Table 1.1 One-to-One Web Marketing Matrix

ONE-TO-ONE WEB TECHNOLOGY	USES
Web site personalization markets	■ Learns more about each user or target. ■ Presents personalized recommendations, especially if you serve a wide variety of target markets or provide a wide range of products or services. ■ Increases ability to convert site browsers to buyers. ■ Automates many processes such as recommendation, cross-selling, and account management. ■ Targets site advertising and promotion to individuals based on their user profiles; presents a unique Web experience to each customer. ■ Conducts membership and loyalty programs; some programs can be premium services for which customers pay. ■ Promotes site and brand loyalty.
E-mail	■ Maintains ongoing company and marketing communications via e-mail announcements and newsletters. ■ Reaches people without requiring a visit to your Web site. Enables recall campaigns to increase loyalty. ■ Targets e-mail advertising on other organizations' e-mail announcements and newsletters.
Advertising and promotion	■ Increases awareness and response from the Internet audience. ■ Conducts targeted and one-to-one advertising to optimize ad budgets. ■ Conducts response- and transaction-oriented Web ads.
Community	■ Creates online discussion forums among users and with organization representatives (management, sales, customer service, etc.). ■ Increases site traffic and site visit longevity. ■ Promotes site and brand loyalty.
Customer care	■ Enhances Web site experience to ensure satisfied buyers.

	■ Increases ability to convert site browsers to buyers. ■ Reduces customer service costs when you apply Web self-service and live help features.
Data analysis and integration	■ Assesses the performance of your Web site analysis or specific sections of your site. ■ Learns more about your Web visitors and customers. ■ Integrates your user profile and other databases with tracking data (what users are viewing/clicking on) on your Web site. ■ Makes other back-end, historical, or live data available to your Web site such as product/service information, customer information, purchase transactions, shipping, and account management. ■ Performs database marketing on your Web site or on the Internet. ■ Performs data mining to segment customers (by profitability, site usage, etc.) and form predictive models about future site or transaction activity.
CRM	■ Reduces customer churn by learning what customers value about your products, services, Web experience, etc. ■ Determines different segments of customers based on their profitability (i.e., highly profitable, potentially profitable, not profitable). ■ Enables you to predict future customer buying behavior. ■ Allows for better service and consistency across media and channels.
Collaboration	■ Allows for online presentations, document sharing, project management, and knowledge management over the Internet. ■ Reduces direct selling costs such as travel and other sales/marketing communications costs. ■ Enables one-on-one selling, marketing, and collaboration to forge tighter bonds with prospects and customers.

willing to pay for the additional value this type of service provides. Some industry pundits believe that the incremental expense to provide personalized marketing and service does not bring the results required to justify the investment. While it is true that personalized Web marketing costs more, one-to-one marketing can pay significant dividends over time in terms of Web site and company loyalty, the ability to stretch your limited marketing budgets by focusing on targeted marketing, higher response rates from targeted advertising, and so on. Each chapter in this book presents some implementation costs associated with each one-to-one Web marketing technology. As we marketers know, there are two variables in the marketing equation: expense and resulting revenue or response. One-to-one marketing, like all marketing efforts, is an investment over the long term.

Technology

Media hype abounds. Artificial intelligence, intelligent agents, personal bots, personalization, collaborative filtering, data mining, and other sci-fi-sounding technologies are all the rage in technology magazines and even in more general magazines. These technologies are being applied to the Web at a feverish pace by still relatively few Web sites. Some of the technology is expensive and takes a long time to implement because almost every site needs a custom solution. The integration of databases to the Web is still in progress. Each of this book's chapters provides an in-depth look at a one-to-one Web marketing technology, including any relevant obstacles.

Privacy

The privacy issue is an emotional one that raised the discussion about protecting users' personal data to new heights when Web marketers began to use profiling technology and encourage users to register with their Web sites. In order for both the user and the marketer to benefit from one-to-one Web marketing, the marketer must protect users' privacy, give users control over their own personal information, and practice self-regulation in order to prevent governments from stepping in to solve problems. Because this issue is so important to the future of relationship building on the Internet, we dedicated Chapter 9, "One-to-One Web Privacy," to the subject.

Up Next

Chapter 2, "One-to-One Web Site Personalization," will provide an in-depth overview of the objectives and applications for personalizing a Web site for online users and customers. There are many ways a site can be personalized; you will learn how and why to use personalization to increase repeat visits or purchases.

One-to-One Web Site Personalization

"Markets are conversations."

Christopher Locke, *The Cluetrain Manifesto*

The ever-fragmenting society has provided more choices for people, who prefer having choices versus not. The incredible number of choices, however, has also caused anxiety and confusion. Although the World Wide Web provides access to any type of information possible, the Web is beginning to become segmented. The first phase of the Web was centered on anonymity and unprecedented access to information. We are now in the second phase, which is characterized by the clustering of information and the need for users to identify themselves in order to receive enhanced value from the Web in the form of time savings and personalized communications.

What Is One-to-One Web Personalization?

The second phase of the Web will be a place where online users gravitate to specialized online communities, super sites, channels, and Web sites that narrowcast specific information to a segment of the online user population. For example, if you visit Excite (www.excite.com), you can find many online communities that are focused on several areas, including books, business, financial, computers, film, games, hobbies, health, learning, lifestyle, music, politics, news, shopping, sports, television, and travel. All of the major search engines now provide users with a personalized news and information service.

In order to save people time and build relationships, the Web is becoming a venue for targeted dialogue between user and Web site owner. Jupiter Communications (www.jup.com) defines this next phase as one that "will be marked by services that enable a more proactive, ongoing dialogue between content provider and consumer."

According to an Intelliquest (www.intelliquest.com) survey, almost half of the respondents stated that information that was tailored to their needs was a reason why they revisited a Web site. Here is how the respondents ranked reasons for repeat visits:

Very entertaining: 56 percent

Grabs my attention: 54 percent

Extremely useful content: 53 percent

Information tailored to my needs: 45 percent

Thought-provoking: 39 percent

Visually appealing: 39 percent

Highly interactive: 36 percent

Loads quickly: 1 percent

According to the 1997 Cybercitizen Report by Yankelovich Partners (www.yankelovich.com), the key to the success of online commerce in the future is the user's ability to personally interact with a Web site. The study revealed that more than two-thirds of respondents prefer more human-like transactions when they shop online. Users want timely answers, product recommendations based on their tastes and preferences, and personalized interaction.

The increasing availability of technology and the decreasing cost of technology have spawned a producer-consumer dynamic that centers on increased choice and competition, which leads to a decline in brand loyalty. The emergence of a clustering of the Web, added to the technological capabilities of the Web to provide an individualized experience, will present a new opportunity and challenge for all Web site owners and marketers. This chapter discusses how a Web marketer can provide personalized information to its online constituents and takes a peek into the future of one-to-one Web site personalization.

Benefits of One-to-One Web Site Personalization

One-to-one Web site personalization will work if you follow the basic idea of value exchange. This means that you will get something of value from your customers and users (e.g., loyal and profitable relationships) if you provide them with something of equivalent value (e.g., personalized attention and increased value).

Benefits to Web Marketers

The benefits of personalization are readily apparent to almost every Web marketer who has tried other forms of direct marketing, target marketing, and loyalty marketing. The key is to target a marketing message to the right people and tailor those messages to match each individual's interests.

Why do some salespeople have a close rate over 50 percent, while most direct mail programs can't sell to more than 2 percent? It's because the best salespeople treat individuals as individuals. In other words, those salespeople respect the privacy of each person while seeking answers to questions they need in order to tailor their sales presentation.

Great salespeople know that the key to selling is the relationship. And the way to achieve a close business relationship is to learn about the prospect's needs and interests, then respond with a tailored presentation that addresses those needs.

In other words, salespeople use the "Three I's" of personalization to gain the trust and respect of the prospect:

Interest. Provide interesting information that is tailored to the individual's interest so he or she will explore your Web site and examine how he or she can use your products.

Interaction. Engage each individual with a variety of interactive experiences that lead an individual to discover how he or she will benefit from your products.

Involvement. Encourage people to share their personal opinions, experiences, and needs to learn more about how you can create a loyal customer who will help promote your products.

These personalization techniques can be implemented on most Web sites without requiring people to provide the kind of personally identifiable information that turns many people away when the request is made too quickly. It's important, though, to guide Web visitors through this process so they will feel comfortable providing the personal information needed to make the experience beneficial to both them and you.

It takes having a well-defined marketing and sales process to build strong relationships with customers, which can be done through a personalized Web site.

One-to-one Web marketers receive several benefits from providing personalization on their sites, including customer loyalty, competitive advantage, lower marketing costs, ability to identify the most profitable customer relationships, additional revenue from premium services, and the ability to adapt and improve their sites, products, and services.

Loyalty

A war is going on among online bookstores. Online merchants like Amazon.com (www.amazon.com) are going up against firmly established, cash-wealthy stores like Barnes & Noble (www.bn.com). Early in the competition for online customers, price was an important differentiating factor. Competing solely on price presents increased risk of failure, especially in a new industry. Now services are the key to a competitive edge. To compete with the established brand awareness of Barnes & Noble, Amazon.com took a technological and service approach to acquiring and retaining customers. Amazon.com offers several personalized services, including cross-selling, recommendations, and easy online ordering. Barnes & Noble now offers book recommendations. Web marketers need to become one-to-one Web marketers in order to increase their customers' loyalty to their Web site or company.

Every organization exists in a competitive industry arena. The benefits of loyalty flow straight to the bottom line. When a customer takes time to invest in teaching your organization more about his or her wants, needs, and purchases, he or she now has ownership in the relationship with you. The cost to the customer to switch to your competitor continues to increase as he or she does more business with you. In his book, *The Loyalty Effect* (Harvard Business School Press, 1996), Frederick Reichheld describes the challenge of loyalty as a leaky bucket. The water in your bucket is your existing customer base. The water filling up the bucket is the new customers you are acquiring. The size of the leak in the bottom of the bucket is the rate of customer attrition. The bigger the leak in the bottom of the bucket (customer attrition), the harder you have to work to fill up the bucket (customer acquisition). Getting new customers is more expensive than selling to existing customers. Thus, it is less expensive to decrease the size of the hole in the bucket than it is to increase the amount of water needed to fill up the bucket. Here are the main benefits of customer loyalty:

Profitability. The revenue growth and cost savings associated with loyal customers lead to increases in profitability over the long term.

Referrals. Loyal customers can be your best and most cost-efficient advertisers. It has been shown that customer referrals produce a better quality of customer versus customers that come to your Web site or business from advertising or other forms of lead-generating communications. These referrals can also translate into profitable and loyal customers much faster.

Second chances. Loyal customers will give you a second chance if you mess up once in a while.

Tailoring your Web site to your customers' needs is the first step in the loyalty process. The next step is to integrate your Web site into other processes, such as sales, marketing, purchasing, account management, customer services, and so forth.

Competitive Advantage

The speed of microprocessors has increased dramatically. In 1965 Gordon Moore predicted the exponential growth in the speed of a computer chip. Known as Moore's Law, it predicted that the advance in the logic density of a transistor would result in a doubling of processor power every 18 months. The increasing speed and decreasing cost of the microprocessor have allowed the rapid adoption of personal computers on corporate desktops and in homes. The computer has aided a significant decrease in production cycle times and a significant increase in the number of products being introduced to the marketplace. The increasing number of products and services has caused the marketplace to become more fragmented and segmented.

According to Regis McKenna, author of *Relationship Marketing* (Addison-Wesley, 1991), computer technology has turned uninformed customers into informed customers. He believes that uninformed customers are easily satisfied. In general, people have much more access to information—especially with the Web—and they can comparison shop more easily. He states:

> Customer technology literacy presents a challenge to manufacturers. Customers are no longer pushovers. They want to understand more about the products they buy. They are skeptical and critical, and more often dissatisfied...As more customers become more knowledgeable—and more critical—about technological products, companies must become more sensitive to customer needs.

The accessibility of information and companies on the Web is a mixed blessing. For online users, the Web gives them unprecedented access to products and companies, which enables users to gather comparative data much more easily than ever before. For online marketers, this has added fuel to competitive fires. The access to and immediacy of the Internet present Web marketers with a new challenge of acquiring and keeping online customers for the long run. Building brand loyalty takes time, but the Web requires marketers to grab the users' loyalties as soon as they visit their Web sites and to continue the process in a very determined and relentless manner.

Web technology itself will not give you a competitive advantage. Making it convenient for your online customers or users to gain a substantial benefit from what your organization offers will be the key to your competitive advantage. One-to-one Web site personalization will help you serve each customer to his or her individual satisfaction, over and over again. When an online customer takes the time to tell you what he or she needs and wants, that customer now has an investment in your service. As long as this personalized service provides your customer with value, he or she will do business with you more often and will think long and hard about switching to your competitor—especially if it means having to go through this investment process all over again with your competitor. If you are in a highly competitive market, where services and products are perceived as equal, then individualized service will help you compete effectively.

In their second book, *Enterprise One to One,* Don Peppers and Martha Rogers presented their *new competitive rules*. They believe that the Interactive Age will require customer-driven competition, also known as one-to-one marketing. Customer-driven competition will become critical to success in a competitive market. The good news is that information technology can help because it can provide the following:

Customer tracking. The combination of databases and Web tracking allows Web marketers to keep track of all interactions with customers on an individual basis.

Interactive dialogue. The Web allows Web marketers to engage in interactive dialogue with customers using online feedback forms and e-mail. With the ability to incorporate video and voice on the Web, communications will become more interactive and will happen in real time.

Mass customization. Web site personalization will enable Web marketers to customize the user's interactions with the site. The Web can also enable companies to deliver information, services, and products more efficiently.

The online search engine business has become extremely competitive. Most of the top search engines such as AltaVista, Excite, Infoseek, and Yahoo! receive most of their revenue from advertising. These top search engines provide a customized service to users, from search preferences to a highly customized news page. Coincidence? No. Because the online advertising market is still relatively young and small, search engines need to attract and keep users in order to attract and keep online advertisers. Advertisers are requiring better demographic information from the search engines' users. The customization services on the search engines assist them in making this kind of data available to advertisers because they capture user profile information, select their customization preferences, and collect information from user interactions with content and advertising.

Lower Marketing Costs

One-to-one Web marketing is now possible because information technology is cheaper and more prevalent. The Web has the potential of minimizing the cost per thousand (CPM) customers that you reach with your marketing messages. By fostering loyalty you also will decrease the costs associated with marketing to each customer over time because existing customers will not need the same level of marketing investment that they did when you first acquired them as customers.

Cost of Information Technology

Information technology has enabled companies to shift dollars that are typically spent on on-site customer visits as well as other, more expensive sales, marketing, and service activities. Face-to-face sales meetings are more expensive than telephone conferences or videoconferences, especially if you want to involve people from more than one remote office. Mailing documentation to a customer is more expensive than directing the customer to your Web site or sending the documentation via e-mail, FTP, or PDF. The cost of a telephone salesperson is greater than an intelligent system that suggests the appropriate item using the same product and customer database the telephone salesperson would use. Order processing by customer service personnel is more expensive than order processing by an electronic commerce system. The Internet is already providing companies with ways to decrease communication, transaction, and account management costs.

Web site personalization will require sites to collect and store user data and interact with other back-end databases and systems. There will be an additional technology and marketing investment to design a personalized site; however, Web sites that are database driven will reduce the time and costs associated with the continuous process of updating and revising.

Acquisition versus Retention

It has been said that it costs five times more to acquire a new customer than it does to get business from an existing customer. Because the Web is still a relatively new medium, all organizations on the Web will need to invest marketing dollars and resources in acquiring new customers. If you start the process of encouraging customer retention by using Web site personalization or other loyalty-building systems, you can move down the path to profitability much more quickly. A customer retention strategy must be mapped out early in your Web plans, and retaining should be as important as attracting customers.

Many Web sites are available to customers, and the amount of time customers have for browsing is limited. Therefore, you want customers to become regular patrons of your site. Your goal should be to make your site an indispensable resource for customers. Web site personalization technology will not accomplish this alone. You should think of the value and benefit behind the reason why you personalize the Web site. This will lead to customer retention. Personalized Web site information is just the first step. What do customers then do with this personalized information?

- Can they view it and store it on your system and their system?
- Can they modify it?
- Can they use it to purchase?
- Can their dedicated sales account manager view it?
- Can they interact with other customers who have similar profiles to exchange ideas?
- Can this information remind them of their next purchase in terms of what to order and when so that they don't run out of inventory?
- Can they be informed of a special offer that is associated with their preferences in the future?
- Can this information be incorporated into the distribution channel or shared with divisions or related companies?

These are just a few of the things that can be done with Web personalization that can help you retain customers beyond the first interaction. Just remember these thoughts about customer retention from Frederick Reichheld in his book, *The Loyalty Effect* (Harvard Business School Press, 1996):

> ...we discovered some years ago that raising customer retention rates by 5 percentage points could increase the value of an average customer by 25 to 100 percent.

Law of Repeat Purchases

In order to increase the return on investment on your Web site, you will want more customers visiting your site more often. The more you interact with or sell to a single customer, the more you will reduce your marketing and technology expenditures on that customer over time. This translates into a higher profit margin per customer in the long term. Don Peppers and Martha Rogers call this concept the law of repeat purchases. This is in contrast to the mass-marketing approach, which requires discounted prices or higher promotional expenses to increase volume. One-to-one Web marketers can take advantage of this concept if they have the ability to interact with and track customers' site visits, requests for information, or online purchases. This enables you to learn more about your customers and return to them the best value for their investment to ensure that they will be back to your site often.

Identifying the Most Profitable Relationships

Not all customers provide the same value to your organization. Web and information technologies can be combined to serve each customer according to his or her individuality. These technologies can also be used to evaluate each customer's value. This allows you to segment your customers into categories, as suggested by Peppers and Rogers in their book, *Enterprise One to One*:

MVCs (most valuable customers). MVCs are those who have the highest lifetime value (LTV). Your objective with this customer group is to center your marketing activities around customer retention.

SVCs (second-tier valuable customers). SVCs are those who have the highest unrealized potential. Your objective with this group is to center your marketing activities around customer growth.

BZs (below-zero). BZ customers are those who will most likely not produce enough profit to justify the costs associated with serving and marketing to them.

LTV is a calculation of your customers' value according to the duration of their relationship with you and the amount of money they spend with you or their number of interactions with you. Once LTVs are determined for your customer base, you can tailor your marketing programs and Web site to each customer's needs and his or her potential worth to your company.

The only way to identify the most profitable relationships with customers or users is through interactive dialogue and interaction tracking. The Web has the unique ability to track customers. Your site can also be tied to databases and other systems such as sales, marketing, purchasing, shipping, and support. Customer data is required to determine which customers are your most profitable ones. This data can be used for all Web site models—with or without electronic transactions. If your site is mostly informational or community oriented, then profitability will not be measured in purely economic terms. If your Web site is advertiser supported, you will have two sets of customers to evaluate: your users and your advertisers. Each customer type will be measured with different factors.

For example, if your site is informational, then you can use technology and services to segment your user population. You can provide a special membership program based on frequency or user profile. Advertiser-supported sites can give discounting or special services based on volume and types of advertising (e.g., banners, sponsorships, editorial features). Transactions, interactions, user profiles, and other data that is useful to identify profitable customer relationships will be stored in databases that can be manipulated using report writing or data mining to discover patterns and make predictions about your customers.

Additional Revenue from Premium Personalization Services

Web site personalization technology can be used to tie into premium services such as frequent flyer or buyer and other membership clubs. Premium services are those types of services for which you can charge the customer to participate. Ticketmaster (www.ticketmaster.com) has a special online club called TMO Plus. The one-year charter membership costs $10. TMO Plus members receive a private ID for secure online ordering, special offers on merchandise, and a special discount on a subscription to its monthly entertainment magazine, *Live! Magazine*. This service gives interested users special advantages and gives Web marketers an easy way to identify, monitor, manage, and reward loyal customers.

Adaptation and Continual Improvement of Products and Services

Customer dialogue is a way to help you continually improve your Web sites and services. Enabling online discussions with some of your organization's representatives and providing online feedback forms can assist the improvement process. Using Web site personalization, one-to-one Web marketers can also tailor enhancements according to different segments of their user population, down to a single customer. Never before has it been easier to get customers and users to give you feedback. Technology has decreased the cost and minimized the time it takes to receive and respond to feedback.

Benefits to Customers and Users

Web site personalization provides your online customers with benefits that include choice, significant time savings, and personalized service.

Choice

In his 1995 article, "Stalking the Information Society," in *Upside* magazine, Regis McKenna states, "Choice in itself has become a paramount value, as important as the goods and services offered. The number of products, services, and options in today's marketplace is mind numbing. This much choice is overwhelming, but most people would rather have many options available to them."

For example, Toyota (www.toyota.com) has many model product lines, such as 4Runner, Avalon, Camry, Celica, Corolla, Land Cruiser, Paseo, RAV4, Sienna, Supra, T100, Tacoma, and Tercel. Each model offers a multitude of features and styles—making hundreds of combinations of models possible, even before choosing style, handling, and other individual options. For example, there are three options for the Toyota Camry: CE, LE, and LXE. Customers can also make choices in car color, upholstery, stereo, wheels, power locks, power windows, sunroof, side-view mirrors, and more. This is a far cry from the introduction of the Ford Model T automobile, when there was one choice of car color—black.

Choice is a two-sided coin on the Web. On the one hand, people want it, and the Web offers it. On the other hand, it presents a challenge to Web marketers. Choice is one of the basic tenets of the Web. With all of the options and choices the Web has to offer, how do you engender loyalty? Ironically, let customers have choices on your Web site. Let them choose how they want information presented and how to communicate their needs and desires to you. If they choose to change their mind, give them the option of changing their preferences. Customers want to find information and services that match their personal preferences, and they want options.

While the Toyota site allows the shopper to click through hundreds of static pages to show descriptions and photos of their products, the CarsDirect (www.carsdirect.com) site takes a different approach. At carsdirect.com a shopper uses a Web form to select exactly which cars to compare, stores a list of cars in his or her profile, explores financing options, and can purchase a car all online.

Web site personalization allows people to build profiles based on their own choices. The registration process itself gives people a sense that they are in control of choosing their preferences. Let your customers opt-in and opt-out of the personalization process. Nothing frustrates an online user more than being forced to provide information to a Web site in order to participate in personalization. If the frustrated user still wants to participate, he or she will give you false information. In fact, you can be guaranteed to lock out many users if you use this practice. If you provide a paid service, then customers know that they must give a certain amount of personal information. You will want to determine what information is necessary for your marketing objectives and what is optional. Optional information should be presented as an option to the user.

Time Savings

Even though people are spending increasingly more time on the Internet, they want the Internet to save them time over alternative ways of gathering information, interacting with others that are geographically distant, and buying products and services. Because the Web is available 24 hours a day, 7 days a week, customers expect to be able to interact and transact with a Web site at any time. In his most recent book, *Real Time* (Harvard Business School Press, 1997), Regis McKenna says that the growing availability of technology has increased the speed of business and the expectation of the consumer to receive instantaneous satisfaction from the organizations with which he or she does business. McKenna opens the book's second chapter with a statement that is evident of the new principle for marketing in the Interactive Age:

> Right here. Right now. Served up just the way I like it. If the new consumers' expectations were spelled out on a billboard, that is what they would read.

According to a Forrester Research (www.forrester.com) report, the size of Web sites will continue to grow dramatically. This study also concluded that companies will be generating more dynamic content in the future. Web site personalization will help ease the user's burden of finding the information that is most pertinent to him or her, without requiring a lot of needless surfing on your ever-growing Web site (i.e., wasting time). If a user is spending the same amount of time doing needful surfing on your site, he or she will perceive it as a good use of time, and thus a time savings. It has been said that if you can get users to visit your site for more than a couple of minutes, then you have a better chance of encouraging users to become regular site visitors.

There is a delicate balance in which the online audience has a need for immediate gratification and the Web marketer has a need to keep visitors on its site for several minutes in order to have a chance to build a relationship. Web site personalization provides the user with immediate gratification. This personalization model appears to be at odds with marketers' needs to have users spend more time on their sites. The key here is to provide an interactive, personal experience that gives the users value. If this is done, then you will no longer have to worry about the time people spend on your site; rather, you will focus on the number of times particular users visit your site over time.

One example of instant gratification and usefulness using Web personalization is Compare Net (www.comparenet.com), which is part of Microsoft's MSN. Compare Net is a free, Web-based service that allows consumers to do customized searches on products. Users can research a variety of topics such as automobiles, electronics, computers, home appliances, home office equipment, and sports equipment. The service is personalized when users make selections from menus and enter data into fields. Users can select categories, products, features, models, and desired price ranges. The system scours the database for products that fit the users' criteria. Once the system provides users with a list of products, they can then do a side-by-side comparison of the products. One personalized feature is Compare Net's Wish List, which allows registered users to store a list of products for future reference. Figure 2.1 shows the results of a Compare Net search.

Personalized Service

It seems like a luxury to go into a retail store and have one of the salespeople remember you, your name, your last purchase, and your favorite products. People want personalized service as long as it isn't intrusive or pushy. This type of personalized service was typical of how customers interacted with merchants before the Industrial Age and mass marketing. During this time, you would go to your local butcher, baker, and candlestick maker. These merchants would remember you and the aggregation of your past purchases. Of course, this wasn't too difficult for the merchant because there were significantly fewer choices in products. The merchants would

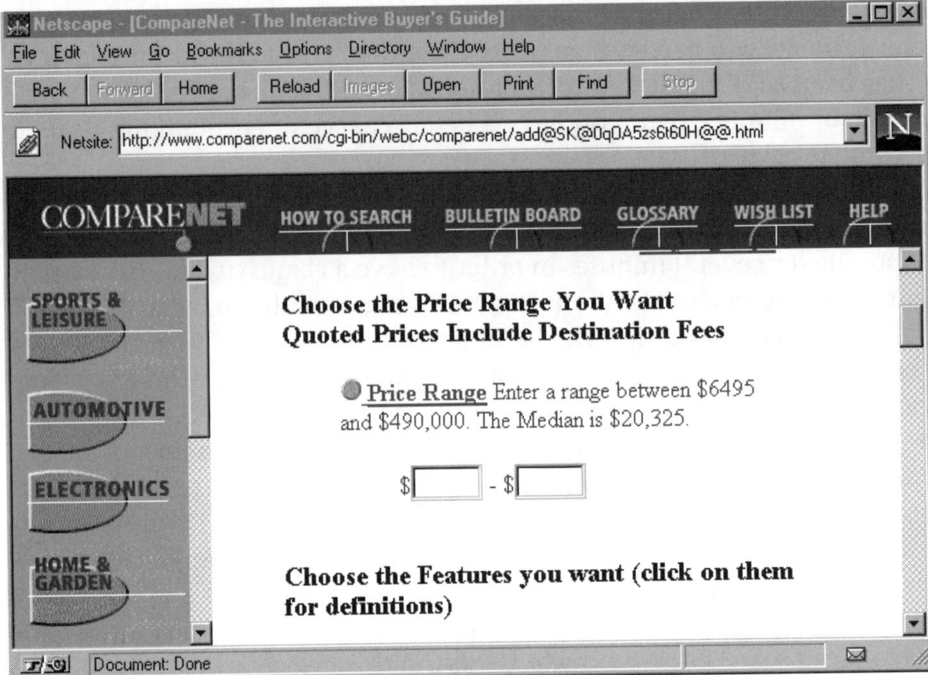

Figure 2.1 Customized product research on Compare Net.

keep this profile information in their heads or on account ledgers. Now, this level of personalized service comes from upscale merchants or technologically advanced companies. The increasing use of computer technology in the sales and marketing process along with the Web will make what was once considered a luxury the norm.

If you are a customer of the leading online bookstore, Amazon.com (www.amazon.com), then you will experience personalized service. When you go to its home page, you will receive Instant Recommendations, which are personalized book recommendations ready for your review. The system makes recommendations based on your past book purchases. Amazon.com also has these other personalized services:

Create a Wish List. This area allows you store a list of products you want to consider purchasing in the future.

Share your purchases with your Trusted Friends. You can add people to your Trusted Friends list and let them see your list of purchases.

1-Click. This service provides easy ordering based on stored user information, including shipping address, preferred shipping method, and

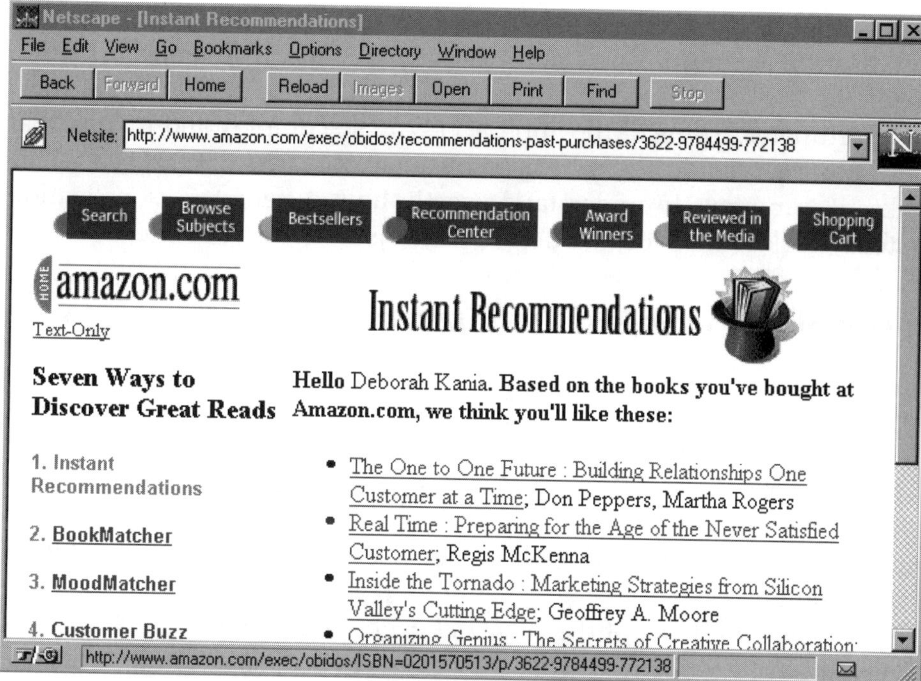

Figure 2.2 Amazon.com's Instant Recommendations feature.

payment information. Customers can store this information, revise the information, and activate the service each time they visit the site.

As you can see, Amazon.com doesn't provide personalization for its own sake; it provides specific benefits to the customer. These types of personalized services can build loyal relationships with customers, especially in competitive markets. Figure 2.2 shows the Instant Recommendations feature on Amazon.com.

Nuts and Bolts of One-to-One Web Personalization

Over the last few years the concept of personalizing content has become very popular. So popular, in fact, that there has been a flood of products on the market that initially look alike, but, in fact, perform very different functions.

Many software companies have rushed to the personalization market with products that meet a very specific set of Web marketing and content management needs. In order to obtain publicity and market awareness, many of these companies have promoted their approach to personalization as unique and appropriate for practically every marketer's needs.

Unfortunately, some of the approaches are so complex and unique that their solutions should really be used by a narrow niche of marketers. This makes it important to understand exactly how different personalization systems work so that you can decide which is right for your site.

Personalization versus Customization

One thing that has occurred is that the term *personalization* has been applied to techniques that, although beneficial to marketers and their audience, may not truly be personalization.

For example, the technique of allowing a user to customize such things as the background color and or the position of objects on the page is called personalization by many sites; however, these features are more akin to customization.

If you have used any of the *my portal* pages at the major search engines then you have experienced what they call personalization. You have control over such things as which stock price should be displayed, where to place news headlines, and other formatting features. When these sites follow your instructions it's like telling the waiter at a restaurant to leave off the onions and put the dressing on the side. There is practically no relationship involved.

When you visit the restaurant the next time and the waiter remembers that you want the dressing on the side and don't like onions, though, it's clear that a one-to-one relationship has begun forming.

On the Web, the difference between customization and personalization usually comes down to who is in control of the content. In the example of altering the background color and placement of content on a Web site, the user is in control.

This would be a personalized site if the user indicated that he or she wants ordinary weather information at the bottom of the page but weather warnings at the top of the page. When the site's editor adds a weather warning to the site, the personalization system would automatically place it at the top of the page.

It's sometimes difficult to tell when a site is customized and when it's personalized because a customized site can provide personalized content. For example, if you add IBM to your stock portfolio and news tracking service at a site, you know you'll see that company (customization), but you don't know what news or stock price data you'll see (personalization).

Both customization and personalization provide benefits to the Web visitor. The real benefit of one-to-one personalization occurs, though, when an individual has an "ah ha!" experience that occurs when the content adapts itself based on the person's profile and provides something new, different, and possibly unexpected.

For the reader to have this experience it's necessary that a team of content creators use a personalized content management system that makes it easy to create and code the content. As we'll see when we get into the different types of personalization, some personalization systems allow the content editor to explicitly code when a particular page should be displayed; other systems use more general rules that allow the server to make those decisions.

One key to providing real benefits to the reader is for there to be sufficient information about the reader's needs and interests for the content creators and the personalization system to know how to meet those needs.

In other words, there almost needs to be a conversation between the content creator and the audience members in order to learn about an individual. This requires more than just personalization technology; it requires an expert team of content creators who have worked with the different types of customers that a company serves and who know their information needs and product requirements.

In this way a company can meet the needs of its audience so that those people will feel comfortable with the Web site, the company, and its products.

Types of Data Available for Personalization

Before we can use data about individuals to personalize their Web experience, we need to look at what data is available. Most companies have more data about Web visitors and customers than they know about—it's just not in a format that's easy to use.

Contact data. One of the easiest types of data to obtain from a person visiting a Web site is basic contact data, such as e-mail address and possibly ZIP code. Many sites now publish an e-mail newsletter, so it's natural to ask for an e-mail address. Sites that provide regional data, such as news, weather, or local event information, can easily ask for a visitor's ZIP code or other information that identifies the geographic location.

Interest profile. When a site promises to tailor content to an individual's interests, it's easy to have visitors fill out a form asking about their interests.

Purchase history data. E-commerce sites that operate their own purchase database probably have access to the product purchase history of each customer visiting their site. Companies that use their Web site for marketing instead of commerce, then sell directly to customers from a call center or with a field sales force may have difficulty in making purchase history data accessible by a Web personalization until an integrated customer relationship management (CRM) system is in place.

Web activity data. As a visitor moves from page to page on a Web site a log of his or her activity is automatically created. Some personalization software systems can add a unique code that identifies each user to each server log entry. When the log file contains this code it's possible to use Web activity data to personalize the Web experience.

Externally obtained data. One of the newest ways, and the most controversial way, to obtain data about Web visitors is to relate a little information obtained from them on the Web to offline data obtained from a specialized vendor. Some vendors are now able to provide the home address and telephone number information based on your providing just an e-mail address.

Types of Personalization

Although there are many ways to use data about an individual to personalize a site, most techniques fall in two categories:

- Explicit personalization
- Implicit personalization

Each type of data collected about Web visitors can be used in both explicit and implicit personalization.

Web personalization is one of the few one-to-one marketing technologies where the marketing team becomes intimately involved with the technology. This usually means using database programming, creating logic rules, and applying the same rigorous testing procedures that programmers use. For this reason, this chapter uses a technique called *pseudo-code* (see www.geocities.com/wayne_bower/ref2.html) to show how different types of personalization systems work.

The following examples use the Web personalization profile data, shown in Table 2.1, about five Web visitors and their clickstream data, shown in Table 2.2.

Table 2.1 Sample Profile Data Used in Examples

ID	First Name	Last Name	ZIP Code	City	State	News-letter	Years Played Golf	Product Purchased
1	Bob	Roberts	90034	Los Angeles	CA	No	10	Glove #4
2	Jill	Jones	72764	Tulsa	OK	Yes	5	Club #1
3	Sam	Spade	27511	Cary	NC	Yes	1	(none)
4						No	(unknown)	(none)
5	Nancy	Dell	29414	Charleston	SC	Yes	1	(none)

Explicit Personalization

When specific data about a person's needs and interests is available it is relatively easy to use explicit techniques to provide content that is almost guaranteed to be appropriate for them. If the data being used to personalize a site is directly related to that person's profile data, then this is explicit personalization.

Much of the data collected about Web visitors when they fill out an interest form provides specific insights into their needs and interests. This allows us to use explicit personalization techniques, such as applying specific business rules, to personalize content on their Web pages and in e-mail messages to them.

When specific profile information is used to personalize a site it is frequently called *rules-based personalization*. Two companies that provide rules-based products are BroadVision (www.broadvision.com) and GuestTrack (www.guesttrack.com).

For example, if you know that a customer is in a particular major metropolitan city where you are scheduled to give a seminar, it's clear that this is appropriate for this person and probably not appropriate for a person in a different state. The pseudo-code that expresses this rule would be:

```
IF state is "CA" and they have purchased a product THEN
  Display a link to the California seminar series
ELSE
  Display a link to the main seminar page
ENDIF
```

Table 2.2 Sample Clickstream Data Used in Examples

VISITOR ID	PAGE SEEN
1	Home
1	Products
1	About Us
1	Contact Us
1	Products
1	Products-Gloves
1	Products-Glove #1
1	Shopping Cart
1	Purchase Confirmation
2	Products-Club #1
2	Shopping Cart
2	Purchase Confirmation
3	Home
3	Contact Us
3	Newsletter
3	Newsletter Confirmation
4	Company
4	Contact Us
4	Privacy Policy
5	Products-Balls
5	Products-Cases
5	Products-Clubs
5	Newsletter
5	Newsletter Confirmation
5	Contact Us

Here is a similar example, but it uses the user-supplied interest information about how long the user has played golf. In this example, the seminar is aimed at experienced golfers, so it is promoted only to people who have played at least five years:

```
IF state is "CA" and years played golf is at least 5 THEN
   Display a link to the California seminar series
ELSE
   Display a link to the main seminar page
ENDIF
```

Another form of explicit personalization is to use Web activity data to determine if a person has seen a particular Web page. The data about which pages each visitor has seen is called *clickstream* data. An explicit personalization rule might be to display a link to the newsletter subscription page if the user is not subscribed. The pseudo-code for this would be:

```
IF newsletter = "No" THEN
   Display a link to the Newsletter Subscription page
ENDIF
```

Here is a slightly more complex example that promotes the products section if clickstream data shows the user hasn't visited that section, or it promotes the newsletter if the user has looked at products. If the user already subscribes, then show the monthly specials page. Here is the pseudo-code for this rule:

```
IF user has not seen the "Products" page THEN
   Display a link to the Products page
ELSE
   IF newsletter = "No" THEN
      Display a link to the Newsletter Subscription page
   ELSE
      Display a link to the Monthly Specials page
   ENDIF
ENDIF
```

Implicit Personalization

Another form of personalization is based on inferences derived from data about a person or a group of people. In this case, statistical techniques use what is known about a person to make projections about what the person wants or will do.

For example, if all you know about a Web visitor is that he or she lives near a golf course and that 30 percent of people who live near golf courses play golf, then you could assume there is a 30 percent chance that your Web visitor plays golf. In this example, once data is added to the process that has uncertainty, the accuracy of the whole assumption takes on uncertainty. In many cases, though, using this approach is more beneficial than not using any information about the person.

Two techniques for analyzing data to make predictions about Web visitors are these:

- Collaborative filtering
- Activity correlation

Collaborative Filtering

This technique is one of the most talked-about techniques for personalizing a Web site, probably because Amazon.com is the best known user of this approach. Collaborative filtering is a statistical technique for matching a Web visitor's data with the data from other people who visited the site in order to make projections about what the current visitor may want to see or purchase. Two companies known for their collaborative filtering products are NetPerceptions (www.netperceptions.com) and the LikeMinds product now owned by Macromedia (www.macromedia.com).

In other words, a collaborative filtering engine tries to match what it knows about a user to the other people in the database. Then, it uses what those other people did (i.e., pages visited, products purchased, and so forth) to display links to those pages or products.

This approach combines the preferences and interactions of similar users. Users build their own profiles, then the system makes recommendations by sifting through the rest of the user profile database to find users who have similar likes, dislikes, and other criteria. These systems are best for online communities and Web sites that provide products and services based on sensory, emotional, psychological, sociological, or cultural criteria. Some examples include movies, music, art, literature, food, hobbies, and leisure activities.

Although the calculations for collaborative filtering are complex, we can represent the overall technique with pseudo-code as we did in earlier examples.

Here is an example of using collaborative filtering to match the pages seen by the current user to the pages seen by customers, then display links to the products purchased by those other customers.

```
CORRELATE the page views of the current user with the page views of
all other users
SELECT the users in the database with the highest correlation and
who made a purchase, limit to 3 users
```

```
    SELECT the pages seen by those users
       DISPLAY links to those pages
    END SELECT
END SELECT
```

Learning Agent

While collaborative filtering looks at what everyone else has done, learning agents look at the user's own Web activity. A learning agent tailors content to match an individual's previous Web activity by learning an individual's interests from past behavior.

This can be done by using a wide range of techniques from simple tabulations of pages seen to complex neural networks that calculate many correlation values to make projections about each user's interests.

Two products that use clickstream and other data are Be Free's BSELECT service (www.befree.com) and Personalogy (www.personalogy.com).

Here is an example of using a learning agent to match the topics of pages seen by the current user to the topics of pages not yet seen by the user.

```
CALCULATE for the current user the frequency of viewing score for
all subject topics
SELECT the pages in the content database with the highest viewing
score and that have not been viewed by the current user, limit to 10
pages
   DISPLAY links to those pages
END SELECT
```

This example shows how a learning agent can match the topics of pages seen by the current user to the types of products purchased by that customer. Then, it displays links to pages not yet seen by the user.

```
CORRELATE the subjects of the pages view for the current user with
purchases they have made
SELECT the pages in the content database with the highest
correlation score and that have not been viewed by the current user,
limit to 10 pages
   DISPLAY links to those pages
END SELECT
```

Peapod (www.peapod.com) is a pioneer in online grocery shopping. Peapod allows people who live in certain cities in the United States to sign up to order groceries online and have them delivered to their doors. They have built a special system called the Universal Event Processor (UEP) that creates and manages its customers' personal account files. The UEP records user preferences such as shipping method and the sorting criteria for their personal shopping list. The UEP serves targeted content, called events, to its customers. An event can be an online coupon, product recommendations, advertising, promotions, sampling, and more. These events are determined by the targeting methodology that incorporates demographics, data warehousing, and real-time behavior. Peapod created its own system to enable one-to-one online grocery shopping and service. There are companies that provide products and services to help you enhance your site with personalization. Most Web site personalization products also log user interaction.

Templates versus Content Management System

There are two general approaches to how personalization systems are implemented:

- Manually embed codes in template files
- Manage the system using a Web-based interface

Most personalization products and tools use both approaches; however, one approach usually dominates. Manually embedding codes in pages is normally thought of as requiring more technical resources, but this is not always the case. Some products, such as those from BeFree, use a small amount of code that can easily be included in pages within the site.

For some products embedding rules in template pages can work very well for some small to medium-sized sites. You add special HTML-type tags to your Web pages and build logic into the system that tells the Web server which data to pull and deliver to the user based on the logic that developed within the Web server personalization application. Figure 2.3 shows an example of what an HTML page template looks like behind the scenes using GuestTrack tags to display a set of golf-related links if the user likes golf.

As the team of content creators grows, it becomes necessary to use a personalization product that allows people in multiple locations to enter, edit, and approve personalized content.

Applying One-to-One Web Personalization

Most Web sites can be personalized. If your business model fits into the following categories, adding personalization will help you serve your online customers more efficiently and effectively:

```
<BODY>
<H1>Hobby Links for #user[name]#</H1>

#user[like-golf|equals|block|yes]#

<H2>Golf Links</H@>

<A HREF="/cgi-bin/guesttrack#user_id#&golf-courses.html>
Links to Golf cources around the country.
</A><P>

<A HREF="/cgi-bin/guesttrack#user_id#&golf-products.html>
Links to catalogs of Golf products.
</A><P>


#end_block#

</BODY>
```

Figure 2.3 Example of a personalization rule embedded in an HTML page template.

- One product/service geared to more than one target market
- One target market and several products/services
- More than one target market and several products/services

Web site personalization can act as a matchmaker between users and your offerings. It can provide users with rapid solutions to their information-gathering needs. Several online models can benefit from one-to-one Web site personalization.

Web Site Personalization and Online Models

There are now many different types of Web site models that provide personalized content and services:

- Advertiser-supported Web sites
  - Free or fee-based news, information, and research services
  - Search engines

- Directories and supersites
- Content networks and channels

- Online commerce/catalogs
  - Consumer
  - Business-to-business
- Online communities
  - Consumer
  - Business-to-business
- Marketing sites for offline businesses
  - Store/dealer locators
  - Product/service information
- Customer service
  - Account management
  - Problem tracking
  - Shipment tracking
  - Service updates/notifications
- Intranet/extranet
  - Employee benefits and travel administration
  - Manufacturer-supplier process integration
  - Reseller information and account management

What Can Be Personalized?

There are many possibilities for using Web site personalization on your site. You could provide something as simple as a personalized home page that gives your users the information they had previously selected each time they visit your site. Web site personalization can become as sophisticated as a recommendation system that uses user preferences, user interaction tracking, user purchase history, and the likes and dislikes of other users based on a similar profile. See the list of Web sites later in this chapter for a sample of one-to-one Web site personalization.

Personalized Web Experience

The user's Web experience itself can be personalized. Everything from a simple targeted message with the user's name to a full-blown personalized consolidation of articles, graphics, information, and online discussion groups can make each user's view of your Web site unique.

Personalized Information

Personalized information can be a simple and effective one-to-one Web marketing feature you can use to enhance your relationship with online users. Personalization doesn't just have to be informational; it can be fun and interactive as well. For example, Gist Communications, Inc. (www.gist.com), provides personalized online television listings.

If you have a lot of products, personalization can make it easy for your customers to sift through information and specifications. You can provide personalized information within a Web site, via e-mail, or using a push vehicle served from your Web site (see Chapter 3, "One-to-One E-Mail," for information about e-mail). The same user profile and customer databases can be used with these other information delivery mechanisms.

Personalized Service

American Airlines (www.aa.com) allows online users to access and administer their AAdvantage frequent traveler account. Customers can redeem their rewards while they are online. They can book travel and access the Web sites of other companies that participate in the program, including providers of rental cars, hotels, and gifts.

About.com (www.about.com) is a great example of an additional level of personal service. Instead of simple database-driven personalization, About.com has enlisted hundreds of people, called guides, to mine the Web for the best content associated with topic areas. The site has about 500 topic areas with plans to have at least 4000 topic areas. The live human guides behind each topic area are accessible by e-mail for one-to-one communications related to the topic area.

Personalized Community

Having online communities in which users can participate based on their own needs can be a powerful marketing and services tool. An online community that provides a place for its customers to chat with company representatives, or one another, is one of the most effective one-to-one Web vehicles (see Chapter 5, "One-to-One Web Community," for a discussion of online communities). You can build communities that are dedicated to certain product lines, subjects, customer segments, and other criteria. iVillage (www.ivillage.com) is a pioneer in the online community concept. iVillage has specialized online communities that provide message boards, surveys, a weekly newsletter, and an extensive chat room for people who are seeking employment and career information and advice. Within the job search area, users can take an interactive quiz to help them find the career best suited to their own criteria. Users can also submit questions to the Job Guru for one-on-one advice about finding a job.

These examples are primarily focused on building online communities—you can translate many of the interactive community features to most any online model to form a one-to-one personalized Web community. For example, if you are a service company that sells water filtration systems, then you could form a community that allows users to share experiences regarding the installation of your systems. You can also host chat systems that discuss topics such as how to determine which filtration system is best for a user's particular needs. The possibilities are limitless.

Personalized Cross-Selling/Upselling

What has been a successful method of personalized selling for mail-order catalogs can now be achieved using a personalized Web site. When a person requests particular information or purchases a product, a personalized Web site should scour its associated databases to come up with other recommendations for the user. Web sites can pull from user profiles, tracking data, and purchasing data to inform the user of related information, products, and services. This is personalized service at its best, and it saves the user lots of time.

For example, if you were ordering a laptop computer, would you find it extremely convenient to also receive information on related products such as a special offer on a leather case, an extra battery, and extended warranty? Amazon.com provides cross-selling each time a customer performs a search on a book. The search results contain additional information such as book subject categories that are related to the book for which you are currently searching.

When the Human Touch Is Required

Many customer interactions cannot be replaced by automated Web site personalization systems. There are times when marketing, sales, and service interactions with customers require a real live human involved in the dialogue with customers. Customer information that has been collected on the Web site can enhance the human interaction. Web sites that use personalization typically will assign a user a unique ID through the use of cookies or by asking the user to provide the Web site with a user name and ID. This information can be added to the customer databases so that when a salesperson or customer service representative is helping the customer, he or she will know much more about that customer. Some highly customized sales cannot be conducted via a Web site, but the Web site and data collected by the site can be involved in the sales process.

How Much Information Should You Capture?

Just enough. Early Web sites enabled cookies and provided guest book registrations only because they were able to do so. This provoked privacy concerns among online users. Users gave information and received little or no value in return. Many Web sites now provide value in exchange for users' information, but users are still tentative about giving personal information (see Chapter 9, "One-to-One Web Privacy," for a discussion of privacy).

The amount of information you request from a user should be directly related to the value you provide to the user in return for his or her information. You should not ask for every bit of information from the beginning. Dialogue and loyalty are long-term processes. As your relationship with your customer evolves, there will be a need to continue the information exchange process. If your site allows users to personalize information based on the types of products you offer, you should ask for just enough information to help users customize their preferences. You should ask for a user's e-mail address only if you are going to provide him or her with a periodic e-mail notification or newsletter service. You should ask for a user's address only if he or she wants to be on your mailing list or if the information is needed for shipping and billing. The bottom line is, asking for information that is not directly tied to personalization will only add to your database resources and cost, and neither you nor your customer will receive added value for the incremental information. You can always ask for necessary information and give users the choice to provide optional information or sign up for optional services such as being added to mailing lists, yours or third-party lists.

Sources of Information for Personalization

There are several sources of data to use to create personalized communications. User profile information can be captured anonymously or in a more candid manner where the user provides more information in order to receive one-to-one communications from the site. Sources of information to enable Web site personalization include the following:

Cookies. Cookies are pieces of information stored in a text file on a user's computer. Cookies are used to customize Web pages based on the information stored in the cookie file. Cookies are an anonymous method in that they are associated with the computer that is being used to access a Web site instead of the people visiting a site. Cookies can be used to store a unique ID as well as a password that will identify the user (the computer) each time the site is visited.

Interaction tracking. Web servers log user site activity. There are also products (such as GuestTrack) that allow Web marketers to track activity according to a particular user. The site can present personalized information based on stored user-tracking information from previous site visits in a real-time manner where information is personalized on the fly as the user interacts with the site.

Online profile/registration. Web registration forms allow users to build unique profiles that the Web site can use to provide personalized content. You will want to use a password-oriented online registration when a customer needs to access account or highly personalized (or personal) content.

Customer databases. Customer databases can be used to store and access information that is specific to each customer. Customer data such as addresses, phone numbers, e-mail, inquiries, and purchases can be used to personalize Web information. Online user profile and preference information can be used in conjunction with customer data to provide one-to-one Web marketing or service.

Customer feedback. In addition to customer satisfaction, online forms and surveys can be a source of information for personalized Web services and information. You can design your site to associate feedback with a particular user.

You can use one or a combination of the aforementioned sources to enable personalization on your site. The best approach for deciding which methods to use to capture user information will be based on the objective of your Web site. If your site is primarily one where users place orders, track deliveries, and perform account management, then you may need a password-protected user registration that ties into one or more back-end databases or systems such as purchasing, inventory, or shipping. If your site is primarily one that provides personalized information and advertising, then you may want to use a combination of cookies, user tracking, and user profile information.

How to Capture Information Online

The key to receiving good, accurate information from a user is to make it an easy and painless process. Users will become quickly exasperated if any of the following situations occur:

- You ask for a lot of information.
- You provide a registration form that has too many pages (you want to stick to just a few).
- You require the users to provide what they consider to be optional information (i.e., information that has no apparent relevance to personalization).

There are two main formats for collecting information from a user: an online registration form and questions/selections embedded in the Web site.

Online Registration Forms

Registration forms are popular to acquire user profile information in order to personalize the Web site according to the information collected. Online forms allow users to enter information into fields, make selections using check boxes or radio buttons, and submit the information to the site database. Web sites should enable users to access and modify user profile information at any time.

Embedded within Web Site Content

In addition to online registration forms, you can build user profiles with questions that are embedded within Web site content. Having questions that are associated with particular content allows you to acquire even more individualized information. Because Web sites are becoming larger and more complex, embedded profile questions can make it easier for users to build their profile on an ongoing basis. Many of your customers have needs that may span multiple product or service categories, so asking for information that is relevant to the part of the site that the user is currently in will increase the impact of your Web site personalization efforts. Once you know several attributes or interests of a user, you can program a Web page to determine what combination of text, graphics, and links to display.

One personalized site that makes extensive use of the ability to continually add to a person's profile is the admissions site for Providence College (www.providence.edu/admiss). Its personalized Web site collects profile data about a student's interests, potential major, living preferences, and other aspects of college life. The site initially used interest data to display links to sections of the site, but it added a feature that uses information about which articles a person has seen to display links to new articles.

By integrating a personalized Web experience with personalized e-mail messages tailored to each student's profile, the school builds a relationship as students gather information and make a decision about applying to colleges. "Our e-mail and Web experience lets us tell our story over time to help them with their application and selection process," says Brian Williams, Associate Dean of Admission.

The site has become an information resource because it allows students to update their interest profiles, link to articles across the Web, and maintain their own personal events calendar.

Since moving to personalized Web and e-mail Providence College has seen the number and quality of applicants increase dramatically. It uses a Web interface for the creation, editing, and delivery of Web and e-mail content. Williams says, "Our goal is to allow our entire campus community to participate in creating our newsletter. We hope that this lets readers see themselves as students here and decide if they would be happy here for four years."

Integration of Tracking and Profile Information

One of the more advanced uses of personalization systems is in relating actual Web page viewing to actual user profile information. Many database programs can be used to join the profile data with the Web server log data so that you can perform queries like these:

- How many people who say they like golf saw a particular golf page versus people who didn't say they like golf?
- What length of time is spent on a particular Web page by the age group of the user?
- How is the length of time spent on certain pages related to the education level of the user?
- Do people who want weather reports for cities with airline hubs spend time on the travel page?

In addition to learning about the Web usage patterns of people according to their demographic characteristics and interests, the profile data can be integrated into your traditional direct-marketing activities. By using traditional merge/purge mailing list management software, you can add new names to your mailing list and update existing names with new data. This means that traditional direct-mail packages can be targeted much more precisely by using information gathered directly from your audience.

For customers who purchase from your Web site on a regular basis, such as in a business-to-business setting, the profile database can store all of the preferences for products, shipping, and special situations. This information can automatically be used each time the customers return to purchase additional products. The system can even store purchase history information and decide to display specials for frequent buyers or especially good customers.

Products and Services

There are several products that allow you to add personalization to your site without building the system yourself from scratch. Table 2.3 contains a list of available products and services. Each product or service varies in approach, complexity, and price. You will want to do a careful evaluation of each product you are considering to make sure it fits your specific personalization objectives. Please visit our companion Web site at www.1to1web.com for in-depth information and updates.

Table 2.3 Web Site Personalization Products and Services

COMPANY	PRODUCTS/SERVICES	URL
Art Technology Group	Dynamo Profile Station	www.atg.com
	Dynamo Retail Station	
Autonomy	Agentware i3	www.autonomy.co.uk
Broadvision	One-to-One Application System	www.broadvision.com
	One-to-One Commerce	
	One-to-One Financial	
	One-to-One Knowledge	
GuestTrack	GuestTrack	www.guesttrack.com
MacroMedia	LikeMinds Preference Server	www.likeminds.com
NetPerceptions	GroupLens	www.netperceptions.com
Personalogic	Personalogic(service)	www.personalogic.com
Perspecta	Perspecta SmartContent System	www.perspecta.com

WEB MARKETER'S GUIDE TO THE CLUETRAIN

APPLYING THE CLUETRAIN MANIFESTO TO ONE-TO-ONE WEB MARKETING

The Web has allowed companies to publish information at an incredible savings over older print methods. It also allows customers to search for information on corporate Web sites without interacting with anyone.

While this can be good for the initial review to see if a company sells products of interest to the person looking for specific products, it doesn't necessarily help the company qualify the prospects or record them in a database so that a salesperson can follow up and close the sale.

Most corporate Web sites are designed to stop most interaction with their employees. They seem to feel that if a prospect is interested enough in buying their products, they will figure out a way to search out and contact a salesperson who can take their order.

Unfortunately, in this competitive economy, companies with this attitude are seeing their Web sites drive customers away instead of capturing sales.

And they wonder why their Web sites aren't producing a return on their investment!

The solution is the same one successful salespeople have used for years—conversing with prospects! By engaging in a conversation we have the greatest likelihood of learning about each person's needs and how our products can help them.

The Cluetrain Manifesto (www.cluetrain.com) advocates that corporate Web sites should do what salespeople do—engage in meaningful conversation with individuals.

BENEFITS OF INTERNET CONVERSATIONS

There are several ways to have conversations with people on the Internet. The technology you use is not as important as how well you engage the other person on a one-to-one basis.

By conversing with an individual you accomplish several things:

- Show that person you regard him or her as special
- Learn which benefits he or she feels are important
- Determine which personality group he or she belongs to regarding your type of product

There are many other benefits of conversing with prospects, customers, stockholders, and employees, but these are the top-level reasons.

The Cluetrain Manifesto points out 95 reasons to add this person-to-person sales technique to your Web marketing site.

The Cluetrain Manifesto, however, doesn't explain exactly why conversation aids in the selling process.

CONVERSATION => COMMUNITY

Great salespeople interact with people in several ways. First, they converse with prospects. High-quality prospects are invited to participate with customers at events such as golf outings, customer-only conferences, and other activities designed to create a sense of community.

It is at these community events that prospects become reassured that other customers are like themselves—they work for companies like theirs, have some of the same needs, and therefore are reassured that the product being considered will work for them, too.

Why does community work well in the selling process? Because prospects want to gather with people like them. It also works because they trust similar people in the community recommending the product being considered.

Even when a vendor is unbiased and helpful, the vendor doesn't use its own product the same ways that customers do.

MAKING THE MANIFESTO MEANINGFUL

With all this talk about conversation, just how do we make the Cluetrain Manifesto work for us?

STEP 1—WEB PERSONALIZATION

The first thing is to upgrade your corporate Web site so that it converses with your visitors. Today, it's easy to add personalization to a site that asks a few questions and personalizes content based on an individual's answers.

By adding Web personalization your Web site can converse with people in many of the ways described in the Cluetrain Manifesto, as well as in one-to-one Web marketing books.

STEP 2—E-MAIL PERSONALIZATION

A trend that is catching on quickly is to use e-mail newsletters and special e-mail promotional messages to increase the frequency of contact and bring people back to a Web site.

This works because e-mail reaches people without their taking any special action. Also, personalized e-mail delivers the most appropriate message to each person, increasing the likelihood that he or she will take action based on what's said in the e-mail.

Personalized e-mail products use a profile database and a set of rules to determine which pieces of text to include in each person's message.

STEP 3—E-MAIL DISCUSSION LISTS

Sending personal e-mails and responding to the e-mails people send back is one way to converse with people. Another way to use personalized e-mail is to publish an e-mail newsletter that includes a "letters to the editor" section of comments from customers. By having the system use profile data to select

continues

WEB MARKETER'S GUIDE TO THE CLUETRAIN (CONTINUED)

which articles and customer comments to include in each individual e-mail, you can cultivate a sense of community in your subscribers. While this isn't the same interactive community as, say, online chat, it does allow a company to improve the efficiency of communicating with the community of customers and prospects.

Of course, the most open form of conversation on the Internet are the 75,000 e-mail discussion lists. This form isn't as controllable as the more moderated or edited forms of communication, which are the focus of the Cluetrain Manifesto, but for many companies it's wise to walk before they run to completely open, unmoderated conversation.

SUMMARY

Whether you implement only Step 1 or use all the steps outlined here, it's clear that the Cluetrain Manifesto will lead to increased communications with the wide range of people who make up a company's community.

Hurdles to Implementing One-to-One Web Site Personalization

In order to take advantage of the relationship-building capabilities of one-to-one Web site personalization, the industry will have to overcome some social and technological hurdles. The future for personalization will hinge on privacy and Web-to-database integration.

Privacy

The privacy issue will be the more significant hurdle to jump. Personal information will enable the most one-to-one communication between users and your company. What makes personalization useful also makes it scary to users. Web sites can be personalized while maintaining a user's anonymity. According to Stephen Tomlin, president of PersonaLogic, "Anonymous is the only, most appropriate way to protect users' privacy." The answer to the privacy question lies somewhere in between anonymity and disclosure. Users are willing to provide a certain level of information if they get value and they have a choice in what happens to their information. This point has been proven with free e-mail services such as Hotmail, where users give personal information and participate in advertising in exchange for their own e-mail accounts. The bottom line is to be up-front with users about how you will be using their information. Just remember these two words: choice and consent. See Chapter 9, "One-to-One Web Privacy," for more information about privacy.

One-to-One Web Site Personalization Resources

Web site personalization is still a relatively new concept, so there are currently only a few resources dedicated to it. Please visit this book's companion site, One-to-One Web Marketing Online (www.1to1web.com), for new and updated information and resources on this subject.

ONLINE RESOURCES

Marketing 1:1	www.1to1.com
One-to-One Web Marketing Online	www.1to1web.com
Personalization.com	www.personalization.com

Sampling of Personalized Web Sites/Services

In the future the majority of Web sites will have some level of personalization. Table 2.4 is a list of sites that provide personalization—some provide a little personalization, and others are highly personalized.

Types of Systems and Processes That Can Be Integrated with the Web

There are many ways to use databases in one-to-one Web marketing, from managing the Web site content to taking orders and providing specialized services for customers. There are so many approaches to using databases, and so many different technologies associated with each use, that we've divided the uses into different categories:

- Content management
    - Customization
    - Commerce
- Customer service

Table 2.4 Examples of Personalized Web Sites

COMPANY	PRODUCTS/SERVICES	URL
Amazon.com	Book recommendation services	www.amazon.com
American Airlines	Travel reservations and frequent flyer member services	www.aa.com
CNN News	Custom news page and clipping service	www.cnn.com
Cisco	Presentation of products by customer type	www.cisco.com
CitySearch	Local business directories and personal scout	www.citysearch.com
Crutchfield	Matching products with particular vehicle	www.crutchfield.com
CyberMeals	Order take-out and delivery meals from local restaurants	www.cybermeals.com
Disney Vacation	Customized vacation planning at Disney resorts	www.disneyvacationclub.com
eToys	Gift registry, occasion reminders, ToySearch	www.etoys.com
Farmer's Almanac	Personalized weather	www.almanac.com
FedEx	Package shipping and tracking	www.fedex.com
FTD	Online flower ordering from local florists, order tracking, and reminder service	www.ftd.com
GM BuyPower	Personalized auto research and purchasing	www.gmbuypower.com
Goodyear	Tire recommendation services	www.goodyear.com
H.O.T. Coupons	Personalized local merchant coupons	www.hotcoupons.com
Jango	Personalized shopping agent	www.jango.com
LookSmart	Personalized Web sources by customer type	www.looksmart.com
MapQuest	Personalized maps	www.mapquest.com
Moviecritic	Movie recommendations	www.moviecritic.com
NetRadio Network	Online music by category	www.netradio.net

continues

Table 2.4 (Continued)

COMPANY	PRODUCTS/SERVICES	URL
NewsBot	Personalized search service for 200 news sources	www.newsbot.com
Overnite	EDGE electronic data services	www.overnite.com
Pacific Bell	Telecommunications solution finder	www.pacbell.com
Quicken	Financial network, personalized portfolio to monitor investments	www.qfn.com
Union Pacific	Railroad invoice and equipment tracing	www.uprr.com
Virtual Emporium	Personal shopper (human) and LiveHelp chat	www.virtualemporium.com
WiseWire	Intelligent Web surfing service	www.wisewire.com

The process of providing information to your Web audience and obtaining information from them is similar to traditional marketing and selling techniques; it's just speeded up considerably. For instance, Edward Nash in his book *Database Marketing, the Ultimate Marketing Tool* (McGraw-Hill, 1993), refers to the two-step selling process of using mass media to generate inquiries from people who think they may be interested in the product being advertised. These people then receive more information than could be provided in an advertisement, along with a reply card that asks a few qualifying questions. Based on answers on the reply card, these people may be elevated to prospect status and receive a telephone call from a salesperson, or they may be placed on a mailing list for periodic mailings.

On the Web the whole process is accelerated dramatically because a Web site can deliver the full range of information—from the general benefits found in an advertisement to detailed product specifications—in one session. This is good for the prospect, but it can be bad for the Web marketer who has provided a great deal of information without obtaining information about the prospect.

This means we need to go beyond having a Web site with just static Web pages in order to create an environment where we can learn about our Web audience. Don Peppers, a noted authority on one-to-one marketing, calls this a "learning relationship." In an *Information Week* article, "Market of One—Ready, Aim, Sell!" (February 17, 1997), John Foley describes how one-to-one marketing on the Web requires the use of three technologies working together to form relationships with customers: customer databases, interactive media, and systems that support mass customization. Peppers and Rogers popularized the term *mass customization*, the concept of using these technologies to provide customers with customized products and services that meet their individual needs.

In industrial manufacturing, design engineers learned early that by specifying components instead of custom manufactured parts, a wide range of products could be made from a small number of subassemblies. In the early 1980s, this became the basis for a class of software called materials requirements planning (MRP) software, which tied every department together with a unified database structure. Sales orders entered into an MRP system immediately influenced the purchase of materials that would be needed weeks later to assemble the product as well as production scheduling, accounting, and other parts of the company.

While later enhancements to MRP systems improved service at manufacturers with a relatively small number of customers, the concept of mass customization has been difficult to implement for a large number of customers until just recently. Easy access to the Internet for field salespeople and customers now allows companies to integrate information systems from the initial inquiry through the sales, manufacturing, and distribution processes.

Content Management

The area of content management on a Web site has started receiving attention because as Web sites become large, the issue of site maintenance becomes even larger. Jesse Berst, editorial director at Ziff-Davis' ZDNet AnchorDesk, is a proponent of using databases to separate the content of a Web site from the format of the Web site. In his article, "The Best Way to Build Web Pages" (www.zdnet.com/anchordesk/story/story_964.html), Berst made the point by describing how his online publication handles content management: "You create the content in a database (type in text, specify which graphics you want, etc.). Then the database pours that content into preformatted templates to create HTML pages. Since content and format are separate, you can change them independently. If you want to give all your pages a new look, you simply change one template. (Compare that to changing each page manually one at a time.)"

When you take a look at previous articles at some news sites, the old article is accompanied by current headlines.

Some of the benefits of using database-driven content Web site tools include the following:

Consistent format. Each page of content is formatted the same way using a limited number of templates.

Content creation separated from graphics creation. Individuals on a Web management team can focus on their skills without concern for interfering with others on the team.

Easy to maintain. Because only a few template pages need to be updated when the format changes, the job of updating a site requires less work.

With different browsers—and different versions of the same browser—supporting different sets of features, it's always been a challenge to develop Web sites that a majority of the audience can see. With the advent of the new Extensible Markup Language (XML) that will be used in place of HTML for many Web sites, it is more important to separate content from format and then let the Web server determine which browser someone is using and which template to use.

Because the whole topic of how XML will affect the format of Web sites is ongoing, be sure to periodically review our One-to-One Web Marketing Online Web site (www.1to1web.com) for updates.

Customization

In addition to maintaining text content, a database is perfect for Web sites that use a significant amount of customized information. An excellent example of displaying information in a table form is a television schedule that is customized for each market.

For example, Gist Communications, Inc., provides TV listings and related content at its Web site (www.gist.com). Gist's software enables users to create a customized television listings guide on the Internet and links to sites related to individual television shows. Because the format of most of the pages is consistent, it is perfect to use a database and templates to display these Web pages on the fly.

Of course, when you gather the information from your audience needed to customize their Web experiences, you are also gathering information you can use offline in your traditional marketing activities. For example, Hewlett-Packard (HP) (www.hp.com) has been enhancing the accuracy of its customer database. Because many of its products are sold through resellers, HP has found it difficult to obtain accurate information about its end customers. Information about customers is gathered in a number of ways, including through its Web site. Periodically HP uses leads and customer data to mail a questionnaire requesting updated contact information that also includes cross-sell and upsell promotions based on the products that had been bought in the past.

Another way databases of information gathered from a Web audience can be used is illustrated by the florist organization FTD. It has recently added a database system that can store a customer's billing information (except credit card information) and recipient information in its database for automatic order entry. This is in addition to the reminder service that stores information about holidays and sends custom reminder e-mail messages. FTD expects to use this database to promote special offers to the tens of thousands of people in the database.

Commerce

One of the most talked-about uses of a Web site is to take orders for products from consumers. When entrepreneurs first saw how inexpensive it was to publish a few pages on the Web, they thought they'd found the silver bullet to competing with large companies. In the early days of the Web, one of the most used phrases was "level playing field."

Unfortunately for small entrepreneurs, the effort required to produce a Web site that can process customer orders is more complex and requires more technical expertise than most do-it-yourself entrepreneurs can muster.

The good news is that tools are becoming available that make it easy to conduct commerce on the Web, and forecasts indicate that both consumer and business-to-business commerce on the Web will continue to experience tremendous growth. Although the leading analyst firms differ in their forecasts, one research group, e-Marketer (www.e-land.com), projects that consumer sales on the Web will grow to $6 billion by the year 2000, while business-to-business commerce on the Web in the year 2000 will reach $140 billion.

"While consumer online revenue is growing rapidly, all researchers agree that the big money in e-commerce will come from business-to-business sales over the Net. This mirrors the physical world where business transactions are worth 10 times as much as consumer sales."

The whole topic of commerce on the Internet is fraught with pitfalls that can catch you in its net (so to speak). Once you decide to take a perfectly good marketing Web site and add the one-to-one aspects of commerce, get ready to learn about databases, security, and federal laws dealing with financial transactions.

On the other hand, the potential for additional revenue is very high. The challenges of conducting commerce on the Internet are much the same as the ones businesses face in the physical world:

Identity. Is the person or company placing the order really who he or she says he or she is, or in the case of orders from companies, does the person actually have authority to commit the company to the purchase?

Credit worthiness. Does the individual placing the order actually have the funds available?

Security. Is the transmitted financial data protected all along the path so that no unscrupulous person can intercept it?

The process of meeting these and other challenges to electronic commerce have, for the most part, been overcome with standards, accepted procedures, and industry-accepted products and services.

Customer Service

One of the most effective uses of one-to-one Web marketing is helping customers by providing them with access to a variety of information as services.

A very easy way to add a database to a Web site that provides customers (and prospects) with a great deal of value is to add a search engine to make it easy to find help documents.

Agfa-Gevaert Group (www.agfa.com), a manufacturer of photographic and imaging products, uses a search engine within its customer support Web site to help customers locate documents based on search criteria. While this is the same technique as providing a search engine for an entire Web site, there are several benefits to restricting a search engine to just customer support documents:

- A restricted search makes it easy to find documents specifically related to solving customer problems.
- The marketing portion of your Web site remains presented in the order designed for it.
- Old or semi-private documents that are not linked are not accessible through the search engine.

Costs of Adding Database Technology

The cost of adding a database to an existing Web site varies according to the type of database being added, but a recent study published in NetMarketing (netb2b.com) found a median cost of $62,000.

Products and Services

A wide range of products and services uses databases and real-time connectivity technologies in Web marketing. The few companies listed here are taken from the more comprehensive listing of resources on our One-to-One Web Marketing Online Web site (www.1to1web.com):

CONTENT MANAGEMENT	
Thunderstone	www.thunderstone.com
Vignette Corporation	www.vignette.com
CUSTOMIZATION	
BroadVision	www.broadvision.com
GuestTrack	www.guesttrack.com
COMMERCE	
Electronic Authorization Systems, Inc.	www.easpays.com
Electronic Card Systems	www.ecsworldwide.com
Automated Transaction Services, Inc.	www.atsbank.com
Anacom Communications, Inc.	www.anacom.com
CUSTOMER SERVICE	
Oracle	www.oracle.com
Sybase	www.sybase.com

The Future of One-to-One Web Site Personalization

One-to-one Web site personalization is used at a number of high-profile sites, but it is still relatively unused at mainstream sites, so it will continue to advance for the foreseeable future. What we will see in the near future is the convergence of real-time and previously collected tracking data. Users who return to a site will receive information based on past visits. This is what Jupiter Communications calls the active pull method. Web site personalization will become more sophisticated and will become more integrated with offline sales, marketing, and customer service processes and systems.

In addition, there will be increased integration of a company's Web site with other points of contact with customers, which is covered in Chapter 7, "One-to-One Web CRM."

As mentioned earlier, the cost to add database technology to a Web site is initially higher than the cost of publishing a Web site using static pages; however, the ongoing cost is much lower. Why go to this extra expense? Many marketing executives have a feeling that customizing the content and customer service of a Web site builds an attraction on the part of the prospect or customer, but they generally don't know why customization and personalization increase affinity.

In his article in *Forbes* (www.forbes.com), "Brands with Feeling," Joshua Levine showed that some marketers understand that there is an emotional aspect to the relationship between marketer and customer—that customers look for emotional satisfaction with their purchases. The two questions for marketers are, of course, what can we do to increase the emotional satisfaction and how can we do that with our Web sites?

The answer to the first question is to understand the personal motivations of your audience and to adapt your message so that it is more understandable and accepted. In his book, *Taking Care of Business* (Pocket Books, 1985), Dr. David Viscott wrote about having identified three main types of people, as well as the goals and driving forces of each type:

- To belong
- To own
- To win

Traditional direct marketers have used buying motives like this for years by providing multiple pieces of sales material in a single mailing, relying on the prospect to pick and choose the piece to read based on his or her personal motivations. This is, of course, an expensive route to "personalization," but for many marketers it has been effective.

Because most Web marketers have created their Web sites based on the assumption that every prospect has the same personal buying motives, it is hard to find examples of Web sites that recognize the personal differences between people. The first step is understanding the differences between people who appear to have the same needs.

Values and Lifestyles

SRI International (www.sri.com), an independent, nonprofit research institute, has conducted a series of research studies since 1978 that take demographics to the next step—psychographics. Traditional demographic consumer-research techniques measure attributes such as age, gender, and income—an approach that is useful for understanding where people stand in society. A psychographic approach takes the analysis a step further, measuring people's attitudes and lifestyle characteristics. Such measurements are excellent indicators of how people are thinking and where they are going with their lives.

SRI's Values and Lifestyles (VALS) program groups people into eight categories:

- Actualizers
- Fulfilleds

- Achievers
- Experiencers
- Believers
- Strivers
- Makers
- Strugglers

The Impact of Empathy

As Web marketers add techniques such as personalization, advanced tracking, and data mining to their one-to-one Web marketing toolbox, a new understanding of the Web audience will emerge. By combining what we learn about each individual's psychographic profile with his or her Web behavior we will be able to tailor the Web experience more closely to each person's needs.

Our experience in developing highly personalized Web sites, combined with our experience in traditional in-person sales and direct marketing, has led us to develop the Five E's of One-to-One Web Marketing:

Empathize. Understand the logical and emotional needs of each person.

Enrich. Provide information about products and services that is based on what you've learned about the individual.

Enhance. Give your message more impact by adding to the value the user expects to receive.

Encourage. Show how the user's quick decision can improve his or her situation sooner.

Enliven. Support your customer with types of extra benefits that appeal to his or her individual motivations.

One aspect of the future of Web-to-database integration will involve better data processing techniques, better security, and faster response to customer needs. An even larger impact will occur as Web marketers learn to use database technology to understand not only the obvious needs of customers, but also the emotional wants and desires that drive all purchase decisions.

Up Next

The next chapter is dedicated to an important adjunct to personalization—one-to-one e-mail.

One-to-One E-Mail

"The marketer's mindset should always be to evaluate the value proposition from the perspective of the user."

John Funk, Founder of InfoBeat

E-mail is one of the most popular uses of the Internet. Practically everyone with access to the Internet uses e-mail to send messages to friends, relatives, and coworkers. In fact, there are more people in the world with access to e-mail than with access to the World Wide Web. This means e-mail marketing can grab attention and interest without requiring users to even start their Web browsers.

One of the reasons that e-mail marketing works so well is that people look forward to receiving e-mail from friends, relatives, and coworkers. This means that their attitude is more open and accepting than in more advertising-oriented media, such as advertising-supported Web sites, as well as traditional print and electronic media and direct mail.

In fact, most of the newer e-mail systems support hyperlinks within the e-mail message that launch a browser and link the reader directly to the Web page. Even more exciting is support for HTML within an e-mail message that makes it look like a Web page, including hyperlinks, graphics, and even multimedia.

Of course, like many Internet-related technologies, there is some controversy, which, in this case, can be summed up in one word: spam (and we're not talking about lunch). Spam is unsolicited e-mail broadcasts that are indiscriminate, untargeted, bandwidth unfriendly, and almost 100 percent of the time unwelcome.

The concept of one-to-one marketing takes a marketer from simply broadcasting a message to a mass audience to speaking to individuals. Whether a marketer writes a message for a narrow target audience or uses personalization to tailor the content of each message individually, one-to-one e-mail marketing can build a relationship between the customer and the company.

A recent report by Jupiter Communications predicts that U.S. online consumers will receive more than 1600 commercial e-mail messages in 2005. This will fuel a $7.3 billion e-mail marketing industry.

Interesting e-mail factoids:

- Telephone directory companies now offer services that let people include their e-mail addresses alongside their standard telephone listing.

On the flip side:

- According to the tenth GVU survey (www.cc.gatech.edu/gvu/user_surveys/), 90 percent of the respondents dislike receiving mass e-mailings. An earlier GVU study found that 61 percent of respondents delete spam without reading the message, 19 percent ask to be removed from the list, 11 percent actually read the e-mail, and 5 percent retaliate against the spammer.
- There is a healthy debate among industry, users, and government organizations on setting guidelines for e-mail broadcasting.
- There are organizations whose purpose is to heighten awareness about spam, and some cyberactivists have resorted to more drastic measures, such as blocking postings.
- Software products are being created to filter messages from known e-mail solicitors. There are also services that help people remove their names from e-mail marketing lists.

The controversy over spam has made e-mail marketing an uphill battle for Web marketers. It will be interesting to see what happens over the next few years. Many people are advocating that the Internet industry self-regulate before the government does. E-mail can be a great tool for one-to-one Web marketers in forming lasting relationships with customers. E-mail can also play a useful role in customer service. In order to make sure that this tool becomes an accepted medium, marketers should listen to their users and customers when it comes to their opinions and preferences regarding e-mail. This chapter covers the fine and delicate art of using e-mail as a very effective and efficient electronic marketing tool.

Benefits of One-to-One E-Mail

In their book, *The One to One Future* (Doubleday, 1993), Don Peppers and Martha Rogers stated that one-to-one media is "individually addressable." Internet technology, such as e-mail, has evolved to become individually addressable via personalization and customization. E-mail makes it easier and cheaper to communicate with users, prospects, and customers. The primary benefits of one-to-one e-mail include its ability to form a lasting relationship with a customer, increase repeat purchases or visits, and provide an inexpensive "push" mechanism in which the information is pushed out to the user, rather than requiring the user to remember to come visit your Web site.

Benefits to Marketers

Online marketers face a number of challenges today to attract attention and bring people to their site on a regular basis. The large number of promotional messages each person sees during the day creates mental clutter that makes it hard for any single company to reach people. Their one-to-one e-mail marketing techniques can cut through such clutter by treating individuals as, well, individuals.

One of these challenges that online marketers face today is to communicate with members of their audience in ways that are appropriate at each stage of the purchase process. E-mail messages can deliver a wide variety of messages based on where an individual is in the purchase process. This requires using what is known about the individual to select the message that will be most appropriate—and have the greatest impact—for that person. This allows marketers to deliver the right message to the right person at the right time.

Forming Relationships with Customers

E-mail broadcasts and one-to-one personalized e-mails enhance a Web marketer's ability to form loyal, long-lasting relationships with customers through a personalized dialogue. The more you know about your customers, the easier it is to provide them with the things they value.

When someone has visited your Web site for the first time and has an interest in the products you sell, it's important to capture the e-mail address so you can communicate with them in the future. Many times customers are looking for information about products and are eager to subscribe to a company's newsletter in order to receive that information. They want to receive this information because they are not yet ready to make a purchase, so they want to research the product category more thoroughly.

This is a great opportunity to stay in touch with a prospective customer right up until he or she makes a purchase decision.

By recognizing that it takes time for a prospect to make a purchase decision, and by providing helpful information in an e-mail newsletter, it's more likely that you will make the sale instead of your competitor.

One of the reasons this works is that the customer has an opportunity to evaluate you and your company over a period of time in a safe environment prior to purchasing. How your company acts toward the individual is seen as an indication of how that person will be treated if he or she makes a purchase from your company. In other words, the e-mail newsletter that you send out each month to people who have not yet purchased is a way to build a relationship with these people.

In addition to building customer relations, e-mail marketing can also help you compete more effectively. Because we are all feeling the pinch of time, we have only enough time to spend on Web sites that provide us with the most value. Therefore, if a customer highly values your e-mail service, he or she will spend more time with you and less with your competitor. If you are applying one-to-one Web marketing, then you have a powerful tool to enhance your competitive position. In their second best-selling book, *Enterprise One to One* (Currency/Doubleday, 1997), Don Peppers and Martha Rogers postulate, "Give your customer the opportunity to teach you what he wants. Remember it, give it back to him, and keep his business forever."

Peppers and Rogers believe that when customers invest time in customizing your offering to their liking, they will continue to invest additional time. One-to-one e-mail can mimic a personalized sales call, which is the most effective one-to-one communication. A sales visit to a customer is the most expensive way to acquire or maintain a customer. E-mail is a highly effective alternative and is relatively low in cost.

Increasing Repeat Customer Visits or Purchases

As the familiar saying goes, "If you build it, they will come." As we Web site owners know, however, this is simply not true. Now, with e-mail: If you tell them to come, they will come. If your site provides a valued experience or service for customers, and if you send them periodic e-mails, you will increase repeat visits by these customers—especially with hyperlinks embedded in the e-mail message. Of course, the e-mails must provide value as well, or customers will not sign up to receive it or will remove themselves from the list. With the increasing number of Web sites still vying for the small, albeit quickly growing, universe of online users and customers, experienced Web marketers know they need to provide a value-added service like e-mail to get people to continue to visit their site.

Benefits to Customers

In addition to helping visitors become customers, one-to-one e-mail marketing can also keep existing customers aware of your offerings and bring them back to your Web site to make repeat purchases.

Even though consumers at home evaluate products differently from business buyers, they have many things in common. Both consumers and those purchasing for companies are increasingly using the Internet to locate the best products at the best possible prices. By sending customers frequent e-mails it's possible to maintain what marketers call "top of mind" awareness. This reminds them of the choice of products you offer, as well as the ease of purchasing by using their account that they have already set up on your Web site.

By using a variety of personalization techniques, it is possible to use interest profile data and purchase history data to suggest very appropriate products to customers.

We recently conducted an online survey to learn how consumers view personalization, including the use of personalized e-mail newsletters. Over half of the respondents (54 percent) wanted to receive a personalized newsletter with the stories and product notices that match their interests. In addition, people want to receive these newsletters frequently. Table 3.1 shows the responses to a question about how often people want to receive an e-mail newsletter from an online merchant with which they shop.

> "You have to make the messages interesting and informative, not just sales pitches. Links within the e-mail that take people to relevant pages work well and encourage people to get more information."
>
> Cyndy Ainsworth, Virtual Vineyards (www.wine.com)

Table 3.1 Survey Responses on How Often Customers Want to Receive an E-Mail Newsletter from an Online Merchant

ANSWER	RESPONSE
Once a week	30%
Twice a month	18%
Once a month	27%
Once a quarter	10%
Not at all	16%

Nuts and Bolts of One-to-One E-Mail

E-mail can be used to deliver material in a variety of formats. The most common uses of e-mail include the following:

- Sending an informational newsletter to a list of subscribers
- Sending promotional announcements (i.e., ads) to an in-house list of visitors and customers who opted into the list
- Renting a list from an e-mail list broker and have the broker distribute a promotional announcement for you
- Creating a discussion list where messages from participants are automatically distributed to all members of the list

In addition to selecting the purpose and type of format for e-mail marketing, you need to determine whether you should manage the mailings in-house or use an outside service.

Managing Your Own Mailing List Server

A mailing list software product is a relatively inexpensive tool to maintain on your own server that enables you to distribute messages to a list of people, such as customers, prospects, and members of a discussion group. Even with its one-to-many orientation, a mailing list server can be an effective one-to-one marketing tool. Some mailing list server software products are free, and the rest are very reasonably priced, especially considering their enhanced features and ease of use.

A mailing list server allows you to maintain a regular dialogue with your Web site visitors or customers. By sending out periodic e-mail notices or e-mail newsletters, your customers will be reminded that your Web site is still out there in cyberspace. Periodic mailings can help "pull" customers to your Web site on a regular basis. Because customers must choose to sign up to receive the electronic mailings, they are less likely to look at these messages as unsolicited e-mail or spam—especially if the information provided is of value to the recipient.

Technology Overview

Mailing list server programs automate the management of Internet mailing lists. If you have hundreds or thousands of customers, a list server will save you a lot of time. The mailing list software allows you to broadcast one e-mail message to many people simultaneously. There are several mailing list software applications available that support Unix, Windows, and Macintosh platforms (see Figure 3.1). If you want to implement and manage the system yourself, some programming skills may be required, as well as some knowledge of operating systems, Web servers, and programming languages.

Once you have selected a mailing list server program, you will need to determine if you will host it on your server, with your ISP, or with a mailing list hosting service. If you do not have a dedicated server to host the mailing list yourself, contact your ISP to host the list for you. When the system is set up, it will typically function as shown in Figure 3.1. The steps associated with the mailing list process are as follows:

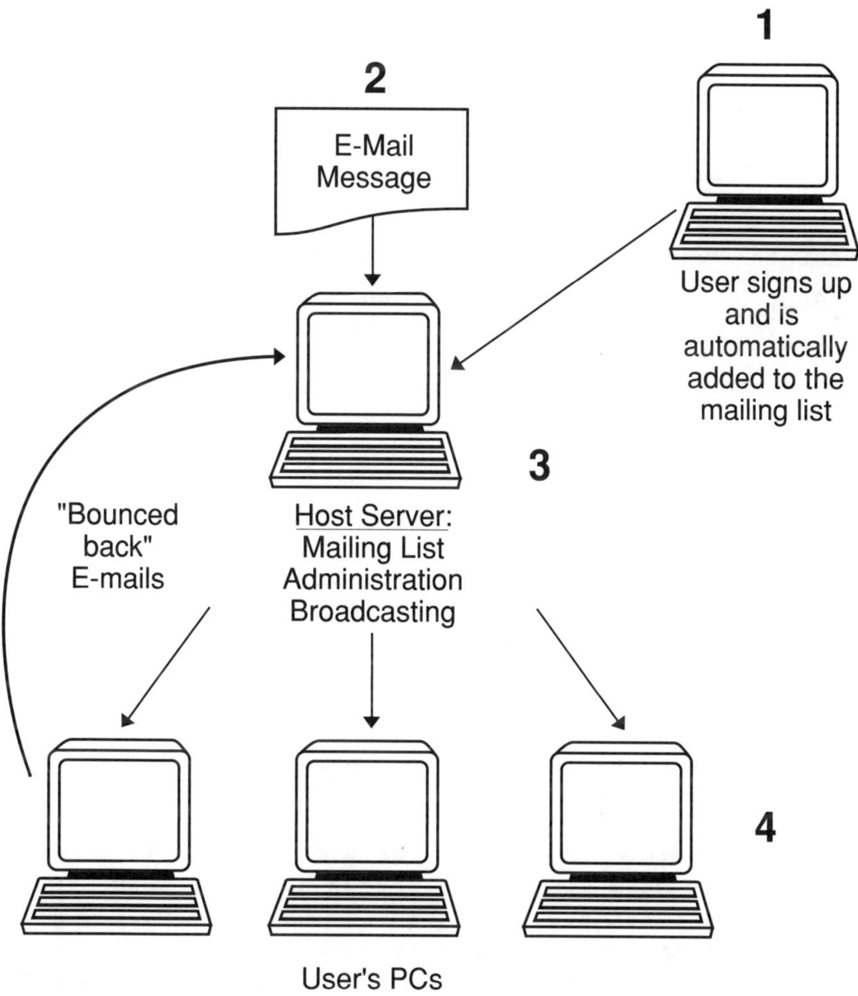

Figure 3.1 Typical mailing list server system.

1. Users sign up for the e-mail notifications or newsletters.
2. You construct the e-mail message.
3. The e-mail message is sent to the address for the mailing list server.
4. The e-mail message is broadcast to all users.

When the user signs up to receive e-mails from a Web site, he or she submits an e-mail address to the site via an e-mail message or online form. The list server automatically adds the user to the mailing list database and sends a confirmation e-mail to the user. Figure 3.2 shows a typical confirmation notice.

When an e-mail message or newsletter is created, it is sent to the list address and is broadcast to all Web site customers who signed up for the service. Including hyperlinks to Web site URLs in the message is a powerful way to pull users to your site—which is the purpose of most one-to-one e-mail campaigns. Hyperlinks and e-mail addresses that are embedded inside e-mails make it easy for the user to take action and increase the likelihood of response. When you send e-mail to a large list keep in mind that

```
X-Persona: <dakania>
Return-Path: <owner-aboutworknews@xanadu.ivillage.com>
Date: Sun, 27 Jul 1997 16:39:56 -0400 (EDT)
To: dakania@mindspring.com
From: Majordomo@ivillage.com
Subject: Welcome to aboutworknews
Reply-To: Majordomo@ivillage.com

 Welcome to the aboutworknews mailing list! Please save
this message for future reference.  Thank you. If you ever
want to remove yourself from this mailing list, you can
send mail to  Majordomo@xanadu.ivillage.com with the fol-
lowing command in the body of your email message:

      unsubscribe aboutworknews dakania@mindspring.com

 Here's the general information for the list you've sub-
scribed to,  in case you don't already have it: Thank you
for taking the first steps to joining the About Work Com-
munity. Expect to receive a weekly newsletter containing
information on what's new at About Work. www.aboutwork.com
```

Figure 3.2 Example of a subscription confirmation message.

not everyone's e-mail program supports embedded hyperlinks, so you may need to instruct users to copy and paste, or manually enter, the link into their Web browsers.

Also keep in mind that for most promotional messages you should rely on several small "sound bites" of information instead of several long articles. This approach is user friendly in that it doesn't require a lot of download time, which can be frustrating to users. It also doesn't require them to scroll through screen after screen of information to find what is beneficial to them.

Costs and Benefits of a Mailing List Server

Mailing list software costs can range from free to a few thousand dollars. The additional Web server usage and traffic will also add to the cost of your site operations. Add to that the human resources required to manage the system and write the editorial and marketing copy. Virtual Vineyards (www.wine.com), a pioneering and leading online merchant that specializes in wine, food, and gifts, provides an e-mail notification service. It states that the cost to implement was minimal, and it has achieved its goal of building community, reminding customers of offerings, and building confidence among patrons regarding recommendations from Peter Granoff, Virtual Vineyards' wine expert, proprietor, cofounder, and general manager. Granoff personally writes the e-mail notifications that are sent using an automated mailing list server.

If your goal is to form lasting relationships with your Web audience or customers, a mailing list will enhance your ability to achieve this goal, at a reasonable expense. What is particularly nice about mailing lists is that you can measure their success very easily. A successful list keeps growing, one user at a time. If people do not find your e-mails valuable, they will unsubscribe. It is perfectly normal to have some turnover or "churn" in your list because experienced marketers know they cannot be all things to all people.

Another way to determine whether your e-mailings are valued is to ask for feedback. An interesting phenomenon about the Internet is that people tend to be more open with their opinions than they would be if they were in a face-to-face meeting or on the telephone. By providing an e-mail address—or a dedicated Web site URL that links a feedback form—in the e-mail message, your customers can readily provide comments, suggestions, and ideas about your service.

Products/Services

There are a few products or services you can use to create and manage a mailing list server. You can choose between an automated or moderated mailing list server based on your marketing objectives or resources. In the section, we have included a list of resources to give you more information about implementing your own mailing list server.

Automated, Receive-Only Mailing Lists

One of the simplest ways to send e-mails to a large group of users—without a lot of human interaction or resources—is to use a broadcast or automated, receive-only method. This allows you to provide useful information to all of your users or subsets of users. The following mailing list server applications and services will handle much of the administration and management associated with maintaining a list server, including handling "bounced back" e-mails that were undeliverable.

FREE MAILING LIST SOFTWARE

Majordomo	www.greatcircle.com/majordomo/
Majordomo FAQ	www.cis.ohio-state.edu/~barr/majordomo-faq.html
Pegasus Mail	www.pegasus.usa.com/

MAILING LIST SOFTWARE

GroupMaster from MessageMedia	www.messagemedia.com (also hosts mailing lists)
ListProc from Corporation for Research and Educational Networking (CREN)	www.cren.net
ListServ from L-Soft International, Inc.	www.lsoft.com (also hosts mailing lists)
ListStar (Macintosh only)	www.starnine.com
Lyris from Shelby Group Ltd.	www.lyris.com

MAILING LIST HOSTING SERVICES

Sling Shot Media	www.slingshotmedia.com
SparkNET's Majordomo Hosting Service	www.sparklist.com
Topica	www.topica.com
EGroups	www.egroups.com
MessageMedia	www.messagemedia.com

Moderated Discussion Lists

Another way to use a mailing list server program (like the ones just mentioned) is to create a discussion list that acts like a forum, similar to Usenet newsgroups. This is a great way to move further down the path to one-to-one e-mail marketing. A discussion list basically allows you to exchange ideas with your users or customers. Typically these e-mail discussion groups allow users to exchange ideas while you moderate the discussion. The discussion list moderator receives and reviews all incoming e-mail messages before they are posted. This process takes time, but it also ensures that the messages are "fit to print" and do not include bad language, irrelevant information, or unsolicited advertising.

Discussion groups are typically administered via e-mail, but more of them are now being conducted using the Web interface. Although a discussion list does not have the "real time" benefits of chat, it can be a way to form a sense of community with your audience. If you would like to see discussion groups in action, visit Liszt, a mailing list directory (www.liszt.com). Figure 3.3 shows its search capability, as well as a few of the categories of discussion lists and newsletters found at Liszt.

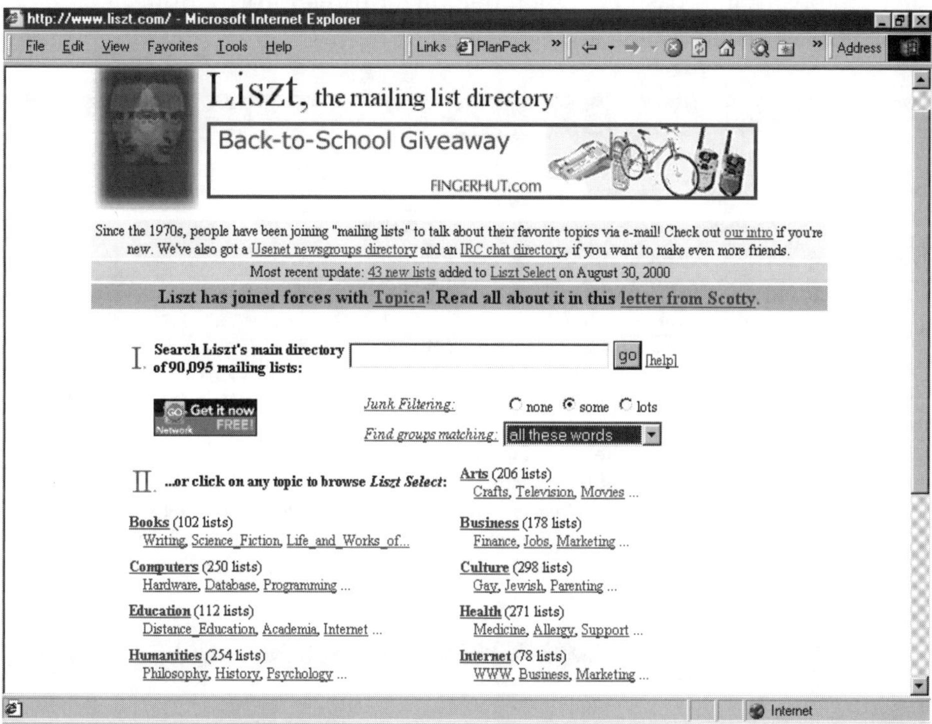

Figure 3.3 Liszt directory of mailing lists.

One alternative to moderated discussion lists are "open" lists. The benefit of having an open list is that it doesn't require the time it takes to moderate the list. The list owner (you) has little control over what is being posted to the discussion lists. Finally, another alternative is to have a "closed" list that restricts the use of the list. One example of this is on *The Wall Street Journal Interactive* Edition Web site (www.wsj.com), which has several discussions at any given time, but restricts them to customers who have signed up and paid for the online edition of the business newspaper (see Figure 3.4).

Managing a Personalized E-Mail Service

With the integration of databases with the Web and e-mail, personalizing content to a user's or customer's profile is a relatively new and rapidly growing electronic marketing application.

One of the features of using the Internet for marketing is its ability to uniquely identify individuals who come to a Web site and to identify who is sent e-mail messages. This allows marketers to use software to target messages to small groups of people and even to individuals. In addition, the power of database marketing allows content of individual e-mail messages to be tailored based on each person's profile information.

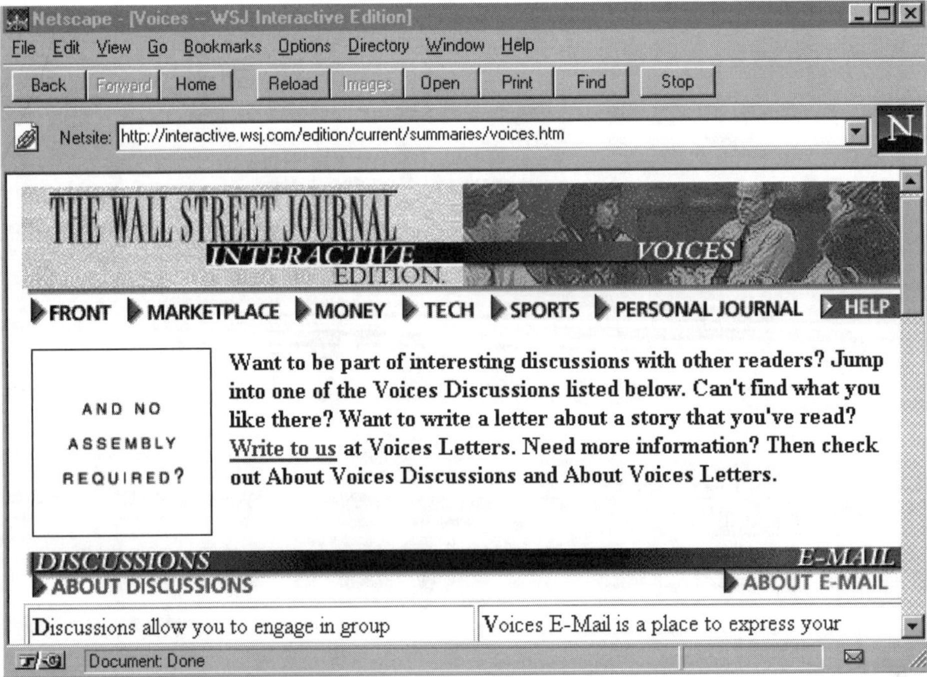

Figure 3.4 *The Wall Street Journal* Interactive Edition discussion forum.

While it's still relatively expensive to convert a static Web site into a dynamic (or database-driven) personalized Web site, e-mail personalization is another story. It has become relatively easy and inexpensive to use personalized e-mail products and services. The easiest way to implement a personalized e-mail newsletter is to outsource the database management and e-mail distribution to a vendor specializing in e-mail management.

The most challenging aspect of managing a personalized e-mail newsletter is usually the subscription process. A database is needed to capture profile data and make it available to the software that creates individualized e-mail messages. When using an outside e-mail distribution service there are two approaches to managing the subscription database.

One approach is to maintain the database on your Web server so that subscribers link to a subscription form on your Web site to create and update their profile. Unfortunately, this means the database must be transmitted to the outside vendor each time a mailing is sent.

The other approach is to maintain the database on the Web server at the vendor's server, such as Sling Shot Media (www.slingshotmedia.com). This means the subscription form used by subscribers to create and update their profile is actually served by the vendor's server.

This makes it easier to create and distribute newsletters and promotional mailings quickly because the database and distribution software are on the same server. Figure 3.5 shows the features of the newsletter content management system used by clients of Sling Shot Media. Each issue's stories are entered via a Web form (see Figure 3.6). Interest profiles provided by readers (see Figure 3.7) are used to automatically select which stories should be included in each reader's own personalized newsletter.

The potential problem with this approach, however, is in keeping the look and feel of the subscription form the same as those of the main site. Fortunately, most sites do not change their overall look and feel very often, so this is usually not a problem.

Most personalized newsletters allow subscribers to choose exactly which topics they are interested in reading about. This means the subscription form needs to have checkboxes next to the descriptions of each topic that update the profile for that individual.

Travelocity (www.travelocity.com) is a leading "one-stop" consumer-direct travel service Web site and is integrated with the well-known SABRE online travel reservation services. Travelocity was launched in March of 1996. Travelocity is a combination of travel-related content, electronic commerce, and community. The site offers a wealth of travel tips, fun and informative travel editorials, discussion and chat forums, interactive maps, travel merchandise, and an online travel booking service for air, car, and hotel reservations. Users can also build a personal travel profile, including

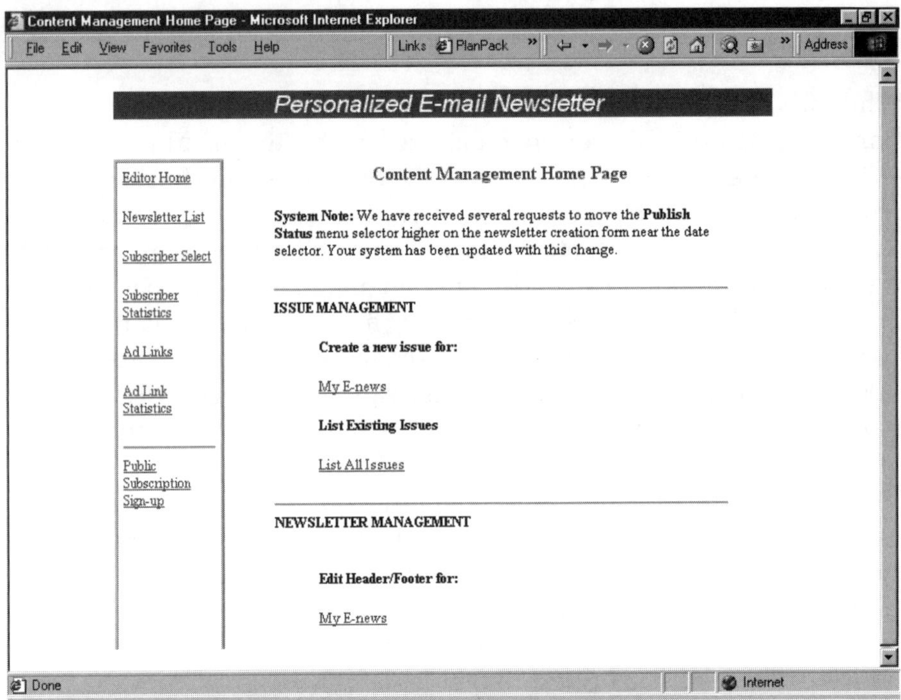

Figure 3.5 Web-based content management system for creating and publishing e-mail newsletters.

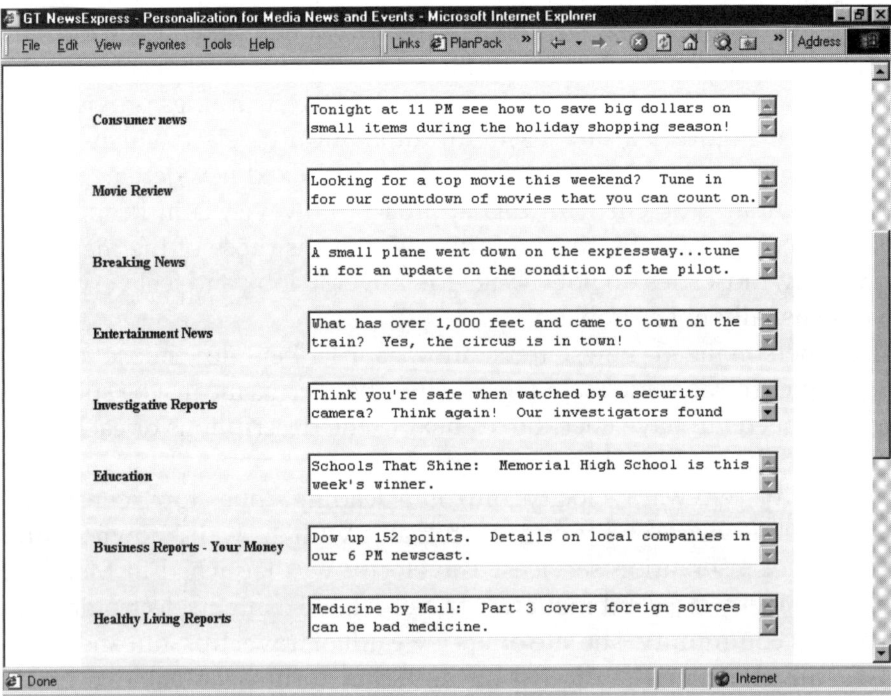

Figure 3.6 Typical newsletter input form used by clients of Sling Shot Media.

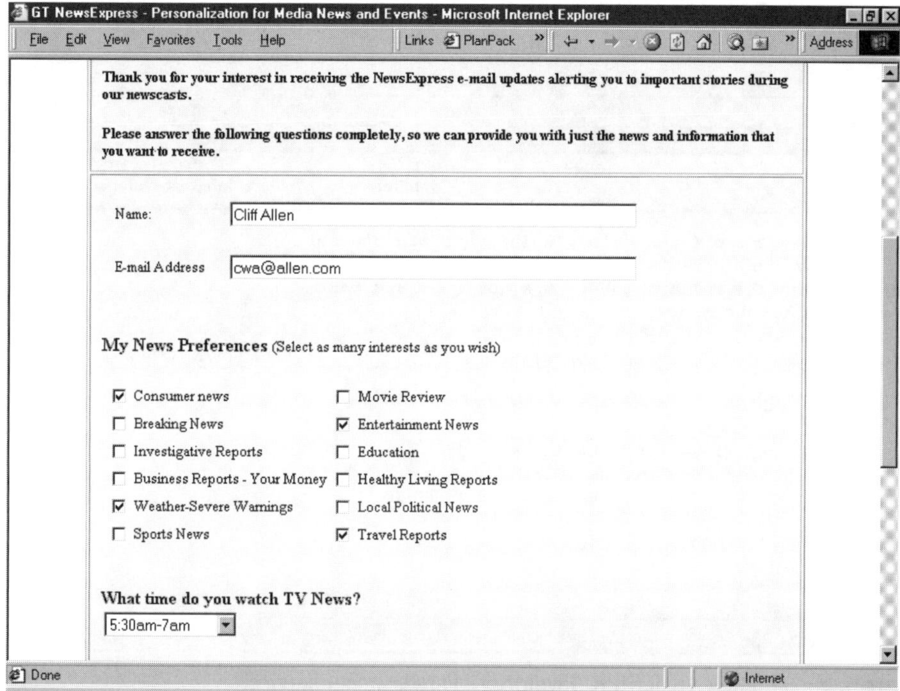

Figure 3.7 A subscription form for selecting interests for a personalized e-mail newsletter.

the location of their travel agency where they can pick up the tickets that they ordered online.

Travelocity offers the free, customizable, and automated Fare Watcher e-mail service to its registered members. The Fare Watcher e-mail service monitors airfares in up to five markets for daily price fluctuations (plus or minus at least $25). A sample personalized e-mail shown in Figure 3.8 shows the fares and includes travel tips, links to travel information, and reservation pages on the Travelocity Web site.

By customizing or personalizing the e-mail to the recipient, it becomes one-to-one marketing communication with the customer. Just as mailing list servers are useful to enhance communications with customers, personalized e-mail services can further enhance a Web marketer's ability to build loyalty or increase sales. According to Bill Binnings, the director of sales and advertising at Travelocity, "The fare special e-mail notification has proven to be a powerful marketing tool. Fare Watcher was a natural fit between technology and customer needs. E-mail messages are sent to Travelocity members to announce the end of a fare special or airline fare war. While SABRE Interactive and Travelocity are very sensitive to the spam issue, we

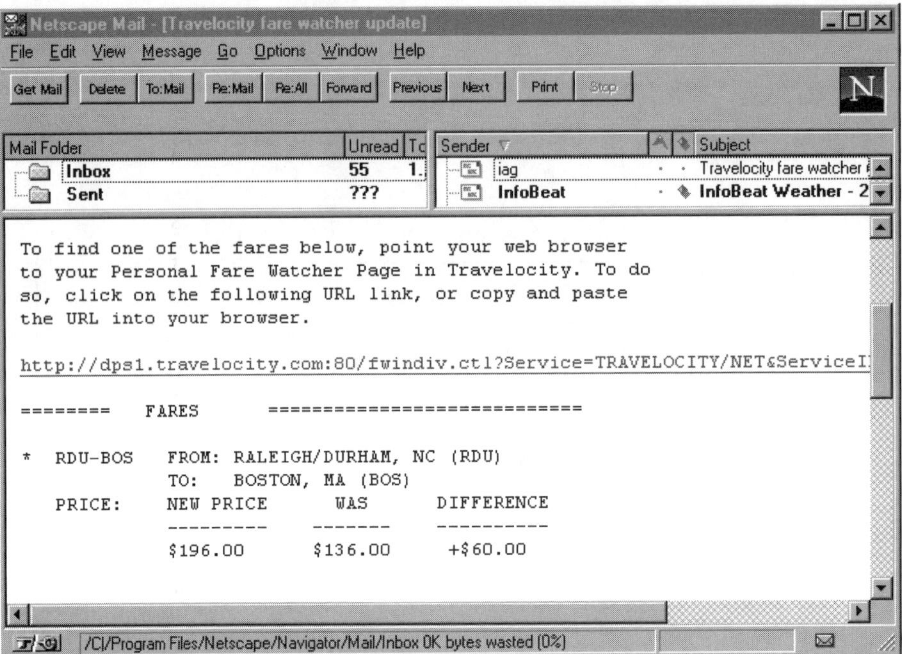

Figure 3.8 Sample e-mail from Travelocity's Fare Watcher service.

have found, through market research, that the vast majority of members appreciate notifications and reminders that can save them money."

TIP **Even with the attractive low cost of conducting e-mail campaigns, you should continue to use other marketing vehicles to gain and retain customers. The Web and e-mail have their unique benefits, just as television, radio, print advertising, direct mail, seminars, trade shows, and other marketing programs have their own value within an integrated marketing campaign.**

The Fare Watcher e-mail service is tied directly to Travelocity's goal of bringing value to its customers so that they will choose Travelocity as their primary source of travel information and transactions. Travelocity also broadcasts a monthly e-mail newsletter that contains useful information about navigating the site, shortcuts, and new online features. The newsletter also contains valuable information about travel in general and tips on how to make trips more pleasant. Travelocity plans to move more toward one-to-one Web marketing by further integrating travel content with the reservation process incorporating each customer's personal information and preferences.

Technology Overview

Personalized e-mail systems are a combination of an e-mail server and a database. To date, most systems have been developed by each site owner, but software products and services are emerging to allow Web marketers to add this functionality to their site without having to build it from scratch. InfoBeat (www.infobeat.com) provides personalized e-mail news and information including finance, sports, entertainment, news, weather, and reminder services. Figure 3.9 shows how the InfoBeat system works.

Three databases are used to create an InfoBeat e-mail message: subscriber information and profile (e.g., which service the user prefers to receive and any personalization specifications), outside information (e.g., weather conditions for the user's specific geographic location), and advertising data. The e-mail engine creates and sends e-mail according to a schedule. Another system logs activity such as successful and unsuccessful e-mail transmissions. A subscription management system handles incoming e-mail messages—for example, people signing up for the service, modifying their profile, or canceling services.

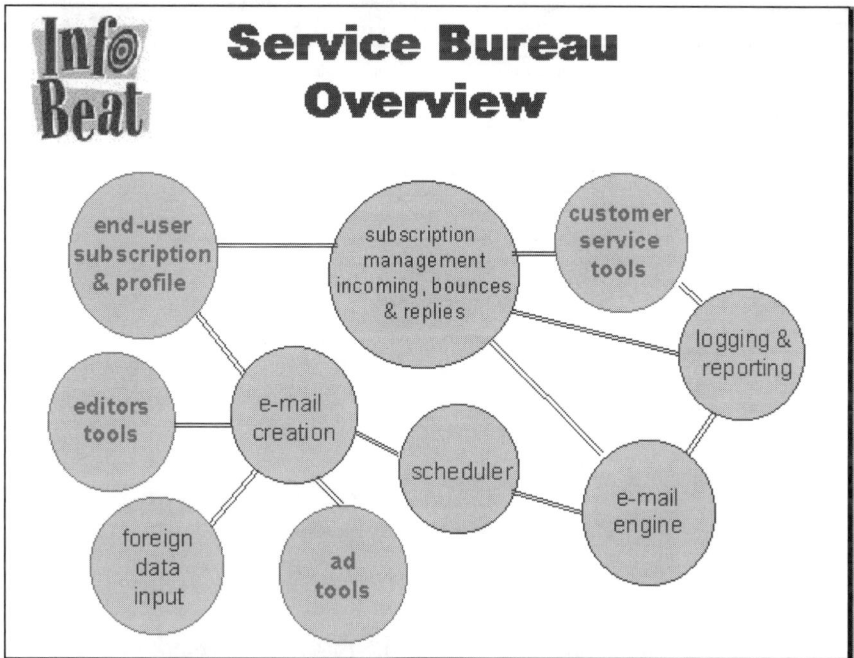

Figure 3.9 InfoBeat's process for creating personalized newsletters.

Costs and Benefits of Personalized E-Mail

The cost for a personalized e-mail system is higher than the cost associated with setting up a mailing list server. The personalized e-mail system also takes more time to implement. If you are already practicing database marketing, you have a head start with the systems, databases, and processes. A personalized e-mail system could take several weeks to implement, depending on the complexity of the desired system and the level of expertise of the people building it.

The added benefit may outweigh the incremental cost over implementing a simple mailing list server. Personalized e-mail systems can deliver one-to-one communications, which can build strong loyalty among users, especially with the prevalence of info glut. Users can choose to receive just the information that is of the most value to them. Recipients look forward to receiving their personalized information, and they are more likely to read the e-mails. Bill Binnings from Travelocity estimated "that the cost would be higher if we 'forced' each interested member to search the system themselves rather than serve the information to them."

In addition to using personalized e-mail for newsletters, the technique can be used to create autoresponder messages that are tailored to each person's needs and interests. Figure 3.10 shows an autoresponder inquiry

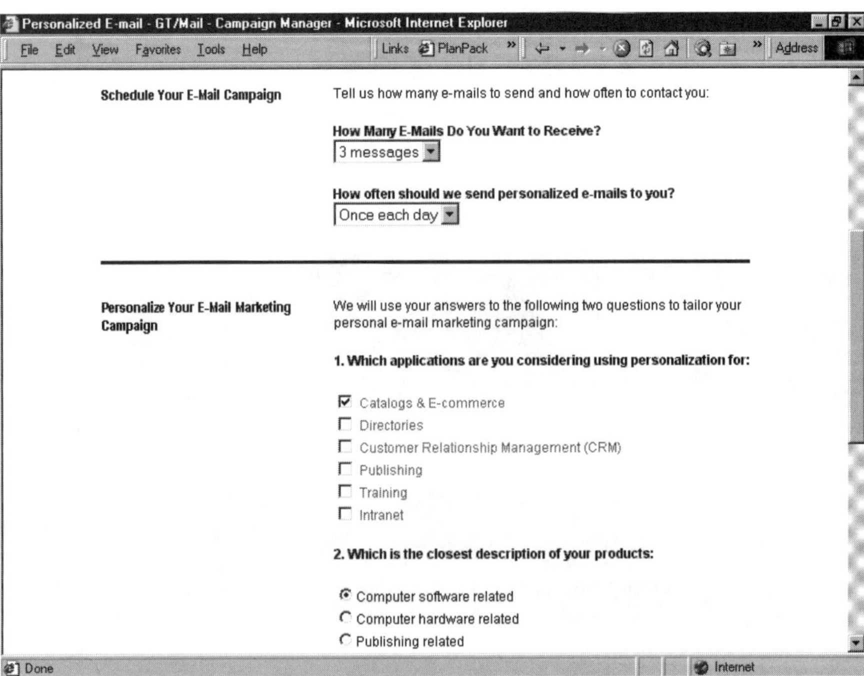

Figure 3.10 Interest profile data used to tailor a personalized autoresponse e-mail about online catalogs.

form where an interest in online catalogs has been checked, and Figure 3.11 shows the e-mail that was created and sent by the personalization system. Figure 3.12 shows the same autoresponder inquiry form with a different interest checked, in this case publishing, and Figure 3.13 shows a slightly different e-mail that was sent.

Products/Services

The market for e-mail marketing products and services is still relatively new, with new solutions becoming available. Each system offers different

```
Subject: Personalization update for Cliff Allen

Thank you for your interest in exploring how personalized
e-mail can help you deliver the right message to the right
people with greater impact.

You indicated an interest in personalizing your online
catalog marketing, so let me share with you a few ways
GT/Mail can apply one-to-one marketing techniques to cre-
ate loyal customers.

So what can GT/Mail do for you? It can:

* Recommend products to people based on their interests
* Bring people back to your site with links to products
based on past purchases
* Send a newsletter with application stories that match
their industry
* Market test different offers and pricing to clusters of
customers
* Obtain feedback from your market with interactive e-mail

If you'd like to learn more about our products, just call
me and we'll discuss your needs.

Regards,

Bob Roberts
```

Figure 3.11 Personalized e-mail sent as a response to inquiring about catalogs.

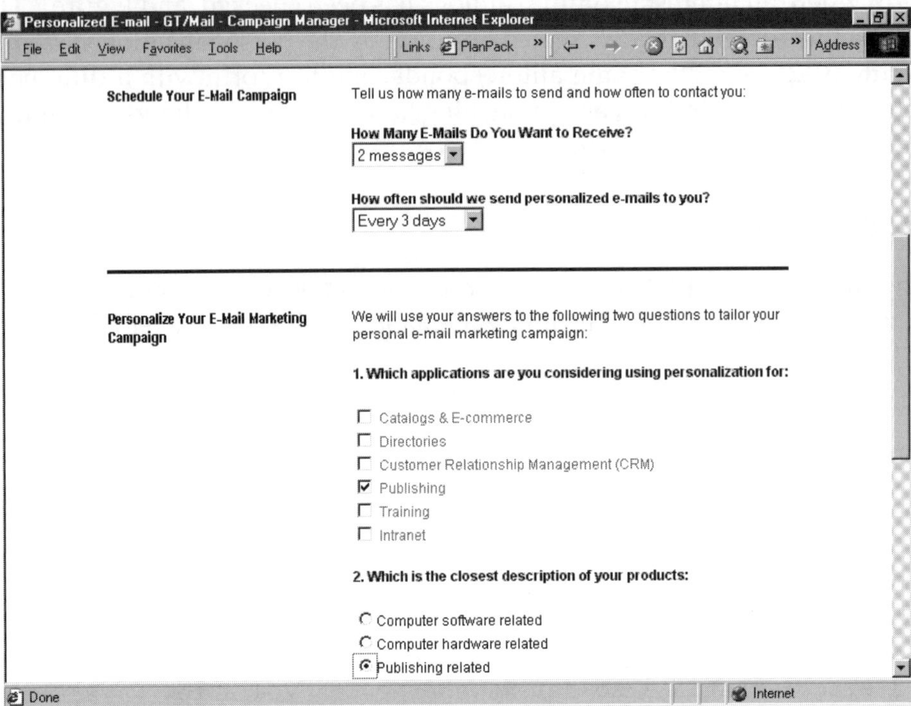

Figure 3.12 Interest profile data used to tailor a personalized autoresponse e-mail about publishing.

features that enable you to create and manage your own personalized e-mail service.

Campaign (Arial Software)

Campaign is an e-mail software program developed by Arial Software (www.arialsoftware.com) that allows Web marketers to create and broadcast targeted e-mail campaigns themselves. Campaign uses Arial Software's ActiveMail engine to provide the ability to create personalized e-mail messages, database integration and filters, message scheduling, and campaign building. Other Arial Software products include the following:

SignUp. Collects Web page form data and puts it into a database.

Respond. Automatically replies to e-mail with information requested by the user.

Director. A package bundle containing three software applications: Campaign, SignUp, and Respond.

```
Subject: Personalization update for Cliff Allen

Thank you for your interest in exploring how personalized
e-mail can help you deliver the right message to the right
people with greater impact.

You indicated an interest in personalizing your online
publishing, so let me share with you a few ways GT/Mail
can be used to create loyal readers.

Many content sites have material that appeals to a broad
range of interests, but most people come to a content site
for a limited range of topics. The way to help readers
quickly find the material they need is to send them an e-
mail newsletter that contains just the headlines and links
they need.

So what can GT/Mail do for you? It can:

* Bring people back to your site with links to new arti-
cles based on their interest areas
* Market products that are related to each reader's inter-
ests
* Deliver targeted ads in the e-mails based on demographic
and interest profile data
* Obtain feedback from your market with interactive e-mail

If you'd like to learn more about our products, call me
and we'll discuss your needs.

Regards,

Bob Roberts
```

Figure 3.13 Personalized e-mail sent as a response to inquiring about publishing.

GT/Mail (GuestTrack)

GT/Mail from GuestTrack (www.guesttrack.com) is a fully personalized system that allows content creators to target groups of people and tailor the content of each person's message based on profile data. The Web interface makes it easy to manage the profile database and the content database, as well as to monitor clickthrough results. The subscription/profile form allows you to gather a wide variety of information, from demographic and psychographic information from consumers, to specific technical needs about products. GT/Mail uses simple or complex decision rules to determine which content to include in each message. In addition, it allows the developer to use SQL database commands within e-mail templates to create selections, tabulations, and complex decision rules. GT/Mail is available as a licensed produce or as a hosted service.

UnityMail (MessageMedia)

UnityMail from MessageMedia (www.messagemedia.com) is a database-driven e-mail system that allows you to create a database of recipients based on user profile information. UnityMail provides database filtering capabilities so you can target specific user segments within a database with e-mail messages that are tailored to each segment. The system also provides tools that allow you to build Web-based forms that capture user data directly into a database from a Web site. It is available as a licensed product or as a hosted service.

The History of Messaging Affects E-Mail Today

It's interesting that many of the features and limitations of today's Internet e-mail are based on how electronic messaging systems were originally designed many years ago.

E-mail is one of the oldest forms of electronic communications, having its origins in the point-to-point teletypewriter devices invented in the early 1900s. One such device was the Teletype from the AT&T Teletype Corporation that was used by corporations to send typed messages to each other.

Then, an improved method of encoding characters, called the American Standard Code for Information Interchange (ASCII) format, was adopted in 1963, which is used today to transmit Internet e-mail. The ASCII (pronounced ASK-ee) format uses 7 on/off bits, which allows 128 keyboard characters to be transmitted.

By the way, don't go looking for 128 keys on your keyboard. This character set is composed of not just the alphabet, numbers, and characters you see on a keyboard, but also includes nonprinting characters you can type by using the shift and control keys.

MIME Headers

In the 1980s, it became clear that people wanted to send a variety of documents to other people via e-mail. Unfortunately, personal computers use 8 bits per character, while ASCII e-mail uses 7 bits per character.

So how can we send 8-bit binary e-mail attachments, such as word processing and graphic files, using a 7-bit e-mail system?

To give you an idea of the problem involved in sending files with larger bit counts, think of how you would solve this car pooling problem. How would you use seven-passenger vans to move several teams of eight players each? The answer, of course, is to put one player from the first team in the second van. But the second team would then need to have two of its players ride in the third van. And so on, and so on.

The solution requires the use of two extra lines in the heading area of an e-mail message to specify that a file has been encoded in a special way that packs 8-bit characters into many 7-bit characters. The general name for this technique is called MIME, which stands for Multipurpose Internet Mail Extensions.

You may have seen MIME mentioned with regard to Web pages because a similar problem exists when using the Internet for Web pages containing 8-bit characters.

E-mail messages containing extended characters are required to have MIME headers that tell the receiving software program how to decode the special file. Some e-mail programs allow you to display the headers that tell how messages are processed as they pass through the Internet. For example, two headers that you might see are these:

```
MIME-Version: 1.0
Content-Type: text/html; charset="ISO-8859-1"
```

There are many more options and capabilities of the MIME headers and related codes used in e-mails. If you're interested in learning more about MIME, take a look at this rather old (circa 1993), but very accurate, document: www.oac.uci.edu/indiv/ehood/MIME/1521/rfc1521ToC.html

Now that we have the technical explanations out of the way, we can explore many new ways to use e-mail as part of a one-to-one marketing program.

HTML-Enabled E-Mail

Most current Internet e-mail programs now support HTML, which is the coding scheme used to format Web pages. The major exception is America Online (AOL), which has not been able to display HTML formatted e-mail messages. Supporting HTML tags enables marketers to send e-mail messages that contain hyperlinks, tables, fonts, and graphics. These elements enhance the e-mail message and make the message look much like a Web page. The *New York Times* online edition (www.nytimes.com) has an e-mail service called "New York Times Direct" that delivers e-mail news to a user's e-mail box. The e-mail message supports HTML and sends a graphical message, including advertising, as shown in Figure 3.14.

HTML-based e-mail can be very appealing technology in that it provides the appeal of graphics without requiring the user to download desktop software or use a Web browser—the messages are delivered via the e-mail. In order to minimize the size of e-mail messages, newsletter publishers usually send the HTML codes that instruct the software to retrieve graphics from the publisher's Web server. Because many people read their e-mail offline they do not see those graphics, but instead see a broken and ill-formatted document. For the benefit of these people, as well as AOL readers, many newsletter publishers offer readers both a text format and an HTML format.

E-Mail Attachments

The ability to send attachments as part of e-mail messages has allowed people to share practically any type of document with friends and coworkers. The

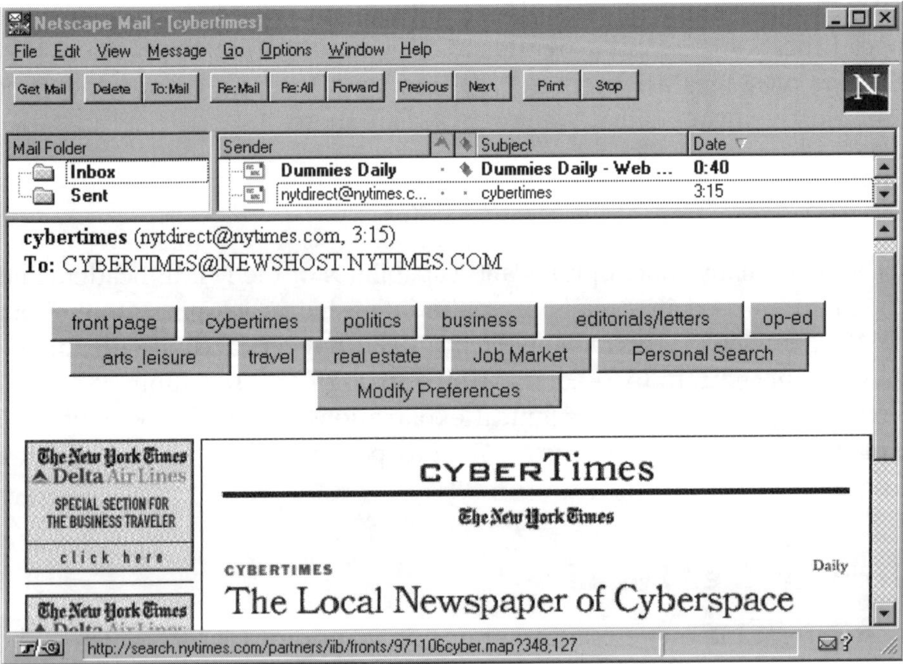

Figure 3.14 HTML-based e-mail from The *New York Times*.

recipient can open an e-mail message containing an attachment, click on the attachment, and launch the application that reads the attachment. And, if the attachment is an executable program, clicking on it launches the new program.

There are two main problems with sending attachments as part of an e-mail marketing program. First, the total size of the message may exceed the maximum allowed by the recipient's ISP or corporate mail system, so the message is not delivered. Second, and generally a bigger problem, is the widespread concern that an attachment contains a virus or other destructive software that will harm the recipient's computer if it's opened. Even when a current anti-virus program is used, users are appropriately cautious about opening attachments because recent viruses have spread so fast that the anti-virus software that is just a few weeks old may not protect users.

Even though there is legitimate concern about opening attachments, they are used to enhance individual productivity. This creates a wide range of marketing opportunities.

Unified Messaging

The number of different ways people receive messages has grown: A person will receive a fax, followed by an e-mail asking about the fax, and perhaps a telephone call asking why the person hasn't responded to the e-mail.

Companies are trying to bring order to this chaos through a technique called "unified messaging" in which multiple types of messages can be managed from a single application program. The types of documents that can be managed with many unified messaging systems include the following:

- Word processing and spreadsheet documents
- Fax documents
- Voicemail messages
- Audio and video files

The ability to send a wide variety of messages and documents allows us to deliver specific highly formatted marketing messages to individuals based on what we know about them.

The Spam Controversy

Spam. It could be the undoing of e-mail. E-mail marketing could be a short-lived marketing method if the Internet industry doesn't take steps toward self-regulating. Spam is unsolicited commercial e-mail that is broadcast to many people without their consent. Why is it called spam? The term reportedly comes from a Monty Python skit in which the word "spam," referring to the canned-meat product, was repeated continually. The word was used within Usenet newsgroups when one posting was sent to many people.

Much of the controversy comes from these companies' "harvesting" e-mail addresses from Web pages, discussion lists, newsgroups, and other sources, then reselling the names to marketers. This is all done without the knowledge of the e-mail address owner. The other issue is that ISPs have to deal with disgruntled customers who receive the e-mail, as well as network traffic problems when the mass e-mailings are broadcast. E-mail list brokers, ISPs, trade organizations, consumer groups, and the Federal Trade Commission (www.ftc.gov) are working together to form guidelines that will protect users from receiving unwanted spam yet allow e-mail to become a legitimate online marketing tool.

"Spam makes you look cheap and sleazy in the eyes of many people online," according to Bob Cortez, president of Total Quality Marketing Inc. "Regardless of how targeted, relevant, or informative you think your message is, unless the recipient specifically agreed to receive the information, you risk alienating a portion of your audience."

In addition to avoiding the negative image of being labeled a spammer, Web marketers are often contractually prohibited from sending spam because the contracts of most ISPs prohibit sending unsolicited e-mail.

TIP **For the benefit of both you and the user, recipients of e-mail should be given the ability to get off your e-mailing list. This will save you the cost of e-mailing messages to people who will never visit your Web site or buy products from your company.**

A survey by World Research confirmed the concern users have about unsolicited commercial e-mail. Two-thirds of the respondents were in favor of regulating spam. Only 7 percent said they "loved" junk e-mails or found them useful. If this survey reflects public opinion, then it is a strong indication that e-mail marketing should be conducted with guidelines set by the e-mail marketing industry. If e-mail marketing is to be accepted, Web marketers should consider practicing these guidelines suggested by industry advocates and organizations:

- Put the word "advertisement" in the subject line of the e-mail.
- Disclose the sender of the e-mail.
- Allow users to get off the e-mail marketing list easily. Include a hyperlink or instructions on how users can remove themselves from the list or "opt-out" from future mailings.
- Do not sell the e-mail list to another marketer without the user's consent.

Organizations and companies have now put services into place to help online users filter out spam and remove themselves from bulk e-mail lists. Mindspring (www.mindspring.com), an ISP, offers free e-mail filtering to its subscribers. This filter checks against a database of known spammers and blocks the e-mail before it gets to the user's e-mailbox.

Applying One-to-One E-Mail

E-mail is a very flexible medium that is being used in many ways to deliver marketing messages to a target audience. In general, there are two approaches to creating an e-mail list:

- Create your own in-house list through online and offline methods.
- Rent a list for one-time use.

Both methods are effective in generating traffic to a Web site; however, the two methods have very different costs and therefore should be used to meet objectives appropriate to each method.

Forrester Research recently interviewed traditional companies and new dot-coms about their results and projections based on experience with direct e-mail marketing techniques. The companies interviewed will triple their e-mail marketing budgets by 2004, and they will spend half of their online marketing budget on e-mail marketing.

In the study, Forrester also compared the cost and response rates of rented lists used for acquisition with in-house lists used for retention. Rented lists cost about $200 per thousand messages sent, while in-house lists cost only $5 per thousand messages sent. Table 3.2 shows that click-through rates for rented lists average 3.5 percent—much lower than the 10 percent average for in-house lists.

In-house list usage is so much lower because it costs very little to add a newsletter subscription form and database to a Web site. In addition, the

Table 3.2 How Successful Are Your E-mail Campaigns?

	COST PER THOUSAND	CLICK-THROUGH RATE	PURCHASE RATE	COST PER SALE
Rented lists	$200	3.5%	2.0%	$286
Sponsored e-mail	$93	2.5%	0.8%	$465
In-house lists	$5	10%	2.5%	$2

cost for using an outside service to distribute e-mail to your own list is much less expensive than renting a list.

E-mail marketing techniques can reach prospects and customers at any stage during the purchase process, from generating awareness and attracting new customers to retaining and serving existing customers. In each stage during the purchase process, different e-mail marketing techniques are needed in order to reach the right people with the right message.

Applying One-to-One E-Mail for Customer Acquisition

Many people visit Web sites in order to learn about products they will need in the near future. Sometimes consumers look for products they know they'll need when their kids go back to school, when they go on vacation, when they start a new hobby, or when they experience many other kinds of changes in their everyday life.

People who work for corporations also look for products before they actually need them, such as for an upcoming project.

This means that many of the visitors coming to your Web site are not prepared to make a purchase immediately, but they are seriously investigating products for future needs. In order to help these people remember your Web site and your products when they are ready to make a purchase, it's important to stay in touch with them through e-mail.

In addition, some people are just beginning to investigate a product category and are looking for education and general information. Other prospects may be further along in their investigation and just need to receive product information when they are ready to make a purchase.

Generating additional traffic to a Web site in order to acquire new customers is probably one of the trickiest aspects of using one-to-one e-mail marketing. Many people become offended when they receive e-mail from a company unexpectedly.

There are several accepted approaches to sending e-mail to people who are not yet customers:

- Rent a list through an opt-in mailing list broker
- Encourage Web site visitors to subscribe to your newsletter
- Offer to periodically send Web site visitors promotional announcements about products

Opt-In or Opt-Out?

The terms *opt-in* and *opt-out* have taken on two different sets of definitions, so it can be a bit confusing at times.

Initially, opt-in was used to mean that someone would have to take an action to indicate that he or she wanted to add his or her name to a mailing list. Conversely, opt-out meant that a checkbox on a form had been prechecked and the person had to take action to keep from being added to a list, such as by unchecking a prechecked checkbox on a Web form.

Later, e-mail list brokers began renting lists of people who agreed to receive promotional mailings. In order to distinguish their lists from spam lists of unsuspecting individuals they called theirs *opt-in lists*—indicating that people on the list had been asked if they wanted to be added to the list.

Then, to keep things from being simple and easy to understand, the industry adopted the term *double opt-in*. When it's important to verify that someone *really* wants to be added to a list, an e-mail is sent asking them to confirm their subscription. The confirmation e-mail asks them to click a link or take some other action before they are actually added to the list.

Rosalind Resnick is president of NetCreations, Inc. (www.netcreations.com) and a leading advocate of requiring use of double opt-in in order to receive e-mail advertisements. This method ensures that the people who are added to their lists really want to receive e-mail promotions. Her company provides the PostMaster Direct Response service that allows marketers to send messages to targeted e-mail lists that are *100 percent opt-in*.

As you can imagine, opt-in lists are different from opt-out lists because opt-out lists contain e-mail addresses of people without their consent (in other words, *spam*) and puts the burden on the user to remove himself or herself from the list, which can sometimes be a very arduous task. Here is an adaptation of a story in one of Resnick's Digital Direct Marketing letters regarding key techniques for successful e-mail campaigns:

Let recipients opt-in before they opt-out. The most politically correct way to build an Internet marketing list is to allow users to come to your Web site and sign up voluntarily to receive e-mail about particular topics, and then give them a chance to get off the list every time you send them a message.

Send recipients only information that they signed up to receive. Marketers have the responsibility to send only the information requested by the user.

Give your recipients value. No matter how politically correct your system, commercial e-mail takes up recipients' time and bandwidth. Also provide incentives to join the list, such as a coupon or a giveaway.

In-House Newsletter

For prospects who are investigating a product category, an informative newsletter can help them learn about the benefits of products in your category while they learn about the specifics of your products.

This means a newsletter needs to be written with the style and tone of helping people learn about your general product category, not necessarily including a great deal of product information aimed at selling your product.

Our experience indicates that a balance of approximately two-thirds educational information combined with about one-third product-specific information is well received and appreciated by most audiences.

The content of this type of newsletter can be original material written in-house or by the company's public relations agency, and it can include links to articles at content Web sites. Of course, it's important to include links back to your own Web site for detailed information, such as white papers, and links to the specific products mentioned in your articles.

Informational newsletters sent to prospects are similar to, but not necessarily the same as, informational newsletters to existing customers. Prospective customers are more interested in features and benefits, and existing customers are more interested in usage tips. It's likely that you'll want to send two different newsletters to these groups.

Product Promotion Campaigns

Prospects who are already familiar with your product category may be interested in receiving periodic promotional mailings about new products and special offers.

At this stage of the purchase cycle, prospects can quickly move from being aware of a product to being interested in purchasing the product, which requires slightly different marketing techniques.

In other words, people with a vague interest would like to receive periodic reminders. Once they have indicated an interest in buying a specific product or in receiving a proposal, marketing messages directed to them should shift from general reminders and promotional offers to very specific information based on their interests and needs.

Because it's never obvious how many e-mail reminders will be needed to help a prospect move from being aware of a product to being very interested, a campaign consisting of a series of reminder messages should be used. Once the prospect has indicated a serious interest the awareness campaign should end and the sales campaign should begin.

This makes it essential to have a way to detect when a prospect mentally shifts from one stage to another. The technique that is frequently used is called *closed loop marketing*. Once a person receives an e-mail and clicks on a link in the message to go to a Web page, that person's profile is updated to reflect the fact that he or she clicked on that link. Many times clicking on a link to a Web page just displays that page, such as information about company, without updating the user profile. When a prospect responds to a description about a particular product by clicking on a link to that product's page, you can use closed-loop marketing techniques to detect that they have indicated a more serious interest in that product.

Normally this is accomplished by including a unique identification code in the URL that is detected when the reader clicks on the link, such as:

```
http://www.mycompany.com/cgi-bin/redirect.html?user=ab1234567890&page=4
```

In this example the page "redirect.html" is used to track all clicks on links in e-mail messages (called *clickthroughs*). The query string (text after the question mark) has the two values needed to identify who is clicking and which link is being clicked. The programming code included in the file redirect.html does the following:

1. Inserts an entry into a log table or log file to store the user's ID, the page identified in the URL, and the date and time the reader clicked the link.
2. Looks up the actual URL for page #4.
3. Redirects the user's browser to the actual URL.

This process takes a fraction of a second in most cases, so the reader doesn't notice any delay in displaying the desired page.

Of course, if the link to the product page is included in a general article about product category, clicking the link is probably not in response to their being interested in the product, but being interested in learning more about an example of the product category. On the other hand, an article in a promotional e-mail may be specifically aimed at generating an action from the prospect. This might include a call to action such as "Click the product link to reserve your discounted price!" This indicates a more serious interest in the product. Once the prospect responds to this call to action, the campaign should shift to a more focused sales approach, such as offering special pricing, special packaging, special delivery options, or other incentives that can help close the sale.

Targeted versus Tailored

Applying the concept of one-to-one e-mail marketing generally means adjusting what is said to reach a person to match what you know about him or her, such as interests and needs.

During the customer acquisition stage of marketing on the Internet you are probably just beginning to gather information about each prospect, which means you could probably group prospects into a small number of market segments. Each of these market segments could receive its own somewhat different promotional e-mail messages. For a group of people who are price sensitive, you might send a message that primarily emphasizes the low price and high-value of the features provided by your products. For a group that is primarily interested in products with features that match their needs, you might send a message emphasizing the features, but also mentioning pricing.

As a prospect shares interest information with you, it becomes possible to tailor each individual e-mail message based on each piece of information learned about the interests of each person.

For instance, you may have learned through inquiry forms and needs analysis forms on your Web site that a prospect is interested in a product with specific dimensions. At the same time you may have learned that the prospect has only a few required features and is looking for the lowest price possible. This combination of needs and requirements may not fit a standard market segment, but it does define exactly what this prospect will buy. A personalized e-mail with content tailored to these specific needs can demonstrate that you can provide the product to meet those needs—and make the sale.

Applying One-to-One E-Mail for Customer Retention

The cost of acquiring a new customer is frequently higher than the revenue obtained from that customer's first order. This makes it essential to bring these customers back to your Web site to purchase additional products and supplies.

One of the first ways to respond after a customer places an initial order is to send an e-mail thanking the customer and inviting him or her back to your Web site.

Many of the techniques used to obtain new customers can also be used to retain customers. This includes sending promotional announcements about product specials, as well as newsletters with information about the features and benefits of the products you provide.

There is a significant difference between e-mail messages sent to prospects and those sent to existing customers. For instance, it is not a good idea to send an e-mail or a direct-mail piece promoting a product that the customer has already purchased.

Applying One-to-One E-Mail for Creating Zealots

You will see throughout this book that we feel customers who are fans of a company are very vocal about helping the company improve the product and promote the company's products through word-of-mouth.

One way to do this is with an e-mail discussion list where raving fans can communicate directly with prospective customers.

The use of moderated discussion lists where a company representative controls the conversation, however, is not a good approach. Many people in the audience will assume that the company is not allowing negative comments to go to the list and will therefore discount the value of comments made on the list.

A better approach is to encourage customers to gather at one of the free Web and e-mail discussion sites. Then, if the list is moderated, it's handled by someone other than a company employee.

A company representative, however, should be an active participant on the list to ensure that official answers are posted to the group to keep speculation and misinformation to a minimum.

Another popular way to allow fans to share their enthusiasm with their friends is with a "send this article to a friend" feature. This allows people to enter the address of a friend and have the server send the content via e-mail. The content can be an article or white paper, a product information page, or practically any other material on the site that someone may want to forward to a friend.

While many sites make this feature available to anyone who visits the site, we suggest that this feature be restricted to people who are registered on the site and, we hope, have been authenticated with a confirmation e-mail. The reduces the potential of abusive usage.

BootsnAll.com is a popular content site for independent travelers. Its Web and e-mail personalization system keeps track of who is registered to access features such as the "send to a friend" feature shown in Figure 3.15.

How to Write Direct E-Mail

As you are already aware, the Internet is a whole new marketing medium that requires a special way to communicate in order to be effective. If you do not want your e-mail to be discarded before it is even read, you need to take some care when writing e-mail messages or newsletters.

There are two main components to e-mails: the subject line and the body. Each component requires a particular style of writing. The subject line is

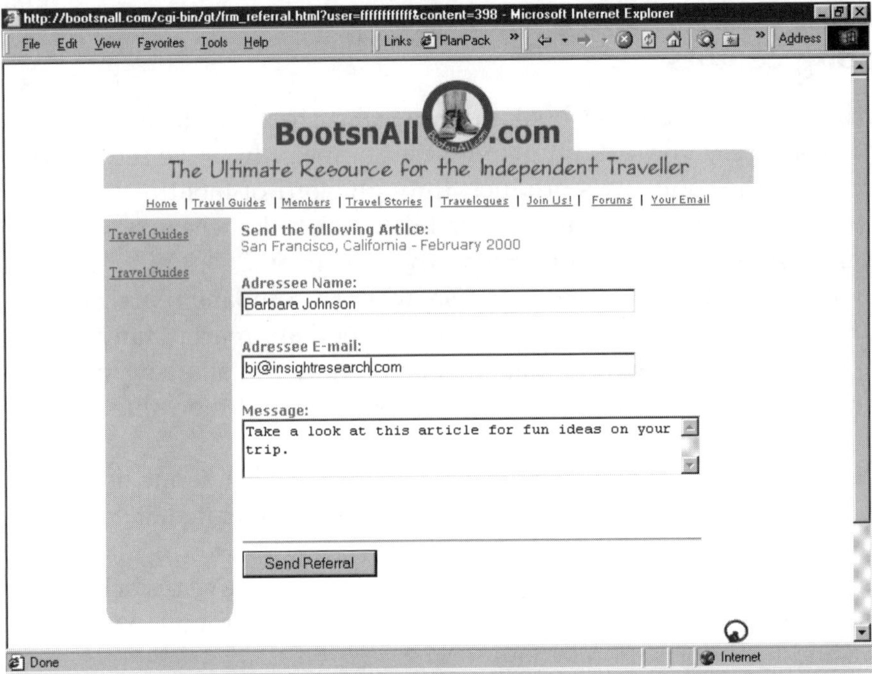

Figure 3.15 Registered users of the BootsnAll.com site can send articles to their friends.

much like an advertising headline or the first line in a letter. The body of the message is where you convey information and entice readers to take action. The body of the message will not be read if the subject line doesn't motivate the recipient to open the message.

Writing Effective Subject Lines

With the controversy regarding spam, one idea e-mail marketers have promoted is to put the word "advertisement" in all unsolicited commercial e-mail. Here is a sample:

```
**AD** Do these prices make you go "Hummmm"?
**AD** Can you find a better deal?
```

There is a fear among marketers that putting the word "ad" or "advertisement" in the subject line of an e-mail will ensure that no one will read your message. If you follow current opt-in procedures, then there is no need to use this "warning" because customers have signed up for or elected to receive the e-mails. You will still need to provide the recipient with an intriguing and/or informational subject line. In his book, *Cyberwriting* (Amacom, 1997), Joe Vitale offers these suggestions:

- The subject line needs to serve as a powerful headline. Think of what would interest readers.
- Don't come across as too sales-oriented.
- Use a benefit headline; that's your safest bet.
- Use your "Unique Selling Proposition." How does your product or service differ from your competition's?
- Put "New" in the subject line if you are offering something new.
- Be specific, and don't tease people with empty phrases.
- Use emotional words.
- Be relevant.

Here are examples of some effective subject lines:

Earn $50,000 in 5 hours	PostMaster Direct teaser to promote a service.
Dummies Daily The Internet	Dummies Daily E-Mail Service, identifying who sent the message.
[THE KEY TO A SAFER WORLD—7/31/97]	The e-mail and a lead for a feature story. This works well when the user signs up to receive the e-mails.
Win a $20,000 Trip	The *New York Times* Direct. Who wouldn't open this e-mail?
New Product Gossip of the Day	TipWorld, an e-mail service for computer enthusiasts.

Writing Effective E-Mail Messages

The body of the e-mail message should be concise. If you are providing news on several topics, dedicate a paragraph for each. If the message has a single purpose, make the message brief, using several paragraphs. Here are some things to consider when writing e-mail:

Write according to your marketing communications objective. Is it a direct-response promotion? Informational news and tips? Teaser? Survey? Each type of communication requires a different "voice." For example, a teaser would have text that is vague and intriguing, whereas informational tips would be very factual and short. In all cases, your objective should be to get users to act on the e-mail, and the e-mail should be worth every minute of your audience's very valuable time.

Be sensitive to your audience. Is the e-mail targeted to consumers? Business professionals? Men? Women? Youths? Remember that your audience comes from all corners of the world. Be careful when using humor; it doesn't translate well in the writing, especially when used in our global marketplace.

People read in a different way on the computer than when they read a book or newspaper. Users typically scan when they read online, versus taking the time to read an article in a magazine from start to finish. E-mail text should be short in length and narrow in width.

Figure 3.16 shows an excerpt from CNET's Digital Dispatch (www.cnet.com), a weekly newsletter that is sent to more than 850,000 recipients. CNET is an experienced distributor of e-mail newsletters. Because their e-mails are longer, they provide a useful table of contents.

Warning: Excessive E-Mail Can Be Hazardous to Your Customer's Health and to Your Marketing Budget

With the information overload most of us are experiencing, one-to-one Web marketers should help to alleviate this problem rather than add to it. A study by the Electronic Messaging Association (www.ema.org) found that more than 70 percent of workers felt overwhelmed by the amount of e-mail they received each day—office workers send and receive an average of 178 e-mails per day.

In David Shenk's book, *Data Smog* (HarperCollins, 1997), he states that we all benefit from the increasing availability and accessibility of information, but we can also suffer from having too much. As human beings, we have a limit to our capacity of receiving and processing information. Shenk believes:

> At a certain level of input, the law of diminishing returns takes effect; the glut of information no longer adds to our quality of life, but instead begins to cultivate stress, confusion, and even ignorance.

In order to avoid creating messages that will get tossed out—much like the junk mail that arrives in all of our mailboxes—you should be sensitive to your customers' or users' capacity for information. You want to make sure that your information or marketing messages are providing value to your customers. By doing this, you will enhance your communications with customers, which in turn will help you meet your marketing, sales, or other goals associated with your e-mail marketing endeavors.

Although e-mail marketing can be conducted at a very reasonable cost, continuing to send e-mailings to users who do not value them is a waste of time and marketing budget.

E-mail marketing is a new field, gaining rapid acceptance. E-mail can range from one-to-many applications to one-to-one applications that are integrated

```
X-Persona: <dakania>
Return-Path: <owner-dispatch@DISPATCH.CNET.COM>
Approved-By: dispatch@CNET.COM
Approved-By:  CNET Digital Dispatch <dispatch@CNET.COM>
Date:         Thu, 7 Aug 1997 15:27:29 -0700
Reply-To: dispatch-faq@CNET.com
Sender: CNET Digital Dispatch <DISPATCH@DISPATCH.CNET.COM>
From: CNET Digital Dispatch <dispatch@CNET.com>
Subject:      CNET Digital Dispatch, August 7, 1997:
email, e-commerce,
              and Apple
To: Multiple recipients of list DISPATCH <DISPATCH@DIS-
PATCH.CNET.COM>


CNET Digital Dispatch: email, e-commerce, and Apple
August 7, 1997
more than 850,000 subscribers


This week on CNET:
1.  Email clients
2.  What is e-commerce?
3.  As the Macworld turns
4.  New product reviews
5.  Glaser: fun with you-know-who
6.  BUILDER.COM: designing for differences
7.  GAMECENTER.COM: 3D games
8.  CNET TV: cyberstalking; U2 on tour; and the Free Tibet
Webcast
9.  EVENTS.COM: Lollapalooza; San Jose Jazz Festival
10. DOWNLOAD.COM: learn how to chat
11. "Your turn": does Microsoft compete unfairly?
12. Top ten reasons Microsoft invested $150 million in
Apple
13. Jobs!
14. Subscribe and unsubscribe
15. Coming soon: Snap! Online


Copyright 1997 CNET, Inc. All rights reserved.
```

Figure 3.16 A sample of CNET's Digital Dispatch.

with customer databases. Following is a discussion of ways to create your own e-mail marketing system for your Web site and what e-mail advertising options are available to promote your site, your company, and your products.

How to Conduct Your Own E-Mail Marketing

E-mails can be a powerful way to strengthen the bond between you and your users or customers. In order to accomplish this you will want to provide e-mail notifications or newsletters that have the primary objective of informing rather than selling. Building relationships with your audience or customers is not a short-term objective, so the horizon for payoff on this endeavor should be a long one. Here is a step-by-step checklist for creating and broadcasting e-mail messages:

1. *Determine goals for the mailing.* Do you want to increase brand awareness, encourage sales transactions, provide an information service, conduct a loyalty program, or provide another outlet for your advertisers?
2. *Develop key information topics.* These can be editorial or editorial plus advertising or sponsorship.
3. *Develop a plan.* Determine period, process, and people.
4. *Promote a new service.* Offer something new and unique on your site and on the Web.
5. *Include "calls to action" in e-mail text.* These could be promotions, feedback, surveys, and so forth.
6. *Reinvent your e-mail service as necessary.* Do not forget to provide customers with a way to give you feedback.

The terms directronic mail, direct e-mail, mailcasting, e-mail push, bulk e-mail, spam, and even electronic trash have all been used to describe using e-mail for direct marketing purposes. There are many e-mail lists available to rent for one-time use; some are opt-in, but others contain people who do not want to be contacted. Unfortunately, it's sometimes difficult to tell the difference. A rented list managed by a reputable broker who distributes the e-mail message on behalf of the advertiser is likely to be an opt-in list of people who have agreed to receive advertising messages via e-mail.

Many lists are not targeted at all, some lists are targeted, and some lists are very targeted and contain only users who have elected, or opted-in, to receive relevant e-mail. The highly targeted e-mail lists move the marketer closer to the one-to-one Web marketing model. For example, if you have a new Web site that provides useful resources for home decorating, as a one-to-one Web marketer, you will want to locate an e-mail list that matches your target audience. You will most likely be interested in renting e-mail lists that contain women aged 25–50, who have a certain level of income, who subscribe to books and magazines related to decorating, who have bought home furnishings, and who share other specific characteristics.

Demographic and psychographic (e.g., lifestyle) information should be supplied by e-mail list brokers to ensure that you are receiving the best and most targeted e-mail list. It will be up to you to investigate each type of list and list owner to determine which one is the most appropriate for your message. Alternatively, nontargeted, bulk lists are usually much larger and less expensive than targeted ones. These types of lists are appropriate for more "mass marketing" campaigns where your product has broad appeal among many types of users.

You should expect a lower percentage of responses from nontargeted e-mail lists than from highly targeted lists. In general, a 2 to 3 percent response is the average response rate for all types of online direct marketing. Targeted lists plus a good promotion can pull a response that is many times larger.

"When using rented lists the most important thing to do is learn exactly how people got on the list," says Michael Mayor, vice president of sales at NetCreations Inc. One key aspect of this is to identify what the individuals on the list signed up for. Some sites have very general interest categories, which can be too broad to be effective.

It's also important to evaluate how people were added to a list. For instance, an opt-in list is one where subscribers have been required to give their active approval, such as checking a checkbox. An even better method to confirm that the people on the list want to receive promotional messages is to look for a broker that rents double opt-in lists. This means the recipients have replied to a confirmation e-mail agreeing that they are signing up to receive promotional advertising offers from companies. "It's important to verify that people want to be on these lists," Mayor says.

Direct e-mail campaigns can be conducted at a fraction of the cost of sending out physical direct mail and have the added benefit of immediate response. Users receive the e-mail, click on a hyperlink at that moment, and increase the likelihood of further transactions such as buying something, filling out a survey, reading an article, clicking on other ads, spending time at your Web site, or becoming a repeat visitor. On the other hand, other traditional direct marketing methods should not be discontinued. Many marketers advocate that an integrated marketing campaign is the most effective approach for gaining and retaining customers. Direct e-mailings are sent by the list owner in much the same way that you would broadcast a message using a mailing list server system. Because they broker lists, the list owners conduct the e-mail broadcasts.

Costs and Benefits of Using Direct E-Mail Lists

The cost of renting a list for an e-mailing varies. The model is similar to traditional list brokering for physical mailings: Highly targeted lists are more expensive than nontargeted e-mail lists. For example, it's common to pay between 10 and 30 cents per name. This price includes the list rental, e-mail distribution, and merge/purge. The postage for sending a physical mailing can range from about 8 cents to almost 30 cents per piece. Add to this the cost of creating and printing a direct-mail piece, which can range from a few cents to a few dollars each.

> "With an advanced e-mail advertising delivery system, users go through profiling steps to get the content delivered, and therefore might represent a more responsive audience. Advertising can be targeted based on demographic profile, geography, or content of interest. These e-mail publishers have the capability of customizing frequency levels to advertisers: high frequency for branding programs and low frequency for response programs."
>
> Kris Pederson, President of KPMedia

It is easy to see how cost-effective direct e-mail can be; however, your message will reach only those prospects or customers who have e-mail or Internet access. The overall benefits of direct e-mail lists include the following:

- They are a cost-effective way to reach online users.
- E-mail campaigns can take a few days or weeks to prepare and send versus the number of weeks or months it may take to complete a physical mailing.
- Direct e-mail lists are highly targeted and are a one-to-one method for reaching prospects.
- They give you the ability to easily motivate immediate response by recipients with embedded hyperlinks.
- They allow you to conduct test mailings as you would for traditional direct mail. The log creation capability of hyperlinks can produce highly granular test data. You can measure right down to the individual recipient.

Products/Services

The e-mail list industry is new, but it is growing at a rapid pace. There are a few types of e-mail list services available to the Web marketer: highly targeted opt-in mailing lists, bulk e-mail lists, discussion groups/lists that can be sponsored or mailed to, and e-mail-based loyalty and promotional programs. Also, many e-mail marketers have been capturing the physical mailing addresses of their e-mail users, and they are now making these lists available for rental.

OPT-IN E-MAIL LISTS	
PostMaster Direct from NetCreations	www.netcreations.com
DIRECT/BULK E-MAIL LISTS	
21st Century Marketing	www.21stcm.com
Electronic Direct Marketing	www.edmarketing.com
Internet Media Group	www.internetmedia.com
Worldata	www.worldata.com
DISCUSSION GROUPS/MAILING LISTS	
Liszt, the mailing list directory	www.liszt.com
Direct E-mail List Source	www.copywriter.com/ lists/index.htm

E-Mail-Related Promotions/ Loyalty Programs

There is a segment of electronic promotions that uses e-mail as the engine to facilitate loyalty programs for Web marketers. One-to-one Web marketers can take advantage of the personalization capabilities of these services. For example, MyPoints (www.mypoints.com) rewards users by giving them points when they receive and view advertisements and additional points if they take advantage of the advertising offer. Marketers pay approximately 10 to 15 cents per advertisement delivered to the user.

Buying Advertising Space on Free E-Mail Services

Several e-mail services are free for users. The only "cost" is that the user has to read advertising sent by the services. Hotmail is the leading provider of free Web-based e-mail with over 5 million users. A Hotmail e-mail user registers for his or her free e-mail account by filling out a questionnaire that captures demographic information. Hotmail delivers about 5 million ad banners per day. Marketers can buy nontargeted and highly targeted ad banners on the Hotmail site.

Juno.com is another of the larger Web-based free e-mail services, with more than 2.5 million users. It has the capability of targeting advertisements based on demographics such as geographic location, age and gender, household income, occupation, level of education, purchasing habits and plans, patterns of computer use, hobbies and interests, marital status, and number of children in the household.

GeoCities (now part of Yahoo!) is an online community where users can receive free e-mail and personal Web pages. The site receives over 60 million visits per month, and it has over 750,000 e-mail subscribers. Just a few of the advertisers include American Airlines, Auto-by-Tel, Honda, IBM, L.L. Bean, Polaroid, Sears, and *The Wall Street Journal*. In addition to online banner ads, GeoCities provides advertising opportunities within each of its communities, e-mail advertising opportunities, and the designing of special e-mail newsletters that marketers can sponsor.

Buying Advertising Space in an E-Mail News or Newsletter Service

E-mail news and newsletters provide added value over e-mail advertising and can be even more effective in pulling higher response rates for Web marketers. The premise behind this ability is that if the e-mail recipient takes time to read the message, the more likely it is he or she will act on the advertising, sponsorship, or promotion included in the e-mail. Because the recipient has elected to receive the news or newsletter and he or she values the information, the organization is more credible in the user's or customer's mind. Thus, the advertising has added credibility by association.

SodaMail (www.sodamail.com) is an example of a family-oriented e-mail newsletter publisher that accepts advertising. Figure 3.17 shows a few of the free newsletters available to subscribers in return for providing demographic data. By using a personalized e-mail ad server, SodaMail's advertisers can target advertising based on editorial content and demographic data.

The Future of One-to-One E-Mail

With the industry becoming more sensitive to online users and their feelings about unsolicited commercial e-mail, e-mail will become a standard and accepted way to provide advertising messages to prospects and customers. E-mail personalization technology will continue to evolve to become easier to implement and administer, as well as easier to integrate

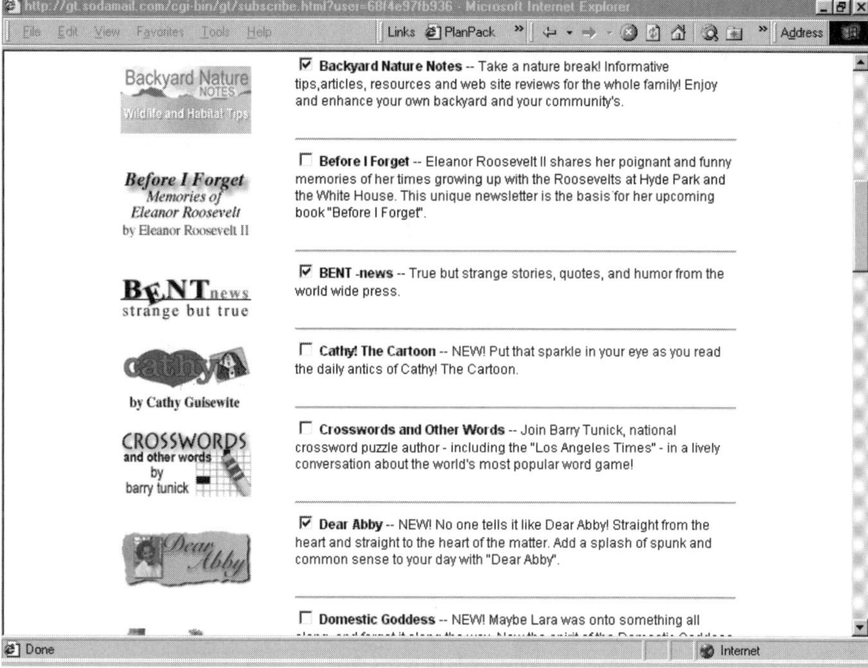

Figure 3.17 SodaMail's network of advertiser-supported newsletters.

with company databases. This will enable Web marketers to benefit from the power of one-to-one marketing. Multimedia e-mail that includes audio and video will also become more prevalent. In addition to multimedia, e-mail will become more customizable and interactive.

E-mail will continue to grow and be the most prevalent activity on the Internet. We have already seen the merger of e-mail and voice technology—people can now call in and listen to their e-mails! There are also products and services available that let people check their e-mail from anywhere—someone else's computer, an airport Internet kiosk—through a Web browser. We may continue to see a morphing of technologies to enhance marketers' ability to communicate with each customer no matter where he or she is located.

Resources

OPT-IN E-MAIL LISTS

NetCreations	www.netcreations.com
YesMail	www.yesmail.com

E-MAIL LIST BROKERS

21st Century Marketing	www.21stcm.com
Electronic Direct Marketing	www.edmarketing.com
Internet Media Group	www.internetmedia.com
Worldata	www.worldata.com

MAILING LIST SOFTWARE

MessageMedia	www.messagemedia.com
L-Soft	www.lsoft.com
ListStar	www.starnine.com
Lyris	www.lyris.com
GuestTrack	www.guesttrack.com

MAILING LIST HOSTING SERVICES

Sling Shot Media	www.slingshotmedia.com
Topica	www.topica.com
EGroups	www.egroups.com
MessageMedia	www.messagemedia.com

WEB SITE **An expanded database of these and other resources is available at www.1to1Web.com.**

Up Next

Chapter 4, "One-to-One Web Advertising and Promotion," discusses the benefits of online advertising on the Web and in e-mail. Whether you are a content provider that depends on advertising for revenue or a marketer looking to promote your products, online advertising plays an important role in your one-to-one marketing.

One-to-One Web Advertising and Promotion

"Propaganda ends where dialogue begins."

Marshall McLuhan

Mass advertising. Direct marketing. Now the next paradigm shift: one-to-one marketing. The computer has enabled this awe-inspiring transformation of the marketing discipline. By 1970, computers were becoming more prevalent, and the cost of computing was declining. At the same time, *market segmentation* and *demographics* were the buzzwords of the day. Add to this lifestyle data, *psychographics*, and a computer at the end of each marketer's fingertips, and we now have a direct-marketing business in excess of $100 billion annually.

No one could have predicted the opportunity for marketers to target their messages to a single user on the World Wide Web. Peppers and Rogers, leaders in the one-to-one marketing arena, had alluded to the possibility of an electronic medium that could individually address the needs of each customer in their first book, *One to One Future* (Doubleday, 1993). Only a very few short years later, the World Wide Web has revolutionized the way we advertise. For example, people cannot click on a magazine advertisement and receive instant information about products or offers—you can do this on the Web. Also, most traditional advertising offers some targeting and response-tracking capabilities, but the Web can target ads and track users in a much more granular and one-to-one manner.

In Joseph Turow's book, *Breaking Up America* (The University of Chicago Press, 1997), he discussed the popular notion among advertisers in the

1980s and early 1990s—*signaling*. Signaling was the practice of trying to reach targets using traditional advertising and publicity methods that would engender affinity among people and the identities of those advertisers. With the emergence of relationship marketing, this practice was an inefficient way to build loyalty among brands. Turow states, "Relying on signaling was no longer enough to ensure loyalty to the company and its output, practitioners generally agreed. What was needed was an ongoing conversation with every desirable customer. This approach to selling therefore implied two other efforts that were then getting much play in the advertising world: database marketing and interactive marketing." The Web is the optimum vehicle to accomplish this with its ability to fine-tune targeting efforts through tracking and user profiling.

In this chapter, we discuss how online advertising is evolving into a one-to-one marketing medium. We show how the Web and advancing technologies, such as tracking and intelligent agents, provide us with the possibility to deliver a single advertising message to each and every customer. In online advertising speak, an online ad reaches the right *eyeballs.* We also provide an overview of each type of advertising format and forum, and we discuss which can be used for targeting and one-to-one advertising. We provide an overview of services and tools, such as advertising networks and ad serving software, that ease the process of creating and managing a targeted advertising campaign. Finally, we take a peek at what is coming in the future of online advertising, including the promising potential of broadband and wireless advertising.

The State of Online Advertising

Early in the history of the Web, there was much backlash against commercial advertising on the Internet. The first Web banner appeared in 1994. Even though we are all still trying to figure out how to optimize the online advertising medium, advertising spending on the Internet is growing fast and steady. According to eMarketer, U.S. online advertising spending was $175 million in 1996, and spending grew quickly to $3.6 billion in 1999, when online advertising passed outdoor advertising spending. This total, however, represents about 1 percent of total U.S. advertising spending of $227 billion in 1999.

The Myers Group and eMarketer estimate that in 2004 online advertising will represent more than 7 percent of total ad spending. In order to fit online advertising in a marketer's media plan, we expect a shift of spending from newspapers, TV, direct mail, and other traditional advertising forms.

Table 4.1 Major Online Milestones

DATE	MILESTONE
November 1993	GNN introduces advertising to the Internet.
October 1994	HotWired site launches with ads from AT&T, Sprint, and others.
March 1995	Ragu is the first packaged-goods marketer to open a Web site.
July 1995	Forrester Research reports online ad spending for 1995 will total $37 million.
October 1995	Poppe Tyson spins off its Web ad sales unit to form DoubleClick.
January 1996	Microsoft pays $200,000 to sponsor Super Bowl Web site.
May 1996	iVillage receives $800,000 in ad commitments.
October 1996	CASIE introduces proposed Web banner ad guidelines.
January 1997	Hewlett-Packard introduces interactive "Pong" banner ad campaign.
August 1997	Jupiter Communications predicts online advertising will total $7.7 billion by the year 2002.

Table 4.1 shows a few major milestones for online advertising with some information from articles appearing in *Advertising Age*.

Analysts now believe that U.S. Internet advertising will reach at least $13 billion in 2002. According to Jupiter Communications, worldwide spending on online advertising will reach $27 billion, with U.S. spending more than half of the total. According to AdKnowledge, there are more than 4000 Web sites selling advertising in 2000, up from 1000 in 1998.

According the Fourth Edition of the Association of National Advertiser's (ANA's) *Web Site Management and Internet Advertising Trends*, 38 percent of survey respondents in early 1997 advertised on the Internet. In early 2000, this has grown to 64 percent of respondents who advertise on the Internet. Also, this study showed that respondents' average annual expenditure per company for online advertising in 1997 was $251,000. In 2000 the average annual expenditure per company grew to $1.9 million. This study also showed that the share of budget for online advertising in 1999 was 2.8 percent and is expected to continue to grow in the future.

Marketers are eager to get their messages online, but has online advertising become accepted by Web users? The answers is: somewhat, but acceptance is growing. Here are some of the facts:

- People are sacrificing TV watching in order to surf the Web. According to a Greenfield Online study, 62 percent of respondents would watch less TV to spend more time on the Internet.
- Clickthrough rates for Web banner ads have declined from about 2 percent in the mid-1990s to less than 0.5 percent today.
- In 1998, Market Facts Telenation found that 21 percent of survey respondents found online advertising "very" acceptable, another 63 percent found online advertising "somewhat" acceptable, and 14 percent thought that online advertising was "not at all" acceptable.
- According to a PC Data survey, 51 percent of women and 43 percent of men occasionally click on banners. About half of men and women listed Internet ads as one of their three primary sources for information about new sites.
- Andersen Consulting found that 25 percent of respondents in a study found a Web site as a result of clicking on a banner, followed by newspapers and magazines (14 percent), TV commercials (11 percent), radio (4 percent), and outdoor billboards (4 percent).

Benefits of One-to-One Web Advertising and Promotion

In their 1997 book, *One to One Enterprise* (Doubleday), Peppers and Rogers present the necessity of building learning relationships, which means, "Give your customer the opportunity to teach you what he wants. Remember it, give it back to him, and keep his business forever."

One-to-one Web advertising and promotion have the capabilities to form loyalty-building relationships with your online customers or users. Loyalty has the benefit of increasing advertising return on investment (ROI) and profitability through increased transactions from existing customers and lower marketing costs. What could be more compelling? The benefits of one-to-one Web advertising include the following:

- Ability to put the right message in front of the right audience at the right time
- Encouraging dialogue with customers

- Taking advantage of one of the lowest costs available to provide hundreds of different messages to different audiences
- Ability to track, report, and actually know if an online ad is successful

The Right Message to the Right Person at the Right Time

As we've discussed previously, the personalization capabilities of the Web are unprecedented. Web sites and online ad networks provide you with the ability to target customer segments or individual customers. Web technologies enable the collection of personal data including Web usage behavior, where every click on a link or a banner ad is added to a profiling database. Then, Web sites can enhance the user profile with transaction and site registration data. Ad networks can serve targeted ads based on the profiling databases they have built with the clickstream of individual Web users within sites and across sites. Targeted ads can be served based on the profile history of a user or in real time as they are clicking through a Web site.

Undoubtedly, the Web has the capability of targeting an ad based on, at a minimum, the user's computer, Web browser, time of day, past purchases, past clicks, geographic location, IP address, and other criteria. With other methods that capture actual user profile information or infer things about one group of users based on another group of users that has *like* attributes and characteristics, online advertisers can finely hone their ad campaigns.

Many Web sites can target banner ads based on "context" or content. For example, if a Web user is browsing a news site and clicks on a health-related link, then a health ad would be served to the Web page. Taking it further, Web sites can target based on demographics. In the case of the Web user browsing the health news, if the user is a women, then the health-related ad could be targeted to a woman. Even further, ads can be targeted based on lifestyle demograhics, or *psychographics*, or even *technographics* (i.e., experienced online buyer, Internet newbie, etc.).

Imagine that you have identified 15 different target markets for your new Web content site. Each target has several idiosyncratic demographic and psychographic attributes. Without doing sophisticated math, you can see that there is the potential for creating hundreds of banners or other online ad types that could be served up on hundreds of Web sites. Not only is it possible, it is a reality with the Web.

The Web is beginning to cluster, where information is being accessed through specialized Web sites, also called "channels" or "communities," that cater to groups with narrow demographic or psychographic characteristics. There are supersites or directories dedicated to specific markets or industries. For example, Manufacturing Marketplace (www.manufacturing.net) is a directory and online community that is solely dedicated to the professional who buys products from the manufacturing industry. Snap! (www.snap.com) is a site dedicated to presenting Web information that is targeted to the user. When a first-time user arrives at the main site, Snap! requests the user's zip code and then presents a Web page that is tailored to the user—plus users can create a personal page. Snap! offers advertisers many opportunities to present ads in a targeted way. There are several channels, including business, computing, health, living, money, shopping, and travel. There has also been significant growth in localized sites where national, regional, or local advertisers can present localized advertising. Hot Coupons! (www.hotcoupons.com) and CitySearch (www.citysearch.com) were pioneers in enabling ad targeting based on local geography. This clustering of the Web will give advertisers the ability to locate and market to specific target groups and measure the success of each ad within each target group. This microanalysis is what makes the Web attractive to direct marketers and advertisers.

Encourage Customer-to-Advertiser Dialog

One-to-one Web marketing requires interaction, or dialog, between customer and advertiser. This interaction can translate to customer loyalty. When customers tell you about themselves and what they like/don't like about you and your competition, you can increase revenue from each customer and increase your ability to compete. The Web has opened up a worldwide opportunity, but it has also changed the competitive landscape. It is easier than ever for customers to shop around on the Internet.

In 1991 Regis McKenna wrote *Relationship Marketing* (Addison-Wesley, 1991), which had a significant impact on changing marketing's focus to be customer-centric. He stated, "Technology is transforming choice, and choice is transforming the marketplace." There are so many choices that customers have become less loyal and more confused. The challenge for online advertisers is to form one-to-one relationships with customers through dialogue—what customers tell you about and how they interact with your advertising. This dialogue opens the door to encouraging ongoing relationships with all of your customer and market segments. It has been said that it is about five times more expensive to acquire a new customer than to get additional business from an existing one. All customers are not created equal, and you can find this out only by establishing a dialogue with them.

The Web facilitates the dialogue between the marketer and the customer—from customers' telling marketers explicitly what their preferences are to capturing customers' data implicitly through capturing click and transaction data. This dialogue process also shortens the feedback loop so that you can learn more about a customer in a shorter period of time. You can test marketing campaigns on the Web and find out quickly if particular campaigns worked or did not work.

Low-Cost and Fast-to-Deliver Multiple Messages to Multiple Audiences

A face-to-face sales meeting can cost thousands of dollars. The fully burdened cost to reach a prospect via a targeted ad in a specialized magazine can be thousands of dollars. A highly targeted direct-mail piece can cost hundreds of dollars. A highly targeted Web banner can cost a few cents to several dollars to reach a likely-to-buy online customer. If you have hundreds of ad messages, the cost to create and place them on the Web is significantly less than traditional media. The cost to create online ads will be increasing in the future with the growing use of animation, video, and audio, but the cost will still not come close to that of producing TV or magazine ads—especially if you need to create 15 different ad campaigns. Also, the time to produce a Web banner ad can be a couple of days versus many weeks to produce a magazine or television ad. According to a report by AdRelevance, Amazon.com had 360 different banner creatives in early 2000, and the average number of creatives per company was 8. AdRelevance found that the number of new banner ad creatives developed each week was around 6000.

Recordability and Accountability

Ad networks, ad management products, and Web traffic analysis products can give online advertisers more data than they ever dreamed of or, in many cases, could ever have the time to assimilate. This is where the Web leaves traditional advertising's and direct marketing's attempts to reach individual customers in the dust. What has been needed is a way to measure advertising ROI. When your objective is oriented to direct response or sales transactions, recordability and accountability are critical elements to the online ad process. If your objective is to build brand awareness among online customers, then a mass advertising model is appropriate where measuring impressions, clickthroughs, and resulting transactions is not as critical. Tracking and analyzing online advertising and promotional campaigns are important—how much data you capture and what you analyze will vary depending on your campaign objective. If an online ad is not working, you can change it in a matter of a few hours, but first you have to know if the ad is not working. The bottom line is, if you want to measure something from numbers of clicks on an ad to what type of ad works best within a particular Web site that reaches a particular target market, you can do it on the Web.

Better Sales Leads

In general, the Web allows people to gather much more information about a product or company than other media. Thus, the prospective customer is better qualified at the point he or she decides to contact the company. The ability to hyper-target ad messages also qualifies prospects up front. The more targeted you make your advertising, the more qualified the sales leads. Direct marketers have found more return on their direct marketing budget by trying to increase the response rate through targeted offers. Mass marketers can go only so far in targeting, so they receive lots of unqualified prospects, which require more resources to sift out the truly qualified sales prospects. Highly targeted Web ads can increase the likelihood of response and conversion to purchase, and they can decrease the cost associated with qualifying the prospects to determine if they are likely to buy.

Minimize Wasted Ad Exposures

Because the Web allows for unprecedented targeting, it can minimize wasted ad impressions. This can make online campaigns hugely cost efficient. Using demographics and other targeting criteria, a marketer can pinpoint who sees what online ad and when. On the flip side, online ads are *not* displayed to Internet users who do not meet the targeting criteria. For example, if you just want to reach online shoppers in Florida, you can target the ads based on zip codes. That way, if a user from Massachusetts visited a Web site, he or she would not see the ad targeted for the Florida audience.

The Nuts and Bolts of One-to-One Web Advertising

In its short history, online advertising has change considerably. We have seen online ad technology grow from simple static banners to fully interactive multimedia ads such as interstitials that include moving images and audio. We have also seen the types of advertising online broaden where many different banner shapes and sizes, sponsorships, e-mail, rich media, and wireless are now more widely available to marketers.

To understand the nature of online advertising and its emerging targeting and one-to-one marketing capabilities, we provide the foundation: the types of advertising, where to advertise, and which online formats and locations are best for mass marketing, target marketing, and one-to-one advertising. First let's take a look at the dynamics of the online advertising market and technologies.

The Online Audience

As mentioned earlier, the Web market could be considered a very large niche or target market to some advertisers. To other advertisers, the online ad medium is just a small segment of their total market. Other advertisers may find that the Web audience represents their entire market. For both types of marketers, it is important to understand the uniqueness of the online audience. It has been rapidly changing and will continue to evolve. Early on, the demographics of the Internet user were skewed to male, younger, higher income, and highly educated. Today, the population of the Internet in the United States is more diversified, looking more like the mainstream population. Also, the growth of the Internet population in Europe and Asia/Pacific is quite rapid. Here are some important facts about today's online audience:

- The U.S. Internet population in 2000 is approximately 135 million, up from 23.4 million in 1996 (*Computer Industry Almanac*, Jupiter Communications).
- The worldwide Internet population will be 490 million people in 2002, with the U.S. market representing one-third of the total population (*Computer Industry Almanac*).
- In the United States, 2001 Internet use by females and males will be a 50/50 split. Outside of the United States, males still dominate Internet usage (*Computer Economics*).
- By the end of 2000, there will be 13 million teens online in the United States, 23 million seniors (50+ years old), 14 million kids between 2 and 12 years old, and 12 million college students (Jupiter Communications).
- The average annual household income of Internet users in 1999 (in U.S. dollars) breaks down this way: United States $59,000, Canada

$50,300, Australia $62,300, United Kingdom $64,600, Italy $36,300, and France $48,300 (Ernst & Young).

- Education breakdown of U.S. Internet users (versus overall U.S. population) is as follows: High school or below is 33 percent (U.S. population 53 percent), vocational/some college is 32 percent (U.S. population 32 percent), and college graduate is 34 percent (U.S. population 20 percent) (Intelliquest).
- U.S. Internet access speed breakdown in September 1998 was as follows: 14.4 Kbps or less was 11.6 percent, 28.8 Kbps was 24.3 percent, 33.6 Kbps was 30.7 percent, 56 Kbps was 30.5 percent, and greater than 56 Kbps was 2.9 percent (ZD Market Intelligence).
- U.S. Internet access speed breakdown by 2003 is expected to be as follows: Analog modem up to 56 Kbps will be 63 percent, cable modem will be 14 percent, xDSL will be 12 percent, and ISDN will be 8 percent (Gartner Group).
- Primary uses of the Web are currently as follows: education (61.4 percent), shopping (52.4 percent), entertainment (60.1 percent), work (65.9 percent), communication (35.4 percent), personal information (73.6 percent), time wasting (37 percent) (*GVU Tenth WWW User Survey*).
- In June 2000, the average monthly U.S. Internet user activity was as follows: 18 sessions per month, 10 unique sites visited, 56 minutes spent per site, 9 hours and 4 minutes spent online, 50 seconds spent viewing a Web page (Nielsen//NetRatings).

The bottom line is that people behave differently and have particular expectations online. Web marketers should be aware of the online audience's idiosyncrasies. We should address online users with different visual and textual cues, offers, and content than what would be provided in traditional media.

Branding or Direct Response?

Both! As the Web population is growing, sites, directories, and search engines are emerging as mass-marketing vehicles. There are also more and more highly targeted, niche sites coming online everyday. Web sites span from sites that are simple awareness vehicles to full-blown, mail-order commerce sites. Depending on what business you are in and the primary reason for your online presence, you can use Web advertising for building your brand or for generating direct response.

Brand building using certain online locations, such as a high-traffic Web site, and certain ad formats, such as the animated interstitial, can be very effective ways to generate brand affinity among online users. Online advertising technologies and formats such as rich media and interstitials have allowed marketers to create ads that have impact on brand awareness and preference. The evolution of online ads to include interactivity, audio, animation, and video will help marketers fulfill brand objectives using the Internet.

For direct response, the interactive and hyperlink nature of the Web allows advertisers to generate traffic and transactions. For example, a Web banner that is promoting a free offer will get people to respond; whether they convert into buyers depends on the degree of targeting of the banner ad. The more the ad is targeted, the higher the response rate. New online ad technologies now let the user respond right in the banner itself. Rather than taking the user to a Web site when they click on a banner ad, the user can complete a transaction within the banner, whether it is placing an order, requesting more information, or playing a game. The Web continues to evolve to be the best direct response medium available.

Mass, Targeted, One-to-One

The Web allows some level of mass marketing, target marketing, and one-to-one marketing. Before proceeding, let's go back to the basics and define each type of marketing:

Mass marketing. One-to-all or one-to-many communications without specialization of message or medium. For example, a company image advertisement in a national, mass appeal magazine such as *Life* magazine.

Target marketing. One-to-many or one-to-few communications with specialization of message and medium for each identified segment of the whole market. For example, Ford Motor Company's sport utility vehicle advertisement in *The Ladies Home Journal* with images and copy geared to women's needs for this type of vehicle.

One-to-one marketing. One-to-few or one-to-one communications with individualized message and medium for each highly targeted market or individual customer. For example, a personalized e-mail advertising message with content geared to that individual's stated preferences or by other targeting criteria such as browser type, computer type, geographical area, prior interactions or transactions, demographic data, or lifestyle data.

Back in 1997, Forrester Research (www.forrester.com) predicted, "Targeted advertising to individual consumers via Web sites will become an industry standard in three years." Now, it has become evident that one-to-one marketing is a reality on the Web. There is an ever-widening range of online advertising options that one-to-one Web marketers can choose from, depending on the objectives of their advertising campaign, from simple banner ads on a search engine to interstitial advertisements that behave like television advertising with animation or full-motion video. Many Web marketers are using a combination of online advertising formats within one campaign. Figure 4.1 shows the spectrum of online advertising.

Targeting and One-to-One Advertising Technologies

The market for targeting and one-to-one Web technologies is booming. Just imagine serving up hundreds, thousands, or millions of unique banner ads to each online user within your prospective market. New technologies and applications are being developed to make this a reality in terms of implementation and affordability. Here is the recipe:

1. Combine one or more of the following ingredients: cookies, user profiling, content personalization, intelligent agents, and neural networking.

One-to-All	One-to-Many	One-to-Few	One-to-Fewer	One-to-One
1 : 1,000,000	*1 : 10,000*	*1 : 1,000*	*1 : 100*	*1 : 1*
Search Engine Home Pages	Targeted Web Sites/ Directories	Personalized Web Sites/ Directories	Personalized Web Sites and Push Channels	Highly Personalized Web Sites and Push Channels
High Traffic/ Mass Appeal Web Sites	Push Channels	Push Channels	Web Sites With Collaborative Filtering	Chat
	Search Engine Keywords	Advertising Networks	Personalized Push	Personalized E-Mail
	Advertising Networks	Targeted E-Mail	Advertising Networks	
	E-Mail		Chat	
			Targeted E-Mail	

Figure 4.1 The online advertising spectrum.

2. Add one or more of the following ingredients: databases, data mining, interaction log files, transaction log files, demographics, and psychographics.
3. Blend the above with savvy direct or one-to-one marketers in partnership with database, information technology, and Web wizards.

Seriously, in order for one-to-one Web marketers to successfully realize the potential of the Internet, they need to bring forward experiences in direct marketing to the Web but apply them in a new way. Also, one-to-one Web marketers will need to work in concert, like never before, with their information technology and Web development counterparts to understand the potential, and drawbacks, of the newer one-to-one technologies such as intelligent agents and data mining.

An Overview of Online Ad Targeting

Online ads can be targeted using a variety of data and criteria. Marketers can target broadly, such as content targeting, or finitely, using several criteria. Marketers can pick one or a combination of many sources of data to target ads. Here is a list of targeting possibilities:

Content/context targeting. Using Web page content to target online ads is one of the most popular forms of targeting. If you manufacturer women's fragrances, you would feature your online ads on iVillage.com or other women's Web sites. Context targeting is more of a time-and-place approach to targeting. For example, if you sell laptops you may want to serve your banner ad on the *USA Today* site within its Tech section.

Web server/browser. A Web server or ad server can deliver ads based on what they know about the user connected to the Web site including IP address, browser, operating system, and the day and time of the server request (i.e., when the user comes to the home page or clicks on a Web page link). A marketer can display targeted ads based on these characteristics. Marketers can also use the information to optimize the ad against the characteristics. For example, IP address can tell the geographic location of the user and the domain (e.g., .com, .org, .edu).

Registration/customer data. A Web site or ad network can serve target ads based on user registration data or data captured from a customer when he or she registers with purchases from a site. Registration data is usually captured when a user joins as a member of a particular site, enters a contest, or participates in other ways. When an online customer makes a purchase from a site, the site collects name, address, and items purchased. A purchase is also an opportunity to ask the customer for user preferences.

Clickstream/behavior data. Online ads can be displayed to Web users as they click through a site and/or based on prior site usage behavior. With ad networks, ads can be targeted based on a particular user's site behavior across sites. For example, an ad for golf clubs can be displayed to a user who has frequented golf sites and golf content.

Collaborative filtering. Online ads can be served to a particular user based on matching his or her user profile with the user profiles of people with similar preferences or Web usage behavior. For example, if you have a profile that indicates you are interested in alternative rock music, the ad server will display a banner ad that was displayed to other online users showing the same interests. (See Chapter 2, "One-to-One Web Site Personalization," for more information about collaborative filtering.)

The goal of online ad targeting is to increase the relevance of the ad and its offer in order to meet goals such as increasing clickthrough, increasing conversion, or minimizing wasted ad impressions.

Important One-to-One Web Advertising Concepts

Cookies are limited to watching the behavior of a computer user. User profiling intelligent agents can make judgments based on user input and input of like people. Profiling and personalization can deliver custom information based on input given by the user on the Web site. Web server log files can give marketers general ideas about which Web pages are the most popular, peak time of day, and percentage of unique visitors who placed an order. Which technology makes the most sense? It depends on the budget and the objective. The more targeted an ad message and placement, the higher the CPM (cost per thousand), the more expensive the ad campaign. The more granularly you want to track performance, the more expensive this endeavor will be. Not every online ad campaign needs to be defined so tightly, especially when the size of the online market is still *growing*. Also, the number of anonymous profiles is growing, so online advertisers can target ads more precisely. There are some caveats, though.

Behavior versus Declaration

Is it better to know how users act or what they tell you about themselves? The answer should be that we want to know a bit of both! With declared information that is usually captured from registration and transaction data, marketers get the benefit of actual user information and preferences. Some online users may not be all that honest, depending on how much they have at stake relative to the offer, content, and so forth. On the other hand, behavior tracked such as Web usage via cookies or tracking software doesn't necessarily tell you what is in the hearts and minds of each user. Guestbooks, registrations, profiling, and surveys are techniques that will enable users to tell you about themselves.

Inferred versus Known

Cookies and intelligent profiling/data mining agents enable advertisers to take behavior tracking to new heights where the preferences and actions can be determined based on something that is inferred rather than known. When products involve emotions, tastes, likes, dislikes, and lifestyle data, an inferred model may be best. Movies, food, clothing, recreation, cars, music, and other lifestyle-oriented interests are very subjective. Thus a marketer cannot draw a black or white conclusion on what an online user may be interested in based on what he or she has told you or how he or she has behaved in the past. This is where a strict set of logic, based on what is known, may not work as well. For example, you operate an online music store. If a particular user has purchased three country music CDs, does this mean he or she will buy only country music? Not necessarily. Most music enthusiasts' interests tend to span several music genres, even if they have a strong affinity toward one. And people change over time as they are exposed to more people and interests in their lives.

Today's One-to-One Web Advertising Technologies

Web technologies that enable the delivery of targeted or individualized advertisements are making many marketers excited, but they are also making many online consumers nervous about their privacy. Most of the current technologies involve some level of personal data; therefore, the future will be precarious for these types of technologies. With self-regulation and building trust among consumers, these one-to-one Web technologies will become the norm. The current technologies include cookies and profiling/personalization.

Cookies

Cookies work in conjunction with the Web browser and extend HTTP (HyperText Transfer Protocol) by allowing a Web server to pass information (a cookie) to the browser, as long as the user has not turned off the cookie capability in his or her browser or has purchased cookie cutter software to block cookies. The cookie usually contains a unique text identifier that allows a Web server to recognize a particular user. Each time a user returns to a Web site, that site's Web server can search a cookie file for only the information that the user had placed there earlier and send it back to the Web server. This is what allows Web sites and advertisers to provide some level of personalized information or messages. Cookies prompt the Web server to access user information that is stored in a database via a unique ID tag stored in the cookie file. Web sites correlate this unique ID with a database on the Web server. Each time the user visits the Web site, the server looks for the associated information in the database (e.g., clickstreams, transactions, survey answers). Editorial and advertising can then be served up to the user based on the user profile data. Cookies can also allow advertisers to limit advertising based on frequency and to rotate ads based on the first, second, or third time the user visited the site or saw a particular ad. Figure 4.2 shows information from the cookie file of one of this book's authors.

There are some downsides to the use of cookies in one-to-one marketing. First, users can block out cookies by changing the configuration in later ver-

cookies - Notepad

File Edit Search Help

```
# Netscape HTTP Cookie File
# http://www.netscape.com/newsref/std/cookie_spec.html
# This is a generated file!  Do not edit.

.cnn.com            TRUE    /customnews     FALSE   946627200       CNN_CUSTOM
.musicblvd.com  TRUE    /cgi-bin/tw     FALSE   946645199       MBNV_SID
www.dummiesdaily.com    FALSE   /cgi-bin/       FALSE   901681743       dumm
www.1800flowers.com     FALSE   /flowers        FALSE   944035200       SHOP
.dummiesdaily.com       TRUE    /cgi-bin        FALSE   908124685       dumm
customnews.cnn.com      FALSE   /cnews  FALSE   946627200       PNAA    :Ktu
customnews.cnn.com      FALSE   /cnews  FALSE   946627200       PNAB    :121
customnews.cnn.com      FALSE   /cnews  FALSE   946627200       PNAC    :DXB
.netscape.com   TRUE    /       FALSE   946684799       NETSCAPE_ID     1000
.focalink.com   TRUE    /       FALSE   946641600       SB_ID   08495472010
.focalink.com   TRUE    /       FALSE   946641600       SB_IMAGE        9.1.
.hardwired.com  TRUE    /       FALSE   946684799       p_uniqid        yM6d
.adobe.com      TRUE    /       FALSE   946684799       INTERSE 207.69.165.1
.isn.com        TRUE    /       FALSE   946684799       session 21732676
.internet.net   TRUE    /       FALSE   946684799       session 21580643
.bmgt.umd.edu   TRUE    /       FALSE   946684799       BMGT    user-37kbsmn
.cyberatlas.com TRUE    /       FALSE   946684799       IPRO_TAG        32a7
.infoseek.com   TRUE    /       FALSE   881610389       InfoseekUserId  386E
www.microsoft.com       FALSE   /       FALSE   937422000       MC1     GUID
.msn.com        TRUE    /       FALSE   937396800       MC1     GUID=38dd6eb
.disney.com     TRUE    /       FALSE   946684799       DISNEY  207.69.165.8
```

Figure 4.2 Sample cookie file.

sions of popular Web browsers. There is also software that allows users to block cookies. Second, users can easily delete the information in their cookie file. Third, proxy servers that allow many users to connect to the Internet through one gateway can block cookies or can make many users appear as one on the Web server. Finally, cookies identify computers and not people. This means that cookies will have somewhat limited targeting and one-to-one online advertising capabilities.

Profiling/Personalization

Today, most of the top Web sites provide some form of personalization. According to eStats, almost 80 percent of Web sites will be using personalization technology by 2002. Beyond Web site tracking and traffic analysis, Web site personalization allows Web publishers who sell advertising to provide in-depth audience information beyond a user's clickstream (via cookies, IP, and referral site) in order to serve relevant ads. With a profile tool, site owners typically use a registration form or transaction to ask users for demographic (e.g., age, income, education, gender, etc.) and psychographic (e.g., lifestyle, interests, attitudes) information that can tell more about each user. Because personalization products also have tracking components, the Web publisher can associate clickstreams with individual user profiles or groups of people based on a single profile characteristic (e.g., gender, favorite type of movie, profession, marital status, and more). Building user profiles helps marketers determine patterns and trends among customers, in whole or in segments.

For online advertising, the common form of profiling is called *anonymous profiling*. Anonymous profiles are data stored without personally identifiable information associated with user profiles. Using data mining, ad networks and web sites using profiling technology from MatchLogic, Engage, DoubleClick, and other providers can determine patterns and make predictions that affect the ability to deliver focused, targeted advertising. Online profiling is powerful, yet there are some drawbacks, including the use of cookies. Cookies are tied to a computer, not a single user. If more than one person uses a single computer, profiling is more challenging. Also, a single Web user has many roles in life. For example, someone who browses and buys on the Internet may be doing so for work and for home, and he or she may be doing so on behalf of others in the case of shopping for gifts for other family members and friends who have very different interests. Of course, the more anonymous profile data collected over time, the better the targeting results.

Some of the companies providing user profiling services for online advertising include MatchLogic, Engage, DoubleClick, and Excite, which are discussed in this chapter. Some of the products and/or services that incorporate user profiling or personalization include Broadvision One-to-One, GuestTrack, Personlify, Vignette, E.piphany, and NetPerceptions. See Chapter 2, "One-to-One Web Site Personalization," for an in-depth discussion of Web profiling and personalization techniques, products, and services.

AN INTERVIEW WITH MIKE GRIFFITHS, CHIEF TECHNOLOGY OFFICER, MATCHLOGIC

MatchLogic is a leading online database marketing solutions provider of online advertising and marketing services. MatchLogic has ad services that allow marketers to target online ads based on demographics. Over the past few years, MatchLogic has gathered anonymous demographic information (profiles) on about 10 million people who have provided their demographic data through site registrations, sweepstakes entries, surveys, and so forth. MatchLogic is able to demographically target ads to the general Web traffic based on the Web usage pattern of the known user in the MatchLogic anonymous profile database. In other words, if the unknown user is browsing a site, his or her clickstream pattern would be matched with the use pattern of the MatchLogic user profile in order to target the right ad.

Authors: **Anonymous profiles are dependent on cookies; do you see this as a drawback of online profiling and ad targeting?**

Griffiths: **Yes, cookies can be generally unreliable if a computer has multiple users and represent "noise" in the online ad model. With cookies, there is no absolute, so marketers should focus on the incremental increases in yield that online targeting can provide.**

Authors: **How effective is online advertising in meeting one-to-one marketing objectives?**

Griffiths: **Currently, online advertising enables marketers to segment markets. It doesn't yet have the ability to target down to the individual. Other online marketing methods, such as e-mail and Web marketing, are more detailed and more reliable because the relationship with the customer is based on explicit data provided by the customer, rather than usage tracking based on cookies.**

Authors: **What does the future look like for online advertising?**

Griffths: **The online advertising industry is anticipating that broadband and wireless access will define Internet advertising in the future. The cell phone and other wireless devices will be more pervasive than PCs connected to the Internet. The expected ratio is five wireless devices to one PC. Wireless access will require advertisers to think about advertising differently. Advertisers will have to provide useful information or services to wireless users instead of overt promotion and advertising. User privacy will be even more important in the wireless advertising medium than in the Internet medium.**

Online Ad Measurement and Return on Investment (ROI)

Measuring the results of an online ad campaign has come a long way since the Web's early days. Early on, the clickthrough rate (CTR) was king. Tracking the percentage of people who clicked on an ad was quite delightful a few years ago, but as the CTR has declined to less than 0.5 percent on average, marketers are adding other measures for their online advertising efforts. Also, as the online medium is becoming more interactive and multimedia, measuring brand awareness is now possible. Selecting which measure(s) is best ultimately depends on the marketing objective (see Table 4.2).

According to the Fourth Edition of the Association of National Advertiser's *Web Site Management and Internet Advertising Trends*, the popular online ad measures ranked by survey respondents were click rate %, ads delivered, clicks (clickthrough, click-down, click within), click-to-purchase, demographics, ROI, delivered CPMs (cost per thousands), e-commerce revenues, and pre-post awareness.

As the online ad medium is progressing, marketers will be able to track the *lag effect* of campaigns. Because online ads are tracked using cookies, advertisers know when a particular banner ad is served to a particular user. If the user did not click at that moment it was displayed but he or she

Table 4.2 Checklist: What Is Your Online Advertising Objective?

✔ OBJECTIVE	MEASURE	DESCRIPTION
Response	Clickthrough (CTR)	Number of clicks divided by number of ad impressions (%)
Inquiry/lead costs	Cost Per Lead (CPL)	Campaign cost divided by number of clickthroughs
Acquire sale/customer	Cost Per Sale (CPS)	Campaign cost divided by number of sales
Advertising effectiveness	Advertising-to-sales	Total cost of advertising divided by online sales during same period
Brand/ad awareness	Recall	Focus/surveys testing recall of advertising (e.g., customer research, MBInteractive's BrandImpact*)
Brand action	Request info/sample	Number of requests divided by number of ad impressions (%), or "interaction rate"

* For more information about BrandImpact, visit www.mbinteractive.com.

visited the Web site at a later date, this can be tracked and reported. Also, users can be tracked when they click on the ad, go to the site, and then visit the site again in the future. For example, an AdKnowledge study showed that within 30–90 days of serving an online ad, almost 50 percent of the activity (i.e., sales, leads) associated with the campaign came from repeat visits, which are in addition to the initial site visits, leads, or sales resulting from the online ad campaign.

Ad Server/Management Software

Online advertising management software products have the power to revolutionize Web advertising campaigns. They target, they track, and they even slice and dice—information, that is. The reporting capabilities of ad management software systems make it possible for Web marketers to know which ad Web site or Web page worked well or didn't work so well. They can tell you if the ad worked better in the morning or at 2:00 P.M. They can juggle multiple ad banners to ensure that the appropriate ad was delivered to the correct eyeballs. These products will become standard among most, if not all, Web sites that sell online advertising; and they will be an essential element in one-to-one Web advertising.

If you are a Web site publisher who sells advertising, then you may want to implement the ad management software yourself or outsource it to a third-party ad management service provider such as AdKnowledge, DoubleClick, or Engage. Typically, for marketers buying advertising on other sites, the ad server is managed by a third-party ad management service company, whether you buy the ad directly from a Web site or through your online advertising agency.

Advertising managers typically can target ads based on the users' computer platform, browser, date, time, host name, geographic location, and the Web site that the user just came from (a.k.a. referrer). The ad management systems are now incorporating additional targeting data. For example, Engage Technologies' AdManager targets ads based on visitor profile information from site registration or external databases, area of content where a visitor is viewing, domain type, browser, time of day, day of the week, computing platform, key word/key phrase, geographic data, and *compound* demographic targets specified by a Web site. Ad management software can deliver ads based on frequency (e.g., the number of times a particular Web user has seen a banner). Ad management software typically tracks user interactions with online ads in real time so that the ads can be optimized based on creative and targeting criteria. In addition to reporting clickthrough rates, ad management software can track the entire process including tracking through to a sale or inquiry. This is known in the industry as *closed loop reporting*. Figure 4.3 shows the management capabilities of Engage.

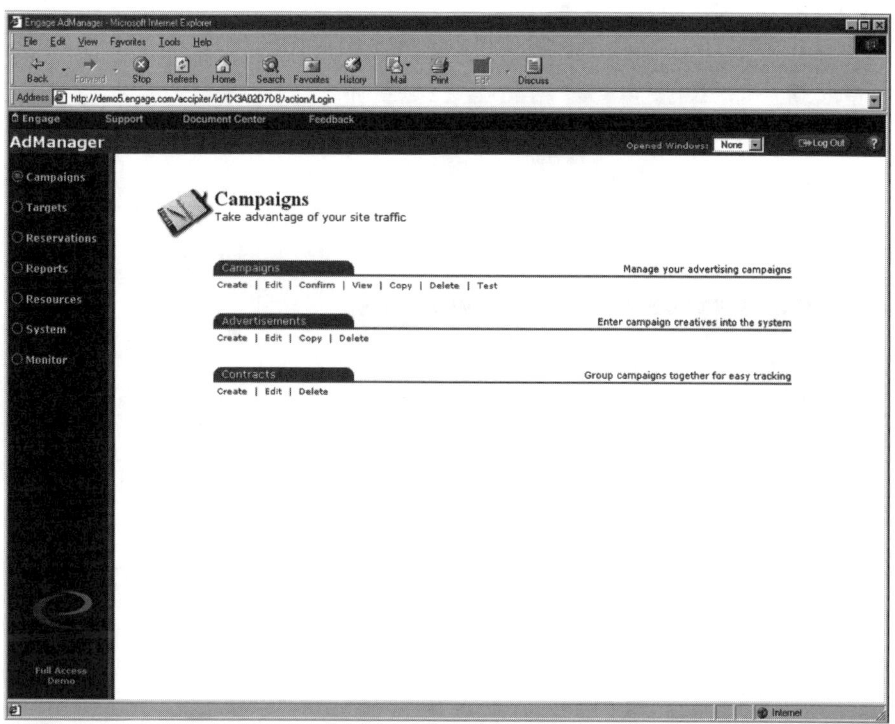

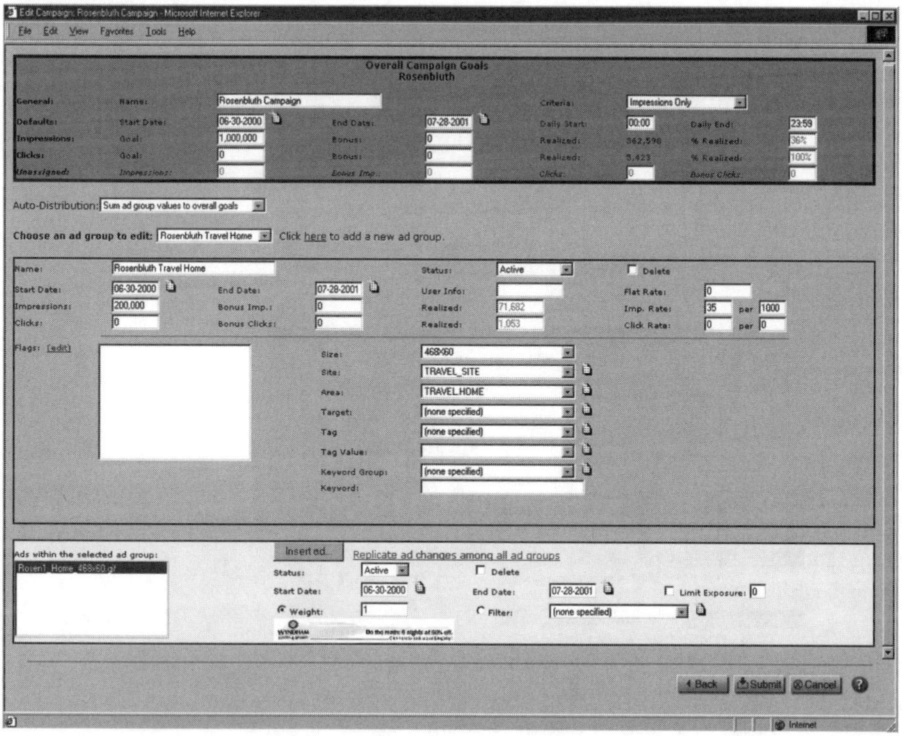

Figure 4.3 Engage AdManager helps advertisers create, monitor, change, and optimize online advertising campaigns.

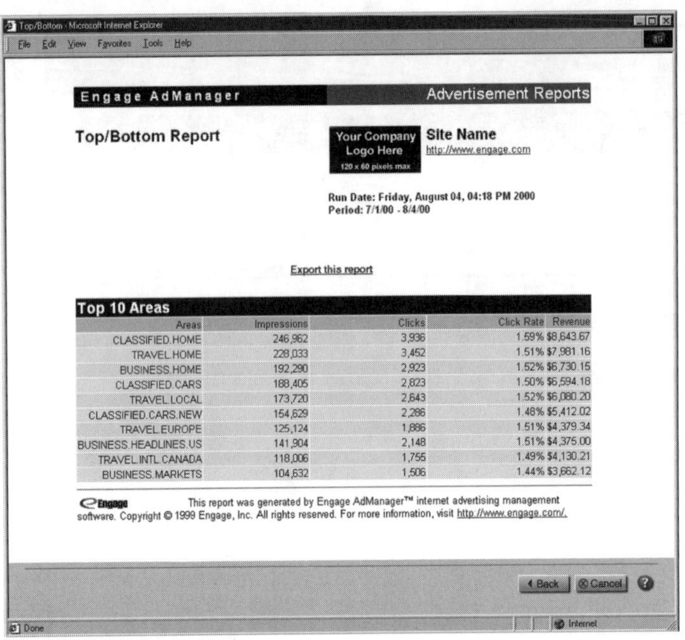

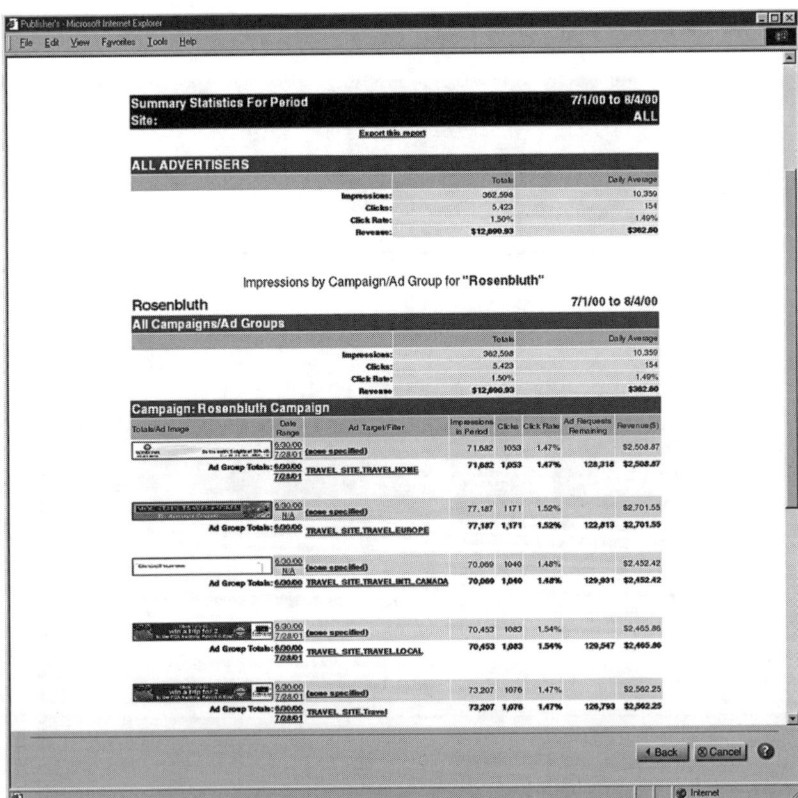

Figure 4.3 Engage AdManager helps advertisers create, monitor, change, and optimize online advertising campaigns. (Continued)

Ad Server/Management Products/Services

Ad server/management software uses artificial intelligence, data mining, and intelligent agents to make decisions based on user input and a community of users or other data. Intelligent agents make predictive responses based on prior Web activity and/or user profiles that include demographic and psychographic information. The agent sifts through information to find relevant information such as content or advertising. The information is then delivered to the user. Agent-based ad networks, online ad serving, and other software products or services that assist the process of targeting can cost a few thousand dollars to hundreds of thousands of dollars. Each advertising serving and management product has its own bells and whistles, but most provide targeting and reporting capabilities. Table 4.3 lists a variety of ad serving and management software products.

Types of Online Advertising

The world of online advertising has grown very quickly in dollars and Web sites, and new types of advertising are being created. In just a short few

Table 4.3 Ad Management Products and Services

COMPANY	PRODUCTS	WEB SITE
24/7 Media	Connect	www.247media.com
AdForce	AdForce, TrackForce	www.adforce.com
AdJuggler	AdJuggler	www.adjuggler.com
AdKnowlege	AdKnowledge, eAnalytics	www.adknowledge.com
Bellcore	Adapt/X	www.bellcore.com
Clickable	AdClick Pro	www.clickables.com
DoubleClick	AdServer, DART	www.doubleclick.net
Engage	AdManager, AdBureau	www.engage.com
Interadnet	Instantadnet	www.interadnet.com
MatchLogic	MatchLogic	www.matchlogic.com
Mediaplex	MOJO	www.mediaplex.com
RealMedia	Open AdStream	www.realmedia.com
Solbright	AdSuite, Dispatch	www.solbright.com
Spinbox	Spinbox	www.spinbox.com

years we have moved from static Web banners to full-blown multimedia ads that fill up the entire browser. Users can now interact with banners, and some advertisers have built comprehensive Web sites with the sole purpose of promoting their brand or brands to the online audience.

Web Site as an Advertising Vehicle

For many companies, especially those with sites that don't conduct e-commerce, the primary objective for a Web site is advertising to inform and market to customers. Web sites are used to increase awareness of a company or brand in the online market. There are two types of sites: whole Web sites and microsites.

Whole Web Sites

Many companies have built Web sites to build their brand image among online users. They aren't necessarily electronic commerce Web sites or corporate image sites—their main objective is to advertise their products and increase brand awareness and brand loyalty. Procter & Gamble (www.pg.com) has built the Tide ClothesLine (www.tide.com), a Web site dedicated to promoting the Tide brand of detergent. The Web site encourages users to "interact" with the Tide brand. The site contains very comprehensive information about laundry and fabric care with several content areas and interactivity. For example, the Tide Stain Detective is a personalized, interactive problem solver for getting stains out of clothing. The site also has contests, product information, and an online store that allows customers to purchase laundry-related merchandise (not Tide products), and it cross-promotes the company-sponsored NASCAR racing team. The site is a good balance of useful content and brand promotion, where the user receives a lot of benefits from the site rather than just a lot of advertising messages. If you have, or plan to have, a brand-building Web site, then the Tide site is a good model for credible brand promotion.

There are many brand Web sites on the Internet. Here is just a sample of sites that do a good job of customer-brand bonding:

Budweiser beer	www.budweiser.com
Burger King	www.burgerking.com
Disney Online	www.disney.com
Excite.com	www.excite.com
Kellogg's	www.kelloggs.com
Kraft Foods	www.kraftfoods.com
L'eggs pantyhose	www.leggs.com

Levi's jeans	www.levi.com
Monster.com	www.monster.com
Nike athletic wear	www.nike.com
Noxema Skin Fitness	www.fitskin.com
Pampers diapers	www.pampers.com
Ragu spaghetti sauce	www.eat.com
Revlon	www.revlon.com
The Body Shop	www.bodyshop.com
Toyota cars	www.toyota.com
Volvo cars	www.volvocars.com

A Web site has the unique ability to provide individualized marketing messages and information when the site uses cookie or HTTP header information. For targeted or one-to-one marketing on your Web site, you can deploy a user profiling mechanism such as site registration, guestbook, or personalization technology such as BroadVision's One-to-One, GuestTrack, and other software or services. (See Chapter 2, "One-to-One Web Site Personalization," for more information on Web site personalization.)

Microsites

Microsites are Web sites that are specifically designed to build relationships between an online customer and an advertiser's brand. There are many benefits to having a microsite—many of the benefits already discussed include flexibility, interactive tools, and delivery of personalized content, advertising messages, and e-commerce. The unique value is that the Web marketer can build a relationship with the customer less clandestinely and more credibly. Here are a couple of examples of microsites:

Dell Computer has created a microsite within the ZDNet (www.zdnet) Web site that allows Web users seeking to buy a new computer to research and purchase from this microsite without having to go the Dell Web site. Web users find the microsite by clicking on banner ads on ZDNet ComputerShopper .com. Figure 4.4 shows the Dell Microsite (www.zdnet.com/computershopper/promos/microsites/dell/dellhome.html).

ROC Dermatologic created a cobranded microsite in conjunction with the women's site iVillage.com that allows site visitors to learn about ROC's products. The microsite is a daughter window (pop-up new browser window) that has in-depth information and includes iVillage.com menus and navigation (www.caringforyourskin.com/roc/index.html).

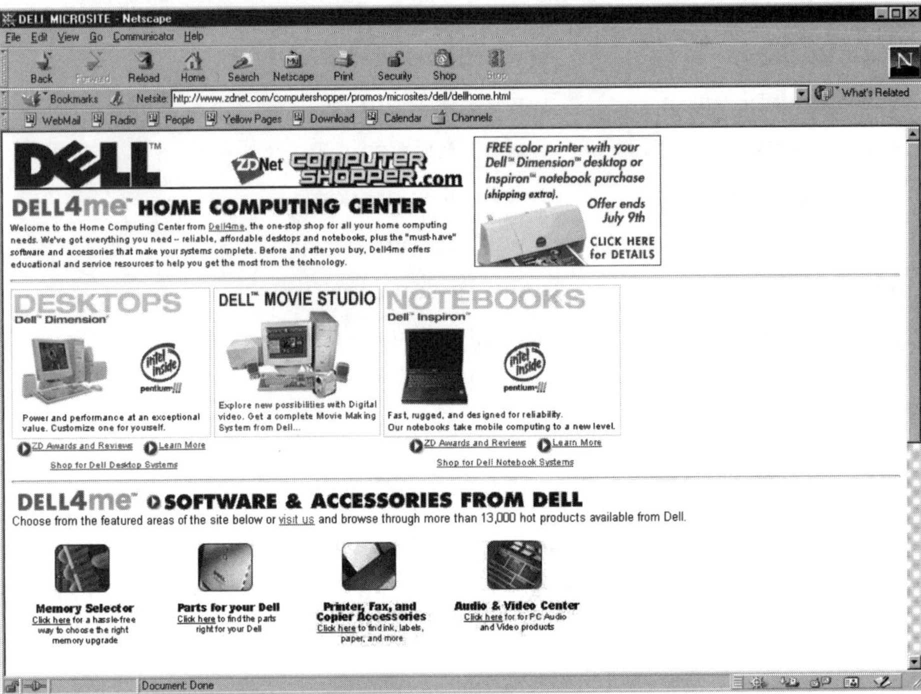

Figure 4.4 Dell microsite on ZDNet Computershopper.com.

Banner Advertising

The oldest and most prevalent online ad format is the banner. Web banner advertisements are rectangular graphical images that carry advertising or promotional messages that link to other Web sites or pages. The most common size is about five inches in length and less than one inch in height. Banners fall into three basic categories: static (fixed, no motion), animated (multiframe rotating), and interactive (rich media). The goal of the Web marketer is to provide enough advertising information to get the user to click on the ad, which takes the user to a Web site or a special section within a Web site. As online ad technology has advanced with animation and rich media technologies, banners can now include much more information and interactivity. In fact, now banners can allow users to interact with them and even request information or purchase right within a banner. (Rich media will be discussed in more detail later in this chapter.)

AdKnowledge follows the acceptance of banner and online ad formats on sites and ad networks. According to AdKnowledge, in early 2000 the most prevalent banner size was still 468x60 pixels. Other banner sizes being accepted by Web sites include 125x125 pixels, 120x60 pixels, and 120x90 pixels. Each type of banner advertisement format is discussed next.

Simple Banners

Simple banners were the first forms of advertising on the Web in 1994. There are a few unique benefits of Web banner advertising versus other forms of traditional advertising such as broadcast TV commercials. You can control who sees which banner advertisement. If a banner ad is not performing, you can change it the same day! You can easily test multiple advertisements and receive rapid or even real-time performance data. The flexibility and accountability of Web banner advertising are what makes the online medium very attractive to Web marketers.

The aim of the advertiser is to receive maximum clickthroughs, which are the number of times an online user clicks on the Web banner ad. In general, banner ads typically receive about a half percent clickthrough rate, which has declined from an all-time high of about 2 percent in the early days of the Web. Many techniques are available to improve clickthrough rates on simple banners, such as adding the phrase "click here," using certain colors (brighter colors versus black and white), providing "free" offers, and introducing something "new."

Buttons

Buttons are an abbreviated version of Web banners. A button is usually rectangular or square and measures about one-half or one-quarter the size of a banner. Buttons can be static or animated and are usually 120x90 pixels or smaller, with the 88x31 button being a popular button size. Although the message is extremely limited, the buttons can be designed and placed according to each target audience you want to reach.

Visit the IAB Web site at www.iab.net/iab_banner_standards/bannersource.html for the standard ad banner sizes.

Targeted Banners/Targeted Sites

If your advertising campaign goal involves reaching several segments of your customer or prospect base, then develop banners for each targeted site or groups of target sites. The ability to target messages enables one-to-one Web marketers to reach just a few customers with a specific marketing message. Many online advertisers have also experienced the higher clickthrough rates associated with targeted Web ads. With the relatively low cost of producing banner ads, companies create several and even hundreds of banners that can be targeted based on keyword searches, targeted content, user profiles, and more. Art.com has created over 400 banner ads to promote its online art store. The Art.com banners feature different well-known artists that are served to Web users who type in search terms in a major search engine like Yahoo!. For example, when the name "Monet" is typed in, a banner from Art.com is displayed that features Claude Monet, the famous Impressionist painter. When a user clicks on that banner, he or she is taken to a specialized Web page on Art.com that features artwork from Monet.

For example, if you sell a sport utility vehicle (SUV), then you probably have several types of customers, or target markets, to which you would like to direct advertising messages. The markets for SUVs can include several groups with in the commercial market and consumer market, such as those shown in Table 4.4.

As you can see, the list for specialized markets for SUVs can include several types. When you design and place targeted Web banner advertising, you will want to create a different message for each type of customer.

On the Web, you have some options when you want to place targeted advertising:

Search engines or online directories. If you want to reach potential buyers of SUVs on a search engine like Yahoo!, then you can purchase general keyword selections such as "sport utility," "sport utility vehicle," and "four-wheel drive." Your Web banners are served up to your audiences when they type in the same keywords. You can also try to reach your target audiences by buying keywords that meet the interests or attributes of each target market. For example, to reach the outdoor enthusiasts, you may want to buy keywords such as "camping," "skiing," and "hiking." If you want to reach people who have boats, then you could choose "boating," "boats," "waterskiing," "fishing," and so forth.

Online magazines, or e-zines. There are thousands of online editions of print magazines, or e-zines. You will be able to place advertising within these sites whose audiences meet your targeting criteria. For

Table 4.4 Commercial and Consumer Market Examples

COMMERCIAL MARKET FOR SUVS	CONSUMER MARKET FOR SUVS
Construction managers for home building	People who own boats
Construction managers for commercial buildings	Large families
Automobile parts retail store chain	Young, high-income couples interested in outdoor activities

example, if you want to reach the young couples interested in your SUV, then you may want to place advertising, with an outdoor adventure theme on SkiNet (www.skinet.com) and Adventure Sports Online (www.adventuresports.com).

Advertising networks. Ad networks, such as DoubleClick, allow you to build a media plan that spans numerous sites that are geared to your target markets. (Advertising networks are discussed later in this chapter.) Targeting banner ads will become a mainstay of online advertising campaigns. For example, Quote.com (www.quote.com), the Internet's leading provider of financial market news and information, created the Target Audience Ad Package. Advertisers are able to display targeted advertising banners based on a stock-ticker symbol.

Links to Jump or Landing Pages

One way to enhance response rate measurement is the use of specialized *jump pages* or *landing pages*. This means that you can direct banner ads to bring users to a specially created promotional Web page, a specific Web page within a Web site, and special versions of the home pages when they click on your ad. The landing page messages can be matched to the banner messages. This approach can help you increase the response and conversion rate of ads by bringing the audience directly to the information related to a particular ad. A popular technique is creating special promotional landing Web pages. This approach is highly trackable, and it helps the marketer increase the conversion to sale or lead. If your banners feature special and distinct promotional or positioning messages, you can create several versions of your home page that match each message. If you have one ad that features the benefit of saving money and another banner that features fast delivery, two different versions of the site's home page can reinforce each benefit.

Online users want instant gratification, so having the promotional information linked directly to the ad enhances the likelihood that these users will convert from prospects to customers. You can build promotional areas on the Web site that map to special target markets. This can help you measure ad campaign effectiveness by isolating the measurement of ad performance to sections of the site versus trying to evaluate a particular campaign's success over the entire Web site, which can be very cumbersome. Imagine having targeted or one-to-one landing pages in the future.

Animated and Interactive Banners

Animated and interactive Web banner advertisements have the benefit of becoming more intrusive and attention getting. They also can increase clickthrough rates and allow one-to-one marketers to lengthen the attention span of the online audience long enough to begin a dialogue or enhance a relationship with the prospect or customer. Animated banners, also known as "animated GIFs," usually have two to several frames that rotate. Interactive banners are created with HTML, where they typically contain a pull-down menu, or with rich media technologies that allow in-banner activity such as entering information, games, or buying something right in the banner. Here are examples of each type of animated or interactive banner:

Animation. According to a study by ZDNet (www.zdnet.com), animation improved clickthrough rates 15–40 percent over static Web banners. There is a trade-off between bandwidth constraints and the ability to tell more of your story. Also, animation is not a replacement for good creative content and call-to-action—both are still required. Figure 4.5 shows how Intel (www.intel.com) uses animation in an advertising campaign for the Pentium II microprocessor.

Pull-down menus. Banners with pull-down menus allow users to make a specific selection from choices within the ad. The pull-down menu makes the banner more interactive and memorable. Pull-down menus allow marketers to tailor the Web site landing pages to each choice within the banner. This type of banner can also help marketers test offers or products to find out what is most appealing to each target customer and which medium performs best with which offer. See Figure 4.6 for a sample banner from a more.com ad campaign.

Figure 4.5 Intel's animated Web advertising campaign.

Figure 4.6 HTML pull-down banner for more.com campaign (created by Freestyle Interactive).

Games. Hewlett-Packard engaged users in a game of pong with a Web banner ad. At the time, it was one of the first uses of interaction in a banner. Other engaging games within banners could include word puzzles, tic-tac-toe, Pac Man, manipulating a game character or logo, among others.

In-banner interaction or transaction. Rich media technologies (e.g., Enliven) allow marketers to create banners that can include contests, printing, purchasing, and other interaction right within the banner.

Rich Media Advertising

Rich media goes beyond animated GIF banners to incorporate HTML, Java, JavaScript, audio, video, animation, 3-D, Flash, Shockwave, and other related technologies. Rich media can incorporate technologies to enhance branding and direct response marketing objectives. Rich media is still not as prevalent as Web banners, but with advances in Internet access speeds and Web technologies rich media will represent the future of online advertising.

Rich media is now enhancing banner ads and inspiring new ad formats such as interstitials that present the Web audience with a full-blown multimedia presentation that increases awareness and response. Rich media will also allow more flexible targeting and one-to-one marketing in online advertising. According to an Excite@Home and IPSOS-ASI study, broadband rich media ads produced 22 percent higher recall and 35 percent more clicks than banner ads. Some of the rich media solutions available today are these:

IBM HotMedia. HotMedia is a Java-based software program that allows marketers to create rich media advertising including adding video, audio, 3D, animations, panoramas, transaction, scrolling, zooming, and other interactivity. HotMedia allows "event tracking" to let marketers track what parts of the ad users click on and record how long the user interacts with the ad. HotMedia allows for "unlimited real estate" where ads can contain as much content as you want. (www-4.ibm.com/software/net.media).

bluestreak. bluestreak developed E*Banners, which are "expandable" banner ads. When a user interacts with a bluestreak-enabled banner, another rich media ad will pop up on the screen and can be interacted with (www.bluestreak.com).

Real Networks. Marketers can create online advertising that includes streaming audio and video. Although the technology doesn't match the level of TV advertising, streaming ads can help marketers bring a fuller marketing presentation that standard banner advertising cannot do. Real Networks requires the RealPlayer and related plug-ins to be downloaded, but the RealPlayer is one of the most popular downloads among Web users (www.realnetworks.com).

Enliven. Enliven banners contain Java that allows in-banner responses and transactions. Enliven banners can include animation, sound and video, expandable ads, downloadable information, and printable information, and they can allow banner interaction tracking to give marketers insight into the effectiveness of the ads (www.enliven.com).

Dynamically assembled ads. Using Enliven and MatchLogic TrueLogic technologies, Excite@Home allows advertisers to optimize the delivery of ads to users based on the users' Internet access speeds. Banner ads have many elements, and they are built and served on the fly, based on access speed. For example, a user with a 28.8 modem may see a banner that includes animation, limited audio, and low-resolution graphics. On the other hand, a user with high-speed access will receive an ad from the same advertiser, but it will be assembled with video, 3-D graphics, and/or high-quality audio (www.excite.com).

AudioBase. AudioBase enables advertisers to add audio to banners and other online ad sizes/formats. AudioBase requires a Java applet to allow about 95 percent of the Internet to play the audio ad without downloading a plug-in. Audiobase detects the Web user's Internet connection speed and streams the correct audio format. In a particular banner ad campaign for the movie *The Flintstones in Viva Rock Vegas,* the play rate was 12 percent and the clickthrough rate was 3.4 percent, which is significantly higher than the less than one-half percent industry average clickthrough rate (www.audiobase.com).

Macromedia Shockwave and Flash. Online advertisers can build Shockwave ads that can contain graphics, sound, text, animation, and video. The ads are delivered in streaming fashion and allow advertisers to create interactive and attention-getting ads. With Flash, advertisers can build streaming interactive multimedia marketing experiences on their Web sites or online ads (i.e., interstitials). Shockwave and Flash require plug-ins that are two of the most widely downloaded plug-ins by Web users (www.macromedia.com).

Rich media is gaining in popularity among advertisers because of its flexibility, targetability, and trackability and for its ability to increase clickthrough and interaction. In a study by MB Interactive, a rich media campaign had a 1.72 percent clickthrough rate versus the .93 percent received by the regular banner ads. As high-speed access to the home grows, the use of rich media by online advertisers will increase. According to Forrester Research, high-speed Internet access will reach 16 million U.S. households in 2002. Currently, the number of Web sites accepting rich media ads is small but growing. Rich media can expand the targeting capability of online ads, as well as impact brand awareness because of the rich experience provide by rich media ad technologies. Of course, rich media ads are more costly to produce. According the Fourth Edition of the Association of National Advertiser's *Web Site Management and Internet Advertising Trends,* the average cost to produce a simple static banner is $1800 versus the average cost of $8900 to produce a rich media ad. Thus, marketers need to determine if a rich media ad has the necessary ROI to justify the additional production expense.

Interstitials

Interstitials are online advertisements that are pop-up windows (i.e., a Web user is surfing a Web site and a new browser window containing an advertisement appears). Interstitials interrupt the user in that they are displayed when the advertiser wants. These types of ads are usually in rich media format (e.g., animation, full-motion video, sound) and can be different sizes. According to MarketAdvisor, interstitial ads produced an average click rate of 5 percent versus 1 percent for banners. Typically, interstitials load invisibly in the background until the entire ad is downloaded and then the interstitial is displayed to the Web user. Unicast (www.unicast.com) is a provider of interstitials, or what it calls its own solution: *Superstitials.* According to an MB Interactive study, Unicast's Superstitials

IS RICH MEDIA RIGHT FOR ADVERTISERS?

Rich media has been growing in popularity because it increases marketer's options. About 20 percent of current online ads contain some form of rich media. Enliven (www.enliven.com) provides rich media advertising solutions that allow marketers to implement e-commerce, lead generation, and brand marketing directly within banner ads. According to Rob Graham, director of production services at Enliven, "Banner clickthrough has been declining to a third of 1 percent. Some of this decline is due to the fact that customers want to stay on the Web page they are on. Rich media ads allow interaction to happen within the banner itself so the Web user isn't taken away to another site. With Enliven rich media banners, users can print out information or promotions, request information, and do other activities within the banner. If an online user isn't ready to go to the site, he or she can at least learn more about the company, or print and save information or offer at that moment."

"If your objective is direct sales or site membership, then you will want to use a direct response banner model, which may not require rich media," stated Graham. Some companies may require the Web prospect to come directly to the Web site. If your objective is to provide information, increase brand awareness/preference, promotion/contests, couponing, sampling, etc., then marketers can take advantage of rich media's higher degree of interaction. In addition to clickthrough, Enliven banners allow marketers to measure the "interaction rate" of banners. This means that marketers can find out if people who didn't click through the banner actually interacted with the banner. Interactions can include clicking on items, playing games, and entering information. According to Enliven, the average interaction rate for their banners has been 15 percent. Enliven can also track how long the person interacted with the banner.

received an ad awareness of 66 percent versus the banner, which had 32 percent ad awareness.

Other Web Advertising Types/Formats

It didn't take long for marketers to yearn for more than static Web banner ads. First, advertisers stretched the Web banner to its interactive limit. Now, online ads are taking many shapes, sizes, and behaviors. The benefit of all of this technological and creative advancement is the ability for the Web marketer to establish dialogue with the user or customer. Other online advertising formats give marketers different paths to awareness and response. Most any online ad format such as pop-up windows, advertorials, and sponsorships can be targeted in order to maximize response and minimize wasted impressions.

Pop-Up Windows

Pop-up windows are online advertisements that are launched when a user goes to or interacts with a Web site. The pop-ups are separate, self-contained windows that are smaller than the browser. In general, these ads get more attention and increase clickthrough rates; plus, they don't whisk users away from the original Web site, which is a very user-friendly factor.

Advertorials and Info-Ads

Advertorials and informational ads are not new ad vehicles in the real world, but they are just emerging in the Web world. These ad formats blend advertising messages with editorial content. This allows advertisers to tell more of the story, which enables higher qualification and conversion rates. In other words, the viewer has more information to make a decision about whether to further pursue the offer. This gives advertisers higher quality and serious sales inquiries rather than what we marketers know as "tire kickers." Many Web marketing gurus already advocate not using vague messages, so the advertorial and info-ad are ways to take this philosophy to the farthest extent. On the other hand, the advertorial must be identified as an advertisement so that it is not confused with true editorial. Advertorials are not new in that they are prevalent in print magazine and newspaper advertising.

Sponsorships

Sponsorships are different from banner ads in that they are more integrated with the Web site on which they are appearing. Instead of selected banners, sponsorships allow users to bond with brands. Instead of outright, in-your-face promotional messages, you can add credibility to your advertising by being associated with a respected company or Web site. Sponsorships typically have a higher impact when coupled with useful content, interactivity, and useful tools (e.g., product finders, calculators, personalization).

Web marketers can monitor the performance of referring links to see if the sponsorship was successful. Web marketers can also provide special offers where they capture user profile information in order to facilitate future promotions based on user demographics. Most major content sites such as iVillage.com, Drkoop.com, and CBS Sportsline.com offer content sponsorships that allow marketers to present a credible image that is omnipresent within the sponsored Web site or section of a site.

Online Ad Types: Availability, CPMs, Production Costs

Web banners are the most prevalent of online ad formats by far. More ad formats are being introduced frequently—now ads can even be sent to wireless devices. Figures 4.7 and 4.8 show the acceptance of advertising in 2000, according to AdKnowledge.

The average cost of online media has been declining to a $33.59 CPM (cost per thousand impressions) in March 2000 from a $39.26 CPM in September of 1997. The more marketers use target advertising, the higher the CPM that marketers will pay. Although the CPM is higher for targeted advertising than for *run of site (ROS)* advertising (i.e., nontargeted), it may be worth it if the response is at a level that justifies the additional cost when the ROI is calculated. As online advertising is advancing, the cost to produce ads has been declining. According to the Fourth Edition of the Association of National Advertiser's *Web Site Management and Internet Advertising Trends,* in 1999 the average cost paid by survey respondents for a still banner ad/button was $4142 versus $1800 in 2000. In 1999, respondents paid an average of $90,964 for a Web site sponsorship, whereas advertisers paid an

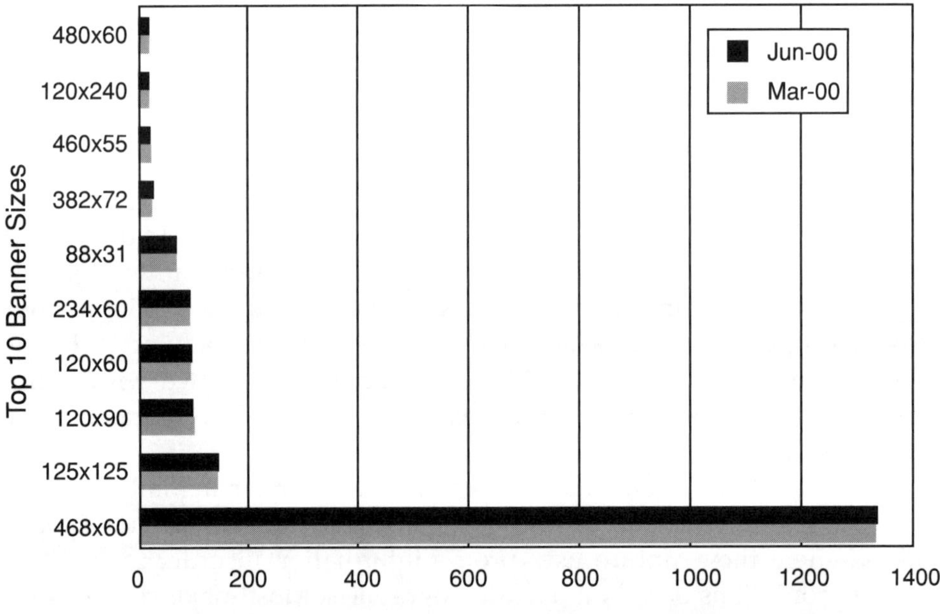

Figure 4.7 Number of Web sites accepting banners of various sizes.
Source: AdKnowledge.

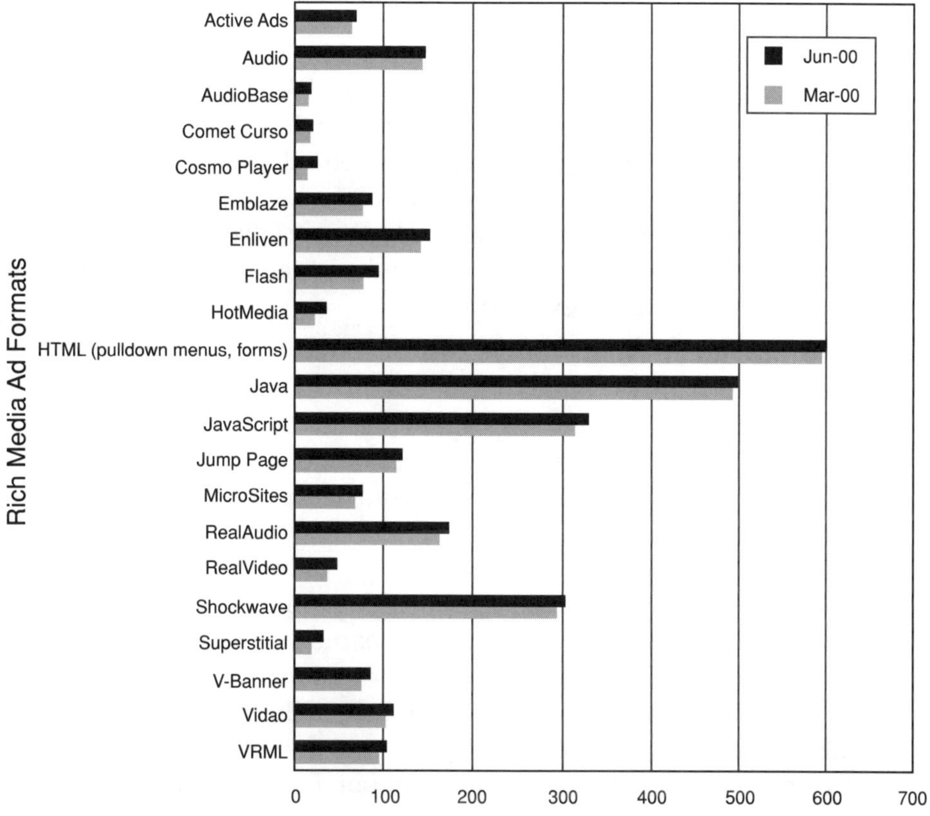

Figure 4.8 Number of Web sites and ad networks accepting rich media formats.
Source: AdKnowledge.

average of $34,900 for a sponsorship in 2000. The average cost to produce a rich media ad in 1999 was $33,675 versus $8900 in 2000.

Places to Advertise Online

Mary Meeker, a managing director at Morgan Stanley, wrote *The Internet Advertising Report*. In this report she classified Web sites as aggregated, content provider, commerce, and hybrid. Each type of site has a different revenue model and therefore a different advertising model. Here is a discussion of each classification:

Aggregated sites. The best-known aggregated Web sites are search engines such as AltaVista, Excite, Go.com, iWon.com, Snap.com, and Yahoo!. Their main reason for existence is advertising, and, while not unexpected, they are at the top of the charts in terms of ad revenue. Typically search engines are better for reaching larger audiences. One-to-one Web marketers, however, can target Web banner ads by keyword, but search engines are advancing in terms of how they can target. Typically, marketers can target based on keyword, key phrase, content, context, domain, computer platform, and browser. Other examples of aggregated Web sites include specialized portals such as @griculture (www.agriculture.com) and virtual tradeshows such as ChemExpo (www.chemexpo.com).

Content providers. Online publishers and traditional publishers with online editions are examples of content providers. These types of sites will provide the best targeting capabilities in the future. There are no-fee content providers such as Ask Jeeves (www.askjeeves.com), C | Net (www.cnet.com), CNN.com, iVillage.com, Gorp.com, Bonus.com, and Internet.com, and fee-based providers such as *The Wall Street Journal Interactive* (www.wsj.com). The fee-based online publishers will be able to get very detailed and accurate user profile information because users will not only be required to give name, address, and telephone number, they will give additional information—all of which can be verified using billing data. No-fee publishers that have highly valued content can also get users to register on the site. The registration process is where online publishers can obtain demographic and geographic data.

Commerce sites. Commerce sites are important to your online marketing program if your goal is to support the sales of your product on these sites. Like content providers, commerce sites can target messages based on product categories and search keywords. The advantage a commerce site has in targeting is in the transaction history and billing information. This information is highly accurate and can be used to provide cross-selling advertising. Commerce sites include CDNow (www.cdnow.com), marthastewart.com, and Ticketmaster.com.

Hybrid sites. The Quicken Financial Network (www.qfn.com) is a support site for its financial software products Quicken and TurboTax and services such as online banking, but it is also a financial information supersite. These sites have the combined targeting capabilities of content providers and commerce capabilities.

Online Advertising Networks

More than 4000 Web sites sell advertising—some are small, and some are large; some attract broad audiences, and some are highly specialized niche sites. Online advertising networks are good if you are trying to reach as many prospects as possible within a narrow target (e.g., women who are between the ages of 18 and 34, have incomes in excess of $80,000, are married, and have children). You will want to enlist an advertising network to aggregate all sites that offer this kind of targeting in order to have a large enough audience. Ad networks now have even more sophisticated targeting and tracking. This enables the one-to-one marketer to reach only the target markets that will be interested in your advertising message, with minimal ad impression waste. This is where advertising networks are attractive. Add to this the ability for ad networks to track and report results, and you have a highly effective online advertising tool.

If your primary marketing objective is to build brand awareness, ad networks enable you to provide separate targeted messages to each segment you want to reach. This allows you to cost-effectively increase brand penetration within segments. Here is a sample list of advertising networks:

@dVENTURE Network	www.ad-venture.com
24/7 Media	www.247media.com
AdClub Network	www.adclub.net
AdFlight	www.adflight.com
AdOutlet.com	www.adoutlet.com
Adsmart Network	www.adsmart.net
B2BWorks	www.b2bworks.net
BannerBrokers Network	www.bannerbrokers.com
Big Bang	www.bigbang.com
CyberFirst	www.cyberfirst.com
DoubleClick	www.doubleclick.net
Flycast Communications	www.flycast.com
FuturePages	www.futurepages.com
L90	www.L90.com
MSN LinkExchange	www.linkexchange.com
Phase2Media	www.phase2media.com
Premium Network	www.premiumnetwork.com
Real Media	www.realmedia.com
Teknosurf.com	www.technosurf.com
ValueClick	www.valueclick.com

Winstar Interactive	www.winstarinteractive.com
WiseAds	www.wiseads.com
INTERNATIONAL	
24/7 Europe	www.247europe.com
Adpepper	www.adpepper.com
Safe-Audit (UK)	www.safe-audit.com

DoubleClick (www.doubleclick.net) is one of the leading ad networks with more than 1200 branded Web sites in 21 international networks. It represent more than 175 premium Web sites in the United States, including The Dilbert Zone (www.dilbert.com), BillBoard Online (www.billboard.com), and *U.S. News and World Report* (www.usnews.com). The DoubleClick network uses DoubleClick's DART (Dynamic Advertising Reporting and Targeting) technology to target ads. According to DoubleClick's Wenda Harris Millard, online advertising can provide highly qualified leads at an impressive ROI, which is the most important yardstick to advertisers. Millard also believes that Web advertising answers all the criteria that is of concern to advertisers that traditional media cannot do as effectively:

- How can I reach my target?
- What is the optimum reach and frequency equation?
- Which creative works best?
- Is the advertising effective?

The Web does a unique thing that traditional advertising cannot. Because of its technology, you can cap the frequency of a particular Web advertisement or banner, which minimizes banner burnout and waste. An I/Pro study showed that by about the third or fourth time a banner ad was displayed to a user, its effectiveness diminished. Imagine that you are reading a magazine and you have seen the same BMW ad for the fourth time. Now, what if someone came up and turned the page so you wouldn't see that particular ad? The Web can do this with its tracking and database integration capabilities. An online ad system can know if you have seen a particular banner one time, two times, three times...Oh, the possibilities.

DoubleClick's DART is a patent-pending system that dynamically delivers targeted banners. It allows advertisers to target ads on sites within its network by the following:

Interest category. Target a group of sites, sites sections, or site pages that attract users who have similar interests.

Search keyword. Target ads on sites that provide a search function where ads are served based on the advertisers keywords.

Editorial targeting. Target specific editorial content within sites to match ad banners with editorial using relevant keywords.

Geographic location. Target sites within specific countries, states or regions, area codes, and zip/postal codes. Advertisers can get really local or global with geographic targeting.

High-level domain type. Target audiences by domain type. For example, serve banner ads on educational sites (e.g., .edu) to target students. Other domains include commercial sites (.com), government (.gov), associations/organizations (.org), network providers (.net), and military (.mil).

Organization type (SIC Code). Target types of companies and organizations using the U.S. government's SIC (Standard Industrial Classification System) code.

Organization name. Target a specific name of a company.

Organization size or revenue. Target a company by size.

Control ad frequency and ad banner series. Control how many times the Web audience views an advertisement to maximize ad performance. Can also track the frequency of ads in order to deliver ads in a series.

Service provider. Target ads based on how users are accessing the Internet—for example, Internet Service Providers (ISP) such as Earthlink.net, Online Service Providers (OSP) such as AOL.

User's operating system. Target ads based on the user's operating system (e.g., Unix, Macintosh, Microsoft Windows or NT).

User's browser type. Target ads based on what browser a user is using to surf the Web. This enables marketers to create ads that are compatible with each of the browser types including Netscape Navigator and Microsoft Internet Explorer.

Days and hours to display an ad. Target ads based on the time of day or particular days in the week.

Ad banner distribution. Control banner distribution to run evenly over a specific period of time with start and end dates, or run ad distribution heavily or lightly at a particular time in the campaign.

As you can see, online ad targeting has gotten more flexible over the past few years. Even with the higher cost for highly targeted advertising, one-to-one Web marketers will gain the advantage of putting the right message in front of the right person, and they will reduce wasteful ad impressions.

Chat/Community

Chat is a highly popular activity among Web users because it lets them connect with others to share thoughts and experiences with people with similar needs and interests. Chat and community sites are natural relationship-building and loyalty-building vehicles. Hosting a chat on your own site or on another site can be beneficial because chat users spend more time online while they are on a chat site or online community. Sponsoring chat areas or specific chats enables advertisers to reach a targeted customer segment at the most opportune time. For example, iVillage (www.ivillage.com), a leading site for women, has hundreds of communities and discussion boards for subjects about women's health, beauty, food, family, pets, and relationships. Advertisers can buy targeted advertising that pertains to any of the subjects. Because many chat sites and online communities serve a target market of their own, this enhances a Web marketer's ability to find a highly targeted audience. With most chat sites requiring registration, this information can be used to target ads by demographics, psychographics, and even by discussion topic. For a detailed discussion about online communities, see Chapter 5, "One-to-One Web Community."

E-Mail

E-mail is emerging as an inexpensive, yet highly targeted advertising vehicle. Even with the controversy surrounding unsolicited e-mail ads (a.k.a. spam), e-mail is being quickly adopted as a main ingredient in online ad campaigns. E-mail reaches more users than the Web, is intrusive, and doesn't require the user to go to the Web to see advertising. E-mail technology is advancing with the support of HTML tags that allow for multimedia e-mails and the integration with database technology. When people sign up for e-mail they fill out a registration form that captures some personal information. For more information on e-mail marketing, see Chapter 3, "One-to-One E-Mail."

Ad-Supported Internet Access/Free E-Mail/Free Web Sites

According to IDC, the number of U.S. users accessing the Internet using free Internet services is 12 million and is expected to grow to 37 million by 2005. Ad-supported Internet service providers such as NetZero (www.netzero

.com) provide Internet access for free or at a discount in exchange for delivering ads to their users. Free Internet access gives advertisers the ability to target much as they would for e-mail advertisements. Free e-mail and free Web sites are also getting users to view advertising, participate in surveys, and do other activities. MSN Hotmail (www.hotmail.com) is a leading free e-mail service that requires users to view advertising in exchange for free e-mail service. Yahoo! GeoCities (www.geocities.com) allows Web users to create their own Web sites for free.

One-to-One Web Promotions

Online promotions are great advertising and publicity interactive events, and they can be done in a targeted or one-to-one manner. Like what was discussed for advertising earlier in the chapter, promotions can be done in a targeted fashion and can be even more powerful in that the user interacts with the promotion and is identified in the process. The benefit of promotions is that the Web marketer can acquire user profile information from online users that participate in the promotion. This information can be used in additional, ongoing communications beyond the promotional event itself.

Keep in mind that online promotions can only kick-start the one-to-one Web marketing process. Promotions are often like a light switch in that while promotions are running, you have a lot of activity (the light is on), and as soon as they are over, activity plummets (the light is off). In your promotional plans, you should already have the after-marketing plan well thought-out and ready to execute at the close of the promotion. Keep in mind these attributes shared by great promotions, according to the author of *Publicity on the Internet* (John Wiley & Sons, 1997) and publicity expert Steve O'Keefe:

Integrity. A promotion grows out of the product being promoted.

Appeal. The promotion is irresistible to the target market.

Scope. The scale is perfectly suited to the product and the audience.

Timing. The right gimmick is used at just the right time.

Novelty. The concept has a unique twist to it.

Preparation. You must be ready to capture the lightning.

Web marketers can use targeted promotions on a Web site, across the Internet, and within special online promotion services.

On Your Web Site

When you launch, relaunch, or want to increase traffic among particular target markets, you can use an online promotion to drive the desired traffic. Within your site you can craft contests, loyalty programs, and offers for free information or classes that will kick-start your Web site marketing. No doubt Web site promotions increase your site's traffic, but can you keep them coming back for the duration? As with other advertising types, promotions can be advertised and promoted in a targeted manner.

Contests/Sweepstakes

Contests are one of the most popular forms of Web site promotions. Contests provide marketers with the ability to increase site traffic and obtain user profile information. Both the contest and site should provide online users with enough excitement and content to make it a memorable experience. Here are some examples of Web site contests:

iQVC goldrush. The TV shopping network QVC launched a special contest on its Web site. iQVC (www.qvc.com) sponsored an online treasure hunt within its 100,000-plus Web pages. Users, or "gold diggers," who found five hidden gold cybernuggets were entered into the drawing for a gold necklace and bracelet set. The online contest was held in conjunction with the company's television program and celebrated the 101st anniversary of the 1896 discovery of gold in the Klondike region of Alaska. The purpose of the contest was to drive traffic to the Web site and promote a large gold sale.

The Palace avatar costume ball. The Palace (www.thepalace.com), a popular online community and software company, relaunched its new Web site with an online costume ball featuring avatars, which are graphical representations of online personas. The Bring Your Own Avatar (BYOA) inaugurated the launch of a new Web site for The Palace. Cash prizes and free memberships were awarded to the most creative avatar costume.

The Weather Channel. The companion Web site for the Weather Channel (www.weather.com) conducted an online contest, "Click, Click and Away," to allow visitors to win a chance for a grand prize of a vacation a year for 20 years. Each contestant who entered the contest received an electronic version of a scratch-off game card. Online contestants used their computer's mouse to virtually scratch off the online game card to reveal a potential prize.

RealTIME Media. RealTIME Media is a company that specializes in creating online contests and sweepstakes (www.realtimemedia.com).

Contests and sweepstakes drive traffic to your Web site so that you can collect leads and achieve new customer sales. Contests also allow marketers to get more information about customers when contest participants enter the contest. A side benefit of running contests and sweepstakes on your Web site is the added publicity your contest and site will get on the numerous contest Web site directories. Free advertising! For more ideas on creating your own contests check out these sites: www.sweepstakesonline.com, www.sweepsadvantage.com, www.contestworld.com, and www.contestguide.com.

Online Loyalty Programs

Web marketers can build loyalty among their customers with quality products and quality service. You can add special reward programs that facilitate loyalty among the best customers. This idea was best practiced by the airline industry with its frequent flyer programs. This method takes into account the basic marketing assumption of "all customers are not created equal." When customers invest time and effort into a loyalty program, they provide Web marketers with a lot of information. Your Web site can conduct affinity programs in which users receive electronic content or traditional rewards such as discounts, affinity merchandise (e.g., watches, T-shirts, and other items with the company or product logo to be earned or even paid for by the customer), and free products and services using a frequency program. These types of programs help you identify and nurture who will be your most loyal and/or profitable customers. The programs can help you delineate segments within your entire customer base and even pare the program down to the individual user.

Across the Internet

Internet-wide promotions can provide a lot of excitement among users as well as the opportunity for a company to build a database of prospects and learn more about their target markets. An Internet promotion can be sponsored by several companies in order to make a bigger impact and facilitate cobranding.

Sponsoring Contests/Sweepstakes

Contests and sweepstakes are quite popular among both marketers and Web users. iWon.com uses a major sweepstakes effort to increase its traffic, repeat visits, and site membership. You can use many types of contests to promote your Web site, products, or company. Sponsoring contests on other sites is a great way to build marketing lists and prospect databases because users must provide some additional user profile information such as birthday, gender, and answers to questions in order to participate.

Online Promotion and Loyalty Networks

Much like the free Internet service and e-mail services, there are online promotion and loyalty networks and services that reward users when they take part in online advertising and promotion. This online promotion category looks more like targeted direct-response marketing than targeted advertising. They interactively involve the online user in building a relationship between user and advertiser. Some Internet marketers have questioned the value of the user involved in these types of promotional services. Web marketers, however, could think of the participants as a target market, enlist these companies in building these campaigns for their own sites, or at least learn from them. Plus, these promotion companies use a pay-for-performance model that can be quite attractive to online advertisers that must measure response and transactions versus general awareness. Some promotional networks and services include the following:

CyberGold. The company's CyberGold program has more than 9 million members and pays users cash rewards starting at 50 cents for reading ads and answering questions. The rewards are transferred to the user's bank account or donated to a nonprofit organization. The company conducted a test on Time Warner's Pathfinder Network where incentive-based advertising produced up to 13 times more clickthrough responses than traditional banner ads. CyberGold is enabling its technology to match ads and other online information to users based on information like personal interests and demographics. In their words, "Eventually we envision a whole marketplace for attention in which every ad is a wanted ad" (www.cybergold.com).

FreeRide. FreeRide is a brand-loyalty marketing program that rewards users with free services or products. Users who participate in surveys and view ads receive points that can be redeemed. Some of the sponsors/brands that have participated in the FreeRide service include Duracell Batteries, Quaker Oatmeal, Oreo Cookies, Kodak Fun Saver Camera, Advil, and over 100 Internet service providers (www.freeride.com).

MyPoints. MyPoints is an online rewards program that includes Web site and e-mail (MyPoints BonusMail) where users earn points for shopping, reading e-mail, filling out surveys, taking advantage of trial offers, visiting Web sites, and referring friends. MyPoints BonusMail sends personalized offers to people by e-mail. According to MyPoints, its program receives 20 percent response and generates 50 percent repeat business on average; in a member survey about 70 percent of members wanted more e-mails (www.mypoints.com).

TIP **Other promotional networks include ClickRewards (www.clickrewards .com), NetCentives (www.netcentives.com), and Webstakes (www.Webstakes.com).**

Applying One-to-One Online Advertising and Promotion

One-to-one online advertising and promotion campaigns can vary to a very large degree from targeted banners, served strategically to the right audience at the right time, to highly interactive online ads that can include rich interaction and personalization. A Standard & Poor's (S&P's) Personal Wealth online ad campaign shows one use of rich media and in-banner transaction methods to meet site registration objectives.

Standard & Poor's Personal Wealth Uses Rich Media to Find Users Looking to Create Their Own Riches

S&P's Personal Wealth found an effective use of rich media advertising to drive user registration. By combining enough information and convenient in-banner registration, its campaign provided better results than other advertising media S&P Personal Wealth used for building its registered user base.

Company

Standard & Poor's Personal Wealth (www.personalwealth.com) is a financial Web site that provides personalized investment news, information, recommendations, real-time stock quotes, personal stock ticker, and other robust financial tools. S&P Personal Wealth provides detailed analysis on more than 11,000 publicly traded stocks and more than 10,000 mutual funds. Because S&P Personal Wealth is the only Internet service to qualify for Securities and Exchange Commission (SEC) Registered Investment Advisory status, the Web site allows registered customers to receive direct, individually tailored advice from Standard & Poor's analysts.

Objectives

The online financial market is quite competitive with many sites vying for online customers. The high level of competition made it challenging for S&P Personal Wealth to acquire and retain registered users. S&P Personal Wealth's objective for its online advertising campaign was twofold: It wanted to increase the number of registered users on the site, and it wanted to decrease the cost per registrant.

Campaign Description

S&P Personal Wealth worked with K2 Digital (www.k2digital.com) and bluestreak (www.bluestreak.com) to create a rich media ad campaign that used bluestreak's expandable banner technology, E*Banner (see Figure 4.9).

The expandable rich media ads had a couple of advantages for the S&P Personal Wealth ad campaign:

- The banner did not require the user to click through to a Web site. In general, many Web users do not like to be taken away from the Web page they are currently on to visit an advertiser's Web site (this is one reason that may explain the low clickthrough rate on banners).
- The bluestreak banner is expandable so it can give enough information to interest the Web user and convert that user to a registered user of the S&P Personal Wealth Web site. The banner featured the free registration.

The rich media campaign ran from November 1999 through February 2000 on Hoovers (www.hoovers.com), Multex (www.multex.com), and 24/7 Media (www.247media) sites.

Results

According to Andrew Portnoy, director of marketing for S&P Personal Wealth, "Attracting and retaining customers in the increasingly competitive world of online finance is a challenge. K2 Digital's banner campaign has proven to be an excellent means of attracting new users at highly competitive acquisition costs." The rich media banner campaign netted a 30 percent registration rate and achieved a cost per registrant that was 75 percent less than that of other media.

Lessons Learned

According to Jeff Hinz, media director at K2 Digital, "We learned that some sites do not accept rich media and that some consumers such as

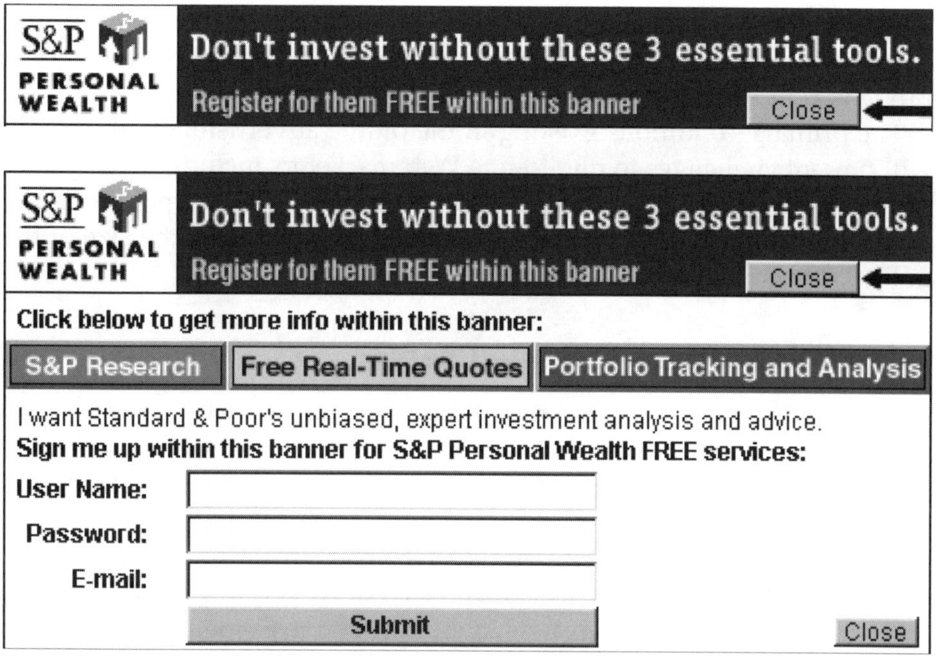

Figure 4.9 S & P Personal Wealth expandable banner using bluestreaks E*Banner technology.

Macintosh computers and AOL users cannot view rich media, thus limiting your potential reach. All other aspects of the rich media ad campaign were similar to existing banner (GIF, HTML) campaigns. We also learned that rich media offers a great opportunity to capture data (e.g., e-mails) if you engage the customer and offer them something of value such as free site registration or information."

Hurdles to One-to-One Web Advertising and Promotion

Internet advertising industry analysts, authors, and practitioners all agree that the biggest potential the Web brings to advertising is its one-to-one capabilities. They predict that online advertising will allow Web marketers to realize this dream. According to a Jupiter Communications' "Online Advertising Report" it is a benefit to know more about an individual customer, but it may not always be worth paying a lot of money for the information. Figures 4.10 and 4.11 show some of the roadblocks to the fabled market of one and the pros and cons of targeting.

The primary conditions existing in the online advertising medium that will present challenges to one-to-one Web marketers include privacy concerns, the higher cost to implement one-to-one online ad campaigns versus nontargeted campaigns, accuracy of user information, and the size of the online market in general.

Privacy Concerns by Online Users

Creating personalized ad messages is dependent on technology and the gathering of information that most online customers are currently not comfortable with. In a 2000 *Business Week*/Harris Poll, 92 percent of Internet users "expressed discomfort about Web sites sharing personal information with other sites." The biggest issue for Web users regarding online advertising is that they don't know who is collecting what information and with whom they are sharing their personal information. Some privacy organizations contend that online advertising's anonymous profiling is no longer anonymous as the user profile contains more data. DoubleClick came under scrutiny when it planned to merge its online anonymous profiles with offline direct marketing data from Abacus. Many felt that the merging of this potentially personally identifiable and private information, without the user's consent, would breach user privacy.

Many marketers and technology companies are frustrated by the misinformation about the cookie technology and other techniques that identify

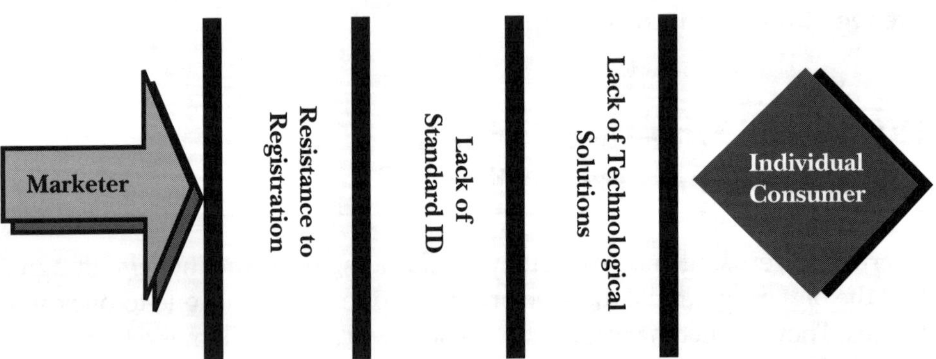

Figure 4.10 Roadblocks to one-to-one advertising.
Source: Jupiter Communications.

	Advertisers	Publishers
Pros	Increased Response Less Waste Increases Creative Impact	Higher CPMs Builds Relationship with Advertiser
Cons	No Clear Proof of Increased ROI after Certain Point	Premier Inventory Shortage Lack of Reach Inventory Management Problems

Figure 4.11 The pros and cons of targeting.
Source: Jupiter Communications.

users to online publishers. Some online consumers think that online marketers can get their social security numbers from a cookie file without the consumer's consent. Not true.

In order to turn this situation around and realize the benefits of one-to-one online advertising, Web marketers will need to embrace privacy standards (and also educate the market!) and practices brought forward by organizations such as the World Wide Web Consortium (www.w3c.org), Direct Marketing Association (www.the-dma.org), and TRUSTe (www.truste.org). Many Web marketing leaders believe that the industry should be self-regulating in order to keep the government, particularly the Federal Trade Commission (www.ftc.gov), from regulating the industry. See Chapter 9, "One-to-One Web Privacy," for an additional discussion about online privacy. Figure 4.12 shows how to turn the privacy problem into a plus.

Higher Cost to Implement One-to-One Online Ad Campaigns

Some online advertising industry representatives believe that the cost of creating one-to-one advertising on the Web outweighs its benefits.

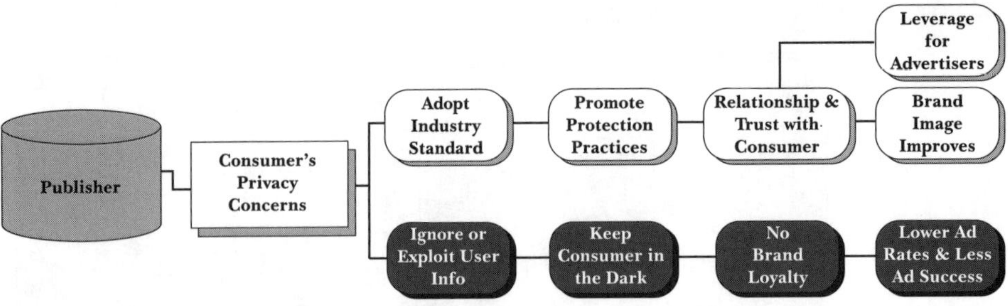

Figure 4.12 Turning the privacy problem into a plus.
Source: Jupiter Communications.

On One Hand

The cost per thousand (CPM) for placing online ads can vary from $1 to $200, depending on the Web site and the level of targeting desired. Today's average CPM is $35. There is usually a charge for each additional target selection chosen when buying an ad placement. For example, it costs $25 CPM for a nontargeted run of site (ROS) banner and $70 CPM for a targeted standard keyword banner on AltaVista. There are also additional creative and production costs associated with each additional ad or campaign versus one Web banner created for one audience as a whole. It will cost more to target your campaign if you need hundreds of banners instead of a couple. A single banner campaign may cost $1800 to produce; if you need 100 banners it will cost you $180,000 to produce. Also, if you want to take advantage of rich media, you will pay more to produce a rich media ad. Table 4.5 outlines an example of the added response required when using rich media and targeting within a single banner campaign.

On the Other Hand

According to Wenda Harris Millard, executive vice president of marketing and programming at DoubleClick, "People don't laugh at John Wanna-

Table 4.5 Example Comparison of an Untargeted Static Banner and a Targeted Rich Media Banner

AD TYPE	PRODUCTION COST	MEDIA COST PER 100,000 IMPRESSIONS	DESIRED COST PER CUSTOMER	RESPONSE NEEDED
Static banner	$1500	$25 CPM untargeted (ROS) = $2500	$4.00	1%
Rich media	$8000	$40 CPM targeted = $4000	$4.00	3%

maker's famous statement, 'Half the money I spend on advertising is wasted, and the trouble is, I don't know which half,' because the Web provides tracking and accountability that solves this mystery." She believes that one-to-one Web marketing isn't cost prohibitive because it is more efficient and, in the long run, less expensive than other traditional methods that can cost hundreds of dollars per qualified lead.

Accuracy of Target Information

With the fears over online privacy, many online consumers have not provided information to online marketers, which has limited the ability to target messages. Or consumers have not given accurate information about themselves, and many online publishers have no real way to verify the information. With software that enables users to block cookies, targeting is further limited. Web sites that have fee-based subscriptions or take online orders have the ability to verify most user information such as address, phone number, credit, and purchases. Even these types of sites, though, cannot verify more qualitative data such as user preferences.

According to the GVU 7th WWW User Survey (www.gvu.gatech.edu/user_surveys/), approximately 40 percent of respondents have provided false information, and a little more than 14 percent gave false information more than 25 percent of the time. Also, if more than one person uses a single computer, cookies can be an unreliable way to target the individual users of that single computer. According to Bill Irvine, director of interactive media at The Wolf Group (www.wolfgroup.com), targeting on the Internet is based on limited information that can be unreliable or incorrect. Irvine does see a promising future for one-to-one marketing on the Web. Even though there is still some guessing when it comes to targeting online, one point to remember is that the Web provides much more information about its audience than any other marketing medium.

Size of Online Advertising Market

Although the Web is growing fast and furiously, for some marketers it is not a big enough marketplace to justify online ad spending or developing a Web site. To some of the largest advertisers, the Web itself looks like a small target market of 318 million worldwide Internet users in 2000 (Source: *Computer Industry Almanac*). To put the Web ad market in perspective, online advertising is currently only about 1 percent of total advertising spending in the United States.

The good news is that the adoption of the Web continues at a breakneck pace. More people are using the Web more times per week and spending more time than ever before. Here is the time it took for each type of media to reach 50 million users, according to a Morgan Stanley Technology Research report:

Radio	38 years
TV	13 years
Cable	10 years
Internet	5 years (estimated)

Although the online market is still relatively small, the types and numbers of Web sites are vast. With this in mind, online targeting makes good marketing sense even at this point in time.

The Future of One-to-One Web Advertising and Promotion

Advertising gurus are predicting that online advertising will be able to make every ad delivered an ad that online users *want* because it is targeted to their likes, dislikes, what neighborhood they live in, what car they drive, what college they went to, and so on. The buzzwords for online advertising and promotion into the near future include interactive, intrusive, broadband, one-to-one, interactive TV, wireless, integration, and local market targeting:

Interactive. With rich media technology, online advertising will become more interactive, giving marketers a better chance to get higher response and more interaction to build relationships with their online audiences.

Intrusive. With interstitials and other online ad formats that pop up when the advertiser chooses, some online ads will become more like TV commercials that interrupt the user.

Broadband. High-speed access to the home will allow advertisers to make more of an impression on the Web user with more interactive and effective online ads.

One-to-one. *True* one-to-one will be the future of the Web advertisement. As time goes by, marketers will collect more in-depth information about the online customer and also have the ability to create an online dialogue with each customer in order to better serve the needs and interests of that customer.

Interactive TV. Interactive TV had a false start a number of years ago, but the Internet will allow for the convergence of TV and the Internet to allow interactive and targeted advertising, programming, and commerce from the television.

Integration. Savvy companies are already integrating ad campaigns across media and channels. Marketers can allow customers receiving a promotional direct mailer to conduct the transaction online or redeem the special offer in the local store. Customers will want to be recognized by the company no matter how they contact the company—by phone, Internet, mail, or store.

Wireless. Wireless devices such as cell phones and personal digital assistants (PDAs) like the Palm Pilot are now receiving Internet information and advertising. Wireless advertising represents a significant growth medium. According to IDC, 61.5 million people will be using wireless devices to access the Internet in 2003. Smart marketers will figure out ways to provide one-to-one services or promotions to these devices, rather than general advertising. There is even less space to advertise on these devices, so the challenge will be to make the promotion relevant and desirable to the cell phone or PDA user.

Local market targeting. Jupiter Communications sees that online ad budgets will incorporate more local advertising, moving from 100 percent of ad budgets going to a national audience in 1995 to 54 percent of online ad budgets going to local marketing advertising in 2002.

We will close this discussion about the future of online advertising with this profound thought:

> "...one thing is certain: In the 1:1 future, the consumer will be the one in the driver's seat, and the advertiser will be thumbing a ride."

Don Peppers and Martha Rogers, Ph.D.,
"Advertising in the One-to-One Future" (*InfoWorld*, 2/12/96).

Resources

Here are some of the many online advertising and marketing resources available:

@d:tech	www.ad-tech.com
AdKnowledge	www.adknowledge.com
Ad Resource	www.adresource.com
Back Channel	www.aaaa.org/bc

BrandEra.com	www.brandera.com
CASIE	www.casie.org
Channel Seven	www.channelseven.com
Cheskin Research	www.cheskin.com
ClickZ	www.clickz.com
Digitrends	www.digitrends.com
EMarketer	www.emarketer.com
FAST	www.fast.org
Internet Advertising Bureau (IAB)	www.iab.net
Internet Advertising Resource Guide	www.admedia.org
Iconocast	www.iconocast.com
Internet Advertising Report	www.internetnews.com/IAR
Web Marketing Info Center	www.wilsonweb.com/webmarket

Up Next

Chapter 5, "One-to-One Web Community," discusses the role online communities and chat will play in one-to-one Web marketing. The chapter shows you how virtual communities can be used for entertaining, consumer retail, and business-to-business applications, and it discusses the heritage and future of online communities.

One-to-One Web Community

"The new electronic independence recreates the world in the image of a global village."

Marshall McLuhan

Online community was one of the earliest uses of the Internet. Although most of these communities were noncommercial or even anticommercial, members took refuge within these communities to share thoughts and ideas, discuss controversies, get advice, and generally socialize. It was the ultimate in one-to-one communications.

These communities were based on *chat.* Realistically, though, participants weren't *chatting* in the true sense of the word. They weren't really talking to anyone, just reading messages that other chat participants had posted. Once they entered a chat *room,* which was really just a Web page, they could choose just to read the exchanges, known as *lurking,* or they could join in and post their own messages.

Today companies are forming communities to better serve their customers. Advertisers are able to better target their messages within focused communities. Investors are putting millions of dollars into community-based technologies and touting communities as the next big use for the World Wide Web.

In this chapter we discuss how one-to-one communities are being created by marketers to build relationships, solve problems, and collaborate with their customers and prospects. We briefly review the history of online communities, discussing two successful business models for creating these communities, and the basis of the interaction needed for success. We examine some of the benefits, controversies, and applications of communities. Finally, we explore some online community resources and some concepts of the future of the one-to-one Web community.

Impact of Community on the Internet

Online community has had a great impact on the Internet. In this chapter, we examine its path in history. We also look at its impact on the future, which will become apparent through the support and enthusiasm of the financial community, the sociological and economical impacts shown in the book *Net Gain* (Harvard Business School Press, 1997), by John Hagel and Arthur Armstrong, and the many one-to-one Web marketing opportunities.

History

Online communities such as chat rooms have been around for years. Chances are that if you meet a *real* Internet guru, he or she will tell you war stories about bulletin boards, posting and flaming, and all the fun he or she had in the pre-Web days.

For many of us who cut our teeth on the World Web Wide with a graphical-based browser like Netscape (or even, God forbid, Mosaic), let's run through a bit of the history of online community. With 3-D virtual worlds and avatars coming into the mainstream now, it will be helpful to take a look back at where we have been in order to fully appreciate the richness of where we are about to go in the world of one-to-one online community.

WEB SITE **Visit the companion Web site to find the article, "3-D Chat Rooms Generate Big Net Investments," from *USA Today*.**

The Well

One of the earliest examples of an online community was The Well (www.Well.com). Stewart Brand and Larry Brilliant founded the Whole Earth 'Lectronic Link in 1985. This community was started with a dialogue between the intelligent, creative, and articulate writers and readers of *The Whole Earth Review.*

The Well started as purely a conversation space, but from 1992 to 1996 The Well gave its members both Internet access and the legendary conferencing environment. In 1996 The Well consolidated the connectivity part of its business with the San Francisco Internet Access Provider, Hooked, forming the new Whole Earth Networks. Whole Earth Networks maintains The Well's servers and billing operations, while the conferencing, content, and cultural aspects are still supported by The Well's staff in Sausalito, California.

The formation of The Well in 1985 set the tone for the open but remarkably literate and uninhibited intellectual gathering that continues today. Over the years members of The Well have been able to do traditional business networking in an untraditional environment and have provided support and mentoring to other members.

The Well members have also founded organizations like the Electronic Frontier Foundation and The River. They have also documented what was emerging in books like Howard Rheingold's *The Virtual Community* (Harper Perennial Library, 1994), John Seabrook's *Deeper* (Simon & Schuster, 1997), and Tom Mandel and Gerard Van Der Leun's *Rules of the Net* (Hyperion, 1996).

Bulletin Boreds—Oops, We Mean Boards

The Well led to the rise of many garage bulletin board systems where basically, if you had a computer, a modem, and a phone line, you were in business. Net enthusiasts began to set up their own bulletin board systems (BBSs) where they could post messages and others could read them and/or respond. These systems mainly focused on subject matter that was of interest to the sysop (the person administrating the bulletin board). They were highly specialized in microtopics and were extremely niche oriented.

Some were actually quite interesting, like discussions of movies and politics, while many could be quite boring—Who would be interested in what time mail messages should move on the network? That, however, is the true beauty of the Internet—there is something for everyone. What's the saying? One man's trash is another man's treasure? Well, the same holds true for the Internet: If you are searching for *any* topic, there is a pretty good chance that someone has a bulletin board system dedicated to that topic and people are chatting about it.

Many BBSs are in operation today, but they often pale to the graphical excitement of community that is now available on the Web.

MUDs, MOOs, MUSH, and Quack?

As early as 1978, MUDs and the world of fantasy gaming captured the hearts of thousands of dedicated techno-adventure seekers. Despite the funny names, these MUDs can be quite addictive.

Table 5.1 MUDs Resources

RESOURCE	URL
The USENET newsgroup	rec.games.mud.announceColin Moock's 51+
Places of Note in the MUD World	watarts.uwaterloo.ca/~camoock/mud_list.html
The MUD Resource Collection	www.godlike.com/muds/
Yahoo!'s List of MUDs	www.yahoo.com/Recreation/Games/ _Internet_GAmes/MUDs_MUSHes_MOOs_etc/

MUDs are role-playing scenarios of the online game Dungeons and Dragons. MUD originally stood for multiuser dungeon; now it stands for multiuser dimensions. Players can interact with one another over extended sessions, even sessions that run for years. Variations on this concept are MUSHes and MUCKs, which extend these programs by including a usable programming language. MOOs, which weren't born until 1990, include a usable object-oriented programming language.

In order to play, users have to telnet into the MUD's Internet Protocol Port. For some MUDs, you may have to register. Some resources to help you find MUDs included in Table 5.1.

Lost Souls (telnet: ux.tcs.uh.edu (129.7.2.110) 3000) is a Dungeons and Dragons-based MUD with a large, open base world—terrains ranging from arctic to desert to jungle. Proclaimed to be possibly the most realistic combat system in existence, Lost Souls uses stats, skills, race, and guilds to enhance a player's individuality.

Commercial Online Services

Quick to follow were content community providers such as America Online (AOL), CompuServe, and Prodigy. AOL is the most successful of these three, largely because it focused on the community/communications model straight out of the gate. AOL also started with an attractive user interface for its content and communities, while CompuServe continued to use a text-only interface. In addition, AOL knew that its success depended on connecting its members to each other. It encouraged chat sessions among its members, and it would set up chat rooms that focused the conversation on specific topics, such as love, money, gardening, waterskiing, and more. That way, people could get together with others who had similar interests.

Be All the Mall That You Can Be

The next progression of online community as we know it was the creation of the online mega mall. These malls catered to everyone for every need. These malls, like Spectropolis (www.spectropolis.com), Minnesota Virtual Mall (mnvirtmall.com), The WholeSale Mega Mall (members.aol.com/wwwpro/wholesale/index.htm), and The Internet Mall (www.internet-mall.com), with more than 20,000 stores have millions of products and services available to the consumer. They can be very impressive, but they can also be overwhelming, especially if you are "mission shopping."

Mission shopping occurs when you are on a mission to find one certain thing. You don't have time to mess around and browse or window shop. You are on a mission! Quite often these mega malls have lots of choices, but when it comes to honing in on one specific item, that focus can be almost impossible to master. And, unfortunately, these venues are not effective in the approaches of one-to-one Web marketing. They are far too general in their breadth and scope, and they try to be all things to all people.

For many consumers, however, these malls were their first introduction into the world of electronic commerce, and this opened the doors for other companies to follow this buying/selling online model but with a bit more focus. The most successful malls are those that are tightly focused on meeting the specialized needs of a specific group of consumers.

Targeted Consumer/Vendor Malls

A good example of this type of site is SciQuest.com (www.sciquest.com), a leading B2B e-marketplace for scientific products. SciQuest is a comprehensive, time-saving, scientific "buyer's guide" on the Internet. The SciQuest database consists of over a million products from thousands of scientific vendors. If you are in the scientific sector and need any type of equipment, instrument, software, product, or service for scientific, laboratory, research, or development work, this is a good place to look.

SciQuest's mission is to streamline the purchasing and communication processes among scientists, buyers, and vendors by leveraging the efficiencies of the Internet and information technology for the maximum benefit and productivity enhancement of the scientific community.

The key features of this site are its search engine and SciMail (a smart e-mail system), which save users time by allowing them to find, qualify, and communicate with multiple vendors in just a few minutes. SciQuest represents suppliers of analytical, biotechnological, biomedical, clinical, and critical environment equipment, supplies, software, and other services. Searches can be conducted via product keywords, supplier location, geography served, distributor of choice, and ISO certification level.

SciQuest was conceived by the first-hand experience of its principles as sales reps for laboratory supply distributors in the scientific industry. Their customers at that time were scientists. One of their biggest frustrations occurred when a scientist was conducting a research project and had to find some new chemical, antibody, instrument, or supply. It was an unbelievably time-consuming task to find out who made the item, how much it cost, how to get the product, and how to communicate with the specific vendor.

The scientific industry is very segmented, with more than 10,000 vendors who sell in excess of $18 billion to more than 500,000 laboratories. Scientists may spend two to six hours per week identifying sources and communicating with this fragmented vendor population. SciQuest chose to use the Web as its vehicle because of the high level of Net sophistication among scientific researchers.

A final impetus to SciQuest's pursuit of this business model was the lead management process within the scientific industry. In the traditional world of journal advertising or trade show marketing, a scientist can fill out a bingo card or inquiry form. This document is normally processed through several people, often taking three to four weeks to arrive on the desk of the person who can take action (sales representative contact, literature fulfillment, sample department, etc.). SciQuest created the SciMail system so that an inquiry would instantaneously route to the appropriate person inside the vendor's organization. This has had tremendous impact on the ability of the vendor to service a customer's request quickly.

Before starting this venture, SciQuest conducted more than 400 one-on-one surveys with researchers who were their current customers from such large companies as Glaxo Wellcome, University of North Carolina at Chapel Hill, and many of the biotech companies.

Following is a copy of that original survey.

SCIQUEST PRE-LAUNCH SURVEY

1. **Please give us your typical information needs and the processes you use to ascertain the information (as they pertain to products and services).**
2. **How do you find out about new products and services? What journals, catalogs, magazines?**
3. **How often do you communicate with manufacturers and distributors directly?**
4. **Does your lab have Internet access?**
5. **What type of access? Browser?**
6. **How often do you use the Net? For what purpose?**
7. **Would you take the time to go on line if you could go to one site for your product and service information needs?**
8. **What would you like to be able to do at the site?**
9. **Would you use a site like SciQuest? Why, or why not?**
10. **How often do you or your lab:**

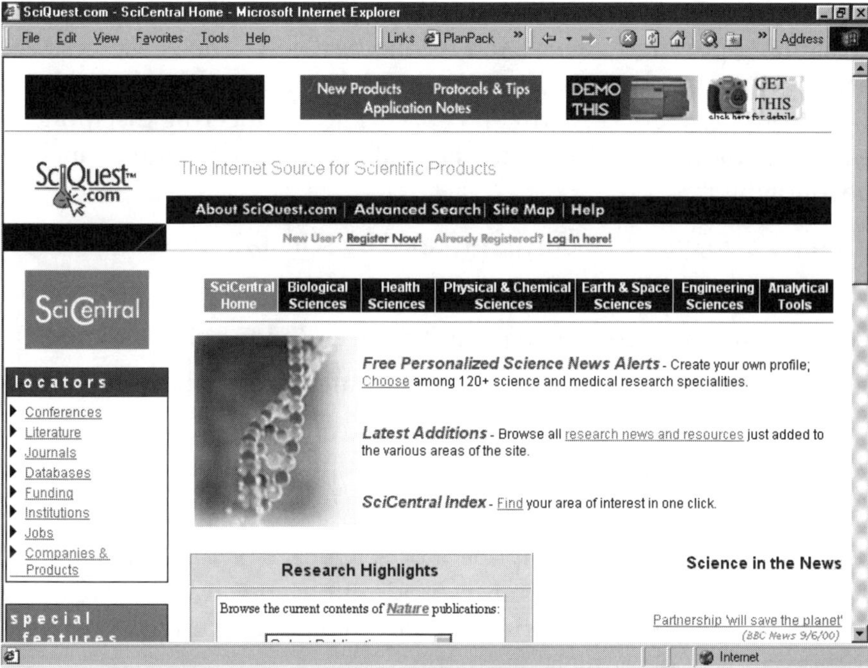

Figure 5.1 SciCentral section of the SciQuest Web site.

In January of 2000, SciQuest acquired SciCentral (www.sciquest.com/scicentral) as the hub of its scientific community (see Figure 5.1). *The Lancet* calls it a "formidable and timely science resource." The American Society

a. **Search for a product for a specific application**
b. **Request pdt samples**
c. **Request pdt literature**
d. **Request quotations**
e. **Register complaints**
f. **Request returns**
g. **Request demos**
h. **Request cross references to equivalent pdts**
I. **Contact sales reps**
j. **Request pdt catalogs**
k. **Place orders**

11. **Do you think you or your company will purchase scientific pdts via the Net?**
12. **If yes, what types of pdts?**
13. **Does your company limit the use of the Net?**

for Microbiology says, "Bookmark this superb web site!" SciCentral is an award-winning portal to science and technology news and resources. The site is made up of thousands of links to the biological, health, physical and chemical, policy and ethics, earth and space, and engineering disciplines.

Created and maintained by scientists, it offers a host of resources, including the following:

- Gateways to online resources grouped by scientific area
- The latest research breakthroughs, updated daily
- A media room with links to print, audio, and video publications
- Locators to help you quickly pinpoint conferences, databases, organizations, and more
- A personalized weekly newsletter with updates covering more than 120 research disciplines

SciCentral has been a key component of SciQuest's community strategy, and it is essential to creating end-user adoption and loyalty. SciQuest's one-to-one Web marketing business model could conceivably be used across thousands of other niche industries.

We're into Money!

As mentioned earlier, early forms of online communities were mainly social, noncommercial exchanges. Today the concept of online community and chat is taking its first baby steps into World Wide Web market success, as illustrated in an article in *USA Today* (3/19/97), which you can find on the companion Web site (www.1to1web.com).

One-to-One Community Business Model

The newest and most effective forms of online community from a one-to-one perspective will be targeted consumer commerce/resource sites and corporate Web site communities.

Targeted Consumer Commerce and Resource Sites

We feel that the most effective one-to-one Web communities will be targeting consumers with specific and focused needs (like SciQuest). Another example of this type of site is The Herp Mall (www.herp.com). This mall is dedicated to information about Herpetology, a branch of zoology having to do with reptiles and amphibians. The site has animal dealers, exporters, supply dealers, food dealers, books and information, upcoming events, and even information about Herp Societies. If you want to buy a snake, this is the place to go.

This Targeted Consumer Commerce and Resource business model will be effective because there are literally millions of niche markets that need access to *information*. Consumers need resources to research, investigate, and compare the specialized niche products that they are seeking. Where else are they to find this information except online? Consumers need access to the highly specialized niche products that they wish to purchase. It's not as if they can go up to the corner store and pick up these items.

Corporate Communities

Another very effective one-to-one community business model will be the corporate community. Corporations that take the time to communicate with their customers and then react by modifying and customizing their offerings will be the big winners in the next decade.

We are moving rapidly into the new business model of one-to-one community as revenue-generating and loyalty-enhancing tools for businesses.

"Web publishers have begun to use chat in ways that extend the application's original purpose as a social medium between users. While a Jupiter study shows that about 16 percent of top consumer Web sites have user-driven chat environments, increasingly chat will be used as a publisher- or merchant-to-consumer medium...Every Web publisher should consider chat as a customer support channel. Shopping sites and service-oriented sites such as travel and banking ventures have been missing a crucial element thus far: live merchant-to-consumer interaction. Companies that use chat in this capacity will form the most profitable online communities in the future," says Kate Doyle, Jupiter Communications analyst.

What Is Community?

In the past, communities were defined by regional areas, such as neighborhoods, cities, or geographic locations. Online communities have redefined that definition of community. Online communities are based on the need for people to interact with others with shared interests and commonalties. The physical boundaries of the world aren't applicable to the Web. Physical location has little to do with the thousands of communities that are actively prospering on the Internet.

In their book, *Net Gain: Expanding Markets through Virtual Communities* (Harvard Business School Press, 1997), John Hagel and Arthur G. Armstrong discuss that interaction in communities is based on people's desires to meet these four basic needs:

Interest. Many early online communities targeted the interest need by aggregating a dispersed group of people who share interest and expertise in a specific topic.

Relationship. Through online communities, people are able to form meaningful and personal relationships because they are free of the constraints of time and space.

Fantasy. Fantasy games like MUDs and MOOs allow people to escape from their daily lives into these online communities.

Transaction. Most people consider online transactions to be electronic commerce exchange, but for many communities, transaction means the giving or receiving of information.

Interest

Communities built around specific interests appear to be the most popular today and probably the easiest for the one-to-one Web marketer to create. If consumers have an interest in something, they will want access to as much information as possible because of that interest. Too often, marketers try to get their messages heard by people who simply aren't interested.

Communities built around the basic need of interest have a ready-made audience. These users are sitting on the edge of their seats waiting to get current, reliable information about their interests. The challenge for the one-to-one Web marketer will be locating these communities and participating in them. Or, if a specific community that you wish to target is not yet created, then take the initiative and create it.

Much of this information can be garnered by interviewing your clients and prospects to see where their interests lie and to determine if your product or service can be tailored to meet those interests. Even if your product or service does not directly mesh with your customers' primary interests, you may be able to create a community based on a related interest that could still give you an audience.

For example, if you sell windows for new houses, it is unlikely that you are going to find a community of people with a window fetish who want to have in-depth conversations about glass thickness, durability, and so on. You may, however, find an audience who would love information about how to select windows properly. You could provide the following:

- Energy-saving tips
- Tips on how to make sure windows are fitted correctly or how to determine when they need replacement
- A guide for checking to see if homeowners are losing heat or air conditioning via their windows
- Instructions for homeowners on how to clean their windows without streaking

You could link your community to other complementary community sites like home buyers' guides, newcomers' sites, relocation sites, home builder and general contractor sites, and Home Depot or Lowes Web sites that target the home-buying or home-improving consumer. The possibilities are endless.

Relationship

In *Clicking* (HarperBusiness, 1996), Faith Popcorn talks about the newest trends of this and future decades—one of them is *clanning*. She defines clanning as "the inclination to join up, belong to, hang out with groups of like kinds, to provide a secure feeling that our own belief systems will somehow be validated by consensus."

The need for relationship is primary and fundamental to all of us. Even in Maslow's hierarchy of needs, the need for belonging is ranked right up there with the need for food and shelter. We are a society of relations, be it through work, school, church, or family.

This need is so strong that many online communities have been popping up solely to fulfill this need. AOL's chat rooms were designed to get people to meet, interact, and form relationships. The Well was an intellectual networking and relationship-building community. Many BBS community participants formed close relationships with others within those communities. They received advice, both professional and personal, and created relationships and contacts that lasted for years. Total relationship services are being born on the Web. From a business perspective, relationship building takes on a whole new meaning. Companies need to build relationships with their customers. Gone are the days of the nameless, faceless consumer. Customers want to be remembered, catered to, and made to feel that their needs are being met by their vendors.

The bottom line is that people do business with people (and companies) that they like. There is too much competition for their business to have to tolerate mistreatment by their vendors. After all, they have the upper hand in this relationship in that they can always walk away. It is your job as a one-to-one Web marketer to delight your customers so much with your service and price and to know them so well (by asking them their needs and predicting their wants) that they wouldn't dream of leaving you!

CROSSING MEDIUMS: NEWSPAPERS CREATING COMMUNITIES ONLINE

COMPANY: Belo Interactive

COMMUNITY: North Texas

OBJECTIVES: As a "traditional media" company, Belo wants to embrace the "new media" of the Internet. Belo's goals include utilizing the Internet in a way that continues to draw the community together and making sure that Belo stays at the center of its local community.

DESCRIPTION: Belo owns and operates a diversified group of television broadcasting, newspaper publishing, cable news, and interactive media assets in 18 markets throughout the country. Belo's Publishing Division is comprised of seven market-leading daily newspapers with a combined circulation that exceeds 900,000 daily and almost 1.3 million on Sunday. *The Dallas Morning News* is Belo's flagship paper and is the nation's ninth largest daily (seventh largest on Sunday). Belo Interactive, Inc., Belo's Internet subsidiary, includes the Web site operations of Belo's television stations and newspapers, interactive alliances and partnerships, and a broad range of Internet-based products and services.

The Internet has opened up a whole new opportunity for local media companies to extend their reach to their local constituents, and Belo understood that making the most of the Internet goes far beyond posting news on a Web site. Because local media organizations have been at the heart of communities for hundreds of years, Belo wanted to utilize the Internet in a way that continues to draw the community together.

After a bit of research, the company found the answer in KOZ.com.

KOZ.com's flagship product, the Community Publishing System (CPS), is the ultimate tool for group publishing on the Web. CPS was developed specifically to help groups who know little about technology to use the Internet as a new way to communicate. Implemented by a local media organization, CPS becomes a tool that helps media companies keep their local community coming to their Web sites.

The first local market Belo decided to address was Dallas. Belo owns *The Dallas Morning News*, WFAA-TV (Channel 8 in the North Texas area), and TXCN (Texas Cable News), and through these properties it launched a new community service Web initiative, community.dallasnews.com, in October 1999. Belo launched the initiative through numerous speaking engagements, advertising, news coverage in *The Dallas Morning News* and public service announcements on WFFA–TV (Channel 8) and TXCN. The site was a quick success.

Belo decided to position its community site as a "free home on the Internet" for all North Texas nonprofit organizations. Through its CPS implementation, Belo offers all area community service groups the ability to easily build and maintain their own Web sites free of charge. Within the first week of its launch, community.dallasnews.com received more than 300 inquiries about the free sites and it is now hosting Web sites for more than 1300 nonprofit organizations.

LESSONS LEARNED: The biggest challenge Belo faced after the launch of community.dallasnews.com was managing the influx of groups interested in creating Web sites. Belo wanted to address the topic of training in a proactive, rather than reactive, way in an effort to make groups, particularly the nonprofits, comfortable from the start. The planned approach was that of a hands-on classroom setting, to help groups use the feature-rich product, CPS, to its full potential. These workshops proved to be extremely popular, and by conducting three workshops a day they were able to train hundreds of people interested in learning how to make the most of their free Web sites.

HOW DO YOU MEASURE YOUR SUCCESS WITH CPS?

"We were thrilled by the response from the community," said Nancy Barry, vice president of community services at *The Dallas Morning News*, who oversees the community.dallasnews.com initiative. "We knew we had a good relationship with the nonprofit organizations in our community, but we never anticipated that so many would want to take advantage of community.dallasnews.com so quickly. There were hundreds of groups that were waiting for training to make the most of their CPS-generated Web sites so we hired additional staff to keep our customer service level high. We had to temporarily stop promoting the service because the demand was so great, but we plan to continue promoting the initiative this fall by creating an ad campaign that features the success stories of our existing nonprofit organizations."

HOW DO YOU RATE YOUR SUCCESS SO FAR?

"Very successful. As community.dallasnews.com continues to add new groups, it becomes increasingly valuable as a community resource. Through a CPS-generated master calendar of community events and activities put on by the nonprofit groups, the site has become the ultimate community connection for the North Texas area."

"Once all the interested groups are up and running, the wealth of community information offered through community.dallasnews.com will be staggering," added Barry. "The community service groups in and around Dallas just love community.dallasnews.com, and from a business perspective, we have made a huge impact on the local community."

FUTURE PLANS?

"We understand that there are more than 8000 nonprofit groups in the North Texas area, and our ultimate goal is to offer them all the opportunity to become a part of community.dallasnews.com, truly the area's ultimate community connection," Barry said.

Fantasy

Escapism is big business on the Internet, and users have the ability to "have it all" either through virtual reality or 3-D chats. The ability to step into another world and experience things even as another person is sure to intrigue even the most cautious Net user. Marketers can cater to this need by creating virtual spaces or "rooms" that are intellectually challenging (for gamers), graphically pleasing, and exciting. The graphical enhancements that have taken the Web by storm have made this a truly satisfying Web experience.

As we discussed earlier, MUDs, MOOs, and MUSEs were the early applications addressing this need. Now fantasy seekers have their choice of 3-D environments in which to fulfill their every dream. Visit places like Honjo Jidai Mura 3D Chat World, where you can walk and see the Japanese old city of Honjo Jidai Mura using Sony's 3-D VRML browser (www.gcoj.com).

Transaction

There is and has been a growing interest in gathering and exchanging information, especially concerning the purchasing of products. People like to hear what others have to say about a specific product that one consumer is using and another is considering purchasing.

In Barnes & Noble's online community (www.bn.com) users can get personalized book recommendations from other readers. Online book groups have also been launched that will be run by bn.com's editorial staff or created and led by readers.

Technology Overview

You may be asking, "How does this chat work anyhow?" It's actually quite simple in the basic, free solutions and can be more complex in the graphical solutions that are being popularized today.

Most Web-based chat systems automatically download a small Java applet into a Web page that handles all of the user functions. The Java applet prompts the user to log in using a unique name and identifies the "channel" or topic associated with the Web page accessed by the user. Once the Java applet connects with the chat server (which can be located practically anywhere on the Internet), the applet displays new chat comments and sends the user's comments to the chat server for broadcast to the group. Because the Java applet interacts directly with the chat server and doesn't communicate with the Web server that served the Web page, the chat server does not need to be located with the Web server—they are two independent operations.

This independence is what allows chat server companies such as iChat to use a centralized chat server to serve thousands of topics associated with thousands of Web pages—without having to interact with the Web servers on the Net. Many chat sites are available off people's Web sites; participants don't need any special software, or if they do, it is often free.

Getting Started

Once you come across a community in which you'd like to participate, you will probably be asked to register. You can use your real name, but most people make up a name. By concealing your identity, you are protecting your privacy, and it also allows you to get deeper into some of the role playing that occurs on some fantasy sites.

After you select a login name, you may also be able to select an icon to represent you. These icons, known as avatars, can be any kind of character—some are cute, and some are ugly. Sometimes, you can even create your own avatar. Avatars were created to give chat a bit more of a personality than the simple text-only chat of earlier days. Once you have your name and avatar, click the Enter button and follow the instructions to choose a room.

Once inside, you may be alone, or you may find yourself in the middle of someone's conversation, so take your time and get your bearings. Scroll through the list of postings to understand what the conversation is about.

You don't have to jump right into the conversation. In fact, many more people watch and listen or lurk, as it is called, and then participate. If you are ready to participate, simply type in your comment or question and hit the Talk button to submit it. Your post will then be put up for others to respond to. The same rules of behavior apply in chat rooms as they do in other online communications, so be sure to review the basic rules of Netiquette to avoid offending anyone. You can also use emoticons and abbreviations to minimize the amount of typing.

TIP **When you put together your plan for your online community, at the same time create a maintenance plan and budget for at least one year. This will ensure that your content will stay up to date and that you won't lose your customers to a better-maintained community.**

Benefits of One-to-One Community

Online communities have the potential to be very strong candidates for one-to-one Web marketing. If companies start implementing community correctly with one-to-one philosophies in the forefront of their plans, they are sure to see a rapid return on investment (ROI). ROI has been a concern among marketing managers—over the past few years, they have been making huge investments in the Web and seeing little return, in part because marketers haven't been implementing one-to-one methodologies.

The Web as a medium was made for one-to-one marketing. Too many marketers are still trying to fit the square peg of mass marketing into the round hole of the Internet, and it just won't fit. No matter how hard you hammer it or throw money at it, mass-marketing techniques do not fit the Web.

Once Web marketers embrace and start to implement these one-to-one Web marketing techniques, they will see the results they are looking for. One-to-one communities have particular marketing advantages in their ability to target an audience, gain access to information to better *customerize* their offerings, and act as a loyalty-building and communications vehicle. *Customerize* was coined by Peppers and Rogers, meaning to customize your products and services to your individual customers. Some of the benefits of one-to-one community are having a targeted audience, being able to customerize your offerings, and creating long-term relationships, better loyalty, and better communications with your customers.

Targeted Audience

By gaining customers one customer at a time, the one-to-one Web marketer is able to target very specific audiences with very specific needs that only a few vendors can meet. If you are one of the few and the proud, you need to take advantage of this position. Communities that are very focused can appeal to a specific audience. That gives you the ability to be the resource for this group.

Someone who collects sharks' teeth may want to buy, sell, or trade them, or just share the story of what beach he or she was on when that really big one was found. These kinds of targeted communities—from pencil buyers to antique car collectors—all need a place. And that place can be an online community.

Ability for Better "Customerization"

By creating online communities, marketers are able to interact with their prospects and customers on a daily basis. Through this interaction, you can gain a better understanding about exactly what your customers want. And when you know what your customers want, you're one step closer to figuring out how to give it to them. With this new insight about your customers, you are better equipped to "customerize" your offerings to your specific audiences. By talking with your customers individually via your community, you are armed with the knowledge to meet their very specific and individual needs.

One-to-one Web marketers will also have access to integrated transaction histories of their audiences. You can learn to predict and anticipate your customers' future needs by analyzing the data that you have gathered from them from their participation with you in your community. For example, say that you are Lands' End and you have a customer who always buys sweaters from your online catalog. The next time he or she visits your site you can give him or her a message like, "Hello, John Smith, we have this new fisherman's sweater on sale today for $59.99. Would you like us to check and see if your size is available?" This can be accomplished through one-to-one personalization, previously discussed in Chapter 2, "One-to-One Web Site Personalization."

Be an Agent for Your Customer

By tabulating and storing your clients' specific needs, you, as a one-to-one Web marketer, in a way become an agent for your customers. No longer are you a simple vendor, but truly more of a partner. You are able to work together with them to come up with a solution that meets their needs. By having the opportunity to collaborate with your customers to find the best solutions for them, you will be a trusted member of their team.

WEB SITE **Visit the companion Web site for "Online Services—Could You Be Found Liable?"—Defamation lawsuits raise troubling issues for providers and users of online information and services."**

Warning: Sometimes you are not the best solution for your customer. Have the integrity and courage to send your customers somewhere else if that is the best thing for them. They will remember this and be loyal to you for life because you put their needs in front of your own self-interests. Reach out and touch someone.

No longer confined by regional constraints in servicing clients, Web marketers can communicate and interact with customers via their online community. As a communications vehicle, online community has been very effective in helping numerous companies, especially in the areas of technical support and sales.

Providing customer-to-customer communications has proven to be most beneficial to many corporations. It's as if you have your own champion of your products, an evangelist who can lead others to experience the greatness of your companies' offerings. Most satisfied customers are more than happy to talk to others about their success, but unfortunately, most marketers (both Web and traditional) don't think to ask them. Isn't that crazy? Start to seek out your existing satisfied customers and get them together with some of your new customers. Your one-to-one community can be a gathering place for both veteran and new customers. The results can be very satisfying for all parties involved.

Some Community Controversies

Since the early days of chat rooms, there was some stigma associated with this type of online community. The rumors of sleazy chat rooms left many users with a bad taste for chat. In the last few years, companies have been focusing on the need for community in our society and have implemented more wholesome communities for the purpose of meeting others with similar interests, forging valuable relationships with a company, or exchanging information. Companies like Talk City position themselves as a "clean, well-lighted" community for chat on the Web. Because we are examining community from a one-to-one Web marketing perspective, the controversies discussed next are mainly from a management perspective including letting customers openly compare you to the competition, issues on the maintenance of content, and lack of control over discussion.

Bad Reputation

As we discussed earlier, many chat rooms are not family or business oriented. You should also be aware that some chat rooms are adult in nature. "Conversations" can be sexually oriented. That stigma is still on some chat rooms, but more companies are setting up communities so that perception will soon be a thing of the past.

We use the word *community* instead of *chat room*. A chat room is just a place to go and chat. What we are encouraging you to do, as one-to-one Web marketers, is to build communities—total places and worlds of useful content, information, and communication for you and your customers. One-to-one community will be the marketing tool of the next decade. You can count on it.

> "The biggest mistake I see marketers making is not modifying their content appropriately. There are many tools available (Well Engaged being one) that will allow the community organizer to tailor both links and ads around the discussion. As a service to your customers, you want to make your content as relevant to their needs as possible. People have the power, it is just changing the mindset and setting the priority to implement it effectively."
>
> Sylvia Lacock, Director of Partner Development at Well Engaged

Open for Competition

If you are a community organizer and not a buyer or seller, this won't concern you. If you are a vendor, however, and you would like to set up a mall where customers can learn about your products, you have two choices:

- You can create a corporate community at your Web site, where it is understood by customers that they will receive only one side of the story because you are conveying your products' features and benefits from your perspective.
- You can create a targeted consumer commerce/resource site in which you and your competitors have equal footing in the race for customers.

This second option is a scary proposition for most marketers. "You mean you want us to help our competition access our customers?" says the concerned marketing communications manager. "Are you crazy?"

Well, actually, we aren't. Allowing for free comparisons of prices and features as well as customers' opinions of your products (and your competitors') has its advantages. Customers will appreciate being able to access this information in one central location and will respect your honesty in putting it out there on the line for everyone to see.

Content and Members Must Stay Fresh

As a community organizer, you have an obligation to your customers (or members, depending on what type of community you maintain, be it content or corporate) to keep your content, meaning articles, news stories, and product information, current. In the last few years, marketers have been dumping thousands of dollars into Web site development and then letting their sites grow stale because no one updates them. This can also happen to online communities if marketers aren't careful.

Also create events and forums that will draw people to your community. By promoting your community correctly, you always have fresh faces online to keep the community alive (see Chapter 4, "One-to-One Web Advertising and Promotion").

One of the reasons that Apple's eWorld failed was that there was no one there. Online communities can fall prey to the same fate that makes a once-popular restaurant close within the first six months: *the fickle public*. Organizers are tasked with always keeping conversations, content, and events both current and engaging.

Control

Many companies are concerned with the control that they may relegate if they actually let their customers talk to one another. The sad truth is that people talk: Wouldn't you rather have them talking *to* you instead of *about* you? If someone is displeased with your product or service, wouldn't you rather he or she share that information with you instead of 30,000 users on a different virtual community?

If you provide your customers with a forum where they can openly discuss both the pros and the cons of your product, you will be surprised at how much you will learn. Be prepared, the truth hurts; however, there is no way that you can correct or improve on your product without knowing what is wrong. It is worth giving up a certain amount of control to receive candid, valuable feedback from your customers that you may not have gotten otherwise.

Another issue to consider is the legal implication of moderated discussions. If you choose to moderate your chat or online posting forum, you could be considered a publisher and can be liable for what your participants say.

Applications of Community and Products

Hagel and Armstrong, in their book *Net Gain* (Harvard Business School Press, 1997), define five criteria for establishing a successful virtual community business model:

Distinctive focus. Communities revolve around a special interest.

Capacity to integrate content and communications. Communities blend chat with articles, ads, and commentary that are appropriate for the specific community.

Appreciation of member-generated content. Community participants can be a great resource for the most interesting and timely content. Their contribution should be nurtured and encouraged.

Access to competing publishers and vendors. The best commerce-based communities will be built by nonpartisan organizers presenting all options to the consumer in an unbiased manner. One-sided, one-vendor malls will be short-lived.

Commercial orientation. Commerce communities will be very successful in organizing products, services, and information in a way that will make it very enjoyable, time saving, and convenient for people to buy.

While many of the community examples discussed next can fall into several of these categories, we have focused on each community's strongest traits in order to illustrate more clearly the criteria for successful community building.

Capacity to Integrate Content and Communications

Another criteria for creating a successful community is the organizer's adeptness at supplementing the discussion with useful articles and advertisements. One company that has mastered this skill is Well Engaged.

Well Engaged

Well Engaged (www.prosperotechnologies.com) was formed in September 1996. It was spun off from The Well, the world-renowned pioneer in online community. It offers Web-based discussion group software and consulting services to leading companies committed to establishing conversation and community on their Web sites.

Sylvia Lacock, director of partner development, said, "One of the first issues we discuss with our clients is how this will affect their bottom line." Well-Engaged is very focused on the building of community to better serve customers and to integrate it as a marketing application.

Its customers have the ability to track individual users, and then they can tailor content and advertising based on the information they get *about* their users and not just *from* their users.

We are an information society bombarded daily with messages. Anything a community organizer can do to make sense of all this data will be greatly appreciated. People don't want many choices, they want only *their* choice. It's great that all this information is available, but it can be very overwhelming and frustrating for users when all they are looking for is one simple fact.

That is why search engines were created, but unfortunately, even they are too broad in scope and breadth. A focused community is a user's best bet in getting the targeted information that he or she is looking for, which has been specifically tailored to his or her needs.

Well Engaged spends a great deal of time consulting with its clients about how to use the information that they glean. Some sites that are presently using Well Engaged are the following:

Warner Music (www.elecktra.com)	Enter Elektra/What's Hot/Halfway down the page you will see the list of BBS topics
Lifetime Lounge (www.lifetimetv.com)	Free to register

The Wall Street Journal (www.wsj.com)	A subscription site with moderated discussions
Minds (www.minds.com)	Free to register
Gamepower (www.gamepower.com)	Free to register

Talk City

Talk City is brought to you by LiveWorld Productions, an Internet content company specializing in online programming that brings together people in shared social, cultural, educational, and recreational experiences. LiveWorld was founded in April 1996, and it has focused on building a reputation for Talk City as a "clean, well-lighted" community for chat on the Web.

Talk City is a live chat environment on the Internet for people who believe in the power of conversation. Its founders share the conviction that communicating ideas with people around the world promotes global understanding and global progress. The Talk City chat network is a community of communities, groups of individuals with specific areas of interest who can entertain and enlighten the rest of us about those interests in hosted chat rooms and on Web pages.

This is an intriguing example of the practical implementation of community: Talk City and Seismic Entertainment run virtual tours of Mars. The centerpiece of the Mars tours is the color 360-degree panoramas of the Mars Pathfinder and Viking landing sites. Visitors can scroll scenes on their computer screens, zoom in for detailed inspection of features, and click on various "hot spots" to get close-up images and information on the different "Rock Stars" (including Barnacle Bill, Yogi, Flat Top, and Wedge), as well as the Sojourner rover and some of Pathfinder's scientific instruments and mechanical parts.

To participate in the ChatZine, connect to www.talkcity.com and click on the Mars icon, connect to www.talkcity.com/seismic, or connect to www.lost-worlds.com.

Imagine the possibilities!

Appreciation of Member-Generated Content

A good community organizer not only organizes and creates good content but also encourages users to create content. Organizers can help their users to help themselves by enlisting them to keep the content current and interesting. This also reduces some of the cost of maintaining an online community. When you collaborate with your members, they feel ownership of their community, again contributing to the loyalty factor.

GeoCities

GeoCities (now part of Yahoo!) is dedicated to offering rich and dynamic content for members and visitors alike. The centerpiece of that strategy is providing free Personal Home Pages in one of its 38 theme communities to anyone with access to the Web. It also offers a free GeoCities e-mail account to everyone who signs up for a free home page. GeoCities has more than 700,000 individuals sharing their thoughts and passions with the world. Users can also subscribe to GeoPlus, the premium service of GeoCities, to have more space for their home page, get a personalized URL, and get lots of free stuff.

GeoCities' philosophy has always been that locations on the Internet become easier to relate to when they are rich with content and closely identified with an actual idea or location. In support of this belief and in keeping with the culture of the Internet, it has developed this free Personal Home Page program and built theme communities to accommodate thousands of home pages.

Tripod

Tripod (www.tripod.com), one of the hottest Internet destinations for twenty-somethings, is now part of Lycos. This personal publishing arena hosts millions of personal home pages created by members with the help of the site's industry-leading home page-building technology and how-to advice. Tripod's innovative Internet community-building approach emphasizes freedom of choice, self-expression, and the ability for anyone to start an online group.

Unlike many Web communities on other sites, the communities within Tripod, called "Pods," feature professionally created content integrated with Tripod members' self-published pages, clustered around topics and issues of interest. In addition, Tripod members can join and participate in as many Pods as desired and can suggest the creation of new Pods. In effect, Pods can be much more cohesive and focused than many other Internet communities.

Each Pod has its own "Poderator," who encourages high-quality expression and interactivity on the site through scheduled weekly chat sessions and/or quizzes on the relevant topic. The weekly chats are well attended and host some spirited debates—everything from women in Hollywood films to the best way to break through writer's block. The Poderator also presents top personal publishers. "Best of Pod" awards are proudly displayed on the Pod's front page to celebrate the most savvy pages or the most thought-provoking content.

Access to Competing Publishers and Vendors

As mentioned earlier in the chapter, SciQuest is a good example of this criteria type in that it brings together all buyers and all sellers within the scientific industry. SciQuest is a true community organizer. It is neither a buyer nor a seller, but the company had the vision to bring these two groups together within this niche market.

This works fine when a neutral party acts as the community organizer or when a company creates a community for its customers, partners, and employees on its Web site, intranet, or extranet. The problem arises when a company, for example, a vacuum cleaner manufacturer, decides to create a community where consumers can learn about and purchase vacuums, but it is the only company represented on this "solution" site. Or, it allows only inferior competitors to participate on the site, giving the host preferred standing. Consumers are smart; they can see through this. Marketers: Do not use the shield of one-to-one for self-congratulatory displays; you must truly be looking to assist your customers in making the best purchasing decisions. You must be an agent for them.

Commercial Orientation

Communities can be built for commercial purposes. There are many advertiser-supported online communities as well as communities sponsored by major advertisers.

iVillage

iVillage (www.ivillage.com) is a good company to examine for successful commercial orientations.

> "iVillage.com ranks 28th among all Digital Media properties and continues to be the leading destination and brand for women online. iVillage.com reaches 8.2% of the Digital Media population; that's more than Women.com Networks (5.9%), CondeNetwork (2.1%), Martha Stewart Sites (1.1%), and Oxygen.com (0.6%)"

Media Metrix Digital Media Audience Ratings report, January 2000.

Each of the 19 iVillage Channels has one common thread: providing its diversified communities with interactive tools, experts, special features, and resources.

Advertisers have the choice of a banner ad that will connect customers directly to their existing Web site or a *bridge site*.

A *bridge site* is a mini-site built within the iVillage channel. It is heavily branded to the advertiser and often links to specific areas within an advertiser's existing Web site. When a visitor clicks on an ad banner, he or she is brought into the bridge site, which contains information that is complementary to the channel. iVillage believes that bridge sites are particularly useful when an advertiser meets the following conditions:

- Has an existing site with broad appeal but wants to attract a more specific demographic group through advertising on an iVillage channel
- Has a corporate Web site with good information but little consumer appeal
- Wants to direct consumers into specific areas within its existing site, not just through the front door
- Wants to align closely with the iVillage channel identity
- Wants to test the latest technology employed on the iVillage channels
- Wants to try a new platform, be it the Web or America Online
- Doesn't have an existing Web site at all

A bridge site can be as small as one page or as large as hundreds of pages. Costs are assessed on a case-by-case basis, but sponsors own any content that is developed for use within their area.

iVillage's goal is to create and build targeted communities online that help people with the real issues of their real lives. The communities are owned by their members, who are the driving force behind the subjects they are most passionate about.

WEB SITE **Visit the companion Web site for a one-to-one case study on "Edmund's Town Hall," a computer-mediated conferencing system where users gather to discuss automobile purchasing decisions.**

The Palace

With more than 2 million users, The Palace Inc., published by Communities.com (www.thepalace.com), is the leading provider of tools for graphical virtual communities on the Internet. The 1000-plus Palace sites that let people chat, attend events, and participate in online games, lectures, and events include Egghead Computer, Syracuse University, 3Com, GameSpot, Merrill Lynch, NEC, The Dallas Cowboys, Sony Pictures, *Entrepreneur Magazine*, *Playboy*, House of Blues, and Fox Broadcasting Network.

The Palace also has strategic relationships with Sun Microsystems, FireFly Network, Microsoft, Intel, and Time Warner. There are also many noncommercial palaces available for users to visit, but in this section we are going to focus on the commercial applications of The Palace.

The Palace Commercial Servers

The Palace provides organizations with tools to develop multimedia virtual communities on the Internet. PalaceServer software allows companies to design and author visually rich environments or "Palaces" that bring users together.

PalaceServer includes PalacePresents, a feature that adds the capability for organizations to host live, moderated auditorium events, including streaming audio and video and an embedded Web browser, all within the familiar Palace user interface. InstantPalace, is the Palace's new Java client, which allows visitors to InstantPalace-enabled Web sites to instantly participate in multimedia virtual communities with no download or installation.

Companies can also leverage the rest of the rich, vibrant, and growing Palace community. With nearly half a million Palace users and over a thousand PalaceServers in place, and with an average of a thousand Palace users logged in at any given moment, marketers can see where the people are and where the places to go are.

ichat

ichat, by KOZ.com, is the leading supplier of interactive, Net-based communications software. ichat delivers several products focused on quick, affordable, online communications. KOZ.com, the leader in extending real-world communities onto the Internet, acquired the ichat suite of products from Acuity Corporation in April 1999.

In a corporate context, ichat's software facilitates low-cost internal collaboration and increases the quality of interaction between customer and supplier. On Internet content sites, ichat's technology enables Web-site community building by increasing user interactivity and promoting repeat visits.

ichat's ROOMS is an integrated, scalable chat server with a feature-rich user interface. ichat's Message Boards is a robust, chat-integrated discussion forum that allows users to search for and post topical messages. The ichat Pager is an Internet paging application providing real-time connections among Internet users. By providing a common directory structure and shared user experience, ichat's ComHub integrates ichat's Pager, Rooms, and Message Boards. All ichat client products are available for free.

In the first three months of 2000, more than 160 new ichat customers, including GovWorks, MOM.com, and Think Inc., were added to the list of more than 2000 licensees, adding to the growing profitability of the ichat family of products.

In May 2000, KOZ.com announced the selection of Lipstream, a leader in live voice communication over the Internet, to voice-enable the ichat 2000 community suite. With just an Internet connection, a Web browser, speakers, and a microphone, visitors to sites enabled with ichat 2000 community suite and Live Voice can be online, talking and chatting, within minutes.

Ideas for Implementing Community as a Marketing Function

We as marketers know that we must build community with our customers or someone else will. Up until now it has been a challenge with the geographic barriers of distance and language. Community was historically built with customers through either phone calls or sales visits.

Today, technology provides us with a new tool for building community. If marketers are creative in their implementations, their customers will reward them with their purchases and feedback. Following are some examples of how companies can use community to grow and nurture their existing customer base, as well as create budding relationships with future customers.

Online Customer Support

Companies can now begin to help their customers help themselves. Through offerings like product-centric chat, customers can answer each other's questions and endorse and recommend products based on first-hand experience. By creating online manuals and FAQ sections, companies can save time and money by reducing the number of calls into their help centers. Technical support departments can create a series of technical tutorial workshops that address frequently asked questions, problems, and issues that their customers have. They can schedule them as moderated online events.

Intranet

More and more companies are realizing the urgency of creating effective intranets within their firewalls. Some applications of intranets are as follows:

Departmental meetings. Marketing can have worldwide weekly strategy meetings online.

Salesforce communications. Sales representatives can access information only they would need.

Project tracking. Multiple layers of management and team members can get immediate status and schedule updates.

Extranet

Many companies are using the community of their extranets to garner valuable customer feedback. For example, Kaiser Permanente has chat in its member services section in which nurse practitioners actively participate. Companies are giving their key customers access to valuable information that they have gathered for them.

Others are using extranets to provide online presentations to prospects in this secure area, giving the prospect a passcode to enter. This allows the company to protect some of its sensitive information that would impress a prospect but also would be of interest to its competition (if it had access to it).

The Future of Community

One-to-one communities will continue to grow and prosper as marketers begin to see the benefits of collaborating with their customers. By treating community content as part of the overall communications experience, companies can take their community-building activities to the next level—creating loyal customers with an emotional investment in their relationship with the company.

In the near future, companies will be using content management tools and editorial techniques that will tie community content to all other Web content. In the first step we will see a company's content editors linking Web and e-mail discussion items directly to product description, service, and online training pages. Later, natural-language processing modules will analyze a person's posting and his or her profile to link readers to appropriate material.

Customers and the company both benefit from this one-to-one approach to integrating community. Customer needs are met while the company becomes a valuable resource of information and a supplier of products to meet those needs.

Up Next

Chapter 6, "One-to-One Web Data Analysis," describes several methods for analyzing a variety of data collected about Web visitors. The chapter shows you how to use data about interests, demographics, and Web activity to learn how to serve Web visitors.

One-to-One Web Data Analysis

"The companies best equipped for the 21st century consider investment in real-time systems to be essential to maintaining their competitive edge and keeping their customers."

Regis McKenna in *Real Time: Preparing for the Age of the Never Satisfied Customer* (Harvard Business School Press, 1997)

Much of this book deals with how to understand the information-gathering process your prospects go through as they learn about your products and services. But there is more to one-to-one marketing than providing the right information in the right place at the right time. You need to be both a good marketer and a good listener, so it's important to know how to observe what your prospects and customers are doing on your Web site, how to ask for information about them, and what to do with that information once you have it.

What Is Web Data Analysis?

This chapter covers techniques you can use to gather this information. First, we cover the behind-the-scenes look at analyzing the log files created by your Web server. Next, we take a look at how to use modern statistical techniques to mine data to learn about the segments of people who come to your Web site. Then, we discuss how databases can be integrated with Web sites for use in one-to-one Web marketing.

Benefits of Analyzing Traffic Data

Before we start observing our Web site visitors, however, we need to know what we want to learn from our observations. As we've talked about in other chapters, prospective customers who come to your Web site are looking for something. Perhaps they are looking for a product to meet an unfilled need. Perhaps they are looking for information to satisfy some curiosity. Perhaps they have arrived at your site accidentally while searching for something else.

Most of the people coming to your Web site will be somewhere along the traditional path of making a purchase decision, so it's important for you to be able to identify which stage in this process people are in so that you can satisfy their individual needs. The data analysis techniques in this chapter will help you turn raw data about Web visitors into an understanding of their wants and needs.

As we move from mass marketing to one-to-one marketing, we need to look for ways to apply what we know about clusters of people—what we sometimes call *market segments* or *niche markets*—and learn how to adjust our marketing to meet the needs of individuals. Only by concentrating on individuals can we truly take advantage of the potential that the Web has to offer.

Marketing research over the years has identified several distinct steps in the purchase of products that require evaluation:

1. Recognition of need.
2. Search for information about alternatives.
3. Evaluation of alternatives.
4. Purchase.
5. Evaluation of purchase.

By using the traffic data we can collect on a Web site, we can spot clusters of behavior that are related to the purchasing process. This means we can adjust the marketing communications process to meet those information needs and meet the product needs of the prospect, too.

Benefits to Marketers of Web Traffic Analysis

Now that we've seen what can be learned from Web logs, let's see how we can evaluate the benefit of investing in the software, processes, and procedures necessary to perform these analyses.

The first element of performing a cost/benefit analysis is to determine the cost. The purchase price of most Web log analysis programs is only a few hundred dollars ($500–$1000), but some analysis programs cost much more. In addition to software products, there are services that will generate traffic reports for you using their computers for as little as a few hundred dollars per month, going up as your needs get more complex. As you can imagine, most products can be installed rather easily, but the cost in terms of time to analyze log reports on an ongoing basis is where you need to focus your analysis of costs.

The primary benefit of investing in traffic analysis products and spending time analyzing your traffic is having information to measure the performance of your Web site. When you are armed with traffic information, you can have actual facts and statistics as to what sections of your Web site are popular among users. You can also see who visits to determine if you are attracting the most desirable target markets. If you have advertising or link campaigns on Web sites, you can assess whether these efforts are working for you. Knowledge is a powerful tool, and traffic analysis can help you easily acquire and assess site traffic.

Benefits to Customers

Visitors to a Web site are in a hurry and will not spend time on a site that doesn't immediately show how they will benefit from using the site. Improvements to a site based on traffic analysis can make it easier to find information and products more quickly.

Many times the improvements made as a result of traffic studies result in customers receiving more personal attention and service when the tools and techniques discussed throughout this book are used.

Nuts and Bolts of Web Traffic Analysis

As pages on your Web site are being seen by thousands or perhaps millions of people, you will naturally become curious about who is seeing your Web site content. In fact, more than curiosity should be driving your interest in learning about your Web visitors because a great deal can be learned about the viewing patterns and habits of your audience, such as why they came to your site, how they got there, and what information they are looking for.

"There is a wealth of information in the log files that many Webmasters don't make use of," said Rick Stout, author of *Web Site Stats* (Osborne McGraw-Hill, 1997). "As the traffic at a Web site increases, there is greater interest in finding out what Web visitors are doing on the site—and that's when they turn to Web traffic analysis programs."

As we move from wanting to use a Web site to broadcast to the masses to using it to focus on individuals, we need to know more about the members of the audience so we can apply the principles of one-to-one Web marketing. It's an overwhelming task to think about the needs of each of the thousands of people coming to your site, but it is possible to think about the individuals coming to your Web site. Part of being able to think with a one-to-one marketing mindset requires that you have the tools to analyze data, but another part is the process of how we think about the people behind the data.

While it would be great to be able to correlate Web traffic to demographic or psychographic information on individuals, there are very few tools available to help us do that (see Chapter 2, "One-to-One Web Site Personalization," for information about building user profiles and the ability to track users based on their profiles). Before we explain how to glean this level of information from the Web server, let's take a look at traditional Web traffic analysis tools and techniques and then cover some advanced technologies and techniques.

Most Web marketers start by asking the question "How many people saw my pages?" and then progress to more in-depth questions. Many of these questions can be answered by tabulating the data found in the log files that are constantly being updated by your Web server software.

This chapter answers many of the questions asked by Web marketers:

- What type of data is stored in the log files?
- How can it be tabulated?
- Can I make graphs of the data?
- What can I learn from the Web log analysis?
- What products are available to create log analysis reports?
- Will the log tell me exactly who is coming to my Web site?
- Can I get a profile of the individuals coming to my Web site?

As you can see, there are many questions that can be answered about Web site activity from the log files that can help you tailor your Web content to the individuals in your target audience, so let's dive right in and review what's available and how to use it.

Technology Overview

In order to gain the most benefit from your Web server log files, it's important to know what files are available and what data they collect. Then, as we get into specific Web analysis tools and techniques, you'll know exactly how the different products do their analysis and why there are limitations on what can be garnered from the logs.

Definitions

In order for the answer to make sense, we need to define the terms used in dealing with Web traffic analysis:

Hit. A *hit* is generally thought of as accessing any file on your Web site, including the HTML files, graphics files, and any other material you provide. For example, if your home page has nine different graphic images, then viewing your home page results in 10 "hits" to your site. Because of the potential misuse of this measurement, many Web managers prefer to measure other activities.

Page view. A *page view* is just what it says: the viewing of a single Web page. This is generally the number of HTML pages that have been served; it excludes the number of graphic images served.

Visits. A *visit* is also called a *session* because it represents all of the material an individual Web visitor sees during one visit. Because standard Web logs include the IP address for each computer coming to your site, it is easy for the analysis programs to count the number of visits by counting the number of different IP addresses in the log. Of course, inaccuracies can creep in because an ISP can give an IP address to a second person later in the day, and that second person would be seen as continuing the first person's visit.

Visitors. A *visitor* should be the number of unique people who came to your site. In other words, it should be a nonduplicated count of visits. Of course, it may be hard for a log analysis program to determine that someone with a different IP address is the same person who visited your site the day before. The use of cookies to identify when a particular computer returns to your site can help improve the accuracy in counting visitors. Some inaccuracy can creep into these numbers, too, because different people can use the same computer to visit the same Web site. Normally this is not a problem, but as families start visiting the same Web site (parents looking for guidance, students looking for homework help, kids looking for games), you could soon face the problem of identifying different people using the same computer—which some of the newer Web browsers handle.

Organizations. The number of different *organizations* coming to your Web site is based on the domain name used by visitors. Of course, with so many people using dial-up services, this measurement may not be as useful as you would like. For instance, the millions of people using America Online are all seen as coming from the same organization.

Data in the Logs

Most Web server software generates a standard set of logs, using a standard file format, so the logs created by your Web server software should match the information and illustrations found in this chapter.

There are a number of changes taking place in the tracking of visitors to Web sites; it will be good to understand the initial tracking ability so that we can cover the latest developments in tracking.

The original Web server programs created a number of log files, including the following:

access_log. Filenames, IP addresses, date, and time.

referer_log. URL of Web site providing links to your site.

error_log. Incomplete requests for files and other error messages.

Figure 6.1 shows the directory of log files for Allen.com's Web server (www.allen.com).

Access Log

When Web server software was initially being created, the National Center for Supercomputing Applications created what is known as the "Common Log Format," which has been used by most Web server software developers. The fields of information stored in the access_log file using the Common Log Format include the following:

- IP address
- ID field (generally not used)

```
-rw-r—r—   1 root     root        739940 Jul 26 15:41 ac-
cess_log
-rw-r—r—   1 root     root        279024 Jul 26 12:29
agent_log
-rw-r—r—   1 root     root        173746 Jul 26 12:29
error_log
-rw-r—r—   1 root     root        411224 Jul 26 12:29 ref-
erer_log
```

Figure 6.1 Directory listing of Web server log files.

- AuthUser field used when ID/password authentication is used for security
- Date, time, and offset from Greenwich Mean Time (GMT)
- Method of request:
  - *get*—indicating a request for an HTML file
  - *post*—data being supplied from a form
  - *head*—usually a request from an *agent* program on the Internet requesting just the header information about a file
- Filename
- Status or error code
- Size of file

The portion of the access_log file in Figure 6.2 shows the information stored in the main log file.

```
207.171.21.62 - - [01/Jul/1997:04:57:53 -0400] "GET /im-
ages/hp-wostars.gif HTTP/1.0" 200 36055

143.117.49.17 - - [01/Jul/1997:04:58:09 -0400] "GET /im-
ages/microsoft-5.gif

HTTP/1.0" 200 57139

143.117.49.17 - - [01/Jul/1997:04:58:50 -0400] "GET
/succ_04.html HTTP/1.0" 200 2762

143.117.49.17 - - [01/Jul/1997:04:58:52 -0400] "GET /im-
ages/cg-med-1t.gif HT

TP/1.0" 200 3137

143.117.49.17 - - [01/Jul/1997:04:58:52 -0400] "GET /im-
ages/microsoft-1t.gif

 HTTP/1.0" 200 5163

143.117.49.17 - - [01/Jul/1997:04:58:53 -0400] "GET /im-
ages/cg-saguaro-1t.gif HTTP/1.0" 200 5434

207.171.21.62 - - [01/Jul/1997:05:01:43 -0400] "GET
/meet.html HTTP/1.0" 200  7157

207.171.21.62 - - [01/Jul/1997:05:01:45 -0400] "GET /im-
ages/gray.jpg HTTP/1.0" 200 1536

207.171.21.62 - - [01/Jul/1997:05:01:45 -0400] "GET /im-
ages/b-meet.gif HTTP/ 1.0" 200 21551

204.62.245.166 - - [01/Jul/1997:05:03:02 -0400] "GET /web-
dev.html HTTP/1.0" 200 9850
```

Figure 6.2 Web server access_log.

Address Field

There are two ways that a user's Internet address can be stored in a log file: as the IP address or the domain name of the computer being used. Figure 6.2 shows IP addresses (e.g., 207.171.21.62), but you may find it helpful to see the actual domain name using the nslookup command, such as that shown in Figure 6.3. The reason many Web managers don't include the domain names in log files is that extra processing power and network bandwidth are used to look up that domain—a task that can be done more efficiently by another computer processing that data in nonprime time.

The first thing you'll want to know is how many different people are visiting your site. The closest estimate is the number of unique sessions, which is determined by how many different IP addresses are in your access log. The addresses of people coming to your Web site are very important in determining the number of distinct people and distinct visits, or sessions. Making these determinations is not as easy as you might think because of a number of factors.

IP addresses always used to be assigned to individual computers, so it was easy to assume that a unique IP address was associated with a unique computer. Because most people always use the same computer to go online, the number of unique IP addresses would equal the number of unique people. A number of changes in the Internet world have made this method of estimating people less accurate. These changes include the following:

- Dial-up users are usually assigned a different IP address each time they connect to their Internet service provider (ISP).
- Users of commercial online services (e.g., America Online, Prodigy, and MSN) access the Internet through a limited number of Internet "gateways," each with its own IP address.
- Corporate users connect through proxy computers, each with its own IP address.
- Community terminals, in libraries and cafés, allow many people to use the same computer.

```
cliff> nslookup 199.171.201.14


Name:     winet.wiley.com
Address:   199.171.201.14
```

Figure 6.3 Results of the nslookup command.

As the Internet becomes more popular, the number of IP addresses in a log file will have less and less relationship to unique people, so we should use the term *unique sessions* instead of *people*. You can do that by adding a profile tracking system to your Web site that identifies individual people.

After determining the number of unique sessions from the Access log, the next information we're interested in determining includes the following:

- The number of accesses to the home page.
- The number of times a graphic unique to the home page is accessed. This indicates how many people came to the site with graphics turned on.
- The number of times the intermediate index pages were accessed from the home page, which shows the interest areas of people. For example, if you believe that a certain link should be popular, but it is not accessed often, check to see if the link is visible when the home page is initially displayed or if the user has to scroll down to find it. If it's low on the page, try moving it up and watch the log to see if that makes a difference.
- The order pages accessed by individual IP addresses. This shows the train of thought people are going through in visiting your site.
- The time spent on each individual page, which can be calculated for individual IP addresses.

TIP **In order to avoid the potential security problems for your audience of passing confidential data into another Web site's logs, consider having your CGI programs written to use the POST method, which passes data to the server directly without being displayed in the URL.**

Date and Time Field

The information in the date and time field looks rather obvious and, for the most part, it is. There are a few potential gotchas with this, though, that can cause difficulty in tabulating logs for large sites that use multiple servers.

As Web sites become larger, it is customary to add multiple computers to the "cluster" of servers and display various pages from different servers in the group. Sometimes a load-balancing front end is used to direct each server request to the system that is least busy. Other large Web sites dedicate certain servers for certain services, such as database requests, transactions, and so forth. Still other Web sites "mirror" the pages of one server at another server, perhaps in a different part of the world. When users are directed to servers in a different time zone, the time zone data can be used to help synchronize log files to a common time, say, GMT (Greenwich Mean Time).

Because it is almost impossible to keep the internal clocks of multiple servers completely synchronized, there will frequently be slight differences in the times for pages. This means that an individual who accesses a series of pages that are served by multiple servers could result in log entries that are out of order, which can affect tabulations for such things as the path through the site.

Method Field

For the most part, the method field will provide you with little information because static HTML files result in a GET, while most form data results in POST entries in the log.

There are a few things to be aware of regarding form data and the use of GET and POST, including a potential security problem for your users.

Without getting into the technical aspects of creating forms and the CGI programs that process form data, we can generalize that forms can use either the GET or POST method of sending data to the server. When the HTML command in the form specifies "method=post," then the form data is passed "behind the scenes" to the CGI program. On the other hand, when the HTML file includes "method=get" in the form tag, then form data is passed in the URL to the server and can be seen in the Location box in the browser. For example, Figure 6.4 shows the results in the browser's Location box after searching for the site PlanPack.

Figure 6.5 shows the referrer field entry after clicking on the links to the PlanPack site displayed by AltaVista.

As you can see, the URL contains the search criteria plus various other internal data used by the search engine. Just imagine if the form had contained sensitive information (such as a credit card number or password), which is now visible to anyone looking over the shoulder of the user. Of course, there isn't much of a security risk with this because most of the time you know who is looking over your shoulder—in the physical world. Unfortunately someone could be looking over the shoulder of your user in the virtual world.

```
http://www.altavista.com/cgi-
bin/query?q=planpack&kl=XX&pg=q&Translate=on
```

Figure 6.4 Results of a form submission at AltaVista.com.

```
"http://www.altavista.com/cgi-
bin/query?q=planpack&kl=XX&pg=q&Translate=on"
```

Figure 6.5 Entry in the referrer field of the server's access_log showing the URL of the user's prior Web page.

One of the two potential security risks involved in sending confidential data with the GET method involves bookmarks. Because the confidential information is in the Location window, a user could decide to bookmark the URL and inadvertently store the information on his or her hard drive in an insecure manner.

The other potential security risk comes from accidentally transmitting confidential information to another Web site. If the Web page that is displayed as a result of the GET command contains links to pages at other Web sites, then any confidential information from your users will be transmitted to the Web site to which you are referring them, and the data will be stored in that other site's referrer log. We'll cover more details about the referrer log in the next section, but be aware of the potential security risk to which you expose your audience if you create a page with these two criteria:

- Form generated by the GET command
- Resulting page contains links to pages at another Web site

Status Field

Web server software generates a variety of status codes that indicate specific results of requests for Web pages, but they fall into a distinct set of categories:

200	Successful delivery of the file
300	Redirect to another file
400	Failure to deliver the file
500	Server error

Of course, most files served by your Web site will result in one of the success codes, so let's turn our attention to the other codes that indicate potential problems.

The redirect code results when one page is requested but the user is redirected to another page. This occurs for a variety of reasons, although they are almost all good.

You've probably experienced redirection on the Web when you've gone to one Web page that automatically sends you to another Web page. That type of redirection is accomplished by a special tag in the head area of the HTML document. Sometimes Web developers use redirection to create a "slide show" effect by taking you through a series of pages without your clicking on any links. At other times Web developers use redirection when a Web site moves or is reorganized and a previously available page has been replaced with another page. Instead of just displaying a link to the new page, the use of redirection can automatically take the user to the new page.

There are other ways a Web administrator can invoke redirection, usually within the configuration settings of the Web server software itself. For instance, when a complete Web site moves from one URL to another, it is easy for the Web administrator to make an entry in the server to redirect users who access any page within the moved site.

While redirection sounds very good, Web managers need to watch for log entries showing redirection because it can indicate that links to your site from a search engine or content site are out of date. If your site moved some time back and you are still receiving redirection, you might want to be concerned that the referring site will eventually discontinue redirecting people to your site.

Size Field

The size of the file served is reported differently by different Web server programs, so be sure you understand what the value represents for your Web server. Some Web servers report the size of the file requested without regard to the amount of data actually served, while other server programs report the actual amount of data served.

As you can imagine, if your audience is frequently choosing not to receive all of a page or a graphic file, then you need to look into why they might be aborting the display. Some common reasons for people to not receive all of a file include the following:

- The page is not relevant to them, and they click Stop or Back.
- The page is not relevant, and they leave the site through a bookmark.
- The page takes too long to download, and they click Stop to read the text.
- Users found the link on the page they were interested in and clicked a link to another page.

As you can see, there are a number of reasons why the display of a page or a graphic would be terminated prior to completion—and some of them are good, such as the user quickly finding what he or she is looking for. But how can you tell which reason applies to a particular user? Many times you can determine which reason was the one motivating the user by looking at later entries in the log. Did that person go to another page a few moments later? If so, it probably indicates that he or she moved to another page more quickly than your graphic was displayed.

Referrer Field

The Referrer data tells how people found your Web site. For example, should you first discover that visitors are entering your Web site through content pages (which may have little image and few navigation buttons) instead of your home page, you'll understand why those visitors link to so few pages.

The key piece of information in the Referrer data is where people were as they linked to your site. Where did they start from to find you? Not only does the Referrer log show the URL, it indicates the search criteria used at the popular search engines, such as Yahoo!, InfoSeek, and others that include that information in the URL. One important action you can take is that after you determine the search criteria people are using to find you, perform those same searches yourself. See which competing Web sites people are seeing in addition to the link to your site.

Figure 6.6 shows three referrals from InfoSeek and the words those users were searching for at the time.

In this example, the person searching entered the three-word phrase "guest script web," which took the person to the Web page guesttrack.html. (Ignore the other characters that are used to direct the database.) The second entry shows another person searching with the phrase "gt catalog" that took the person to the file gt-cat.html. The third entry shows someone linking from a page at an ISP to the Web page index.html that is stored on our Web server in the "thought" directory.

As you can see, you can glean many valuable pieces of data from your Web logs, but you have to keep in mind just how they are determined and how accurate the data is.

```
www.infoseek.com/Titles?qt=%2Bguest+%2Bscript+%2Bweb&sn=50
3633203&lk=ip-noframes&st=30 -> /guesttrack.html

www.infoseek.com/Titles?qt=gt%2Fcatalog&col=WW&sv=IS&lk=no
frames&nh=10 -> /gt-cat.html

www.peterboro.net/page1.htm -> /thought/index.html
```

Figure 6.6 Entries from the Referrer log referer_log.

An example of how log data can be helpful in analyzing the design of a site involves studying log data about graphic images on the site. When you find people leaving a key page, such as your home page, and going to another page on your Web site without downloading all of your graphics, you are losing an opportunity to establish an image, or brand awareness. You may want to reimplement this part of your Web site to download graphics faster so that these audiences will see the same imagery as the newcomers to your site.

One easy way to make graphics appear to download more quickly is to use *the low src* attribute that can be used to display a smaller graphic file prior to displaying a larger file. This technique is usually used to display a lower-resolution version of a graphic first, followed by the higher-resolution version of the same image. If your graphics are used for navigation (i.e., have words describing links), then you may want to combine this technique with another technique: making a black-and-white version of the color file.

These are just a few of the design techniques Web developers can use to display graphics to that most important group of Web visitors, those with whom you have a relationship and want to emphasize the relationship through graphics without delaying their movement through your Web site. For more tips on designing a Web site to improve the relationship with your audience, see the companion Web site at www.1to1web.com.

Analyzing Logs

The first question most people want answered from their Web server logs is "How many people came to my site?" With current log analysis programs, you can actually answer that question.

In order to derive insights into your audience that can help you achieve one-to-one marketing success, it's important to know what questions to answer and what actions you can take to improve your Web marketing based on those answers. First, let's go over the things you can change and improve because those will lead us to asking other questions.

Situation

Too few leads are being generated from the Web site.

Question: How many people saw the inquiry form?

Action: If many people are seeing your inquiry form but only a small percentage of people are filling it out, then you need to look at reorganizing the form, reducing the questions, or breaking the form into multiple, sequential forms. People like to be guided through giving information. A long scrolling form can keep people from filling it out.

Situation

Too few people are seeing the inquiry form.

Question: How many people are seeing the pages leading to the inquiry form? How long, on average, do they read those content pages? Is the path to the inquiry form inviting?

Action: If you just have a text link or a graphical icon linking to the inquiry form, consider adding the other type of link. Research into how people react to direct-mail pieces shows there are multiple types of people and multiple ways they take action on what they learn. This means that you need to have both text links and graphical links in your site.

Another technique that pulls people through a Web site to the action location is to personalize the presentation of links and descriptive material. For instance, consider using personalization software to recognize why they would complete the inquiry form, and display text that will appeal to them. For instance, if your Web site sells a guide to earning more income and a guide to great vacations, use the information in your users' profiles to determine which is more important to them and then display an inviting sales message.

Example #1. Let us send you the top 10 tips to earning more income.

Example #2. Let us send you a set of colorful brochures about your favorite vacation spots.

By combining what you learn from your log analysis with what you want to accomplish in your one-to-one Web marketing, you can use your log analysis reports to pinpoint where changes need to be made in your Web site.

Applying Web Traffic Analysis

Now let's take a look at how to apply the data you'll derive from a more detailed analysis of your traffic by reviewing what actions you might take based on the data available in the traffic tabulations, as shown in Table 6.1.

Applying Direct Marketing to the Web

Traditional marketing people who have wanted to improve their ability to target prospective customers have done such things as rent lists of people who have been observed doing a particular behavior. For instance, if you

Table 6.1 What Web Site Traffic Can Reveal and Action Steps

TRAFFIC INFORMATION	ACTION
Popular pages indicate the appeal of your site.	Promote the popular topics in online and traditional promotion.
Less popular pages indicate lack of interest.	See if less popular pages are read by certain types of people (e.g., registered customers). Perhaps you should add links to those pages in other parts of the site.
Length of time spent on pages shows whether material is actually read or just skimmed.	Short durations on long Web pages indicate people found them too difficult to read or the material didn't meet their expectations. You may need to rewrite material into a more "Web friendly" style.
Starting pages other than your home page should be reviewed for "image."	Review starting pages to see if they tell enough of your story to newcomers or if you need to add more image graphics (e.g., logos, navigation bars, etc.).

sell safety equipment, such as lab coats to protect the person working in a laboratory, then you'll be interested in using a mailing list of laboratories that have purchased related products. By targeting your communications to people who have demonstrated an interest in an area in which you sell products, you can increase the likelihood that any particular person in that audience will buy your products.

The key aspect here is not to try to find people who have bought a competitive product in the past—they may be loyal customers of the other company—but to identify people who have a concern in an area in which you sell products. Finding and targeting your competitors' dissatisfied customers may yield excellent results, however, and the Web is one of the best ways to accomplish this. In the direct-mail industry, these mailing lists are called hotline lists.

The principles of excellent marketing don't change when the media changes—only how we apply those principles changes. With the Web, you can use traffic analysis to develop statistical analysis of clusters of Web visitors. What makes up a cluster? Common behavior. By using the analytical capabilities of your log analysis software, or by using a database, you can select the "hits" from all users matching a set of criteria.

Example #1

Suppose you have a daily newspaper Web site that covers national news, business news, and sports news. Within the business news section, you cover stock prices, commodity prices, and bond prices.

By identifying a cluster of users who spend above-average time with your stock price pages, you can infer that those individuals would be interested in seeing ads for stockbrokers and stock information services. These people are different from people who read only a few of your stock price pages but spend more time on the company news pages and are less likely to be interested in ads related to buying and selling stock.

Example #2

Continuing our newspaper Web site example, we're now looking to identify people for an advertorial (sponsored articles) about management training products. In order to create a cluster of readers appropriate for this advertiser, we need to determine the types of pages we can use to identify these prospects. In this case we might look for people who spend an above-average amount of time with news stories dealing with changes in company management.

Because the key stories that we can use to identify this cluster might be located in different parts of your Web site, we may now be able to use the sections reports of many traffic analysis programs, so we will need to identify the filenames of stories appropriate for this cluster and create a macro, or mini-program, to tabulate the logs for these people. What we are attempting to do by creating various clusters of people with different behaviors is to differentiate members of our audience.

Testing a Business Concept

Market testing is a fundamental technique in traditional marketing, and it's a fundamental technique of successful Web marketing as well. With Web marketing we have so much more data available on each individual—information that marketers using traditional mass media don't have—that it takes combining our traditional marketing techniques with this new source of data to become focused on the individual.

Traffic analysis can be used in market testing in a number of ways. We've all probably heard the traditional admonition of "Ready, aim, fire" rearranged to represent a marketer's view: "Ready, fire, aim!" While no one would suggest investing millions of dollars in a business without having a clear goal, market testing of a concept or offer can be done very easily on the Web without expensive focus groups and delays.

You can do a similar type of coding with your Web site to identify which source of leads and customers is most valuable. Sevio Software, a division of Robert A. Sevio, Inc. (www.sevio.com), needed to know which uses of its

MarketView software, a marketing analysis tool, were most important to its target market, so multiple introductory Web pages were created. Each introductory Web page highlighted a different application, or benefit, of the software product. By analyzing the hits to each introductory page, Sevio was able to easily identify which application descriptions were generating the most leads to its Web site. "We learned a great deal about which benefits people are looking for to help improve their own marketing analysis," said Bob Sevio, president of Sevio Software.

Of course, the real question we need to ask is whether those leads produce actual revenue, so it's important to track those individuals through their complete information-gathering process—perhaps over multiple visits to the Web site—to determine with precision which sources of traffic really pay off. By analyzing the path prospects took through its site, Sevio Software was able to identify not only the most popular uses for its software, but which uses generated the most leads and customers. "We've seen that the referrer log can tell us the search criteria used to link to our site, and we've seen that having multiple home pages can give us data on the source of links to our site," said Sevio.

If you have been wondering if your site is appealing to as many people as it can, or if you have multiple target markets, here is a technique to test everything from a business concept to a special offer. This technique uses different Web pages to describe your Web site to several of the leading search engines.

Here are the steps to follow to conduct this test:

1. Make a copy of the home page. For most tests, you will want to keep the graphical look and feel the same and change just the visible text on the page used by the search engines to rank the page.
2. Edit the meta tag for description to reflect the new benefit or concept you are testing. Make sure your description is short enough to be completely displayed by the various search engines.
3. Edit the Title tag to include keywords that will appeal to the target group for this test.
4. Store this test home page on your Web site and test the page and its links to the rest of your Web site.
5. Submit the test home page to a number of search engines such as AltaVista and Infoseek.

Because search engines such as AltaVista and Infoseek generally update their databases very quickly, you should start seeing results within a few days. What results? By watching your traffic analysis reports for the number of hits to the test home page you can see the popularity of the test concept and compare it to your original home page.

If your traffic analysis program allows you to trace the path of visitors from page to page, then you can also determine the number of people who come in through the test home page and reach an inquiry page and compare that to the number of people who reach that same inquiry page starting with your original home page.

In addition to just counting hits to the test home page, you can also review the referrer data to see the search criteria used to reach the test home page. Once you see the search criteria that brings people to your test home page, look for other keywords being used that you may not have included in your pages.

After you've gathered sufficient data on how well the initial text did in bringing people to your test home page, you can adjust the text and repeat the process. Just be sure to resubmit the test home page to the search engines so they will use the new text for the next test.

Once you know the search criteria being used by your audience, then you can see what they see by performing the same searches. Just enter the same keywords in the same search engines and see where your test home page appears in the list of links. Are you on the first page or further back? To get a feeling for the mindset of your audience when they reach your test home page, continue to use the same searching techniques they are likely to have used in order to reach your site. This means looking at the descriptions on the search engines results pages, determining if you (as a potential buyer) would click on the first link. If so, then go ahead and explore that site until you determine it doesn't meet your needs (as a prospect). If your prospects normally compare multiple brands before they make a purchase, then proceed with the next site recommended by the search engine.

By the time you reach the link to your test home page, think about what you (as a prospect) have learned. Have you been educated about how to buy this particular product? Have you learned some features that other brands have that you've added to your list of evaluation criteria? Are you seeing that many of the products in this category are so similar that it's hard to find criteria on which to make a buying decision?

If you are feeling at this point in your test that your prospects may be confused and may randomly pick a vendor, then you're ready to apply more of the concepts of one-to-one Web marketing in order to build a relationship with your prospects. Just as a salesperson attempts to build a relationship with each of the individuals he or she deals with, you may quickly see that a relationship with individual prospects may be the only differentiating characteristic you have in order to rise above your competitors and bring in the sale.

Product Evaluation

There is a wide variety of options available in selecting a Web traffic analysis program, so here are a number of features you will want to consider and rank before you make a decision on which product is best for you.

Platform

Some analysis programs run on the Web server itself; others require you to move the log files to your PC for processing; others are services that process your log files on their computers. There are benefits to all methods, so you need to consider whether you are more interested in reducing the processing load of your server or keeping data files on the central server.

In addition, most programs are designed to run on only certain platforms, so you need to consider whether a product is a server-based program and if it runs on the type of server you use.

If your Web site runs in a shared server environment at a Web hosting service, then you will need to coordinate your selection of an analysis tool with its system administrator because the hosting service may have policies against adding such programs to its equipment. Many Web hosting services provide their customers with some level of analysis reporting as part of their service. Because Web log analysis programs consume a great deal of processing power, they have found it's easier to manage this need than let each of their customers handle it themselves.

File Size

As your Web site receives more traffic, your log files each month will become very large, and they may become too large for your analysis program to process. Therefore, take into consideration the future growth of your site and its needs. If your site uses multiple dedicated servers, then you will want to be sure to evaluate analysis products that are designed to aggregate logs for a cluster of Web servers.

Viewer Program

Some traffic analysis programs use a special viewer program that must be installed on your PC in order for you to view your reports, whether they are processed on your computer or at a service bureau. Other analysis programs use standard Web browsers to view files, and some have incorporated Java applets that can provide additional flexibility in selecting and viewing reports.

With a browser, you are more likely to be able to view reports remotely, whether you administer a remote server or just want to display reports to a group in the conference room. With products that use special viewers, you may be limited in how you access and view reports, especially when the log files have been downloaded to a specific desktop computer in another office.

In addition, some analysis programs are designed for you to access reports (with a browser or special program), while others automatically deliver reports to you via e-mail. For most needs, the viewing of reports on demand versus e-mail is a matter of personal choice, but high-traffic sites that need instant analysis can benefit from having reports delivered via e-mail. In situations where a group of people are interested in receiving traffic reports, such as marketing, sales, and the Webmaster, it is easy to establish a single e-mail address that forwards mail to the entire group.

Log Files versus Database

One of the latest features of Web traffic analysis programs is to build a database of traffic information as it is created, instead of processing a log file created by the server. While using a database to store information instead of a traditional text file may sound like a whizbang selling point, there are situations in which this is very beneficial.

Some analysis programs that use a database are able to reduce processing load using a database technique to process only certain data and not process data that is not needed for a report.

A wide variety of Web log tracking products and services are available to meet a wide range of needs. Some Web site managers need real-time tracking so that they can make instant decisions on the content they are serving. Other managers are more interested in balancing the load between multiple Web servers in a cluster. The product summaries here are intended to help you prepare a "short list" of vendors on which to focus your attention. In addition to the summaries in this book, be sure to take a look at the updated articles and links available to you on our Web site.

Questions to ask about log analysis programs that you consider include the following:

- Can it handle data from multiple servers?
- Is it a service or a product?

- How often can it process data?
- Does it process data in real time or only when run?
- Will it run on a Web hosting company's shared server?
- What kind of customization is possible?
- Can demographic/psychographic data be integrated?

As you determine how you will use a Web traffic analysis program, you will also want to consider the types of preformatted reports available. Figure 6.7 shows a list of reports typically found in traffic analysis programs; you can determine which reports you need and then evaluate the products on the market.

While tabular reports provide a great deal of data, it's the graphical reports that most managers look for to get a quick overview of Web traffic. Figure 6.8 shows one of the trend line graphs produced by WebTrends (www.webtrends.com).

Reports Available from Traffic Analysis Products

Top referring sites
Top requested pages
Top requested directories
Visits by day/time
Most active countries
Most active organizations (i.e., domains)
File activity by hour of day
Activity by day of week
Errors and abandonment
Most used browsers and versions
Most used platforms (i.e., operating systems)
Number of visits
Average number of pages displayed per visit
Average length of visit
Top entry pages for visits
Top exit pages for visits
Top referring URLs

Figure 6.7 Typical reports available in many Web traffic analysis programs.

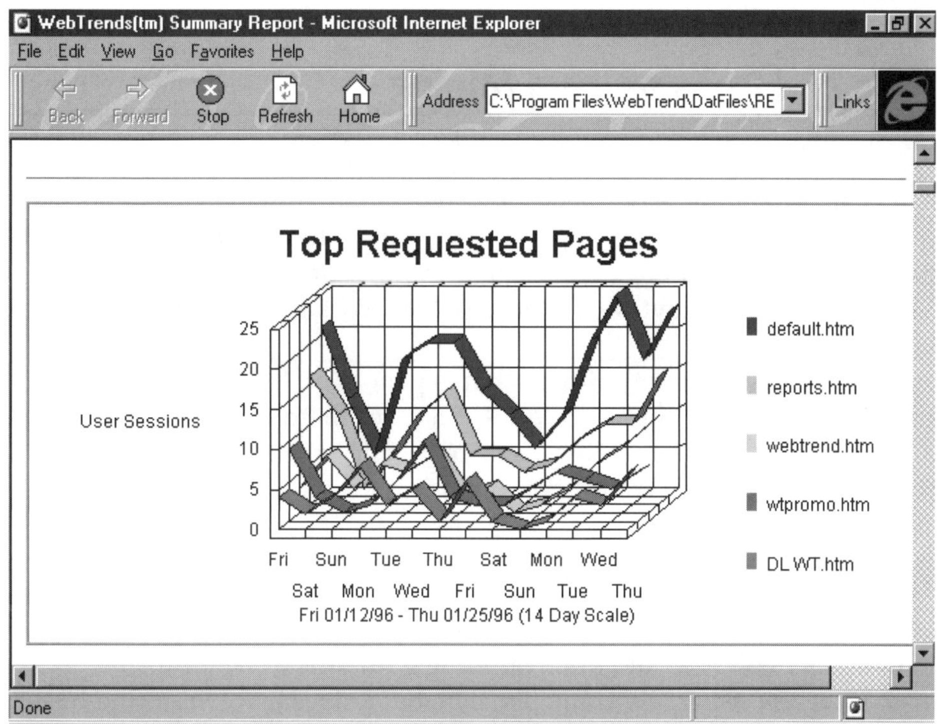

Figure 6.8 Trend graphic from WebTrends' log analysis program.

CASE STUDY: TRACKING TRAFFIC AT A PORTAL

SportSitio.com is a portal for U.S. Hispanic and Latin American sports fans. With content available in English, Spanish, and Portuguese, SportSitio.com serves a diverse Internet audience. In order to learn more about their audience, the marketing staff at SportSitio.com started using the HitBox Enterprise service from WebSideStory to analyze traffic.

Their initial objective was to learn which sites were sending the most traffic to their site in order to budget marketing resources more effectively. "Once we saw that people who entered through a content page chose to view more pages than people who came in through the home page, we knew we needed to make a few changes," said Priscilla Vieira. After changing the home page, the average number of pages viewed went up dramatically.

Vieira says they are seeing people go deeper into the site, which creates an opportunity for increased advertising revenue.

Even though all log analysis programs and services have essentially the same raw data to work with, Vieira offers a few tips to Web marketers. First, she says, choose a product or service that is easy to administer. Second, look for a vendor with very flexible reporting that lets you choose the time periods and types of data to report.

Nuts and Bolts of Data Mining

As the amount and complexity of data continue to grow, new data management techniques have been developed that provide marketers with quicker access to analytical reports. Two of these techniques are data warehousing and data mining. Although one is for storing data and the other is a set of advanced analytical techniques, they work together to help manage large sets of data.

With the large amount of data that is generated by a Web site, such as tracking, purchases, and profile information, these advanced data management techniques are being used more and more to build one-to-one relationships with the Web audience.

What Is Data Warehousing?

What a term—*data warehousing*. It sounds like we're boxing up old bills and hauling them off to an old brick building with broken windows.

Data warehousing is nothing like that, but it does involve storing historical data for use in analyzing business conditions and making decisions. In fact, making decisions should be the focus of creating and maintaining a data warehouse.

The staff and researchers at The Data Warehousing Institute (www.dw-institute.com) have included in their statement of purpose a succinct description of data warehousing: "Data warehousing is broad in scope, including: extracting data from legacy systems and other data sources; cleaning, scrubbing, and preparing data for decision support; maintaining data in appropriate data stores; accessing and analyzing data using a variety of end-user tools; and mining data for significant relationships. The primary purpose of these efforts is to provide easy access to specially prepared data that can be used with decision support applications such as management report, queries, decision support systems, executive information systems, and data mining."

The early attempts to build enterprise-wide systems to facilitate decisions used real-time queries into large corporate databases. In some cases, the real-time nature of these systems was so critical to the operation of the company that the processing delays caused by executives using the system caused more problems than they solved.

The solution has been to create a "snapshot" of the real-time database systems and warehouse this data on a computing system that is designed to perform analytical calculations without affecting the production computing systems. Because there are a number of ways that production computing can be affected when trying to perform an analysis, let's touch on the potential problems, including the difficulties of integrating data from the Web site.

As Michael Berry and Gordon Linoff point out in their book *Data Mining Techniques* (John Wiley & Sons, 1997), a number of factors in large corporations can make it necessary to create a data warehouse in order to have an effective decision support system and a responsive production computing system.

For companies that have acquired various companies that must work together in the manufacture of a line of products, the various data processing systems in use generally don't use a common set of data. In order for management to have an overall picture of these business units, data must be collected from each unit and converted into a consistent format before trying to mine the data for information and insights.

In addition, many companies have added automation to various functions, from order processing to computerized manufacturing equipment, all creating data about their individual parts of the process. These different databases with different data formats were not designed to share data with a centralized analytical system, so data warehouse techniques are needed to pull this disparate data into a centralized location.

Berry and Gordon point out another important reason to use data warehousing—the one that is most important to those of us interested in one-to-one Web marketing: the change in emphasis that is taking place. As management realizes that the concept of one-to-one marketing is becoming the dominant approach to meeting customer needs, companies will devote the analytical resources needed to understand small groups of customers.

What Is Data Mining?

With the prediction models that are possible with database marketing techniques, you might think that you don't need any more tools, but such is not the case. In fact, the predictive capabilities of linear regression models have several limitations that data mining techniques can overcome.

The main problem with the linear regression model is, well, that it's linear! The statistical principles behind this method depend on data being symmetrical: ups equal downs, the number of A's equals the number of F's, and other aspects of human behavior that just don't apply. In fact, have you noticed that the stock market goes down faster than it goes up?

Although these calculation problems are significant, there are a number of data processing problems that data mining techniques can overcome as well, many of which we touch on in this section. In fact, because most of the techniques used in data mining have been in existence for many years, one of the main questions people have about data mining is "Why is it becoming popular now?"

Berry and Linoff describe the influences that have come together to allow this set of tools to become one of the hottest quantitative developments in years:

- More data is being created.
- Data is being warehoused for easy access.
- Computing power is more affordable and accessible.
- Competitive pressure makes it essential to become more productive.
- Data mining software tools are becoming available.

Data Grows on You

One of the results of the growth in population and computers is that there is more data available now to describe what people are doing. Years ago, when a company purchased a product from a supplier, the paper purchase order, followed by a paper invoice and a paper check, were eventually boxed up and stored in a warehouse. In that situation, there was very little likelihood that data, as we know it, would have been created or tabulated.

Today, transactions like this are handled almost entirely through computers, using what's called *Online Transaction Processing* (OLTP). While it may seem that "transaction" represents a financial transaction, actually data processing people refer to the processes of storing and retrieving data from a database as transactions.

These OLTP systems are designed to quickly access individual data items in order to respond to customer orders, inquiries, and other needs. Data is stored in formats that minimize the amount of disk space needed, which assumes that any calculated value can be recalculated from the raw data anytime it's needed. For instance, a relational database system can be used to calculate the sum of orders in the Western Region.

Data Is Being Warehoused

As the amount of data about transactions has grown, so has the time required to run extensive analysis reports for management. The ability to store summarized data in a data warehouse for use in calculating extensive analysis reports now allows the intensive data mining techniques to be used.

The creation of a data warehouse for use in data mining involves reformatting data to make it easier for these calculations to be performed in a timely fashion. Just imagine an executive requesting an analysis such as "Rank the average change in sales for each of the past three years by region." The steps to handle this with a traditional relational database system that is used for order processing (providing all of the data was still online) would be as follows:

1. Sum all invoices for a region for the most recent year and store it in a temporary location.
2. Repeat the sum function for a region for each of the preceding two years and store the results.
3. Calculate the average change from year to year for a region.
4. Repeat steps 1 through 3 for each region.
5. Rank the results of each region.

As you can see, what sounds like a simple analysis results in every record in the database being accessed, plus additional calculations to create the final results. OLTP systems are designed to access just a few records within the database—not the entire database—so it's clear that the decision analysis needs of management must be handled by a system that is more efficient.

The approach to creating a data warehouse for use in data mining is similar to creating a spreadsheet where certain columns are used for summary data, while other cells contain zeroes to show that no data was available for that area.

Reporting and OLAP

Because much of the data mining needs involve analyzing data over time, called "time series analysis," the structure of the data warehouse should take this need into consideration. For example, if you create a spreadsheet for data about products (rows) sold in each region (columns) for a particular period of time, such as a year, and then create similar additional spreadsheets behind the first one for past years, you have created a three-dimensional set of data. If you then turn the data cube one-quarter turn so that products are on the rows and each year's data is represented in the columns, then it is much easier to calculate a wide range of management analyses.

Analytical reporting generally includes three types of analysis: complex tables, descriptive statistics, and online analytical processing (OLAP) cubes. Complex tables of data present a single view of data. Descriptive statistics provide a wide variety of summary statistics about the data, such as mean, median, mode, standard deviation, variance, percentiles, and more. OLAP enables you to examine data from several different views.

Because data mining techniques involve many more elements of data than just products, regions, and years, the complexity of data needed in the data warehouse grows quickly.

Competitive Pressure Makes It Essential to Become More Productive

The almost automatic growth that occurred in our economy in past decades has not continued into the present, which presents a challenge for corporate executives today. This has forced many companies to seek out new ways to serve customers, become more productive, and increase profits. This competitive pressure has given marketing executives additional motivation to explore complex procedures such as data mining.

The other motivating factor for using data mining is the move toward identifying smaller groups of prospects and customers that can be served profitably. The interest in one-to-one Web marketing is adding to this motivation as the Web presents an opportunity to compete on a new level.

Data Mining Software Tools

The statistical techniques and artificial intelligence techniques that are part of the data mining category have been used for many years by researchers who are accustomed to adjusting the many configurations necessary to obtain satisfactory results.

Today, the software industry provides a number of excellent data mining products that automate much of the work that used to require a Ph.D. in statistics or similar expertise. International Data Corp. has recently projected that the market for data mining tools will grow to $1.78 billion by 2003! In addition, the advent of a *graphical user interface* (GUI) that most of us now take for granted has contributed to the approachability of complex products such as data mining.

Data Mining Techniques

As we said earlier, many of the statistical techniques used in data mining have been around for years, but they have had limited use because they require lots of data and lots of processing power. Two of the most commonly used techniques in data mining include the following:

Neural networks. Nonlinear predictive models that learn (i.e., adjust the weights themselves) through training.

Decision trees. Tree-shaped decision points that represent a path to a solution or result. Each decision point uses a rule to analyze a particular data element (e.g., is Age over 30?). By using a large number of rules and data elements, a large number of paths can be handled, which allows for extremely complex groups of rules. Two decision tree methods include *Classification and Regression Trees* (CART) and *Chi Square Automatic Interaction Detection* (CHAID).

Data mining is not a single technique, but a set of statistical techniques that are used to identify trends, patterns, and relationships in the data. Most data mining tools can create several different mathematical models from data, but two models are especially valuable to marketers looking to understand the segments of their market—classification and clustering.

Classification techniques can assign people to predetermined classes based on their profile data. For instance, you might be interested in analyzing Web site data to group people into customers and noncustomers who had either visited the Web site or not. This set of classes can easily be represented by a 2-by-2 table, but as the number of data items increases, it quickly grows beyond simple tables.

In addition to classification is clustering, a technique that identifies occurrences in the database with similar characteristics and then groups them into clusters. Unlike classification, the clusters are not specified ahead of time, so the results of clustering may or may not be valuable.

One of the challenges of analyzing Web data is knowing which technique to use, especially when the mathematical techniques seem to overlap in capability and use. In addition to the complexity of the data available, the experience of the analyst in using these tools helps determine which technique to use. Figure 6.9 shows how these factors influence which data analysis technique to use.

There are several reasons why data mining techniques require so much data. Several of the techniques require a tremendous amount of data for use in training, or adjusting the formulas, so that they accurately predict behavior. After a set of formulas has been trained, then another tremendous amount of different data is needed to test the predictive ability of the formulas.

Applying Web Data Mining

Databases are everywhere. It seems that everything we do goes into a database that collects data on where we go, what we do, and what we buy. When used correctly, the integrated systems of computers that we interact with can help make our lives much more fulfilling. That's the focus of this

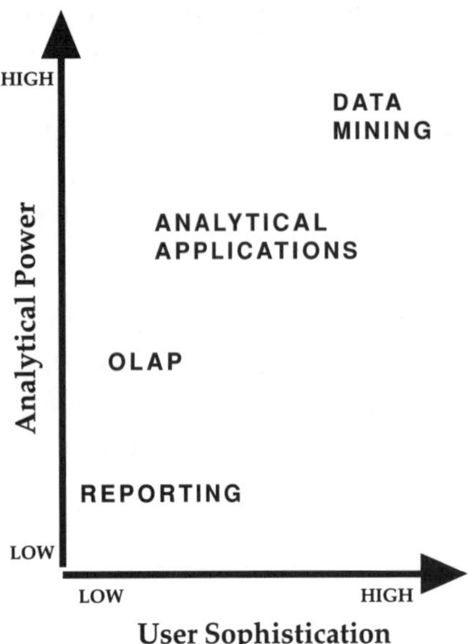

Figure 6.9 The choice of an analytical tool depends on the need and experience of the analyst.

FROM *DATA MINING: CREATING A NEW PARTNERSHIP WITH CUSTOMERS* BY NISSAN LEVIN AND JACOB ZAHAVI

The knowledge discovery process, better known as KDD—Knowledge Discovery in Databases—is a multistep process that can help us translate data into information.

SELECTING TARGET DATA

Databases are heterogeneous, containing a wide variety of data, not all of which may be appropriate for the analysis. For example, in marketing high-ticket items, it may not make sense to consider low-income people. One therefore needs to extract the target data to analyze to match the business problem involved and its objectives.

DATA PREPARATION

Data sets for the KDD process are frequently compiled from different sources using merge/purge procedures. Large depositories of data contain duplicate records that are hard to cull together.

TRANSFORMATIONS

Usually, the predictive power of data resides in its transformation. Typical transformations include: categorical representation to account for nonlinear relationships, interactions, content-specific features, summarizing data elements and collapsing others, taking care of missing values, outliers and other data irregularities, etc. Data analysis, visualization and domain

chapter: to help you help your customers through the integration of databases and other computing systems into your Web site.

In an article written by Lee Marc Stein for the Direct Marketing Association, "The Whys and Hows of Prospect/Customer Self-Qualification," he said, "Being relevant is of increasing relevance." He went on to point out that our customers want to be part of the information flow. He said, "The benefits go beyond getting relevant answers: Consumers want to be part of the marketing process from the beginning, and answering questions makes them a part of this process."

With one in every four American adults now online, according to a recent survey by IntelliQuest, the number of people looking to buy products online is growing at a rapid rate. In fact, IntelliQuest found growth was up 34 percent in one year.

The focus here is to help you analyze your one-to-one Web marketing activities so that you can learn more about how to help customers and generate revenue and profits.

knowledge play an important role in defining the appropriate transformations for the application.

DATA MINING

Most data mining models belong to two major categories, predictive modeling and descriptive modeling. Predictive modeling uses known observations to predict future events, e.g., predicting the probability of responding to a mailing solicitation. It is arguably the strongest goal of data mining. Descriptive models interrogate the database to identify patterns and relationships, e.g., forming clusters by finding natural groupings of data items, finding association and sequencing rules, detecting deviations from normal use, profiling an audience, and others. The core of the modeling process is the feature selection process—choosing the most influential features, typically only a handful of them, that explain the phenomenon under study.

KNOWLEDGE EVALUATION AND DECISION MAKING

Regardless of what data mining technology is used, the solution must withstand economic criteria. Thus, economic analysis should be an integral component of the decision process. This could vary between applications. For example, in cross-selling applications, one should contact only customers whose expected net profit, predicted by data mining, exceeds the promotion cost.

—Nissan Levin and Jacob Zahavi, *Data Mining: Creating a New Partnership with Customers* (2/21/2000), www.urbanscience.com/story11.html.

This means you have an opportunity to learn about the needs of your customers and provide just the information they need about the products you offer.

One of the interesting changes in shopping that the Internet is bringing about is the shift in where people are making their purchases. According to a survey by NFO Interactive, nearly one-third of online shoppers spend less money in retail stores and on catalog items as a result of shopping online.

What are people buying online? About 24 percent of Net users have made a purchase over the Internet, according to Deloitte & Touch LLP/ National Retail Federation. Top purchases are software (31 percent), CDs/ tapes (24 percent), women's apparel (17 percent), men's apparel (17 percent), sporting goods (17 percent), toys (14 percent), electronics (13 percent), jewelry (12 percent), and computers (12 percent).

As intriguing as online shopping is for companies, most people use the Web as they use other media: to gather information. According to the Tenth Graphics, Visualization, & Usability (GVU) Center's World Wide Web User Survey (www.cc.gatech.edu/gvu/user_surveys), Web shoppers are comfortable buying apparel and video and electronics products online. Making purchases, however, is not as important as gathering information. The survey found that quality information on a site was slightly more important than factors such as easy ordering and security.

The story behind these statistics is that the Web audience is growing and looking for more sophistication in the sites they visit and use. This means that more and more sites will use a variety of database technologies in order to manage the vast quantity of data that allows them to apply one-to-one Web marketing techniques and principles.

Identifying Clusters of Individuals

Despite the quality of today's Web traffic analysis programs, sometimes you need to perform an analysis that is either unique to your situation or beyond what current traffic analysis applications can perform. When this happens, it's best to switch to a comprehensive statistical analysis tool that you are familiar with in order to have complete control over the data and the statistical techniques you need.

Identifying Actual People

As we've seen, the Web logs do not actually track individual people; they track the Internet addresses currently being used. As one-to-one Web marketers, we need to know more about the individual people coming to our Web site, so it's important to use additional technology to track individuals.

Using Cookies to Identify Computers

Much has been written about the "cookies" that are stored on the computers of Web users by some Web servers. Some privacy advocates are concerned that personal information is being gathered about individuals in a way that violates their right to privacy.

The study on almost 60,000 Internet users at the University of Michigan for the Hermes Project (www-personal.umich.edu/~sgupta/hermes) indicates that over 81 percent felt cookies were undesirable. This very high negative feeling is a symptom of the media's coverage—sometimes incorrect coverage—of the potential for invading Web users' privacy without their knowledge.

In fact, a *cookie* is usually just an identifying code the browser is instructed to save in a specially named file where all of the cookie information is stored. The specification that Netscape developed for cookies requires that only the Web server that originally sends a particular cookie can retrieve that cookie. This means that identifying codes written to your computer by one Web site are not allowed to be retrieved by a different Web site. In addition, cookies normally don't contain any more than an identifying code used by that site to identify your computer when you return on later visits. The last item on each line in Figure 6.10 shows the type of codes used to identify computers.

Many Web users are not sure what cookies are, but concern about cookies is less important to them than what is done with the information. Cyber Dialogue, an Internet customer relationship management company, found that more than 40 percent of users don't know or understand what cookies are or how they work. Yet Cyber Dialogue also found that more than 80 percent of users are willing to provide personal information, including name, education level, age, and hobbies, in exchange for customized content.

```
webcrawler.com    FALSE  /          FALSE  1022364724Anon-
Track  3C488F3333899z34
www.sun.com:80    FALSE  /          FALSE   978307200
AM_UserIDdq3b066a36693580
```

Figure 6.10 Typical entries in a browser's cookie file.

Advantages of Using Cookies

There are many reasons why you as a Web manager would want to use cookies, beyond the benefits of traffic analysis, such as in personalization and other services you can provide to your audience.

Because IP addresses are reused by different people dialing into an ISP, trying to identify sessions using IP addresses doesn't always produce accurate results.

Limitations of Cookies

Although cookies do add a degree of identification, they are limited in that they identify only computers, not necessarily the people who use them. It's important to make this distinction because there are multiple ways to identify users other than with cookies, some of which overcome the limitations of cookies. Here are three types of projects where cookies won't work:

- Identify customers using a computer at home, office, or an in-store kiosk.
- Track customers across a group of Web sites to cross-sell products.
- Allow multiple employees to use the same computer to receive personalized notices.

Tagging and Tracking Individuals

Several techniques are used to identify individual people when cookies will not work, but all of them require the assistance of a system administrator who can add the necessary programs and system files to your Web site.

IDs and Passwords

The oldest method of identifying users on the Web is to require the user to enter an ID and a password to gain access to certain sections of a Web site. It's technically easy to activate this feature, but Web users generally are not able to remember their IDs and passwords. This means you should use this feature only for important, frequently accessed areas where the value to the user is much greater than the annoyance of having to remember an ID and password.

You'll recall that the Web server log files have a field reserved for user IDs, the AuthUser field, so if you decide to use IDs and passwords, you'll find that your logs can identify specific users.

Session IDs Stored in URLs

A more popular method of identifying people when they return to your Web site is through the use of a session or personal ID that is embedded in the URL that they choose to store in their bookmark file.

Some Web catalog software uses session IDs while a person is shopping in order to know which person is adding products to his or her shopping cart. These session IDs normally persist during only one session or visit to a Web site, but they can be helpful if your Web traffic analysis program is flexible enough to separate them.

Several of the Web personalization software products use IDs in URLs to identify people by having them bookmark pages on the Web site. When these people use their bookmark to return to the Web site, the personalization software automatically recognizes who they are and acts accordingly. The GuestTrack personalization and tracking software uses this technique:

```
www.backyardnature.com/cgi-bin/gt/index.html?user=1234567890ab
```

The use of personalization is covered in Chapter 2, "One-to-One Web Site Personalization," so if your Web site uses this technique you will want to make sure your Web traffic analysis software can handle log entries with both an ID and a Web page on the same line of the log entries.

Once a site is able to identify Web visitors across sessions separated by several hours or days, it is possible to answer a wide range of questions about behavior.

A few of these questions include the following:

- Number of visits per sale?
- Number of days between visits?
- Number of return visits to the site?
- Number of visits for customers versus non-customers?

Take a look at the questions you would like answered and the types of data that is available at your site by tracking individuals to see if moderately simple database tabulations can help you understand your visitors.

Sometimes the questions require going beyond simple tabulations into more complex data gathering and processing.

Understanding Visitor Behavior

There are a number of ways to evaluate data about Web visitors, such as monitoring the various paths that people take through a Web site. People looking for product information so that they can make an offline purchase display a different set of pages—in a different order—than shoppers planning to make a purchase online.

By using a data analysis tool, such as eMine from SPSS (www.spss.com), it is possible to create profiles of your most desired customers and target new visitors who fit the same profile. In addition, you can use tools like this to lead visitors to important content more easily when you can use their profile to identify where they will want to go in your site.

When purchase history data is part of the profile data, it can be combined with path data to refine predictions about behavior and revenue.

In addition to predicting desired behavior and removing navigation roadblocks, there is another use for path analysis data. When you know the heavily traveled paths through your site, you can create real-time monitoring tools to track behavior. By using exception rules the monitoring tool can notify the site managers if a large number of people deviate from the traditional paths, which could indicate a problem with the hardware, software, or content.

While some sites need to acquire tracking and monitoring software for use on their own server, other sites want to outsource this function and use a service such as HitBox Enterprise from WebSideStory (www.websidestory.com). Products like this eliminate the system administration task of maintaining server log files and tabulation software because the log data and processing are handled by the outside service. Figure 6.11 shows a graphical report of the popular paths used by Web visitors.

Using Databases in One-to-One Web Marketing

Many of the database techniques we've covered in this chapter lend themselves to helping improve the effectiveness of our one-to-one Web marketing efforts. Some of these techniques can be implemented easily, while others, such as data mining, will require more effort.

For a Web site promoting products to consumers at home or to businesses, the process of integrating your Web site into your existing computing environment is similar:

Decide on your objectives. Are you looking to generate leads for salespeople, product orders, or some other item that needs "back-end" fulfillment?

Determine the process. Map the movement of data from the point of origin through fulfillment of the customer's needs (and back).

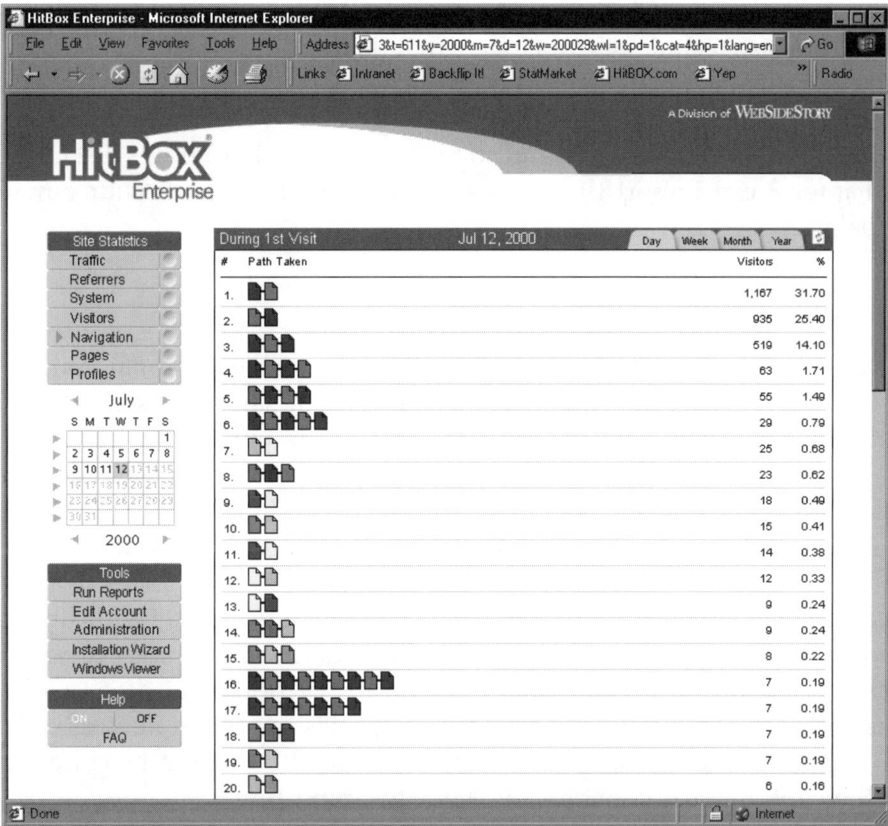

Figure 6.11 Popularity of paths through a Web site.

Design the implementation plan. Make sure that every department affected has ample opportunity to help make the project a success.

Develop the software to perform the integration. Allow sufficient time for the technical team to create a quality system because blending the different technologies is a complex process.

Deploy the system. Launch the new system, invite friends and family to test the system prior to its public launch, and then tell the world.

Direct E-Mail to Prospects and Customers

One of the easiest database techniques to implement is to collect names and e-mail addresses from people registering with your guestbook and automatically generate e-mails to those people. The content of these e-mails was covered in Chapter 3, "One-to-One E-Mail," so here we'll touch on the database techniques to manage that data.

You use a contact manager program such as GoldMine or ACT! that can select records based on criteria you specify, such as interested in certain products, live in certain areas, and so forth. The e-mail programs discussed in Chapter 3 can import these e-mail addresses and launch your e-mail campaign.

Sales Lead Management

One of the easiest ways to integrate a Web site with traditional marketing is to start with automating the processing of sales leads generated by the Web site. Let's cover how to take the data entered by prospects and move the data to people who can respond to the needs of your prospects.

Sales contact programs such as GoldMine (www.goldminesw.com) now offer supplementary programs that move data from Web forms to their contact management system. GoldMine users can now direct GoldMine to import and process contact data created from an incoming Internet e-mail message. The message can contain special instructions that direct GoldMine to check for duplicates, schedule activities, or create new records. This feature allows prospect data entered on a Web page to be collected and then automatically sent to GoldMine for importing.

One of the earliest uses of this technique of moving prospect data from a Web site to a fulfillment database was on the CORT Furniture Web site (www.cort1.com), where leads from the Web site's inquiry form (see Figure 6.12) are converted to CSV records and sent via e-mail to a fulfillment operation. They are then e-mailed to headquarters marketing staff. When the fulfillment operation receives the e-mails, the data is imported in CORT's database, where certain data fields tell which brochures and other material have been requested.

Turn Web Log Files into Predictors of Prospect Behavior

Until recently the log files created by Web servers could be used only for relatively simple tabulations. By using data mining techniques such as decision tree analysis, the almost infinite number of paths through a Web site can be analyzed to determine the patterns Web site users follow and tell which patterns are used by customers versus the paths followed by people who don't make purchases or inquiries.

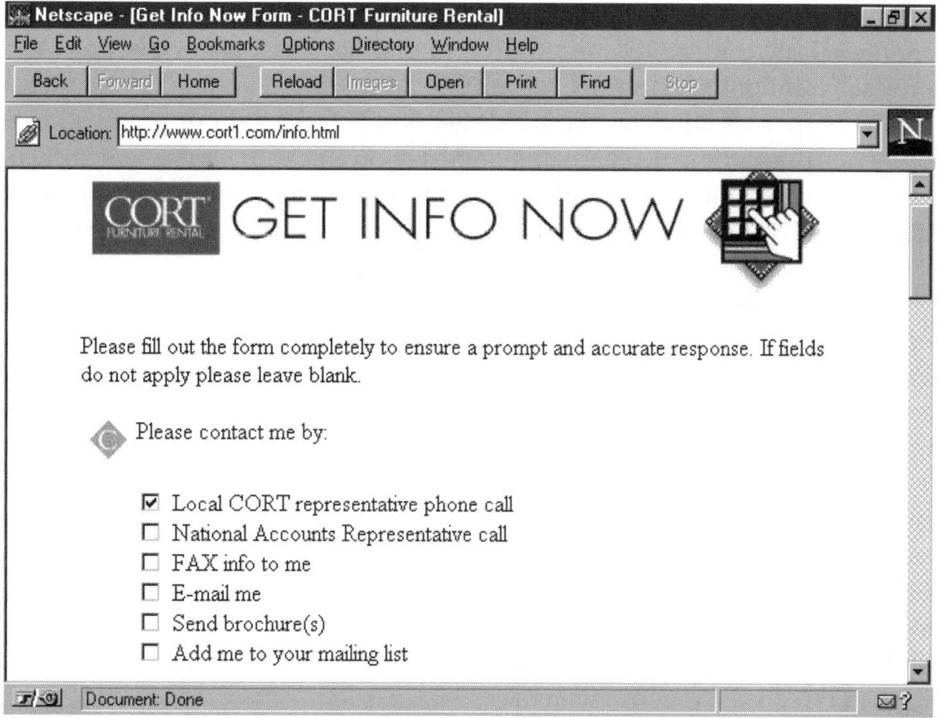

Figure 6.12 CORT Furniture Rental inquiry form generates data that is automatically imported into a fulfillment database.

Some Web log analysis programs have difficulty in processing files larger than 50 megabytes, but data mining software can be used on files of several hundred gigabytes. For Web sites that receive 50,000 visitors per day who retrieve anywhere from 10 to 30 pages from the site, the log file will grow by several megabytes each day.

When the log file data is combined with the profile data collected on a personalized Web site, the opportunity to understand the behavior of Web visitors becomes possible using data mining techniques.

State of Web-to-Database Integration

Database technology is typically used when manual methods of managing data become, well, unmanageable. One of the more difficult decisions to make is to determine that the effort and investment of moving to a database outweigh the cost of continuing with the manual process.

With Web site content, many companies find that practically all of the content on their Web site is static, in that it doesn't change from day to day or week to week. For high-traffic media Web sites, however, the content changes daily, and sometimes hourly, so manual methods of creating Web pages are out of the question.

For companies wishing to provide access to a selected portion of a large body of information, a searchable database on the Web server will suffice. For other companies to provide access to order entry and order status systems, a fully integrated Web-to-database system is needed to provide instantaneous results of the query.

There are other ways database technology can help achieve the benefits of one-to-one Web marketing, such as in analyzing data collected about Web visitors and customers. This data can be used to identify ways in which to serve the audience better on the Web site and in the back-end operations of fulfillment and customer service.

Many of the traditional database software companies have added capabilities to their core products that allow a data processing organization to integrate a Web site into their traditional server environment. For instance, Oracle (www.oracle.com) and Sybase (www.sybase.com) provide several Web development tools, while PowerSoft (www.powersoft.com), a subsidiary of Sybase that sells advanced database development tools, has incorporated the Web into its tools.

Other companies sell products that help companies turn their mainframe legacy applications into Web applications, which not only reduces the need for expensive mainframe terminals but also allows more employees to have access to essential mainframe applications.

Benefits of Web-to-Database Integration

The growth of economies has led marketers to look for more efficient ways to reach their target audience with sales messages. The move to reach a mass audience with a small number of media vehicles had several effects on marketing:

- A small number of media outlets were being used, such as the three leading broadcast networks and a small number of high-circulation publications.
- The marketing message became more general and emotional because it was inefficient to target the message to small clusters of customers.
- Selling to individuals, at home and at work, became an effective, although expensive, way to deliver a customized sales message to individuals.

As computer technology became inexpensive enough for marketers to use, other forms of marketing communications became cost effective, which led to the use of direct mail and specialized catalogs—and fewer salespeople making individual sales calls on customers. The problems with direct mail are the same as with mass media advertising, just not as large. Direct mail, like mass advertising, is a one-way form of communication that is aimed at a large number of people.

Even with today's large number of cable television channels, most television advertising budgets are spent on commercials that reach millions of people each time they run. Not what we'd call targeted advertising! Even direct-mail campaigns are aimed at tens of thousands of people.

As we've seen in every chapter of this book, true one-to-one Web marketing provides the benefits of communicating with people as individuals, much as a salesperson does in customizing a sales presentation based on the needs, wants, and desires of the prospect. This chapter describes several ways to use database technologies, internetworking, and statistical techniques to improve communication with prospects and customers and to provide products and services that meet the needs and expectations of customers. By applying these techniques, businesses can meet the needs of their Web audiences, but because the technique of database marketing is integral to a discussion of using databases on the Web for marketing, we need to understand the basics of database marketing.

The idea of storing information about consumers has been in use since there were customers. Salespeople have kept notes on cards, in notebooks, and now in computers that help them tailor their sales message to the customers they see.

Even though personal selling is augmented by the use of Web-based presentations, the need to store information about your customer hasn't gone away. In fact, the more a company applies computer power to understanding and serving customers, the more it uses the concept of database marketing.

What Is Database Marketing?

The term "database marketing" has been used to mean many things because there are many ways to create a database. Although no single definition is necessarily more correct than another, Swanson Russell Associates, a marketing communications firm in Lincoln, Nebraska (www.sramarketing.com), has developed a definition that works well for most companies:

Database marketing: Creating a computer file of a company's customers and/or best prospects and then marketing to those people as individuals.

USING RFM ANALYSIS TO IDENTIFY CLUSTERS OF CUSTOMERS

RFM is a technique that has been used for many years by large direct mail operations, such as national consumer catalogs. With over 50,000 customers, companies have a monumental task of identifying the needs and desires of groups of customers because several factors influence each person's buying behavior.

Direct marketers discovered that three factors taken together were helpful in identifying clusters of customers and predicting future behavior. These three factors—recency, frequency, and monetary—can normally be *coded* in a database and tabulations run to help marketing managers learn which groups are important to the company. Basically, the process is to assign each customer to one of five groups for each of the three characteristics.

Recency. The date of the most recent purchase.

Frequency. The total number of purchases that person has made since he or she started doing business with you.

Monetary. The total amount of money the customer has spent with you since he or she started doing business with you.

You might think that by knowing the oldest date, the largest order, and the customer with the most orders, the customer database could be coded in one pass; however, it is not quite that simple. The reason multiple passes through the database are needed is that each of the five groups is not an even distribution of customers over its range, but an equal number of customers in each group.

The first step is to sort your entire database by the recency date, with the most recent at the top. Then, code the top 20 percent with a "5," the next 20 percent as "4," and so on. Each customer then has a 5, 4, 3, 2, or 1 recency code

In addition, the executives at Swanson Russell Associates also define the term "database marketing communications," which they use to refer to all the communications (letters, mailing pieces, newsletters, brochures, telephone calls, company magazines, videos, faxes, electronic mail, etc.) directed to the people whose names are stored in a database.

Because we are engaging in one-to-one Web marketing to sell our products and services, it's appropriate for us to cover traditional database marketing systems and see how they can be integrated with our Web marketing activities.

For many years salespeople have used contact manager software that collects name and address information, next contact dates, and comments about recent sales calls. For individual salespeople, this may be enough use of a database to help jog their memory about their prospects and customers in order to build a relationship. With the decline in personal selling and the

in his or her database record. Be sure that each of the five groups (called "quintiles") are the same size (i.e., has one-fifth of the total file).

Next, code Frequency the same way, with the top 20 percent coded with a "5," and so on. Then, code monetary with its code.

The next step is to create a three-digit number from the three codes we've created so that each customer has a number from "555" down to "111" in the RFM field of the database for a total of 125 groups, or *cells*.

To use the RFM codes to predict results, you will need to select a portion of the total customer database and send those people the next mailing you plan to send to the entire customer base. After the test customers have had an opportunity to respond to the test mailing, determine the response rate for each RFM cell. You can then use a variety of analysis techniques to determine whether to contact particular cells of customers in the master database, such as response rate, average order size, average profitability, and so forth.

The use of this technique in one-to-one Web marketing needs to be adjusted based on whether all of your customers use the Web or whether a large portion of your customers haven't told you about their online capability.

Since the RFM technique doesn't use any advanced statistical calculations, it can be implemented very easily with simple database updating procedures. Statisticians sometimes feel this technique is subject to error because recent customers also have a small number of orders and, of course, your oldest customers have more orders than average. This reduces the predictive ability of these two characteristics; however, from a practical standpoint, RFM provides a great deal of predictive ability for very little investment.

increase in selling through a distribution channel, it has become hard to monitor and track customers. With database tools, marketers now have the ability to use the massive amounts of data that can be accumulated to learn the needs of at least clusters, or groups, of customers, and sometimes of individuals themselves.

As the demographics of Web users approaches that of the general population, data gathered on a Web site will more nearly represent a company's total market, not just those customers who are also Internet users. Even before the online and offline markets become homogeneous we can gain tremendous benefits from current database marketing techniques.

In their book, *Strategic Database Marketing* (NTC Publishing Group, 1994), Rob Jackson and Paul Wang identified several benefits of database marketing techniques that apply to the one-to-one Web marketer:

- The ability to target marketing efforts only to people likely to be interested
- The ability to create long-term relationships
- The ability to offer varied messages to different prospective customers
- An advantage in product distribution
- Increased knowledge about customers

Each of these benefits is based on developing a database of customer information, some of which you can obtain directly from visitors to your Web site, but some that you may need to obtain from other sources. Before we cover sources of external data, let's go over several specific projects you can conduct using database marketing techniques.

Identify the best customers. Use RFM analysis (see the sidebar titled *Using RFM Analysis to Identify Clusters of Customers*) to determine which customers are profitable to market to and which ones are not.

Develop new customers. Obtain data files from companies that develop comprehensive databases of potential customers that you can incorporate into your master database.

Tailor messages based on customer usage. With a complete history of each customer's purchase profile you can tailor your mail or e-mail based on the types of products he or she uses, frequency of purchase, combinations of products, and more.

Recognize customers after their purchase. Reinforce the correctness of a purchase decision by letting them know they made the right decision and that you appreciate their business.

Cross-sell related and complementary products. Some products are naturally used with other products you sell, so use your customer purchase database to identify opportunities to suggest additional products during the buying session.

Communicate with customers without telling your competition. Some forms of marketing communication, such as advertising and mass mailings, notify your competition about your plans before the message reaches your customers. By sending messages directly to good customers in your database you eliminate the possibility of the competition countering your campaign.

Conduct product research. The more information you have about how customers use your products, the better equipped you are to create better products. Data such as time between repeat purchases, warranty work, and other contact with customers indicates how your products are being used.

Personalize customer service. When customers contact your customer service operation, an online database of purchasing history can help the service representative show you are interested in solving their problems and meeting their needs.

Eliminate conflicting or confusing communications. It's important to present a single image to customers, even if you treat groups of customers differently. For example, you don't want customers who purchase frequently to receive a "get acquainted with us" offer because it looks as if you have forgotten what good customers they are!

Rob Jackson, senior vice president of KnowledgeBase Marketing, Inc., illustrates the underlying concept of serving your customer through one-to-one Web marketing principles with his Customer Driven Strategy. Table 6.2 shows the distinctions he makes between the traditional approach of inside-out thinking, where the company decides what to sell to the customer, versus the approach of outside-in thinking, where the company listens to the customer.

Modeling Your Market

A number of statistical techniques can be used to improve on the accuracy of RFM to predict the behavior of customers. In his book, *Database Marketing: The Ultimate Marketing Tool* (McGraw-Hill, 1993), Edward Nash suggests that the traditional statistical method called "regression analysis" is a better tool for prediction than RFM because it can take into account more elements that are probably in the customer database.

In order to illustrate how the results of a regression analysis are used in a formula to predict behavior, let's use two of the data elements used earlier in the RFM analysis sidebar:

Table 6.2 Customer Driven Strategy

INSIDE-OUT THINKING	OUTSIDE-IN THINKING
What we want the customers to buy	What the customers want to buy
How we want to communicate to them	How they want us to communicate with them
What we want them to hear/see/understand	What they want us to say, show, and tell

Source: KnowledgeBase Marketing, Inc.

Recency. Number of months since last order.

Frequency. Number of orders placed by the customer.

A typical model used to predict behavior has coefficients, or weights, that are multiplied times the data element. Then the results of these multiplications are added together along with some base value (i.e., starting point):

Order Size = $25 + (–2.50 x Recency) + (+1.50 x Frequency)

This model says that for each month that has passed since his or her last order (i.e., Recency), a particular customer's order will be $2.50 lower, and that for each additional order placed (i.e., Frequency), that customer's order will be $1.50 higher. For example, for a customer with a Recency of three months and a Frequency of six orders, the model predicts his or her next order will be:

Order Size = $25.00 + (–2.50 x 3) + (+ 1.50 x 6) = $25.00 – $7.50 + $9.00 = $26.50.

For a customer who placed one order 10 months ago, the model predicts that the next order will be:

Order Size = $25.00 + (–2.50 x 10) + (+1.50 x 1) = $25.00 – 25.00 + 1.50 = $1.50.

Obviously it is not profitable to even try to market to an old customer like this because the expected order size is much lower than is needed to make a profit.

By using additional data elements commonly found in the master customer database, the accuracy of the regression model and other statistical techniques goes up dramatically. While most businesses do not sell directly to consumers, the types of data that can be obtained through a consumer-oriented Web site illustrate the types of data that can be used in creating database marketing models:

- Age
- Gender
- Income
- Education level
- Occupation
- Marital status
- Home location (e.g., urban, suburban, rural)

- Lifestyle characteristics (e.g., hobbies, interests, community concerns, etc.)

Where this type of data may not be available directly from individuals, consider purchasing data from companies that gather demographic and psychographic data about consumers and similar data about businesses, such as the following:

Claritas	www.claritas.com
Acxiom	www.acxiom.com
CACI Marketing Systems	demographics.caci.com

Security on the Web

Several technical challenges face information technology executives in integrating Web servers, whether public or internal, into traditional data processing. One of the problems inherent in the Internet is that it is a stateless environment, which means that the connection between the server and the browser is active only while a Web page is being served. Cookies are currently used to store codes on users' computers that uniquely identify the user, but efforts are underway by various standards groups to improve on this technique.

Another challenge facing IT is security: how to allow access for only authorized users and how to keep private data on the public Internet private. The technique of making data secure from unauthorized access on the Internet is called *encryption*, which is done by substituting different characters for the actual characters and then reversing the process at the receiving end.

To illustrate how encryption works, imagine telling someone that you will be changing every letter in a message to the next letter in the alphabet and that they should do the opposite. Of course, that pattern would be obvious in a document of just a few words, so it's important to use an encryption method that has a significant amount of difficulty.

Just as a chain is only as strong as its weakest link, so it is with security on your Web site. One of the most visible forms of security is the secure Web server software you use because individuals making purchases on the Web have come to expect to see the indicators in their browser window that a secure server is being used for their credit card and other private data. Netscape heavily promoted the idea that a blue bar across the top of the window and a solid blue key at the bottom meant secure.

Products

The Netcraft Web Server Survey (www.netcraft.com/survey) can give you an idea of the market share of each major brand of Web server software in use. The survey of Web server software usage (Table 6.3) is accomplished by sending an HTTP request for the server name that identifies the server. As you can see, the most popular server is the Apache server (63 percent), which runs on Unix platforms, followed by Microsoft's servers (19 percent), which run on the NT and Windows platforms.

Before you start planning to add commerce to your site, be sure to experience online commerce yourself so you'll know just how it feels to a customer to search for the product you're looking for, entering your credit card number, and wait for the confirmation—and the product. If you haven't purchased products online yet, then it's time you did a little surfing for fun (or business) and bought your next book or hobby-related item on the Web.

A commerce-based Web server presents more technical and procedural challenges for a company than most other marketing activities it will undertake. This is because the system provides the one-to-one Web marketing function to customers while it is integrated with the internal computing environment that only employees have traditionally used. The combined need for a very high level of customer service on the Web site and tight security makes it essential that every department within a company that will be affected by the commerce operation be involved, starting

Table 6.3 Top Web Servers

SERVER	ACTIVE SERVERS	PERCENT
Apache	11,412,233	62.81
Microsoft-IIS	3,608,415	19.86
Netscape-Enterprise	1,255,085	6.91
Rapidsite	293,957	1.62
WebLogic	291,067	1.60
Zeus	227,043	1.25
thttpd	220,937	1.22
WebSitePro	101,174	0.56
Stronghold	91,556	0.50
WebSTAR	88,653	0.49

with the planning stages. As you prepare for adding commerce to your Web site, be sure to check out the latest information at our *One-to-One Web Marketing* Online Web site (www.1to1web.com).

The Future of Web Data Analysis

The tracking techniques covered in this chapter can help you improve your success on the Web by showing what people are doing on your Web site and can allow you to gather information from individuals.

The Web personalization software covered in Chapter 2, "One-to-One Web Personalization," points the way to improved one-to-one marketing, but the Web traffic software companies will need to quickly catch up so that their products will continue to be helpful.

One of the challenges facing vendors of traffic analysis software is how to track the intrapage activity. In other words, personalization software can display different content to each user, but the traffic analysis software shows that the same page was accessed by these different people. Because pages are created "dynamically" on the fly, making content decisions based on each person's profile, these activities are not included in the log files. As Web personalization becomes more common, look for the Web traffic analysis software vendors to find ways to track individuals and the content they see with greater precision so that you can meet the needs of the individual.

Checklist for Data Analysis

The process of selecting and implementing appropriate analysis techniques is based largely on the types of data available for analysis. This checklist helps clarify the data required for the three types of data analysis techniques covered in this chapter:

- Web server traffic analysis
- Web mining
- Data mining

Review the following questions to identify the types of data you have available. Then, in the recommendation section use the letters for questions you answered "yes" to determine which analysis techniques you can use.

Questions

A. Do you have Web server log data files available?

B. Does the server log contain unique identification of individuals?

C. Do you collect profiles that can be associated with Web activity in the server log?

D. Do you have customer data available?

E. Can the customer data be associated with each person's Web activity in the server log?

Recommendations

Match the letters from the questions to which you responded "yes" with these recommendations.

ANSWERS	DATA ANALYSIS TECHNIQUE
A	Use Web server log analysis tools to report on pages visited.
A + B + C	Use advanced Web traffic analysis tools with database connectivity to compare demographic profiles with traffic patterns (i.e., Web data mining).
D	Use traditional data mining products to identify most profitable customers for promotions.
A + B + C + D + E	Use sophisticated data mining products to compare demographic profiles and purchase data with traffic patterns.

Resources

There are a growing number of traffic analysis and data mining products available that provide access to these analytical techniques. The products listed here are part of a continually updated list of resources on our *One-to-One Web Marketing* Online Web site (www.1to1Web.com).

LOG ANALYSIS PRODUCTS

Accrue	www.accrue.com
Macromedia	www.macromedia.com
net.Genesis	www.netgen.com
WebTrends	www.WebTrends.com

WebSideStory	www.WebSideStory.com

DATA MINING PRODUCTS

Angos Software	www.angoss.com
Digital Archaeology	www.digarch.com
HNC Software	www.hncs.com
IBM	www.software.ibm.com
MINEit	www.MINEit.com
SAS	www.sas.com
SPSS	www.spss.com
Trajecta	www.Trajecta.com

Up Next

Chapter 7, "One-to-One Web CRM," describes how a number of one-to-one techniques are brought together into a comprehensive system across an entire enterprise. It provides an overview of integrating personalization, e-mail, community, and other methods of building relationships with customers.

One-to-One Web CRM

"Dynamic trade will push the traditional model of customer relationship management beyond its limits. Companies need a new approach, eRelationship management, to leverage the Web's unique strengths for capturing and publishing a single view of consumers."

Forrester Research, Inc.

What Is CRM?

CRM is really nothing new. It stands for *Customer Relationship Management*, and it is an application of the One-to-One Marketing philosophy, which has been around for years. Much of the media coverage has focused on the enabling technology of CRM. But, we must remember that CRM is really a process, *not* a software product or technology. It is the *process* that manages interactions between a company and its customers. Components of CRM do include hardware, software, and services, but those should only *support* the strategy of Customer Relationship Management.

Gartner Group defines CRM as, "a business strategy designed to optimize profitability, revenue, and customer satisfaction." That truly is the end game. But, in order to execute on that promise, *you must put the customer in the center and integrate all processes around a single view of the customer*. This is the fundamental concept of CRM, and one that makes it so difficult to do. In order to have a complete CRM system; a company must coordinate all customer contact points, which means capturing *all* company/customer interactions across *all* channels.

Customer Relationship Management allows companies to be customer-focused, customer-driven, and customer-centric. This knowledge creates better understanding of what each customer relationship entails in order to provide personalized services, build mutual value and respect, and foster a mutual commitment to the relationship itself.

This is clear in the views of Barton Goldenberg, founder and president of ISM, a CRM research and consulting firm:

> "CRM is a comprehensive approach that provides seamless coordination between sales, customer service, marketing, field support and other customer-touching functions. CRM integrates people, process and technology to maximize relationships with all your customers including eCustomers, distribution channel members, internal customers and suppliers. CRM increasingly leverages the Internet."
>
> www.ismguide.com/html/crm.htm

While that definition sounds as if it relies on technology, Goldenberg has frequently said that CRM today is best accomplished "through the integration of people, process and technology, while taking advantage of the revolutionary impact of the Internet." (www.ismguide.com/html/barton_menu.htm)

While the definition of CRM will continue to evolve as technology and business needs change, the research done by ISM indicates that 13 components will be in the CRM systems of most corporations for the next few years:

Sales functionality

Sales management functionality

Telemarketing/telesales functionality

Time management functionality

Customer service and support functionality

Marketing functionality

Executive information functionality

Field service support functionality

Enterprise portals

E-commerce functionality

ERP integration functionality

Data synchronization functionality

Multimodal access

One of the key objectives of CRM is to optimize profitability. CRM seeks to provide answers to the following questions:

- Which customers are most profitable to me? Why?
- Which customers would be interested in which products?

CRM enables companies to follow the customer through the lifecycle. Trajecta, a firm that specializes in optimization solutions, which include CRM, data mining, and decision support, depicts how this is done in Figure 7.1.

Beyond CRM, there is also eCRM, which has been receiving attention. eCRM, coined by Forrester Research, is a Web-centric approach to synchronizing customer relationships across communication channels, business functions, and audiences. eCRM is basically the marriage of CRM and e-commerce. Successful eCRM empowers customers to access tailored information and services tied to products that are less expensive and far more convenient than the traditional ways of helping customers evaluate and purchase products. By making services more convenient and less expensive for customers, companies can deliver on the promise of CRM, which is to *increase revenues* and *reduce costs*, thereby improving profitability and customer satisfaction.

eCRM represents a shift from having a company's employee take care of customers directly to allowing customers to use self-service tools that allow them to become active players in the purchase and service process. In this environment, the Web is used not just to make it easier to know more about each customer, but to empower the customer to manage and control the process via the Web.

Many Web users have found that a well-constructed Web site provides better on-demand services than they usually receive through a company's human-based contacts. The Web site lets customers easily obtain product and service information that helps them investigate product features, make purchases, and solve problems without help from the more costly sales and support staff.

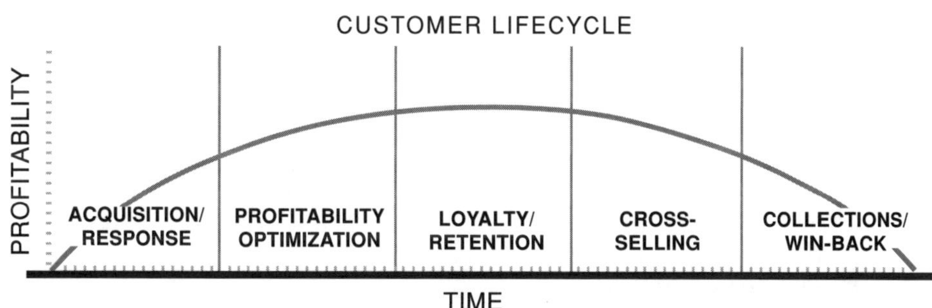

Figure 7.1 Customer lifecycle.

Power of Information

In the March 2000 issue of *Business 2.0*, an article entitled "10 Driving Principles of the New Economy" had a very interesting first principle. Driving principle number one was "Matter. It matters less. It's a cliché, but it's the key to the New Economy: Processing information is dramatically more powerful and cost-effective than moving physical products. Increasingly, the value of a company is to be found not in its tangible assets, but in intangibles: people, ideas, and the *strategic aggregation of key information-driven assets.*"

This is a powerful statement for marketers exploring CRM. Data is becoming a major asset. Not simply data, but truly the *information* that a company will be able to garner from that date. Many of the meta markets, such as Amazon.com and Garden.com, are creating great market awareness about the value of aggregated data.

While there are some debates about the aggregation of data and privacy, in terms of CRM, we are really talking about the "dis-aggregation" of data—basically, dissecting it down to the individual customer level and having all of the data surrounding that one customer available in real-time so that we can personalize their experience.

CRM is about harnessing the power of information. We have the data! But, the challenge is: How do we turn that data into useful information that we can leverage to better serve our customers? It doesn't do them any good for us to *know* them if we still treat them like everyone else.

Currently, thousands of companies are collecting lots of data from their Web sites; however, very few are doing anything for their customers with that data because there are many challenges to overcome. CRM is tricky because it is truly a combination of art and science.

The art is anticipating human nature in order to build your system. The science is that of predictive modeling and statistics. The miracle is making it all work together.

Traditional Uses of CRM

The main applications of CRM fall into three major categories:

- Sales force automation (SFA)
- Marketing
- Customer care

Sales Force Automation

These applications are built to increase sales revenues through better selling processes and to provide better information for strategic sales planning. Strategic selling is possible when a sales executive has access to a comprehensive customer profile. SFA also helps to shorten the sales cycle and helps managers deploy their best sales executives to the accounts with the highest potential revenue opportunities.

Marketing

CRM allows marketers to plan, execute, and analyze campaigns for improving ROI. Later in the chapter, we focus on the specific benefits of CRM for marketers. This means that marketers can finally know how prospects learn about the company's products, how they respond to advertising, and what promotions actually result in sales. In addition, a total CRM system can help marketers better understand the needs and desires of the various segments of their market so that they can better apply one-to-one marketing techniques.

Customer Care

Many companies have been criticized for their poor e-mail response to online customers. Also, customers now want to be recognized no matter how they contact the company they are doing business with, whether it is online, over the phone, or in a retail setting. CRM helps companies manage the integration of customer data from these sources. A company's Web site should be treated like other touch points with the customer where companies practice the same, or better, service-level standards. Web customer care is so important to the success of a Web site that we decided it needed dedicated coverage in this chapter. At the end of this chapter, you will find an in-depth look at what is available to provide and manage customer care on your Web site.

Benefits of One-to-One Web CRM

As Barton Goldenberg pointed out in his definition of CRM earlier in this chapter, CRM is a process of integrating technologies that allow a company to communicate with each customer in several ways. Each time a customer contacts a company that has an effective CRM system in place, the customer is recognized and receives appropriate information and attention. This provides many benefits to both the company and its customers.

Benefits to Marketers

The increase in the number of different ways that a customer can interact with a company has added to the complexity of keeping up with these "touch points" of customer interaction. The multiple levels in the distribution channel for consumer products illustrates this challenge. For many years consumer products were available only through local retailers, such as grocery stores, drugstores, and department stores. Even when specialty stores and large discount stores became popular, consumers still relied on these local merchants for these products. This meant that it was nearly impossible for consumers to communicate directly with the manufacturer to provide feedback and suggestions.

Today, consumers and business customers are obtaining products and support services from a number of sources in the distribution channel.

The travel industry is a perfect example of how customers interact with a number of business partners from the start of the sales cycle through the delivery of services. Travel agents have traditionally sold airline tickets and hotel reservations on behalf of major airlines and hotels. With the growth of online airline reservation Web sites, a new type of touch point has been created.

After tickets have been issued travelers are likely to interact with airline employees at a telephone call center and at the airport while boarding and deplaning the aircraft. The food served while in the air has normally been provided by an outside vendor—a vendor that taps into the reservation system to know which special meals are needed on each flight. At each step along the way, it is important for airline employees, and the companies representing the airline, to understand and meet the traveler's needs.

Complex customer interactions have replaced direct contact in practically every sector of our economy. In the consumer mail-order sector, SkyMall (www.skymall.com) has demonstrated that catalog and online marketing can be done in a number of different ways. Their print catalog and online Web site sell products from multiple mail-order catalogs. SkyMall aggregates orders for products supplied by multiple companies, then uses a sophisticated electronic transaction network to transmit orders directly to each vendor. While SkyMall handles practically all of the customer interaction during the sales process, each vendor ships its particular product directly to the consumer on SkyMall's behalf. Because SkyMall's catalog is constantly in front of airline passengers, it's important for SkyMall to maintain a good relationship with customers so that they will be encouraged to become repeat customers.

These examples illustrate the complexity of today's sales and service process, as well as the importance of obtaining the benefits of CRM.

Reduce Churn

Once we acquire a customer, we really want to hold on to him or her. Churn is becoming a major concern as sites duke it out for market share and loyal customers. By providing advanced personalization and customized solutions using an effective CRM system, marketers have a better chance of retaining customers.

Companies like SciQuest (www.sciquest.com), a leading B2B e-marketplace for scientific products, are providing their customers with this advanced personalization and custom solution. With the Web features shown in Figure 7.2, such as Fast Track, Quick Order, My Favorites, Order History, and Track Orders, researchers can be more efficient in their ordering of products, which helps to reduce their procurement costs while increasing their productivity. SciQuest also provides an automatic routing system that supports the researcher's internal approval process and individual spending limits.

In addition to its public Web site, SciQuest has a customized Internet ordering solution called SelectSite. Customers with a SelectSite have a private Web site that they access through their company intranet that has *their approved suppliers* and *their negotiated prices*. Companies like Dow Chemical, DuPont Pharmaceuticals, Merck, and Monsanto all use their SelectSites built by SciQuest to do their scientific purchasing.

Create Switching Costs

Customers who make repeat purchases from a company obtain more than products—they begin to have an investment in the information about their purchases.

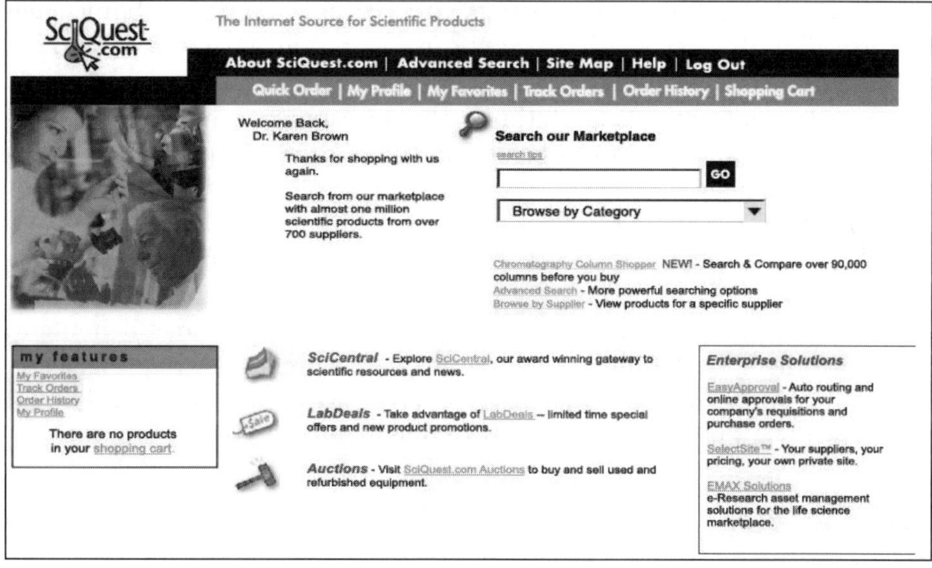

Figure 7.2 SciQuest offers several features that help customers select products to purchase.

E-commerce sites like Staples (www.staples.com) and HomeGrocer (www.homegrocer.com) allow customers to store shopping lists and see previous purchases. This information is a valuable part of the shopping experience because it saves the customer time. The more an individual customer purchases from a site with information features like this, the less likely he or she is to switch to another vendor.

Cross-Selling

One of the biggest benefits marketers realize when using CRM is the ability to use purchase history and interest profile data to recommend appropriate products to customers. The ability to cross-sell is possible when a central database is used to store all customer information.

Each product purchased by a customer can be correlated with the purchases made by other customers. When combined with the expressed needs and interests of the customer, it is possible to identify patterns of buying behavior that can be used to project future needs and interests.

Valuation of the Customer

What is this customer worth to me? It comes back to basic one-to-one principles of treating different customers differently. With the advent of CRM, marketers can now truly measure the value of each of their customers.

The cost of obtaining each new customer is quite high, so it's important to market additional products to existing customers. Some customers, though, just don't have the same value as other customers because their needs and situations are different. This means that it's important to determine the lifetime value of each customer so that marketing efforts can be tailored based on the expected revenue and profitability of each customer.

Benefits to Customers

Just as CRM provides benefits to companies, it also provides benefits to their customers. Each time a customer makes a purchase or requests a service from a company that has implemented CRM, the sense of loyalty and the investment in the relationship are likely to grow.

Better Service

Customers can expect much better service as more companies invest in CRM. Customer care agents will have critical information about each customer at their fingertips.

Better Experience

We now have the ability to make product recommendations based on the data that was collected about each customer compared to the data we've collected from other customers

Time Savings

As companies become more efficient in integrating their offline systems with their online systems, customers can expect better "self-service" options. They will be able to access online information about their orders, shipping, and more. This will save a tremendous amount of time for customers so that they don't have to wait on the phone for help.

Nuts and Bolts of One-to-One Web CRM

The concepts behind CRM are relatively easy to understand; however, there are a number of integration details that can make implementing CRM extremely complex. In order for marketers to apply CRM input to one-to-one marketing, they don't need to understand all of the technical details. It is helpful, though, to have a broad understanding of how the different pieces need to work together.

Technology Overview

The essence of CRM is to have a single comprehensive database that can be accessed from any of the customer touch points.

In general, most customers have four types of interaction with a company as they purchase and use a product. These correspond to distinct operations, or departments, within a company:

Marketing. Builds awareness through advertising and other mass communications and targeted marketing communications.

Sales. Handles inquiries, prepares custom proposals, and processes orders through a call center, Web site, or field sales force.

Fulfillment. Ships products to the customer, invoices customers, and collects accounts receivable.

Service. Provides the customer with technical assistance in using the product or repair service.

As a company begins to implement CRM, it usually finds itself with a number of standalone systems that do not share information with each other. It is technically possible for a company to create or purchase a brand new, totally integrated CRM system; however, there are a number of reasons why this may not be the best approach. Instead, it may be better to look for ways to integrate the existing software systems in order to gain some experience with integrated systems prior to creating a new integrated CRM system (see Figure 7.3).

For most companies, the customer database, which includes the accounting system, contains the core data for the operations of the company. In addition to having current contact data for customers and their shipping addresses, the system also contains current payment records. While the files and databases used in other departments may have some customer information, many times those departments rely on the central customer database for their needs.

For example, a technical support operator might need to tap into the customer database to confirm that a caller has actually purchased the product for which help is being requested. When a customer tells a salesperson that he or she wants to purchase a particular accessory, the salesperson may need to refer to the customer database to learn exactly which model the customer had purchased.

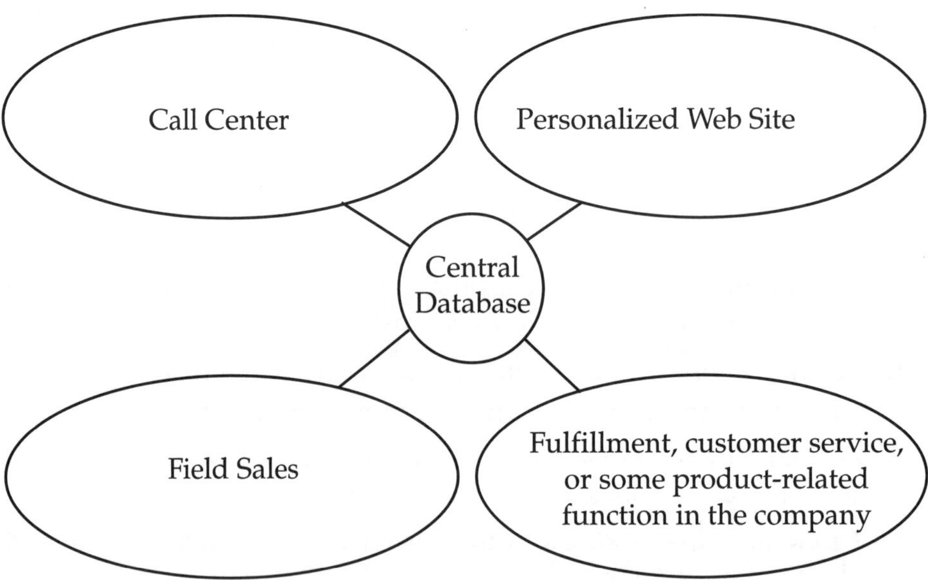

Figure 7.3 A CRM system where each customer contact point has access to the complete history of the prospect or customer.

This means that one of the first challenges in integrating disparate systems is to look at how the central customer database can feed information to the systems used in other departments.

The next challenge is to allow the systems used in these other departments to update information in the central customer database so that each department will have access to all customer information. This also means that the company's Web site needs to provide customers with access to specific pieces of data, as well as allow customers access to certain ordering and tracking functions.

E-Commerce

Many e-commerce Web sites use a "batch" technique to process orders. These sites transmit orders at least once each day from the Web server located at their ISP to the in-house customer and order processing system and database. Another piece of data that needs to be shared between the systems is which products are in stock and available for shipping. This data is transmitted from the in-house system to the Web server at least once a day as well.

This means that a customer using one of these Web sites may see that a product is "in stock" and place an order, thinking that the product might be shipped that day. In actuality, the product could already be out of stock, and their order would not be transmitted to the in-house system until the following day.

Real-time CRM systems connect the Web server database to the in-house database to provide the customer with up-to-the-minute product and inventory information and to transmit the order immediately to the in-house system for processing.

Sales Force Automation

Just as real-time information needs to be made available to customers via the Web site, it's also important to make sure that field salespeople are kept up to date as well.

Most field sales teams today use one of the popular sales force automation (SFA) software products to enter and update information about prospects and customers. Over the last few years features have been added to these products to allow them to easily share information with other salespeople and sales management. This is especially helpful when teams of people, such as an account manager and a team of application engineers, work together to create a custom proposal.

The challenge is in making sure that the databases on multiple laptop computers all have the same information about a prospect or customer. These laptops are not always connected to the Internet as desktop computers are in the office. The technique of sharing changes between members of the team is called synchronization. SFA products use several different techniques to synchronize members of the team, but one of the most popular techniques is to automatically transmit updates via e-mail.

This is done by automatically e-mailing changes in profile data to other copies of the software within the sales team. The data received by the copies of the SFA software is used to automatically update that salesperson's prospect database. These e-mail messages generally move over the Internet without the knowledge or intervention of the salespeople. This means that the next time the salesperson runs his or her SFA program, updated data will appear.

SFA products such as GoldMine from FrontRange Solutions (www.frontrange.com) also allow for a centralized database to store customer and prospect data for all of a company's sales force. When this technique is used it becomes relatively easy to integrate the master SFA database with the central customer and order database.

This allows field salespeople to have almost instantaneous access to up-to-date customer and ordering information.

Web CRM Technologies

There are so many CRM technologies that we can't mention them all, but we can list a few to get you started. The major players include Siebel, Kana (which recently bought Silknet), Onyx, Oracle, Pivotal, Brightware, Clarify, HyperParallel (recently bought by Yahoo!—very interesting! What do you think that their focus is turning to?), Surf Aid (both IBM and Hilton Hotels use this), Blue Martini (used by Levi's), Netperceptions, RightPoint, NeuralWare, and Thinking Machines, bought by Oracle.

Push Vendors Moving into CRM

If you happen to have a copy of our first version of *One-to-One Web Marketing* you may have noticed that we had a chapter on Push. You also may have noticed in this second edition that we do not have a chapter on Push. Push was the hot thing in 1998, and then it kind of fell apart. There was a big shakeout in which many of the companies merged or died. Diffusion appears to have reinvented itself in the CRM space. Nationsbank now uses Diffusion software to automatically notify its largest corporate customers of wire transfers. Wit Capital, an online brokerage firm, also is using Diffusion to automatically notify clients of impending IPOs.

WANT A DATE?

When two people agree to get together for a fun activity they commonly call it a "date." The origin of this term comes, as you might expect, from their looking at their calendars and agreeing on a specific date to meet. Today, it's taken for granted that all calendars have the same dates, so we quickly assume that when we refer to a date such as "10/7/2000" that everyone knows what we mean.

The problem with this assumption is that in some countries the month comes before the day, while in other countries the day of the month comes before the month. Just imagine what would happen if our two people planning a date have different calendar customs—they won't know they are talking about two different dates!

Many of the challenges of integrating existing software applications are caused by how data is stored in each system's database. Here are just a few ways dates are stored in computers:

12/1/2002

12-1-2002

12012002

2002-12-01

1038729600

While most of these versions of the date December 1, 2002, are easy to understand, the last one is probably unfamiliar. That format is used by Unix systems to represent the number of seconds since "1970-01-01 00:00:00," which makes it unambiguous in any language.

Dates are just one of the many common formatting problems that programmers face when trying to integrate multiple systems. Other common problems involve the following:

- Size of text fields for name, address, and other personally identifiable information
- Size of text blocks with narrations or descriptions
- Names of fields that mean the same thing (e.g., "date_of_invoice" versus "invoice-date")
- Codes identify people, companies, products, and departments (e.g., a customer may be the company with a code of "GE-001," while another department might refer to the customer by the contact person at the company, such as "CA132")

Programmers are occasionally able to modify their software to match the formatting of other programs. It's usually not possible, though, to convince a

continues

WANT A DATE? (CONTINUED)

vendor to change its commercial products to match the methods of another company. In these cases, software conversion programs need to be developed that move data between applications and make the necessary conversions along the way.

So, when you're ready to integrate two products that will be part of your CRM system, set a date with the technical team early to go over the data conversion challenges. Just be sure you're looking at the same calendar when you make that date!

PRICELINE.COM

Priceline.com does a good job of leveraging CRM, as seen in Figure 7.4.

It created the Bonus Money Page to display Priceline Partners. The purpose is to get the user, in the middle of making a bid for an airline ticket, to sign up for a Discover credit card, Sprint Long Distance, and other offers. If the customer signs up, then the partner will add the displayed dollar amount to the airline ticket bid.

The enabler here is a technology called Prime Response. It executes the logic to determine which partner programs are to be displayed. In this instance, the user has never accepted the Discover card offer, or the Sprint long distance

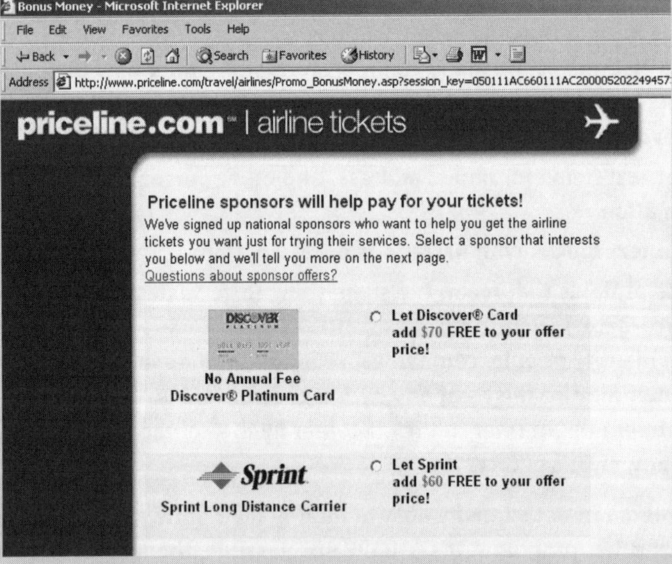

Figure 7.4 Priceline partners.

Applying One-to-One Web CRM

Throughout this chapter we have tried to show that CRM is more than a technology; it's also the philosophy for how to implement one-to-one marketing.

The techniques and technologies covered earlier in this book, such as personalization, data mining, and e-mail, are all components of effective CRM systems. This makes it both easy and difficult to describe how to apply a one-to-one Web CRM—we're really pulling together much of what has been covered in other chapters.

offer, or any of the others displayed, so Prime Response checks the available data, determines that the user had not taken any of these promos, and returns content for the Web page.

Prime Response checks the following:

- **The user's cookie**
- **The user's session information to see if the user has taken a Discover card while bidding on a rental car, hotel room, or groceries**
- **The database (if I'm a registered user) to see if the user has taken a Discover card in a previous Web site visit**

If Prime Response determines that the user has indeed taken the Discover card offer previously, then Prime Response will return no content, and all subsequent promotions will be "moved up" on the page (no slots are left empty).

As a Priceline user makes a bid on an airline ticket, certain critical information is captured. For example, the origin airport and the destination airport are captured as well as the city and state of the billing address and the e-mail address for notification.

Once a user has finished making his or her bid and entering critical information, his or her last page in the process is called the Confirmation Page. This page lets the user know that the transaction is complete and the user will receive an e-mail within an hour letting him or her know if the bid was accepted. At this point, the user is done with his or her business and could easily leave the Web site; however, Priceline is not through with the customer. At this time the site suggests offers from other companies that are related to the purchase just completed. While affiliate or partner linking like this is common on sites, the Priceline site uses simple business rules to determine which offers are most appropriate for the customer.

Applying One-to-One Web CRM for Customer Acquisition

Acquisition initiatives become much more focused and targeted when leveraging CRM. Companies have a better profile of their "ideal customer" and can be more specific about criteria when purchasing mailing lists for direct-mail campaigns or e-mail campaigns. Also, with these campaigns companies can make the right offer to the right person at the right time. It is much easier for these marketers to generate a response because they know that they have what the customer is likely to want.

Acquiring new customers by using CRM involves tracking prospective customers, starting as they contact the company for the first time and tracking them all the way through making their first order. This means that marketers should be able to look at their customer records with analytical tools and determine things such as the following:

- Which advertising vehicle, both online and offline, produced the best customers?
- Did offline media generate initial online inquiries or just calls to the call center?
- Do more initial customers who purchase the more expensive and higher-margin products purchase through the Web or through the call center?
- How many calls to the call center and visits to the Web site are typically made by new customers before they make their first purchase?
- How does the number of a follow-up e-mail messages sent to a prospect affect the likelihood of making the sale?
- Is the number of salesperson calls or visits prior to making a sale lower for prospects who visit the Web site?

When a CRM system integrates all the marketing communications and inquiry contacts with initial orders, marketers have a better view of what works—and how to apply their marketing budget.

Applying One-to-One Web CRM for Customer Retention

Marketers can retain their customers better through convenience and support. Through one-to-one Web CRM marketers can provide what customers want, how they want it, and when they want it.

When the prospect becomes a customer the goal then becomes finding ways to continually help the customer learn additional uses for products from the company (i.e., create repeat orders).

When a CRM system integrates data from the Web site as well as person-to-person contacts, and when the system provides the marketer with comprehensive data mining tools to do statistical analysis, it becomes relatively easy to spot patterns and trends in customer behavior that can be used to alter or update marketing and sales activities.

Many Web and e-mail personalization systems routinely collect data on which pages were seen, the paths taken through the site, and other observational data. They also collect profile data that gives them a clearer picture of a person's interests and needs. When this data is combined with purchase data, and perhaps with other offline or purchased data, it becomes easier to automatically assign people to various market segments. This profile information can be used to update a profile database on the Web site and guide customers to information and products in which they are more likely to be interested.

Applying One-to-One Web CRM for Creating Zealots

In today's competitive environments to keep customers, you must convert them into raving fans or zealots. Once a customer is a zealot he or she can be your customer forever—but it takes much work and effort to get the customer there. We think that to create zealots, marketers must really push the envelope in the user's Web experience. Many Web sites allow customers to add products to a list of favorites and check on order status. A key to success is to go beyond that.

For example, Lands' End offers features such as the following:

Lands' End Live. Allows customers to chat live with a customer service representative. That representative can even take control of the shopper's browser to help him or her find the right products.

Shop with a Friend. Lets two shoppers access the site together to browse and shop.

Your Personal Model. Allows customers to enter and save their measurements for easier clothing sizing.

Customers who are fans of a company and its products are some of the most vocal enthusiasts who help promote products through word-of-mouth; however, these customers require special attention. An integrated CRM system is especially helpful because it can recognize and reward these customers for their loyalty.

Airline frequent-flyer programs were one of the first loyalty programs to recognize people for continuing to purchase from a particular company. They initially provided frequent travelers with more travel—something the frequent flyer may not look forward to! Those programs have evolved over the years to provide other benefits to these special people, such as recognition and nontravel rewards.

A few of the programs that can be implemented through a CRM system include the following:

- Frequent purchase program
- Recognition program
- Community sharing program

Frequency Marketing Program

There are many ways to create a frequent purchase program that rewards customers for continuing to purchase your products. There are outside vendors that can provide points programs that allow customers to accumulate points toward products from your company as well as others. Most of the points programs managed by outside vendors allow customers to accumulate points by making purchases from multiple companies. Unfortunately, this creates a sense of loyalty on the part of the customer to the points program—not to the products he or she purchases.

In many cases, it is best to operate and manage your own loyalty program with assistance from a consulting firm specializing in this area.

Recognition Programs

Recognizing special customers can be done with many CRM systems by simply storing each customer's category in his or her profile. Like many nonprofit fund-raising organizations, you may want to attach names to each level of recognition, such as platinum, gold, silver, and bronze. Then, when these customers come to your Web site, call your call center, or shop in one of your physical stores, the CRM system should recognize these people so that they may be given special treatment.

Community Participation

Because customers who are raving fans like to talk about their favorite products, you can help them by providing Web-based opportunities to share their feelings and product knowledge with other customers through an online community.

It All Starts with the Data

As you might imagine, data mining must come first in order to have a high-quality CRM system. Data mining automates the detection of relevant patterns in the data and then is able to build models to predict customer behavior.

First, marketers want to identify the segment of customers that has high-profit potential. By examining buying behaviors, marketers can find patterns that are good predictors of purchasing behaviors. The key is to look for meaningful and new correlations, patterns, and trends in order to build predictive models rather than retrospective models. Relationships between a variable and behaviors that are nonintuitive are the jewels that data mining hopes to find.

After mining the data, marketers must feed the results into software that manages the campaign directed at defined market segments. Data mining allows marketers to align their campaigns more closely with the needs, wants, and attitudes of customers and prospects. We can model virtually any customer activity; the key is to find patterns relevant to current business problems.

CRM assumes that disparate data sources will be unified in a data warehouse. A *data warehouse* is the focal point for data integration. Data warehousing is a technique of calculating and storing summary data that can be used in management and marketing analysis.

Challenges of One-to-One Web CRM

Every company faces a different set of challenges in adopting the CRM concept because every company has different procedures and systems in place. Most companies, however, will benefit by including in their CRM implementation an employee education phase and a software integration phase.

Educating the Enterprise

"The single greatest barrier to mass customization within today's organizations lies not with the technology or the strategy, but rather with the organization's own inability to truly understand where the value lies," warns Sean Kelly, author of *Data Warehousing: The Route to Mass Customiza-*

tion (John Wiley & Sons, 1996). "Without this clear business perspective, CRM can never be delivered."

This makes it important to educate employees on the value of a CRM system, as well as the important role each employee plays in maintaining a quality CRM database.

Integration

With everyone we talk with, integration ranks high as the big technical challenge to implementing CRM. One aspect is that many companies have legacy systems that don't easily integrate with others. But we're finding that even in relatively new enterprises, integration is still a large challenge.

Expense

Effective CRM is not cheap. And the price range is vast. For example, GoIndustry.com spent $500,000 on the Onyx installation, including two heavy-duty servers from Compaq, to provide a reliable hardware engine to run the software. Sun Microsystems uses $4 million worth of smart software from Californian software house Quintus in its support centers around the world. Quintus supplies a program called eContact that uses a lexicon to scan through the words contained in e-mails and extract meaning from these electronic messages.

Analysis and Action

It doesn't do any good to collect the data if you're not going to do anything with it. Too often marketers bury themselves in reams of data that never gets analyzed. Or, once analyzed, it doesn't turn into action that will improve the user experience. Bottom line: If you can tell what is different about your customers, use that knowledge to *do something*; as Peppers and Rogers always say, "Treat different customers differently."

Privacy

And, finally, something that has been, and will continue to be, a major issue on the Web: privacy. With even more data collection points, customers are going to be even more concerned about what companies are doing with that data. *Tell them*! Nothing is more annoying than going to a

CRM: SIX UNAVOIDABLE TRUTHS

By David Sims, sharpAngle

Advice comes at you in all shapes, sizes, and values. It's easy to follow a tangential piece of advice—"interview your vendor thoroughly with these 20 questions"—and lose focus of the overall picture. Saratoga Systems VP of Technical Services, Pat Nestiuk, reminds you of the fundamentals.

UNDERSTAND THE NEED

Why are you doing all this again? Oh yeah, to improve efficiency while building customer loyalty. In today's highly competitive markets, companies must differentiate themselves. Just delivering quality products and services is no longer enough. Customer loyalty is a strategic aim for any successful organization since it is far more expensive to attract new customers than it is to sell to and support existing ones. A CRM system means everyone in the organization, or even external trading partners, can look at information regarding the customer: contact information, inquiries made, historical notes, purchasing requirements, and more. Clearly define how you want the system to impact your business and what value it will create for your company.

GET THE RIGHT SPONSORSHIP

CRM is a strategic, cross-functional business initiative. A CRM implementation should be a strategic thrust of the company and requires the appropriate sponsorship across the company. The sponsorship will establish the business goals and objectives expected from the CRM implementation. They could include targets for increasing sales, more effective support resolutions, or higher customer satisfaction ratings. The right sponsor will present it as a strategic, business-led initiative, not just a technology implementation, and ensure the company-wide buy-in and sponsorship of the project.

COMMUNICATE THE CONCEPT INTERNALLY

This is a critical phase of any successful CRM that rarely gets the emphasis it deserves. Cross-functional buy-in goes well beyond upper management. A successful implementation touches nearly all aspects of an organization, so a real need exists at the beginning of a project for early preparation and communication. One of the main reasons early CRM projects failed, Nestiuk believes, was that participants didn't fully understand the purpose and company-wide benefits the system would create. Change should be introduced in a well-managed and supportive environment. In selling the concept throughout the organization, plan for training and acceptance workshops before the system is ready to be deployed—it needs to be a forethought, not an afterthought.

continues

CRM: SIX UNAVOIDABLE TRUTHS (CONTINUED)

ANALYZE CUSTOMER NEEDS AND ASPIRATIONS

Don't forget the "C" in CRM. Understand your customers' needs thoroughly. It's easier than ever before, since the Internet presents new opportunities to identify rapidly changing customer buying characteristics, and to leverage new electronic marketing and e-commerce possibilities. Your sales and support organizations can do the same. Companies interact electronically and personally with their customers and are provided a wealth of data that needs to be analyzed and understood to provide the right information and services at the right time to the right target. Through the proactive accumulation of customer data, any organization can transform customer information into customer intelligence, allowing them to better serve their customer by designing, developing, and refining future products and services tailored to customer needs.

SET PRIORITIES AND SELECTION CONSIDERATIONS

When selecting technology, compare the scope and capabilities of different systems to your needs—don't just run out and buy the latest thing. Organizations have numerous departments, divisions, groups, and task forces, each with its own set of priorities. A CRM solution enhances—or should enhance—the interaction between many of these disparate entities. A key contributing success factor is the need to set the business drivers that the CRM system will solve and improve. Different solutions have different levels of functionality, capabilities, strengths, and pricing structures and are better suited for some organizations, industries, and user requirements. When choosing a CRM vendor and solution, choose the system that works best for your interactions with customers and business partners and that uses the right business processes the right way to achieve your goals.

FACE FEARS ABOUT IT

Hey, it's okay. Not everyone wants to share information, even though the success of a CRM solution depends on broad acceptance and use throughout the organization. Some users aren't accustomed to working with IT, and sales people often don't want to share their information with the rest of the organization. Communicate the benefits. Make certain the system is designed to deliver information that is important to them—information that helps them sell products and services to customers. Incentives will help in ensuring a successful project. Consider providing commissions that are available via the system, allowing the sales people to see exactly what commissions they could make on a particular approach. Provide mobile devices that enable them to easily access and input data into the system. Most of all, design the system to be efficient. Don't include every conceivable option that may make it too cumbersome or difficult to use.

Web site, registering, providing lots of information about preferences, and then *nothing* happens. We always wonder, "Why bother?" What is the point of my disclosure if the company isn't going to tailor my Web experience based on that information? Is the company saving it for a rainy day? Unfortunately, the answer is yes. Many companies are doing very little with personalization relative to how much customer data they have. But they all want that data, just in case.

Marketers have an obligation to tell their customers what they are doing with the information that the customer provides or, as the case may be, what they *intend* to do with it. Honesty is the best policy, and it will be appreciated by your customers, especially as the paranoia continues to rise around the topic of privacy.

The Future of One-to-One CRM

CRM has a long was to go. We predict that there will be much tighter integration of sales and marketing information in the future. Also, there will be better combinations of CRM and ERP. Resource allocation will continue to be a major issue with implementation.

Forrester Research reports that an increasing proportion of contact with customers is coming via the Web rather than the phone. It found that 1 percent of the customer interactions came from the Web in 1997, and up to 14 percent in 2000 and 56 percent by 2003 will come from the Web. Also, companies will better accept and understand CRM and therefore will *spend*. According to a new report by Business Intelligence, a London-based research company, between $5 billion and $7.5 billion will be spent in 2003 on hardware, software, and services for CRM.

We anticipate great advances in voice over IP, interactive TV, and more and better self-service via the Web as people become more comfortable with these technologies.

Rapidly, the worlds of Internet and wireless technologies are coming together. We tend to think of PCs as being pretty commonplace; for a sense of scale, though, consider that by 2004 some 1.3 billion people are expected to have wireless access to the Web, up from just 5.7 million last year (according to IDC). Additionally, in places like Scandinavia and Japan, one in two people already owns a cell phone. We will have reach in which the Web will extend into every aspect of a customer's life if he or she so chooses. What marketers do with that access remains to be seen.

CARING FOR YOUR ONLINE CUSTOMERS

We define one-to-one customer care as simply Web-enabled call centers, where customer contact is handled through the Internet. That service can be a simple e-mail response all the way to a multimedia interaction between a customer service representative (CSR) and a customer.

Now, it has progressed all the way to sophisticated e-mail management systems, real-time interactive text chat, and voice over IP (VoIP). CSRs now help guide their customers through the Web site by "taking control" of the customer's browser, all while having a conversation either through instant messaging (text-based chat) or by actually taking over the customer's browser (with the computer's microphone and speakers acting as a telephone). On many sites, there is now a "Need Help" button in which customers can click to access a live person in real time to walk them through the site. Now, customers can receive true one-to-one service from a Web site, making each shopping experience a personal one.

Web customer care is just one aspect of a total one-to-one Web CRM process. Many Web sites can effectively implement Web customer care now, and it can be integrated into a larger CRM-based system in the future or one that may already be in place.

Benefits to Marketers

CRM is a concept that companies can embrace for several years as new technologies provide marketers with increased value for their CRM investment.

Real-time touch. The standards of online customer service are rising. Customers need more than simple product information and online ordering capability. They need true buying guidance and the real-time personal interaction that Web customer applications can bring to a Web site. Companies need to be able to do request-for-bid, pricing negotiation, and custom product configuration, all in real time. This requires customers to better serve themselves and marketers to build customer-facing applications that empower customers to "serve themselves."

Real-time sales. Web-enabled call centers can allow CSRs to engage the customers when they would be most willing to buy. One of the "problems" inherent in e-commerce is abandoned shopping carts. Many times these carts aren't taken to the checkout point because of questions that customers want answered before they buy. Web-enabled call centers can answer these questions. Statistics show that when a potential customer speaks with a CSR while perusing a site, 60 to 70 percent of these browsers place orders.

Reduce costs. Web customer care systems can reduce the costs of serving customers. Web customer care applications allow companies to create many self-serve applications such as search engine databases housing specific problems/solutions, product finders, frequently asked questions (FAQs), and others. You can reduce customer service costs because customers can be more efficient in getting what they need, when they need it and how they need it.

Benefits to Customers

As new CRM techniques are integrated into a company's operations, their customers will receive additional benefits from being loyal to those companies.

Immediate service. The name of the game for e-commerce sites is service. And it is proving to be critical to the success of Web-based businesses. Customers are finding that they are getting better service online. They no longer will stand to be left on hold on the phone for too long when they can get online and get immediate satisfaction. In many instances, the call center CSRs are accessed through "click to talk" buttons positioned strategically throughout an e-commerce site. If a user revisits a page several times, a sign that he or she is either having second thoughts or has some questions, the button becomes bigger and more prominent.

Customer, serve thyself. Customers can help themselves on the Web at any time, from anywhere. With Web customer care applications, they can get answers to their questions after your business has closed for the day (unless you promise 24x7 operations). Online customers are now more comfortable with accessing information about their orders online. The beauty of a well-developed Web self-serve application is that customers will be more confident in their purchase upfront; therefore, they will return items much less often.

Web Customer Care Technologies

Much of the Web customer care technology has been around for years; many of these applications date back as far as 1992. Lately one-to-one Web customer care has been getting a lot of attention, primarily because an estimated 60 percent of the U.S. population now has Internet access and 40 percent of households today have a second phone line to accommodate Internet access. Also, with better and faster access more customers can utilize the "speech" capabilities of their computers (which is pretty cool if you haven't tried it yet).

Many of the Web customer care applications are hosted solutions, meaning that they are hosted on that company's Web servers. There are pros and cons to hosted solutions. Some of the pros are that you don't have to mess with the technology as much; it is already prepackaged and served up to you. You need to worry about hardware and software investment. Often hosted solution are more efficient in that you can "go live" much more quickly and efficiently. Often they also can provide an array of services regarding implementation, integration, and processes that may assist in making your one-to-one Web customer care launch a success. Some of the major players include the following companies:

eGain. eGain offers many solutions including Self-Service, Live Web, e-mail, and Call Center applications. eGain Call Center Bridge is a solution for blending Internet communication channels with call centers and enabling CSRs to handle communications across channels. eGain has provided solutions for customers such as America Online, Earthlink Network, Egg, Freddie Mac, GE Capital, Lloyds, Lucent Technologies, Northern Light, Quick & Reilly, Suretrade, Xerox Corporation, and 3Com (www.egain.com).

eshare. eshare's Online Customer Interaction Solutions include the following:

Net Agent: Combines live online communications and inbound phone calls in a single view to build strong customer service and maximize agent productivity.

Re:Sponse: Routes and responds to all of those incoming e-mails.

Expressions: Builds an interactive community for your customers using chat rooms, discussion forums, and online presentations.

eshare offers easy-to-define and updated FAQ pages for easy access by your customers. Some of its customers include Lycos, AT&T WorldNet, and Citigroup (www.eshare.com).

Talisma. Talisma provides e-mail, self-help, and chat as part of its customer care solution. The largest vacation property site on the Web, Vacationspot.com, uses Talisma to provide immediate, personalized, and consistent responses to the hundreds of e-mail inquiries that flood its customer service department (www.talisma.com).

Kana. Kana's multiple communication channels, including e-mail, Web, chat, instant messaging, voice over the Internet, phone, and person-to-person, enable companies to offer a wide range of interaction methods to communicate with their customers throughout the lifecycle, from proactive or virtually assisted service, to assisted and self-service (www.kana.com).

Quintus. Ticketmaster uses Quintus eContact to sell tickets and provide customers with personalized, consistent service via the phone, Web, and e-mail. As part of the eContact deployment, Ticketmaster implemented Quintus WebCenter, customer interaction management software designed exclusively for Web-based transactions (www.quintus.com).

Edify. City National Bank of Taylor, Texas, had two goals: It needed to replace its outdated interactive voice response system, and it aimed to make its static Web page more dynamic. The Electronic Workforce was the only proven solution that could retain the same logic to access its back-office SQL database for both phone and Web. And no competitor could offer host legacy balance transfer over 3270 terminal emulation, in real time. With the Electronic Workforce, City National Bank has provided its customers with 24x7 access to all their banking needs. Customers can now access their bank via the Web and verify account balances, calculate interest on loan payments, and gather information on CD and IRA options (www.edify.com).

Right Now. RightNow Web effectively automates customer service and technical support through three Web-based modes of query: self-service, e-mail management, and live chat (rightnowtech.com).

liveperson.com. As the world's leading virtual shopping mall, iQVC upholds the three pledges of quality, value, and convenience from which QVC derives its name. iQVC began using LivePerson to communicate with its online customers in September 1999 with 14 operators. Based on the service's success, iQVC now plans to host 100 operator seats and continue its tradition of service 24 hours a day. A subsidiary of General Motors Acceptance Corporation (GMAC), ditech.com is one of the most innovative online mortgage lenders. LivePerson is available on every page of ditech.com's Web site with 70 operators providing real-time customer service (www.liveperson.com).

Using One-to-One Web Customer Care to Create Loyal Customers from the Start

Forrester Research reports that 90 percent of online purchasers say that good customer service is critical in choosing a Web site on which to shop. Moreover, 37 percent of online customers say they use customer service

CHECKLIST: ARE YOU READY FOR REAL-TIME WEB CUSTOMER CARE?

While the technology of a Web-enabled call center can help make CSRs more effective, a number of issues need to be resolved before seeking this technology out. The following is a checklist of questions from Chris Stanwick of Kowal Associates that need to be answered before looking for a Web-enabled call center:

- ✔ **Am I prepared to have service available 24 hours a day, 7 days a week? The Web is always open; offering Web-based service some of the time may not be enough.**
- ✔ **Do I want to build this capability in-house, or will hiring an outsourcer be a better solution for me? Outsourcers have added Web customer service to their list of offerings.**
- ✔ **What level of service offering am I prepared to support—e-mail, chat, voice, cobrowsing? Each level has increasing complexity.**
- ✔ **Do I have phone reps who can be cross-trained for Web support? When writing skills weren't part of the hiring profile, a job writing e-mails and chatting may not be a good fit.**
- ✔ **How sophisticated is my customer base? Will they have microphone-equipped PCs for online chat, or do I need to be "lower tech"?**
- ✔ **How much quality control do I need over Web communications? Phone conversations are gone once you hang up, but e-mails provide a ready audit trail showing what the company said.**
- ✔ **Are my current supervisors and managers equipped to deal with multimedia? Having "techno-comfort" is important when coaching a techno-rep.**
- ✔ **Is my telephone system ready to support data as well as voice? Am I looking at an upgrade or a forklift?**
- ✔ **Does my technology allow me to use home-based Web agents? It's a great way to accommodate after-hours support needs.**
- ✔ **Am I ready to have my customer service contacts increase by 15–40 percent? Many Web interactions are incremental and don't replace a phone call.**

more when they shop online than when they do offline. A great example of applying one-to-one Web customer care for customer acquisition came from icontact and its customer, Steve Romley, Director of Marketing of CyberStateU.com.

"CyberStateU.com chose icontact.com for an e-business solution," Romley noted, "We were looking for a customer acquisition technology that would allow us to reach Web site surfers in a seamless manner. We wanted a technology that didn't make any assumptions or requirements of the end user. At the same time, we were seeking a high level of customization and integration with our existing architecture. The last thing we wanted to do would be to frustrate a customer who we are trying to assist."

icontact is the only such technology that allows e-businesses to profile their Web site traffic based on site behavior, prioritize the sales potential of surfers, proactively engage high-value surfers in a text-based conversation, and personalize one-on-one interactions, all in real time. The interaction is completely trouble-free for the end user. There are no invasive downloads, applets, or plug-ins. Web site customers are completely free to use the full functionality of their browsers to surf the site while simultaneously engaging in a conversation with a NetRep, the online customer service agent.

In October of 1999, icontact was implemented on CSU's Web site. CSU sought to filter the site traffic and set a profile for surfers searching for course information. icontact took that approach and provided CSU with the ability to distinguish the surfer with potential interest from the casual browser, engage site visitors who met their criteria, and offer those visitors assistance.

The process was simple. NetReps engaged eligible surfers in HTML-based text conversations, offering their assistance. Once a surfer responded, the NetRep would then provide the desired information to the surfer. These conversations would occur on a customized, one-on-one level. While the information provided by the NetRep could be tailored specifically to the surfer, icontact empowers CSU to employ prewritten responses to commonly asked questions. Use of such preset messages allows CSU to ensure the quality of service its customers receive from all NetReps, while at the same time providing personalized service.

Through its online interactions, CSU was able qualify the interest of potential customers and provide immediate, relevant information to the surfer, as well as to "guide" him or her through the Web site. If a surfer wanted to speak with a salesperson, the NetRep would ask for the surfer's name, phone number, and e-mail address and pass that information on to the inside sales division of CSU to conduct outbound calling.

After six months, the results are in. According to CyberstateU.com, the close rate on icontact leads is 36 percent higher than the average close rate from their other leads. Romley notes, "icontact has enabled us to reach customers on our Web site at the point at which they are evaluating our courses, qualify their interest, and pass them to our sales representatives. This has cut our normal sales cycle in half and resulted in increased efficiency by starting out with prequalified leads. The ability of our sales representatives to close deals on leads generated through icontact is second only to student referrals, and that's second out of the 125 different lead generation methods we employ."

Romley adds, "Being able to converse with surfers while they are on the site and give them timely information on the products without forcing them to guess how to access information...I think that is just crucial for any e-business."

Going forward, CSU intends to expand its utilization of the icontact solution to its partner program. CSU is actively partnering with learning portals, systems integrators, VARs, instructor-led training companies, software/hardware vendors, and content providers to bring their e-learning solutions to a global audience. Romley explains, "There is so much interest in e-learning right now, and we receive an enormous amount of requests for information about our partner program. What we really want to do is prescreen those requests. We envision using NetReps to prequalify those leads on the Web site before routing them to our business development department. With icontact, we know we can reach potential partners on our site, ensure a consistent message to our target market, provide personalized interactions, and sign more contracts." That shows how truly important quality customer care is during the acquisition phase. This can make or break an initial visit to your site.

Blurring the Lines between Sales and Service

Furniture.com uses NewChannel to help it with retention. NewChannel analyzes visitors browsing Furniture.com's Web site and determines whether they are serious prospects or casual browsers. Visitors who spend a specified amount of time on the site or visit certain pages are identified as prospects, based on the company's own criteria. Furniture.com's sales consultants can then select a prospect and issue an invitation, which "pops" up in a box on the visitor's desktop, offering the prospect a personal consultation. Visitors can either accept or decline invitations, and those who decline are flagged to help salespeople avoid issuing repeated invitations. This permission-based sales approach allows Furniture.com to protect its customers' privacy and ensure their satisfaction. "Thousands of people visit our Web site every day, so choosing the best candidates for engagement is essential to our profitability," says Brooks. "With NewChannel, we can focus the efforts of our sales staff on the most qualified prospects at the optimum time in the sales cycle, while they're visiting our virtual store."

Once an invitation is accepted, Furniture.com's sales consultants engage prospects via a new browser window, which appears automatically on the visitor's screen. Prescripted suggestions and responses help guide the consultants through the sales process, making upselling or cross-selling suggestions based on current sales promotions or on the customer's preferences for certain styles or colors. In addition, sales consultants can push information to the visitor's browser, such as photos, manufacturers' catalogs, and pricing information. They can also collaborate with customers on orders and provide comparisons of different types of furniture.

According to Brooks, most visitors are surprised and delighted at the opportunity to engage in an interactive dialogue. "Our customers love it. We get a lot of positive feedback from customers who are thrilled with the personal attention and assistance they receive on our site. It's that kind of service that builds long-term relationships and repeat business."

Web-to-Call Center Integration

It would be great if our Web sites could provide customers with all of the product and support information they need; however, many customers have unique needs that must be handled by a human. By integrating call center support into the Web site it is possible to improve the Web experience, and even generate additional revenue that might have been lost due to shopping cart abandonment. In the past, when a customer attempted to obtain service over the telephone from a call center he or she frequently waited on hold for 5, 10, and sometimes as much as 15 minutes or more. Not only does that create frustration on the part of the customer, it's also expensive to keep people on hold. Today it's possible to connect a Web customer needing service directly to a customer service representative over the Internet. A number of technologies can be used to interact with customers, such as voice, chat, and instant messaging. Each of these methods has its own benefits and challenges, so it's important to analyze your market and your resources to determine which is best for you.

Instant messaging. One of the easiest ways to add live customer service to your Web site is to use one of the popular instant messaging programs, such as ICQ or Instant Messenger. Millions of Internet users have already downloaded and installed one of these programs, so it's easy for customers to click a link on your Web site or enter the instant messaging address of your customer service operation. While these popular instant messaging programs are already installed on millions of computers, they don't provide any of the customer service features or reports found in products designed for this purpose. One of the benefits of using instant messaging technology is that a good CSR can work with multiple customers simultaneously, which increases productivity. Another benefit of using written communications in supporting customers is that there is a record of exactly what was said.

Real-time text chat. Sometimes it's desirable to allow the customer and the CSR to type messages to each other more quickly in real time. This calls for using chat technology that allows for a more highly interactive conversation. Chat products that use Java applets have become more stable over the past few years, so this technology can be used with greater confidence than when this technique was originally introduced. Commonly coupled with real-time chat is "cobrowsing," where the CSR and customer can be browsing the same Web pages at the same time. Also, CSRs can "push" Web pages to the customer and can even fill out Web-based forms for the customer while the customer is browsing.

Voice over the Internet. The newest approach to providing live customer service to Web customers is the use of a true voice conversation using VoIP technologies between the CSR and customer. A number of products and services have become available recently that make it easy for a customer to click a button on the Web site and be connected by voice to a CSR. Of course, if the customer does not have a PC equipped for multimedia the customer needs to talk to a call center rep using the traditional telephone. Even this approach can be enhanced with Web technology by allowing customers to transmit their phone number and request to be called directly to a call center rep. The use of voice over the Internet is starting to become more popular as consumers switch to faster access to the Internet. The use of cable modems and DSL connections in homes is fueling this increased interest in voice support over the Internet.

Challenges of One-to-One Web Customer Care

Implementing Web access to call center support, like many other one-to-one techniques, requires more than technology—it requires human resources as well. Some of the questions that need be answered before you can implement this type of system include the following:

- Which type of online support technology is your market prepared to accept?
- Do you need to provide around-the-clock support, or will your customers be satisfied with support only during business hours?
- Can your current call center personnel be trained to handle Web-based support?

- Can the call center in use be adapted for Web-based support?
- Should Web-based support be provided by in-house personnel or be outsourced and handled by a vendor specializing in providing this service?
- Does this system allow for home-based customer service personnel to provide support over the Internet?

The Future of One-to-One Customer Care

We predict that companies will leverage their Web-enabled self-service to give customers an even more extended view of their relationship with the company, reaching out to provide information on interactions with affiliates and partners as well. Just a small example of futuristic usage of Web customer care technologies is Bluetooth.com. Bluetooth.com uses audio, ISPs, wireless broadband, and VoIP with mobile or hand-held devices to give us a virtual assistant to speak to us and recognize voice commands.

Resources

The following sections offer lists of vendors you might consider when you begin to apply CRM in your company.

CRM/SFA Vendors

SMALL BUSINESSES

ACT!	www.act.com
GoldMine	www.frontrange.com

MEDIUM BUSINESSES

Applix	www.applix.com
Epicor	www.epicor.com
Onyx	www.onyx.com
Remedy	www.remedy.com
Sales Logix	www.saleslogix.com
Siebel	www.siebel.com

LARGE BUSINESSES

Clarify	www.clarify.com
Pegasystems	www.pegasystems.com
Siebel	www.siebel.com
PeopleSoft	www.peoplesoft.com

Organizations and Education

Customer Relationship Management Association	enterprise.supersites.net/ssnn2/crma
ITtoolbox Portal for CRM	www.crmassist.com
CRMCommunity	www.crmcommunity.com
CRM-Forum	www.crm-forum.com

Up Next

Chapter 8, "One-to-One Web Collaboration," shows how to use the Internet to communicate with prospects and customers one-to-one. Whether you need simple slide shows or real-time videoconferencing, the chapter will help you take advantage of the communications potential of the Internet.

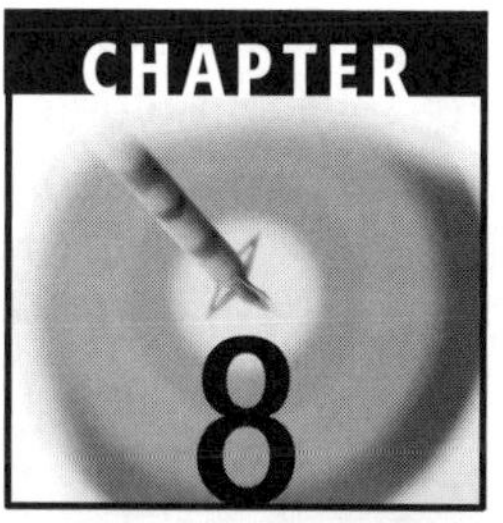

One-to-One Web Collaboration

"Man's mind, once stretched by a new idea, never regains its original dimensions."

Oliver Wendell Holmes

People have enjoyed the feeling of one-to-one communication since the beginning of time and have always looked for ways to enhance that feeling. Since AT&T demonstrated the videophone at the World's Fair in 1964, the expectation of communicating with people who are at a distance—and seeing them—has remained one of the "future" benefits of this technological age—until now.

A number of improvements in computing and communications technologies now allow us to apply one-to-one marketing concepts using real-time audio and video on the Internet. Although it is still very new and requires more coordination than just sending e-mail, the value is there now.

In their report, "Teleconferencing Markets and Strategies: From Novelty to Necessity," analysts at the market research firm Forward Concepts expect the amount of videoconferencing equipment and services to grow dramatically from the estimated $300 million in 1996 to $3 billion in 2001. Why after all these years are we seeing this level of growth? The maturity and convergence of the various technologies are now allowing the growth in online conferencing, much like the growth in PCs that was experienced in the 1980s and 1990s. The current strong demand for PCs with enhanced processor chips capable of better graphics and video shows that the market is looking for the technologies that will allow it to communicate better and faster.

The first question is "Why use multimedia when *monomedia* would work?" The answer, of course, is that the type of media used should fit the type of presentation you are making—and that depends on the audience and its needs.

This chapter helps answer questions about what multimedia technologies are available to deliver a marketing message to individuals and how to help sales and support personnel communicate directly with online users, prospects, and customers. You'll see that the blending of graphics, audio, and video allows Web marketers to make maximum use of the sometimes limited Internet bandwidth to build relationships using one-to-one Web marketing techniques.

What Is One-to-One Web Collaboration?

All new technologies require frequent review to see when they should be used in an organization. In the case of videoconferencing, the cost of installing equipment for a single location has dropped from over $10,000 to well under $1000. When compared to the travel costs of sending a person to a meeting, the lower cost of using videoconferencing produces a quick return on investment. The real challenge of deciding when to use Internet-based conferencing today is not cost, but other issues of time, content, and group dynamics.

How do you measure the value of a timely response? Most of the time it's easy—the prospect or customer says he or she needs information *now*, and your experts are located in multiple locations. Telephone conference calls can meet most of these needs for focused information, but Web conferencing can enhance many of the electronic meetings we have now and replace some of the one-on-one presentations without losing the personal communications dynamics.

In the 1980s and early 1990s, 3M sponsored research conducted by the Wharton Center for Applied Research and the University of Minnesota's Management Information Systems Research Center. The research indicates the value of using dynamic presentation materials to help an audience understand the presenter's material.

- When visual aids are used in a presentation, the audience remembers as much as 10 percent more of the information presented.
- Using visual aids can reduce the length of the average meeting by as much as 28 percent.
- Using visual aids increases audience attention (7.5 percent) and comprehension (8.5 percent).

With the various technologies available today for audio, video, and collaboration using the Internet, the type of interaction and its content are key determiners of what technology to use. Gregg Keizer described the new possibilities of using the Internet for meetings in his article, "Meeting of the Minds" (CNET, 5/21/97):

> And while at one time accomplishing this teamwork required you to spend four hours in a stuffy conference room sitting next to a smelly guy named Vinnie, the Internet has shattered that shackle. Net-based conferencing software lets you take part in group meetings from the comfort of your own desk, from whatever corner of the world you happen to be in. You can collect opinions from several people simultaneously, throw ideas on a whiteboard, work on shared documents, type chatty comments back and forth, and even watch the Young Turks smirk while they trash others' ideas.

While it's obvious that the public setting of online conferencing should not be used to criticize others, this technology can be used very effectively in certain key situations:

- Audio and video can be used together, with a presenter responding to questions from the audience.
- Group brainstorming is enhanced by seeing calculated results of scenarios displayed instantly.
- Collaboration of a group strengthens development of a document (text, tabular, or graphic).
- Training on the use of computer-based systems is improved with immediate feedback and participation.

In their book, *Net Gain* (Harvard Business School Press, 1997), John Hagel and Arthur Armstrong discuss how virtual communities can reshape companies:

> Within businesses, they [virtual communities] may improve management effectiveness by speeding up the emergence of "communities of process" that link together cross-functional teams that are focused on the same set of business processes...The answer in the past was to get all the relevant managers together for meetings. In practice this led to organizational paralysis, as capable managers spent hours in meetings where their contribution could have been limited to minutes. Applying the principle of the virtual community to this problem by establishing electronic billboards and meeting areas, supplemented by e-mail and even videoconferencing facilities that allow people to communicate electronically without leaving their desks, could reinforce informal networks that already exist and strengthen integration across organizational divides.

This idea can also be applied to relationships with prospects, customers, and suppliers. It doesn't take too much imagination to figure out the benefits of bringing people together using the Internet and its conferencing capabilities.

Types of Presentations

Let's make sure that we know the type of presentation we are making so we can make effective choices for media, content, and presentation. In his book, *Effective Business and Technical Presentations* (Addison-Wesley, 1975), George Morrisey describes many techniques for effective communications, but he first sets the stage, so to speak, by describing four types of presentations commonly used to motivate an audience:

Persuasive. Selling an audience on the credibility of the material in order for the audience to feel that the material is worthwhile (i.e., worth its time and worthy of its belief). This form of presentation is used to *sell* members of the audience on believing the material being presented so that they will *act* on that belief. This *action* could be investing time to research a product, persuade others in their organization, or actually buy the product being presented. The commonality for all of these objectives is for an action to be taken by the audience. The persuasive form of communicating on the Web is most applicable for helping visitors feel that your products are *exactly* what they need.

Explanatory. Providing a general familiarization of the topic being presented, sometimes used to present information about recent developments, new products, or other new information. Here, the primary objective is *not* to try to sell a product, but rather to provide the audience with new or renewed knowledge and understanding and problem solving. This works well on a Web site for strengthening a one-to-one relationship with customers who already know the value of your products but are looking for additional information.

Instructional. Teaching the audience about how to use a tool, process, or procedure. This requires greater involvement on the part of the audience than other types of presentations. With Web-based training, you can engender your company to customers by providing personalized training on demand, wherever they are in the world.

Briefing. Bringing the audience up to date on a topic it is already familiar with. This type of presentation may or may not involve heavy detail, based on the needs and interests of the specific audience. The wide range of Web-based multimedia techniques available can be used to strengthen the one-to-one relationships between partners, whether those partnerships are with customers or vendors.

The recent trend in companies to adopt Internet-based *collaborative* techniques builds on Morrisey's explanatory type of presentation and becomes an effective approach to actually getting work done, which we'll see later in this chapter when we cover the latest collaborative tools.

Benefits of One-to-One Web Collaboration

Throughout this book, we've covered techniques and technologies that can provide words written by one individual to be sent to another individual (plus the associated graphics, audio files, etc.). In this chapter we help you integrate audio, video, document sharing, and project management into your one-to-one Web marketing in order to help you build relationships, provide information more quickly, and satisfy the needs of your audience.

First, let's define your audiences and who can benefit from the different Web-based multimedia technologies. In the world of the Web there are, in general, two types of Web sites: content Web sites and marketing Web sites. While content sites market their material and marketing sites have content, Table 8.1 shows that the general distinction is that content Web sites provide information that leads to other Web sites that sell products.

Content Web sites have the same dilemma that other news media organizations face: how to attract an audience that will eventually leave the media presentation and go buy the advertiser's products, then later return to the media's presentation for more news and information! The other almost schizophrenic characteristic of content media is the need to serve two masters: advertisers and the audience.

Table 8.1 Characteristics of Content Web Sites versus Marketing Web Sites

ATTRIBUTES	CONTENT WEB SITES	MARKETING WEB SITES
Articles with links to other Web sites	Yes	No
Advertising links to other Web sites	Yes	No
Comparison of different products	Yes	No
Product description sheets	No	Yes
Products available for sale	No	Yes

Web marketers whose goal is to sell products that meet customers' needs face similar challenges, but the path to success is somewhat more straightforward because a product company's audiences are the following:

- Prospects
- Customers
- Employees
- Vendors
- The financial community

Each of these audiences has different interests, needs, goals, and—something that is important in one-to-one Web marketing—relatively short attention spans!

As one-to-one Web marketers, we need to take all of these—plus the benefits and constraints of the technologies—into consideration when creating multimedia material for Web marketing.

Table 8.2 shows how the depth of content and amount of interaction enter into your decision on what type of multimedia technology will help you effectively convey your message.

Prospects

Individuals who are gathering information about your products and services move from a general information-gathering state to a very specific questioning state. In fact, when the purchase price is high, the amount of presale technical information you need to provide is much greater than for less expensive products. In addition, the number of people involved at a prospect's organization increases when the impact on their organization is high.

One of the ways you can minimize your sales expenses while providing personalized, real-time answers to prospects is to conduct meetings and conferences using the Internet. For years, McGraw-Hill has published its research results on the cost of an in-person sales call to demonstrate the value of advertising. Recent studies show the cost is approaching $500 for each sales call. As the number of sales calls needed to make a sale increases, the pressure mounts to reduce time and costs.

Table 8.2 Use of Content and Interaction in Types of Presentations

DEPTH OF CONTENT	CONTENT	INTERACTION
High	Persuasive presentation	Low interaction
Low	Collaboration	High interaction

Prospective customers have a set of needs that are very different from those of other groups with which your company communicates because they know the least about your products and have the least commitment to buying them. While other groups might give you a second chance to communicate clearly, prospects need to be led through the process of learning about you in terms to which they can relate.

If you've seen an audience in a dark room slowly sink in their seats as the speaker drones on and on about a mundane topic, then you've experienced the compete antithesis of dynamic one-to-one marketing!

One of the reasons audiences have a hard time keeping their attention focused on speakers is that presentations aren't customized for each individual in real time, nor do they take the audience's needs into consideration or match the presentation technique to the needs of each individual.

Customers

Customers who buy from one supplier over and over are the life's blood of most corporations because the cost of selling to an existing customer is much less than the cost of obtaining a new one.

Customers who have purchased your product or service need more detailed information than prospects in order for them to use your products better—and this allows you to grow the relationship.

Most industries have experienced changes in how products are sold and distributed. More time is being required to provide personalized service to customers in order to maintain the relationship and help ensure that future orders will be received. This has traditionally meant that salespeople and their support people have been spending more time making smaller sales.

This trend has sales managers looking for ways to increase the efficiency of their sales team. One-to-one marketing techniques are being explored in both new sales and customer support.

Vendors

One of the support groups your company depends on is its vendors. Each company has its own way of dealing with vendors, but with today's economy it's important to develop "partner" relationships with vendors. This means you need to update vendors on your needs and help them understand how they can effectively help you meet your challenges.

With the growth of electronic data interchange (EDI), which connects the purchasing computer of one company to the order entry computer of another, it's becoming important for the employees of both to develop ways to work well together.

Steve Young, director of the electronic commerce research program at INPUT, a Mountain View, California-based research firm, has observed that the industry is composed of established EDI companies, who are all pretty aggressive and technologically astute, but growing at quite handsome rates according to most standards—25–35 percent—and then you've got this enormous tidal wave of the Internet companies moving ahead at much faster growth rates and with a history behind them of much quicker adoption of standards.

The growing reliance on vendors as partners requires a new level of information sharing. With vendors using the Internet to transmit orders, it's clear that the Internet can be used to allow people at both vendor and customer locations to update each other. The types of communications that can help two companies coordinate their activities include research updates, new product briefings, sales training seminars, prospect presentations, customer training, and project coordination.

Nuts and Bolts of One-to-One Collaboration

With the combination of Internet technologies for making presentations and traditional multimedia presentation technologies, one of the early challenges is in selecting the right technology for the right audience. As Tim Tully points out in his survey of presentation tools ("Net-Savvy Tools for Dynamic Presentations," *Netguide*, May 1997):

> These tools allow you to bolster your presentations with live links to the Net. For example, by clicking on a button, you can dynamically update those humble pie charts with information from your database back at headquarters. Or you can prepare relevant bookmarks ahead of time and seamlessly transition to the Web to glean additional information.

Many of us like to use the "latest and greatest" presentation tool to wow the audience, but there are times when a tool gets in the way of the message. Web-based presentation tools range from the simplest approach to complex, real-time video extravaganzas—slides, near-real-time video images, streaming video with audio, Internet telephony, and videoconferencing.

A basic approach that can help you decide which technology to use is to compare the strength of the need for the information on the part of the individual with the effort he or she must go through to obtain that information. In the case of viewing static Web pages, the effort is next to none. Compare this to the effort required to download and install a plug-in in order to participate in a videoconference. When considering the technology, consider the appropriateness to the specific audience by applying George Morrisey's "six A's" for selecting the appropriate technique:

Audibility or visibility. Can the use of audio or video enhance the message?

Accessibility or availability. Can members of the audience access the presentation?

Adaptability. Does the presentation technique enhance some particular point you are making?

Appropriateness. Does the technique match the subject (e.g., audio to sell music CDs, video to highlight a DNA string, interactivity to conform audience attentiveness)?

Arresting quality. Will the presentation technique gain attention and keep it on the subject matter rather than on the technique itself?

Auxiliary nature. Does the presentation technique strengthen the message?

Applying Morrisey's "six A's" to your selection of the right technology for effective one-to-one Web marketing requires applying the right combination of interaction and depth of material. Table 8.3 shows our recommendations for the technology appropriate for a particular type of presentation to a particular audience.

As we've seen, the right technology can enhance meetings by encouraging one-to-one communications, so let's take a look at the different types of Web-based presentation technologies for one-to-one Web marketers.

Table 8.3 Communication Technologies and Appropriate Target Audiences

	PROSPECTS	CUSTOMERS	EMPLOYEES	VENDORS	FINANCIAL COMMUNITY
Slides	Sales presentation	Briefing	Training		
Telephone		Support			
Audio	Promotion		News	News	News
Images (Web cameras)	Information	Information	Status		
Streaming	Promotion	Training	Training		News video
Video-conferencing	Large complex			Briefing	Briefing

Using Slides on the Net

One of the easiest ways to incorporate "multimedia" into your presentations is to take advantage of those existing presentations in your library!

For the last few years, most business presentations have been created in presentation design programs such as Microsoft's PowerPoint or one of its competitors. Most of these programs have some way—although it is not always easy—to convert these for use on the Web.

We've all seen presentations that are made up of still-frame slides with an individual presenting to a single person or an audience, using a standard telephone line to present the speech portion of the presentation. Why not use the Internet for the audio? Most of the occasions when you want to present a set of slides will involve an audience that does not want to go to any extra effort to view your Internet-based presentation, and the Internet connection is likely to be no higher than 56 kbps. In order to keep the presentation looking good and moving quickly, you won't want to try to combine displaying pages and audioconferencing on the Internet.

A better approach is to use an ordinary telephone connection for the audio portion of your presentation. Just arrange for a speakerphone in the room with the audience and a computer with a connection to the Internet. You'll be in constant touch with the audience and can utilize good one-to-one Web marketing techniques to build your relationship with the audience. This use of two technologies is more reliable and flexible than stressing one technology to its fullest potential. Keep in mind how to create a fast, seamless communication setting.

Products for Producing Presentations

Now let's look at two of the more popular presentation programs used to create slides for use on the Web.

Microsoft PowerPoint

Recent versions of Microsoft's product (www.microsoft.com) allow you to save presentations in HTML format. It creates both a graphical version of what's seen on the screen and a text-only version. Figure 8.1 shows a typical example of the graphical version that includes a mini-screen shot of the whole slide with navigation graphics to move forward and backward in the presentation.

The text version of converted PowerPoint slides is not much better because the default template doesn't use any art to enhance the look of the slide. When planning to convert a number of PowerPoint presentations for use on the Web, consider modifying the default text template to make

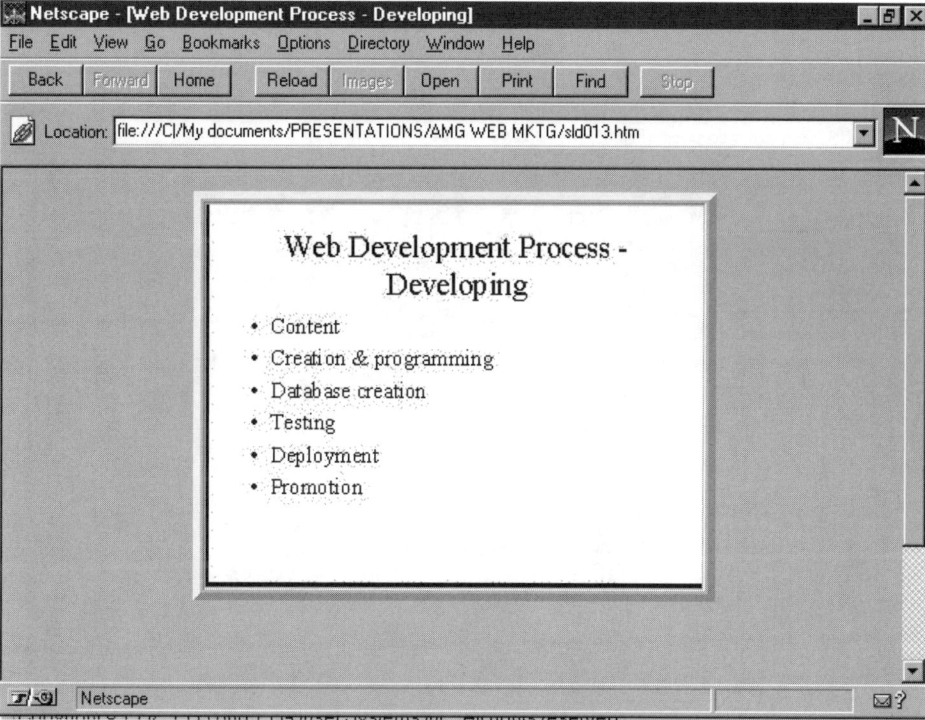

Figure 8.1 PowerPoint slide for the Web using a standard graphical template.

slides that are more professional and more like your original slides. Figure 8.2 shows one of our training slides that has been converted to HTML using a modified version of the template file. Notice how the heading and bullets fill the window. In addition, these bullets can easily be turned into links that access other Web pages.

Astound

Astound (www.astound.com) has been used for many years to create high-end presentations, but recent enhancements to PowerPoint have eroded this product's appeal in the market for most business presentations. The company has enhanced its high-end products to make them more powerful and more attractive for creating fancy Web presentations.

In order to use traditional Astound presentations on the Web, you can use the Astound tools to place presentations on a Web page to be viewed by other Web users. The product formats the presentation for Web playback by breaking the file into small files that load while the project plays, so it begins quickly.

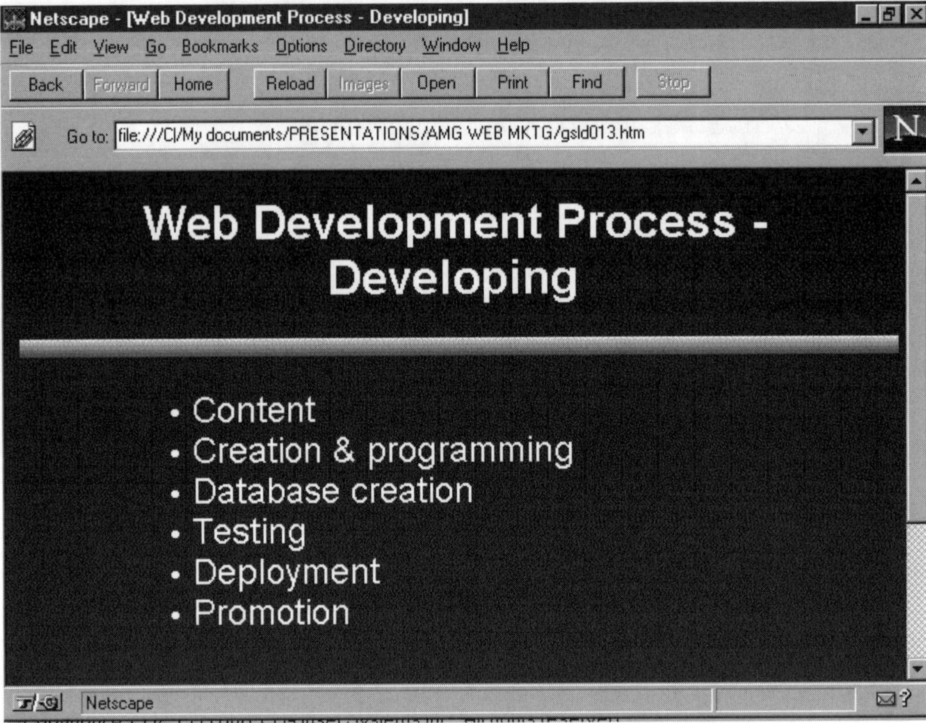

Figure 8.2 PowerPoint slide for the Web using a modified text format.

Examples of Presentations on the Web

There are many PowerPoint presentations on the Web—a search with AltaVista (www.altavista.com) lists more than 4000 slide presentations in its database. Here are some examples of presentations available on various Web sites that can give you an idea of how they look to an audience:

- To view a variety of slides used by Mark Gallagher to help companies understand intranets, visit www.gallagher.com (see Figure 8.3).
- Conferences and trade shows on the Internet are the topic of this presentation on the Web site of Lehman Associates, a consulting firm. Visit www.ansible.com/asae1296/sld001.htm.

Using a Web Camera

One of the most popular ways to incorporate video on your Web site is with "semi-real-time" video, showing frequent updates of a live video feed

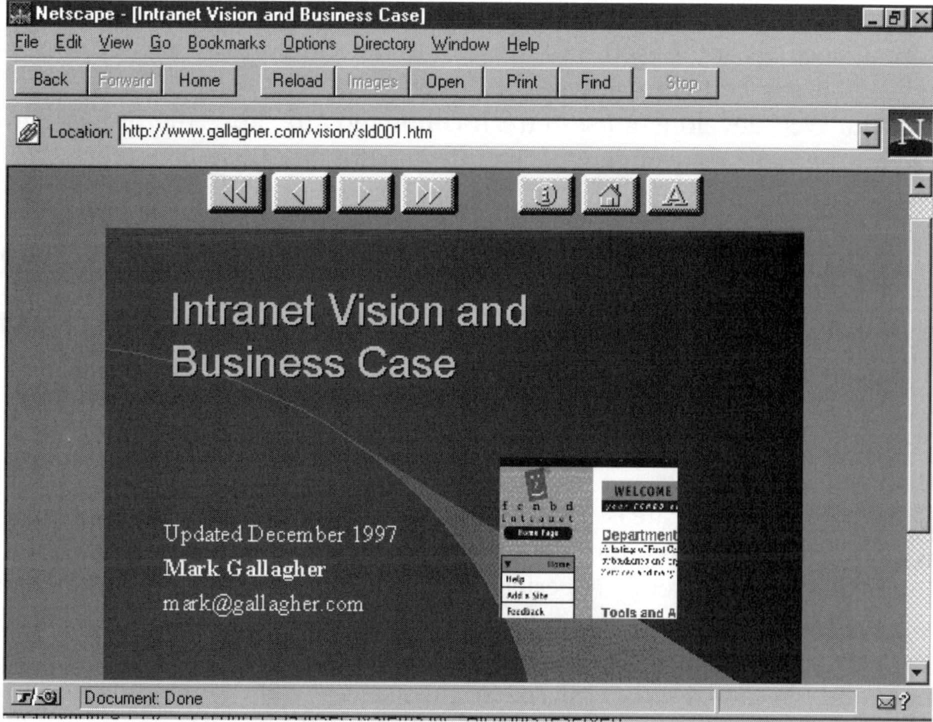

Figure 8.3 Mark Gallagher's opening slide about intranet usage.

from a changing scene. As one-to-one Web marketers look for ways to communicate directly with an audience, we need to remember to give them just what they're looking for!

If you're looking for a way to get started with video but don't want to invest in producing video programming and publishing it with a video server, a *Web Cam* can get you started.

Technology Overview of Web Cameras

Until recently, the process of connecting cameras to a Web site involved custom software and complex electronics. Now a number of off-the-shelf products make using Web cameras very easy.

The technology needed to display instantaneous photos on the Web requires two pieces: Web server software and a camera that is designed to respond to requests from the Web software. Many of the video cameras on the market require the use of a *video capture board* in the PC that can convert video into the digital files we are accustomed to using when creating Web sites.

The software that runs on the Web server is designed to receive requests for images from the browser and then send a signal to the camera requesting an image. The camera then takes the current image, converts it into the format needed for the Web, and passes it to the software on the Web server where it is served to the browser.

Some Web developers use refresh commands to cause the browser to request periodic refreshment of the image automatically, while other Web managers prefer to serve images only once per visit.

Web Cameras Helping Tourism Industry

Tourist destinations that depend on favorable weather conditions are using Web cameras to provide customers with a look at actual conditions at their locations. By providing tourists with an actual look at up-to-the-minute conditions at their locations they are able to provide better information than weather forecasts.

For seasonal resort areas, live cameras showing the current weather are a real boon to the local economy. For the North Carolina Outer Banks area, the tourist industry frequently experiences a significant number of cancellations when a hurricane is reported in the Atlantic. By providing a current look at the beach (www.rsn.com/cams/hattys/), along with current weather conditions and forecasts, tourists can see for themselves when a hurricane is actually approaching or will not affect their vacation plans.

The Resort Sports Network (www.rsn.com) has a number of other Resort Cam Web pages that show how many resort areas around the country look at any given time.

Web Camera Products

There is a wide range of products available to display still images on a Web site, from inexpensive cameras designed for the Web to near broadcast-quality cameras. In this section, we've chosen to focus on an inexpensive camera and software combination that is proven to work well together, leaving the high-end products for the videoconferencing section later in the chapter.

Logitech

One of the most popular low-cost cameras used to create video on the Web is the QuickCam (www.logitech.com). While the quality of the image created with the QuickCam is not as high as that of professional video cameras, the under-$300 cost makes it very affordable.

Installation of the QuickCam is easier than that of other cameras because the PC version connects to the parallel port (the Macintosh version connects to the serial port). This means that no special video board is required, so you save the cost of adding a board to your system.

Webcam 32

Webcam32 (www.surveyorcorp.com/webcam32/) is a Windows 95/NT application that allows video camera images to be displayed within a Web page. This product can deliver images to your Web audience in a number of ways, such as publishing periodic updates to a Web page or continuously pushing images to users.

Webcam 32 can provide instantaneous images on the server, or it can be configured to show only the last image it uploaded, so it works in a wide variety of environments.

Examples of Web Cameras

It will be helpful to experience Web cameras so that you can understand their value in one-to-one Web marketing. Here is a list of a few *sights to see* on the Web:

- The Arizona Department of Transportation wants you to see the traffic situation, such as this Web camera showing Durango Curve—watch out, partner! Visit www.azfms.com/Images/Cameras/camera33.html.
- Want to know what's shaking in Los Angeles? When the Earth moves in Southern California, you can see it live on the NBC 4 Seismo-Cam. Visit www.nbc4la.com/tvsd/seismo.
- If you are planning a vacation—or want to remember one—take a look at Front Street, Lahaina, Maui, Hawaii. Visit www.mauigateway.com/~video/.

Using Streaming Video on the Web

Because we live in a TV age it's natural for marketers as well as Web users to expect that video will be the next big technology to become available. The difficulty, of course, is in overcoming the bandwidth limitations of today's Internet and the modem speeds used by many people. This makes it important to consider not only the value of video to convey your message, but also the bandwidth available to members of your audience. Some of the uses for video include training materials, news broadcasts, and product demonstrations.

Technology Overview

The first few videos used on the Web were large files that needed to be completely downloaded before they could be viewed. Once the technique of *streaming audio* became a proven technology, companies went to work on applying the same technique to video so that motion could be viewed as the file is being downloaded.

When video files were just downloaded and played locally, a variety of network problems were hidden because a five-minute increase in download time from 30 minutes to 35 minutes wasn't very noticeable. With streaming video, those delays could cause havoc with the program. Part of the solution is to compress the files by identifying repeating patterns and sending each pattern only once, but that doesn't solve all of the problems.

In his white paper "Broadcasting Video on the World Wide Web," Tom Arnold provides a detailed explanation of the difficulty of producing and distributing streaming video on the Web (www.inproduction.com)—for example, the amount of data being sent, network traffic, and the speed of users' computers and connections.

After the technical challenges of compression have been dealt with, the other two challenges deal with the variability of the Internet to deliver a continuous flow of data. The original design of the Internet allowed small groups of data, called "packets," to move through the network of computers at whatever speed the network would allow. That was okay when the Internet was used primarily for e-mail because it didn't matter if an e-mail message was delayed a few seconds (or in some cases, a few minutes). Now that we're trying to push a continuous stream of data, it's critical that the flow of video frames be seen as continuous.

How is this done? The same way that most municipal water systems deliver water today—accumulate water in storage tanks during low usage and empty the tanks during high consumption.

With streaming video, the storage tank is a temporary storage buffer at the viewer's computer. The trick, of course, is to store enough in the buffer so that the display is continuous, but not so much that it takes too long to start displaying the video. Each streaming video product has its own way to adjust the speed, balance of audio versus video, buffer, and other factors that make each product unique.

Streaming Video Products

The streaming video products available to serve video on your Web site generally have three major components: a creation software tool, Web video server software, and browser plug-in software.

There are two leading suppliers of streaming video products:

- RealVideo (www.real.com)
- Microsoft Media Player (www.microsoft.com)

Examples of Streaming Video on the Web

As we've discussed, the lack of bandwidth for most Internet users to deliver full 30-frame-per-second (television quality) video makes the use of streaming video for marketing somewhat difficult.

At the present time, streaming video is used mostly by content providers, those journalistic Web sites that provide the news, information, and entertainment that allow the rest of us to see the innovative edge of what can be done today. You can find hundreds of sites listed at various online directories, such as these:

- Real Networks (realguide.real.com)
- Yahoo Broadcast (www.broadcast.com)

Internet Telephony

Using the Internet to carry voice conversations has had its share of appeal but, until recently, has been slow to take off. Now that standards have been adopted and vendors have begun selling second-generation VON (voice over the Internet) products, voice over the Internet is becoming much more doable.

Benefits of Internet Telephony

The most striking benefit of using the Internet to deliver telephone-type audio conversations is the lower cost. Companies that can install compatible equipment in remote offices are already reducing long distance charges. As these companies install products adhering to international protocols, conversations between companies via the Internet will become commonplace.

Technology Overview

The basic technologies used with Internet telephony combine the analog-to-digital techniques similar to those of music CDs with the file compression technologies used for years to reduce file transfer time.

While compressing files to maximize the amount of information transferred over the Internet is a big challenge, a larger challenge is managing network delays inherent in the Internet. Because data travels over the Internet in small *packets*, as opposed to a continuous stream of data, there are frequent pauses and delays. The technique that has been used to overcome these pauses and delays is to *buffer* data, filling a reservoir of packets that are then used at a constant rate. When the Internet causes delays in packets arriving, the buffer is drained until it is empty (which causes the pause). Of course, storing more packets in the buffer to reduce pauses causes a delay in content reaching the receiver, so the size of the buffer needs to be adjusted dynamically, based on the speed of the Internet at that particular moment.

Fortunately, new research and new standards are being developed to help eliminate this problem. The voice-compression algorithm used in VON applications known as the G.723.1 standard is being used in several telecommunications applications, including private networks.

Now that a standard is in place, router manufacturers are creating prioritization schemes to give voice traffic higher priority. The developing Resource Reservation Protocol (RSVP) standard will allow gateways to negotiate with routers between end points to reserve bandwidth for a particular voice session. Because this will require new network hardware to be designed, manufactured, and installed, it will be some time before the Internet will be ready to move streaming traffic faster than ordinary traffic (e.g., e-mail, Web, etc.).

Internet Telephony Products

Internet telephony products include products that connect people when one or both people are using the Internet. Some products just connect two individuals, and a new category of products is starting to arrive on the market that handles the switching usually performed by corporate PBX systems.

Jeff Pulver's Voice over the Net Web site (www.pulver.com) has a continually updated list of Internet telephony products, but you can start by reviewing the following products to get an idea of what is available:

- Internet Phone from VocalTec (www.vocaltec.com)
- Intel Internet Phone from Intel Corp (www.intel.com)

Videoconferencing on the Internet

We've all been enamored with the stars we see on television, so it's no wonder that we want to see ourselves on television, too. While today's videoconferencing can't deliver broadcast-quality video without tremendous expense, we can experience conversations with people, individually or as a group, that are as productive as face-to-face meetings.

In the past, dedicated videoconferencing systems were so expensive that they were usually installed in conference rooms that could be used by a large number of employees. Equipment compatibility restricted who you could talk to, so most videoconferencing was done within a company.

In addition to corporate meetings within a company, other typical uses of these dedicated videoconferencing facilities have been in health care, where doctors consult with patients in another location, and distance learning, where students can watch an instructor in a centralized facility.

Technology Overview

Videoconferencing technology can be divided two ways: the type of use and the equipment needed to implement it.

Until recently, desktop videoconferencing products could display only one other location on the screen, which limited its use to a little more than a telephone call—hardly a group collaboration technology.

Recent advances in desktop videoconferencing technology now allow what's sometimes called "continuous presence," which is the ability to handle audio and video channels from multiple locations. These signals are mixed by a videoconference server and sent to all participants so that everyone can be heard and seen at the same time on the screen. Steve Nill, chief financial officer of VideoServer, Inc., says continuous presence is just one advance that will help bring about large-scale acceptance of videoconferencing.

An additional technology that has been added to videoconferencing products is the ability to experience the use of a computer application by all participants in the conference. By displaying the changing elements of a computer window—including mouse movements—and allowing each participant to control the application being run, members of the audience can become involved in ways that have not been possible in the past.

Standards for Videoconferencing

Advances in computer design are just one reason for today's popularity of videoconferencing. Another reason for acceptance is the use of standards for handling audio and video data over multiple types of networking systems.

For instance, the International Telecommunication Union, an international telecommunications organization, has helped set standards that many manufacturers and software companies are agreeing to use. The standard, called H.324, establishes how videoconferencing will take place over standard telephone lines. And, yes, there is a generally accepted acronym for plain old telephone service—POTS.

In order to videoconference with multiple locations, vendors have agreed to use the H.323 standard, which covers Internet videoconferencing. So, with H.323 and H.324, videoconferencing has taken a new turn to pull people together.

If you're looking for a few more acronyms to toss out at the next party of people who couldn't gather over a videoconference, try saying that you look for high QoS and then explain that that means *Quality of Service*. And if the guy next to you tries to one-up you and starts talking about things like G.711, H.263, or the old H.320 standard, just remind him that they all got rolled up into the H.323 and H.324 standards.

Equipment for Videoconferencing

Now that we have the standards out of the way, let's talk about cameras ("Makeup, get the shine off this guy's head") and how they're connected to the computer screen at the other end of the line. In general, the products needed at each location for a videoconference include a camera, video capture board in the PC, videoconference software, and an Internet connection. High-end video cameras need to be connected to a specialized video capture board that converts the video signal into the digital signal that can be transmitted by the videoconference software to compatible (thank goodness for standards) software at another location.

As we saw earlier in the chapter in the section on Web cameras, not all cameras require a specialized video capture board. The QuickCam plugs into the parallel port of PCs (the Macintosh version connects to the serial port), so it doesn't need a video capture board.

Evaluating Products for Internet Videoconferencing

The number of products on the market today for use in videoconferencing using ordinary telephone lines as well as the Internet is growing. Some of the products are individual pieces that need to be combined with other products; some products are sold as complete systems.

In addition, not all videoconferencing products have all of the features—or support all of the standards—that you may need, so here are a few features to keep in mind when evaluating these products:

Audio-only versus audio and video. Some conferencing products support sharing of applications, whiteboards, and other handy features, but they don't support video. If video is important, make sure it's included.

Interaction with other brands. While manufacturers may say they support certain standards, their products may or may not work well with products from other manufacturers. Until interaction with other brands becomes common, be sure to evaluate which products are compatible.

Ease of setup. Plan for how you will install and set up equipment at each of your company's locations, as well as those of your customers who will be using the system. Sometimes the extra cost of complete turnkey systems is outweighed by the savings in time and resources to install systems across an enterprise.

Multiperson conference. Some videoconference products allow for multiple people to participate in text-only "chats" without video or audio, while other products support full multiperson videoconferences (splitting the screen into multiple views).

Application sharing. Allowing the audience to see how a particular computer program looks as a presenter uses it gives the audience a real sense of interacting without having to overcome the initial concern about training everyone. Some videoconference products allow for easy sharing of practically any computer application (i.e., software program), while others require each location to have a copy of the shared program installed.

Collaboration. Whiteboard sharing of applications and notes is one of the most valuable features of videoconferencing, but it is handled in different ways by different vendors.

As you can see, evaluating videoconference products requires careful consideration of the features you will need now, as well as those in the near term, in order for your trials and full implementation to be successful. When starting to evaluate Internet-based videoconferencing, please visit our companion site, *One-to-One Web Marketing* Online (www.1to1web.com), for new and updated information and resources.

Software Products for Internet Videoconferencing

Now let's discuss some examples of the software products on the market and take a brief look at their distinctive features.

CUseeMe

Originally developed and provided by Cornell University (thus, the CU) and now available as a commercial product from CUseeMe Networks (www.cuseeme.com), CUseeMe was the first popular Internet product to allow for multipoint audioconferencing and videoconferencing.

NetMeeting

Microsoft (www.microsoft.com) has provided NetMeeting free of charge on its Web site for some time and has generated a considerable user base experienced in using this product. It has the most popular features used in business today—audio, video, file transfer, chat, application sharing, and whiteboard—so it meets the needs of many people looking to conference over the Internet. The product is available only for the Windows platforms, so take that into consideration.

Hardware Products for Internet Videoconferencing

Here are some examples of more hardware-based products, some of which include computers, cameras, and everything you need for plug-and-play installations.

ProShare

The Intel ProShare Video System (www.intel.com) is a PC-based desktop videoconferencing solution that brings full video, audio, and data conferencing capabilities to business PC users. It works over ISDN phone lines, LAN connections, or broadband Internet connections. The technology complies with H.320, H.323, and T.120 interoperability standards.

Internet Video Phone

The Intel Internet Video Phone allows Internet users to see and talk to each other while using other Internet applications, such as browsing the Web. The Intel Internet Video Phone works on Pentium processor-based PCs running the Windows, and it complies with the ITU H.323 interoperability standard.

Complete Videoconference Systems

Complete videoconference systems that include the computer, monitor, camera, and other equipment save time and reduce the opportunity for misconfiguration. The three complete systems discussed next illustrate the type of products available.

Intel's TeamStation

Intel's TeamStation system, a PC-based multifunction videoconferencing solution, delivers video/audio/data conferencing and presentation capabilities, plus Internet and corporate network access. The Intel TeamStation system's standard configuration includes a 233 MHz Pentium II processor, Intel ProShare technology, and an auto-tracking, high-resolution camera. The TeamStation system supports the H.320, H.323, and T.120 international communication standards, as well as Microsoft Net Meeting for interoperability.

PictureTel's LiveLAN

The LiveLAN videoconferencing system (www.picturetel.com) works on corporate LANs and delivers full-screen and full-motion video. It runs on a Pentium PC running Windows and is H.323 and T.120 standard compliant. Like other complete solutions, it provides for data collaboration, application sharing, shared whiteboard, file transfer, and messaging. And because LiveLAN's application sharing is interoperable with Microsoft's Net Meeting, you can conference with Net Meeting users in your LAN.

PolyCom's ShowStation IP

ShowStation IP (www.polycom.com) allows for both formal and ad hoc Web presentations involving 10 multipoint conferences. ShowStation IP can connect to any number of remote sites that have either a ShowStation or a PC via the Internet, an existing corporate intranet, or ordinary analog phone lines. Conference participants at any number of sites can use ShowStation IP's electronic pen to write, draw, highlight, or erase on the unit's display just as with an overhead transparency, and all notes and comments are immediately visible at all sites simultaneously. ShowStation IP supports common software such as Microsoft's Net Meeting, which allows users to load and store presentations directly from the ShowStation IP's floppy disk drive. ShowStation IP also supports printing of the presentation and can read Microsoft Office files.

Videoconferencing Service

When you need special features that are part of the network itself, such as encryption or extremely high speeds, then an outside service may be the best solution.

Group Conferencing for Training

The high cost of in-person training is causing many companies to look more closely at using Internet-based training techniques.

Cisco Systems, the leading provider of Internet routers (the devices that decide which path to take through the maze of possible Internet connections), faces the challenges of growth and training everyone on their new technologies. The audiences they communicate with start with prospects, customers, and market analysts and include everyone inside the company—from salespeople to engineers and manufacturing personnel.

While their internal television network provides the capability for real-time broadcasts, their training needs extend beyond the set schedule that is inherent in live broadcasts.

By allowing a person to select the material, the time of delivery, and the location of delivery, one-to-one communication is put in the hands of the individual.

Videoconferencing with Prospective Customers

One of the benefits of the work to make videoconferencing equipment compatible with multiple standards is the ability to have conferences using the Internet and ordinary telephone lines (POTS), depending on the need.

For example, Mentor Graphics is using Intel's ProShare conferencing systems at its trade shows to increase customer communication and to "bring the factory to the conference." At a recent trade show, Mentor used videoconferencing systems in its product demo suites so that qualified customers could communicate directly with the software developers at the company headquarters.

Videoconferencing with Customers

There are many opportunities to use videoconferencing to interact with customers to provide better customer service and reduce costs; however, each of these opportunities must be approached with care. It is important to understand how customers feel about replacing in-person experiences with videoconferencing experiences.

Conferencing within an Organization

One of the easiest approaches to introducing videoconferencing is to use it within an organization where you have control over the computing environment and the training and support environments.

By using videoconferencing within an organization, you gain experience with the many technologies involved, and you have an opportunity to understand how people interact with these systems.

Using Online Project Management

Online collaboration involves more than just holding meetings using the latest audio or video technology. Most people collaborate over the Internet with other members of their project team to share documents, project plans, or ideas about the project.

E-mail can be used with small groups to send project notes and distribute documents via e-mail attachments. Mailing list software and Web forums have also been used by some teams to maintain contact. Most project teams with more than just a few people, though, can benefit by using one of the online project management Web sites. These sites are more than just group calendars because they provide enhanced features and functions that help a project manager actually manage tasks, resources, and schedules.

For example, PlanPack (www.planpack.com) is a free Web-based project planning tool that uses a program/project/task approach:

- Programs are ongoing groups of projects.
- Projects are groups of tasks that end with a well-defined deliverable.
- Tasks are short-term work items that are assigned to a particular person.

PlanPack is a collaborative tools that combines the assignments from multiple project managers into a prioritized "to do" list for each person. Figure 8.4 shows a task list for an individual who has been assigned tasks by two project managers.

In addition to PlanPack, a number of fee-based sites are available for project managers, such as OnProject (www.onproject.com) and eProject (www.eproject.com).

Applying One-to-One Web Collaboration

Each of the technologies we've explored relies on the same basic communication need: Move information into the minds of individuals in your audience. This communications need hasn't changed over the ages, but our understanding of how to impart information has grown. Human factors research has identified a number of details about how the human brain absorbs information.

In his book, *Multimedia Authoring* (Academic Press, 1994), Scott Fisher reviews the findings of research into developing interactive presentations

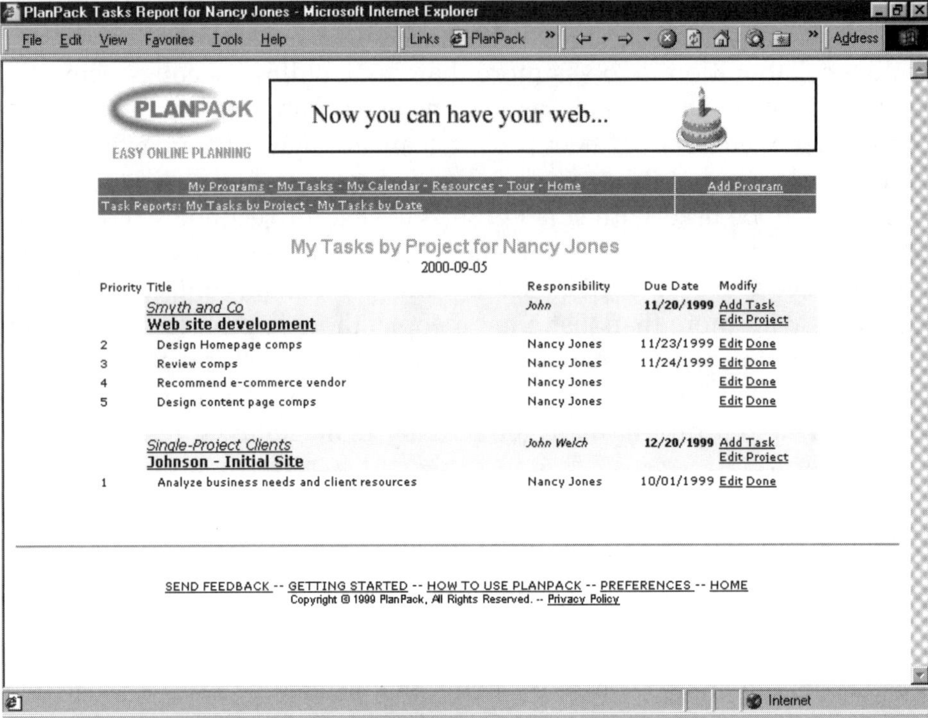

Figure 8.4 PlanPack task list by project priority.

that truly communicate. He lists several key points to consider when you create your presentation:

- Most people can keep track of 5 items of information in short-term memory.
- The length of time these 5 items can be retained is about 15 to 30 seconds.
- Short-term memory works best when the information is in the form of visual and textual material.

These concepts have different impacts in different types of presentations. For example, prospects looking for general information can be expected to remember five general benefits of your product. On the other hand, customers in a technical training session might have a hard time remembering five detailed steps to using your product. As Fisher points out, information that requires the audience member to turn away from the presentation to perform the task consumes the retention time and makes it essential to reduce the amount of material presented within a given time.

Applying these concepts to presentations requires carefully following the steps to preparing and presenting presentations, which George Morrisey covers in his book, *Effective Business and Technical Presentations* (Addison-Wesley, 1975):

1. Establish objectives for the presentation.
2. Analyze your audience.
3. Prepare a preliminary plan for the presentation.
4. Select the right resource material required for the message.
5. Organize material for effective presentation.
6. Practice the presentation.

It seems that most of us know these steps; we just don't always follow them! As presentation technology has become more complex, the need to practice using the technology has become more important. You've probably sat through the executive's speech where the slides didn't match, or the microphone wasn't loud enough, or the lights were too bright for the slides. With Internet presentations, just think of all of the *additional* problems you can face when trying to impress your audience, and then rehearse until you can deal with any eventuality.

The Future of One-to-One Web Collaboration

One of the keys to improving relationships with prospects and customers is increasing the attention, involvement, and interaction of the audience whether that audience is 1 person or 1000 people. The appeal of television and movies is the combination of motion and audio. The immediate challenge for using Internet-based multimedia is obtaining sufficient bandwidth for all users to allow full-motion (i.e., 30 frames per second) video and CD-quality audio. Corporations with high-speed internal networks are currently achieving near-broadcast quality video, but the bandwidth consumption limits the availability.

After bandwidth limitations are overcome, the next breakthrough will be greater audience involvement. One type of audience involvement will be real-time voting, much as presenters do now when speaking to an audience. Additional techniques to attract and hold an audience's attention will be 3-D graphical environments for individuals to interact, personalized multimedia on demand, and improved workgroup collaboration. While it's clear that the technological products will continue to be developed at a quick pace, the greater challenge is providing presenters with training on these technologies so that they are effective in delivering their presentation with Internet-based multimedia.

Resources

Here is a list of companies that provide products and services for one-to-one Web collaboration:

Intel	www.intel.com
Astound	www.astound.com
Microsoft	www.microsoft.com
Logitech	www.logitech.com
RealNetworks	www.real.com
VocalTec	www.vocaltec.com
CUseeMe Networks	www.cuseeme.com
PictureTel	www.picturetel.com
PolyCom	www.polycom.com

Here are companies that provide products and services for one-to-one Web project management:

PlanPack	www.planpack.com
OnProject	www.onproject.com
eProject	www.eproject.com

Additional resources for collaboration can be found at www.1to1web.com.

Up Next

Chapter 9, "One-to-One Web Privacy," discusses the role of privacy in one-to-one marketing. Some Web visitors appreciate a personal touch in meeting their needs, other visitors feel their privacy has been invaded. The chapter provides insights into maximizing the benefit of a Web site to both types of people.

One-to-One Web Privacy

"Good one-to-one marketers will become jealous guardians of their customers' privacy."

Martha Rogers, Ph.D., interview in *Wired* magazine, March 1996

Online users are personalizing Web sites at an incredible rate. According to Cyber Dialogue, by April 2000, more than 28.2 million online consumers personalized a Web page, which is up from 2.8 million in April 1997. On the other hand, a study by AT&T, *Beyond Concern: Understanding Net User's Attitudes about Online Privacy*, found that 87 percent of respondents were somewhat or very concerned about threats to their personal privacy while online. Other surveys have shown that Web users are very willing to give personal data as long as their data is protected and they feel they are getting enough *value* in exchange from companies.

Although the direct-marketing industry is noted for buying and selling customer data without the customer's consent, the Internet is being held to a higher standard. The issue of privacy has come to a critical mass where marketers must address it to the satisfaction of customers, privacy advocates, and governments. In order for marketers and customers to get the most out of one-to-one Web marketing, personal data must be collected. The privacy debate centers around two key areas: informing customers about what data is being collected and how it is being used, and allowing customers to choose whether they want to participate in the data profiling process.

Marketers want to approach a solution to the uproar with self-regulation, but governments do not think marketers are acting fast enough. The bottom line is that for one-to-one Web marketing to work, customers must be willing to reveal information about themselves, from public to private. A loyal relationship is built on trust. If marketers want to achieve the customer loyalty levels that are possible with one-to-one marketing, then customers must feel confident that their personal information is safe and secure. Otherwise, customers will hold back and, in turn, marketers won't achieve their desired results. Privacy protection is inevitable. Marketers do have some choices about how they are going to build an online privacy process and policy.

The bottom line is that it will be up to marketers to do the right thing to protect the privacy of online customers in order to facilitate the growth and adoption of e-commerce.

The Two Sides of the One-to-One Web Marketing Coin

The fact is, one-to-one Web marketing is not possible without the customer's participation. If the current negative perceptions of online marketers continue to persist, then both the customer and the Web marketer will lose. On one hand, the benefits of one-to-one marketing to both the Web marketer and the customer are great. On the other hand, the online audience has spoken out against spam, cookies, anonymous profiling, and other activities that may be perceived as an invasion of privacy. For both the Web marketer and the online customer to realize benefits, a lot of trust will need to be established.

The Benefits of One-to-One Web Marketing

There are benefits on both sides of the one-to-one marketing equation. In a March 1996 interview in *Wired* magazine with one-to-one marketing guru Martha Rogers, she made the following statement about the benefits of one-to-one marketing to both the marketers and their customers: "Simply the more I know about you, the more I'm able to meet your needs—better than someone who doesn't know you. Ultimately, if I do it right, it's a great advantage to both of us."

Benefits to the Web Marketer

Throughout our book we discuss the incredible opportunity the combination of one-to-one and the Web brings to the Web marketer. Imagine being able to have information and insight into what makes each customer the most satisfied with your products and services. This information can help you repeat this success over and over, at a lower and lower marketing cost each time. The information also reduces waste associated with mass marketing and even some direct marketing. A 2 percent response rate on online offers is not what Web marketers should be expecting. With the Web you have the power of matching offers with the people most likely to respond. In fact, savvy Web advertisers are already trying to increase response rates to 20 percent and higher, and we can expect even better results in the near future as Web sites and marketing campaigns become more targeted and more user profile information is available.

In order to accomplish this task, one-to-one Web marketers need to know what makes our online audience, prospects, or customers tick and click. The more you know about each customer, or groups of customers, the more you can tailor marketing and sales messages. You cannot distinguish between two online customers without some basic information. For example, how does a Web marketer know the gender of an online customer without asking? Beyond the demographics, what about psychographic information? True one-to-one marketing can be done not with just clickstream tracking (behavioral data), it also needs information provided by the customer himself or herself (declared data). Ultimately, the best possible results coming from one-to-one marketing depend on the customer's participation in providing and managing the information marketers collect on them. This will give marketers a more accurate view of the customer and a better possibility to build a relationship with the customer.

All of this information-gathering activity translates into increased profitability and lower customer attrition and turnover. In some cases, personalized delivery of goods and services can be provided to the discerning customer at a premium—providing these specialized services at a higher rate.

Benefits to the Web Audience

Online customers will give information to Web marketers if they see value in it. The overall benefit of one-to-one Web marketing to customers is that they no longer waste a lot of time wading through numerous offers to find the one most appropriate to their tastes or situation. With the Web adding to the information-overload problems in today's information society, customers will benefit from the assistance the one-to-one Web marketer gives them by providing personalized information. According to the NEC Research Institute and Inktomi, there are more than a billion unique documents on the Web. According to Giga Information Group, the Web is expanding at over 100GB of data per week. Online users will appreciate the help one-to-one Web marketing can bring in making the time they spend online more efficient and therefore more rewarding.

One-to-one Web marketing can also provide users with the benefit of convenience. When ordering books from Amazon.com, existing customers don't have to fill out the entire online order form every time they order. They simply type in their unique password and verify or modify any information Amazon.com has stored from past orders. This makes it very convenient to order from Amazon.com; therefore, their customers see the benefit of this ease and convenience.

Another benefit is how important the customer feels. Don't you feel important when you receive special, individualized attention when you go to your favorite restaurant or store? Feeling important is of great benefit to a customer. This feeling of importance by the customer translates into affinity and loyalty.

One spark of hope for Web marketers has been the acceptance of personalization on the Web. According to a study by the Personalization Consortium, 51 percent of survey respondents said they would share personal information in exchange for better service. In a Cyber Dialogue report, *Personalization: A Threat to Privacy?*, many respondents were willing to provide personal information to a site including name, level of education, age, hobbies/special interests, and household income. These same respondents were less willing to provide credit card and salary information. In the same study, 71 percent of respondents personalized a site to receive more relevant content, 65 percent personalize so that a site can "remember" their preferences and interests based on their input, 43 percent found that sites that can automatically "learn" their interests were beneficial, and 38 percent see a benefit from sites that can deliver more relevant marketing messages. Web users are warming up to personalization features online. Personalization can be expected to become a mainstay on the Web. The future of one-to-one marketing online is great, as long as marketers address the concerns, issues, and challenges surrounding privacy.

The Challenges

Although the challenges surrounding privacy policy seem large, the key issues center on simple principles: notification and choice. Online customers want to know if a site is collecting data, what data the site is collecting, and how the data is being used. Online customers want to have the choice of participating in online profiling or not.

With new opportunities come new challenges. One-to-one Web marketing efforts will be on an uphill slope on the information highway. As more Web sites are capable of collecting personal data now, more incidents have raised online customer fears: invasive viruses, lawsuits against Web sites that are collecting information without informing customers, legal actions against unsolicited e-mail, and uprisings against third-party ad servers that want to marry the online profile data with offline direct marketing data. Here are a few facts to give you a sense of the privacy challenges presented to Web marketers:

According to the "Internet Privacy Study" by Boston Consulting Group (www.bcg.com), over 70 percent of the respondents are more concerned about privacy and information exchanged on the Internet versus phone or e-mail. More than 41 percent of the respondents left Web sites that asked users to provide registration information. Twenty-seven percent of these online users entered false information on Web site registration forms.

The "1996 Equifax/Harris Consumer Privacy Survey" (www.equifax.com) found that 43 percent of Internet users disagreed strongly with this statement: "Providers of online services should be able to track the places users go on the Internet in order to send these users targeted marketing offers." A total of 71 percent of respondents disagreed somewhat or strongly, and only 4 percent agreed strongly with this statement.

According to Giga Group (www.gigaweb.com) and Arthur D. Little (www.adlittle.com), privacy was ranked second behind security in a ranking of barriers to adoption of electronic commerce.

The Graphic, Visualization, & Usability Center's (GVU) 7th WWW User Survey results showed that about 40 percent of respondents provided false information to a Web site when they registered. Also in this survey, the most prevalent reasons why users do not register on a Web site are that the terms and conditions of how the collected information is going to be used are not clearly specified and that users feel that the information they reveal is not worth being able to access the Web site.

According to a recent study conducted by Dr. Alan Westin of Columbia University, 94 percent of Americans reported being concerned about privacy, which compares to 1978 when 68 percent were concerned about their privacy.

In a 2000 *Business Week*/Harris Poll, 92 percent of Internet users "expressed discomfort about Web sites sharing personal information with other sites." In the same poll, 56 percent would "always" choose not to have their personal information collected, and another 34 percent would "sometimes" opt-out of the data collection. Only 6 percent would "never" opt out.

According to the AT&T study, *Beyond Concern: Understanding Net User's Attitudes about Online Privacy*, 52 percent found that unsolicited e-mail

> is very serious, and 80 percent found that Web sites collecting e-mail addresses from visitors without their consent to compile e-mail marketing lists is very serious.

Cookies, spam, hackers, and other strange-sounding cyberphenomena are making Web surfers uneasy. Online consumers feel that cookies—technology that keeps track of what people are doing online—violate a person's right to privacy. Unsolicited commercial e-mail, or spam, is an invasion of privacy and very unwelcome to many because the spammer did not ask the user's permission: The spammer covertly obtained the user's e-mail address. There is the ever-present fear of hackers, people who take pleasure in finding the Achilles' heel of a Web server and breaking through security barriers just to lurk or sometimes even steal information from the computer. With this going on, and a lot of misinformation is covered in the media, we can all agree that there is legitimacy to the fears of online consumers. As you can see, Web marketers will not be able to hide from the inevitable, which is to build enough trust to alleviate the online population's privacy concerns.

Privacy Issues

Although there is much hype and media attention to privacy on the Internet, online users are skittish. Misinformation about cookies and privacy missteps by Web marketers have escalated the privacy issue. Now there are several groups pitted against online marketers, and the Federal Trade Commission has a pivotal role in ensuring that the marketing industry satisfactorily addresses the privacy needs of the online audience.

Perception Is Reality

During June 1997 Federal Trade Commission hearings, Dr. Alan Westin, publisher of the *Privacy & American Business Newsletter*, stated, "So the media, in a standard fashion, have emphasized to people that [the Internet] is not a safe place, this is not a secure place for your confidential information." This statement was a conclusion to a contradiction in findings in a study conducted by Dr. Westin and Lou Harris and Associates. The survey results indicated that the majority of Internet users see a need for privacy protection, while there has been a small percentage (5 percent) of Internet users who have actually suffered an invasion of privacy. The study also asked similar questions about privacy in the *offline* world, and upward of 25–35 percent of respondents reported incidences of invasion of privacy.

Hackers, spammers, and viruses have contributed to the lack of confidence in the Internet—for example, when hackers hacked their way into AOL to get access to personal information about some members. There have been a few hacker incidents that put online customers' credit cards at risk. According to a study commissioned by EDS, more than two-thirds of Americans are concerned about the threat of hackers and cybercriminals. It will take privacy protection practices and significant public education to change this perception.

Perception is reality. As we marketers know, this is one of the golden rules of marketing. More importantly, this is how Web marketers should approach the privacy concerns of the online consumer. Even if you may not agree that there is a legitimate basis for a lot of the media reports and opinions, Web marketers should consider the other golden rule: The customer is always right. Marketers who protect Web customer data and provide a secure online experience will only benefit from increased visits and sales. Marketers should clearly communicate and educate the customer about how safe their Web site is in order see potential growth in new and repeat customers.

All about Cookies

As you are probably already aware, cookies are bits of information collected and stored by a Web browser when a person navigates the Web. A cookie can be an identification tag that Web sites have placed in the cookie file, and it can pick up information about your computer operating system, browser, and username. There is what is called the *"bad" cookie*, which is information that tracks and records user activity across the Web. There are two types of cookies, a *session* cookie and a *persistent* cookie. A session cookie tracks user activity only during a single Web session. Once the customer leaves the site and closes the browser, the session cookie expires. The persistent cookie is an identifier that will always remember a particular visitor that returns to a Web site. All of this is going on without much notice to the user.

The cookie technology was built with good intentions, but it has gotten a scarred reputation. Lou Montulli is an engineer at Netscape and was one of the inventors of cookies. He states in a *Red Herring Hits* magazine article that "the only way cookies can contain personal information is if users freely volunteer information about themselves." According to Montulli, cookies cannot access other parts of an online user's hard drive. At one point during the cookie controversy, Microsoft and Netscape were considering releasing the next versions of their browsers with the cookies *turned off* as the default. Luckily for marketers, things have calmed down, and this has not occurred.

The benefit to the user is that when he or she continues to visit a Web site, the user can receive personalized information because the cookie enables the site to remember the returning customer. There are limits to what a cookie can do for one-to-one Web marketing. Cookies track computers, not users. When cookie information, or other tracking technologies, is coupled with on-site registration information, it can be a very powerful source of information for the Web marketer. The mixture of what is known (user profile) with what has been tracked (cookie file) can give Web marketers a clear and more accurate view of what is important to online customers. The tracking information can also serve as an indication of what is successful in an online marketing campaign or within a Web site.

The best way for marketers to increase adoption of their personalization efforts is to educate customers about the use and benefits of cookies. Marketers should inform their customers about what type of cookies their sites use, how these cookies work, and what benefits customers will receive from the personalized marketing and service that the cookies enable. In their book, *Enterprise One to One*, Peppers and Rogers believed that for any cookie format to gain wide acceptance, the user should have a large degree of control over his or her information.

Walking the Tightrope of Online Profiling

The practice of online profiling, aggregating data about customers by tracking their clickstream, is coming under scrutiny. Much of the data collection will tell marketers what these customers' preferences and interests are. The concern is that this collection is taking place without the customers' knowledge or consent. If marketers are able to gather enough clickstream data and add to that any personal information the customer provided through site registration or online transactions, then the anonymous profiling is no longer anonymous, so customers should know that it is being done. At the center of the controversy over anonymous profiling are third-party ad servers like DoubleClick and ad networks. Tracking and gathering data about customers over many Web sites call into question the level of anonymity where if enough data is collected, the profile is no longer anonymous.

The benefits of profiling to users is that the user will see online ads and targeted marketing messages that are relevant to his or her unique likes. The obvious benefits of online profiling to marketers are the potential to enhance response because the ads are highly relevant to the audience, and marketers can minimize wasted ad impressions. Cookies allow ad networks to stop displaying the same ad to the same user over and over, once the user has viewed and/or clicked on the banner ad.

The Federal Trade Commission (FTC) and privacy advocacy groups are calling for standards for online profiling. It has been suggested that Web users should be notified that online profiling is occurring and that they have the ability to opt-out of the profiling process.

Privacy Standards and Initiatives

Those involved with the Internet and online marketing have already taken steps to increase customer confidence, including privacy initiatives, legislation, practices, policies, technologies, and standards. The common wish of Web marketers is to swiftly implement self-regulation so that the government will not step in with what could be very limiting privacy laws.

Online Privacy Standards, Initiatives, and Legislation

In order to ensure that the Web becomes a viable commerce platform, governments and industry trade organizations have responded swiftly to the online privacy controversy and have proactively addressed the concerns of the online audience and vocal privacy advocacy groups. Many initiatives, standards, technologies, and legislation are continuing to emerge for the protection of privacy and for enabling the collection of user information.

Platform for Privacy Preferences (P3P) Project

The World Wide Web Consortium (www.w3c.org), also known as W3C, is a guiding organization that is led by Tim Berners-Lee, the creator of the Web, and is dedicated to the creation of common protocols as the Web evolves. The W3C has created the Platform for Privacy Preferences Project (P3P), which is an industry standard to allow Web users to gain more control over the personal information that is being collected on the Web and to make privacy policies easier to find and understand. P3P is standards and software that standardize privacy policies and encode privacy questions into machine-readable format. The P3P technology allows users as they are visiting Web sites to determine their own privacy preferences, and then it automatically determines if Web sites' privacy policies match users' privacy needs.

The P3P technologies allow marketers to create their privacy policies in the P3P standard so that user's P3P-enabled browsers can easily read the policies on P3P-encoded Web sites. P3P would alert users before they visit Web sites that would collect more personal information than users want to provide. P3P promotes the idea of informed consent in order to establish trust between the user and the Web marketer and the idea that protocols can be at the heart of privacy statements and data collection technologies. For more information, visit www.w3.org/P3P.

Federal Trade Commission (FTC)

Since early in the consumer adoption of the Internet, the Federal Trade Commission (FTC) has taken a proactive role in determining guidelines and standards for online privacy in the United States. The FTC has been favoring industry self-regulation. In the FTC's May 2000 report to the United States Congress, *Privacy Online: Fair Information Practices in the Electronic Marketplace*, the commission suggested the government step in to set up legislation since, in the commission's opinion, the industry has not moved quickly enough to improve privacy protection. The FTC is looking for the industry to follow its Fair Information Practice principles:

Notice. Web sites must disclose information practices before collecting data on visitors/customers.

Choice. Web users must be given options to whether and how information is collected by the site and for any other uses beyond the Web site (i.e., providing the information to third parties).

Access. Web sites should give online customers/visitors access to the information that is being collected, and users should be able to "view and contest the accuracy and completeness of the date being collected about them."

Security. Web sites must take reasonable steps to protect the accuracy and security of the data they collect from their online customers/visitors, and they must protect their users' data from unauthorized use.

An FTC study found in 1998 that 92 percent of commercial Web sites were collecting a lot of personal information, but only 14 percent disclosed any information about their data collection practices. Does privacy protection pay off? FTC found that only 8 percent of its random sample of Web sites participated in a privacy seal program (e.g., BBBOnline, TrustE), but

45 percent of the most popular sites, according to Nielsen//NetRatings, displayed these seals. Could it be that popular sites have better adoption because they put privacy protection as a priority?

The FTC has also established guidelines for companies that market to children under the age of 13. The Children's Online Privacy Protection Act (COPPA) protects children against Web sites that collect information. Web sites that collect information from young Web visitors must have "verifiable parental consent" before collecting, using, or disclosing a child's personal information collected on the Web sites.

European Data Protection Directive

Privacy protection is taken a lot more seriously in Europe than in the United States. In order for Web sites to be successful in doing business with European businesses and consumers, they must follow the European Data Protection Directive. According to the Directive, online users have basic rights where they must be told the identity of the organization collecting their information and what they are doing with the information; users have the right to access the data being collected, they have the right to correct any data that they believe is inaccurate, and they have the right to opt-out of allowing their data to be used for marketing. For more sensitive personal information, such as medical information, the data can be collected and used only if the Web site has explicit permission from the Web user (i.e., opt-in). For more information visit: http://europa.eu.int/comm/internal_market/en/media/dataprot/news/925.htm.

The Direct Marketing Association

The Direct Marketing Association (www.the-dma.org) has historically taken the initiative to give consumers a way to *opt-out* of marketing. The organization is an advocate of self-regulation and has taken these steps in order to prevent government intervention. The DMA created the Mail Preference and Telephone Preference Services to enable consumers to remove their names from nonprofit and commercial marketing lists of DMA members. The DMA has created a similar service for online marketing called the e-Mail Preference Service (e-MPS).

The DMA has created many guidelines for direct marketers, which are available on the organization's Web site. The organization directs marketers to provide notice, allow customers to opt-out, maintain an in-house suppression file, and use the DMA Preference Services to protect customers' wishes for privacy protection and against unsolicited marketing.

The DMA created a Privacy Policy Generator that any company can use to create its own Web site privacy policy. DMA suggests making the privacy policy easy to read, promoting the policy inside the company, promoting your policy to all stakeholders, and updating the policy as needed. The policy generator is available on the organization's site at www.the-dma.org/library/privacy/creating.shtml.

Online Privacy Legislation (United States)

There are many proposed bills related to online privacy currently under consideration. More than 80 privacy-related bills were introduced in the U.S. Congress in 1999, and more than 50 before midyear 2000. Here is a sample of legislation:

Unsolicited Electronic Mail Act of 1999. This bill protects online users against receiving unsolicited e-mail (i.e., spam). Any person/company that initiates unsolicited e-mail must have a reply e-mail address in the e-mail message. Anyone who receives the unsolicited e-mail must be able to get off the e-mail list.

Consumer Privacy Act of 2000. This legislation proposes that all Internet service providers, online service providers, and Web site operators cannot collect personally identifiable information unless the provider gives notice, obtains consent, provides access to information, ensures security of the data collected, provides notice of privacy policy change, provides notice of any privacy breach, and ensures that the privacy protection applies to third parties.

Online Privacy and Disclosure Act of 2000. This legislation proposes the use of a seal that Web sites that comply with the "Principles for Fair Personal Information Practices" can display. The practices would include the lawful and fair collection of data with the knowledge of the user, that the personal data would be accurate, complete, and current, the specific disclosure about how the data is being used, that the online user should be able to find out if the Web site is collecting data from him or her, and that he or she should be able to challenge the Web site to delete, rectify, complete, or amend the data.

Marketers should expect much more legislation; however, many studies have shown that most Web users would prefer industry self-regulation to government intervention. Self-regulation is the best option because many Web marketers are now finding that it only makes good business sense to provide privacy policies and protection.

Opt-in or Opt-out?

One of the most debated aspects of privacy is whether Web marketers should use an *opt-in* or *opt-out* practice. An opt-in practice allows online customers to participate in the data collection process by choice. These Web users are *not* automatically added to the profiling process by default; they must elect to participate. An opt-out practice will automatically add customers to the profiling process unless the customers takes themselves out of the process. How it usually works is that a customer completes an online transaction or site registration and he or she checks (opt-in) or unchecks (opt-out) the boxes relating to e-mailing list subscriptions and sharing customer information third-party companies.

Which practice should a marketer use—opt-in or opt-out? It depends on the company's objective, the nature of the data being collected (i.e., sensitivity of data), and the company's relationship with its customers. Seth Godin, author of *Permission Marketing*, believes that if a customer chooses to give a company permission, via opt-in, then the customer will be more receptive and responsive to all marketing by the company. In fact, opt-in can help marketers identify their best customers. According to Godin, permission marketing is as follows:

Anticipated. Customers look forward to hearing from companies.

Personal. Marketing messages are directly related to the individual customer.

Relevant. Marketing messages are something the customers are interested in.

Although marketers worry that an opt-in model will have many fewer customers signing up than opt-out, these customers will be more qualified and more profitable to marketers. At a minimum, marketers who are collecting information from online customers should follow a practice of opt-out. The most popular business-to-consumer Web sites typically follow an opt-out practice.

An opt-in process should come into play when a Web site collects sensitive customer data such as medical information. A site should also use an opt-in practice regarding the sharing of customer data with third parties. In general, customers will entrust companies they do business with directly with their personal information; however, customers don't feel confident that a third party will protect their interests. Marketers should know what third parties will be doing with their customer data, and they should inform customers of what the third parties will be doing with the data also so that customers can determine whether they want to do business with other companies.

Online Privacy Options, Recommendations, Policies, and Seals

The common theme of the online industry is self-regulation. Companies involved prefer to build trust with their online audience instead of relying on government legislation. For Web marketers, there is no single solution to preserve online privacy while enabling one-to-one online marketing. There are common beliefs that will help a one-to-one Web marketer succeed in protecting his or her customers' privacy. Web marketers who ask for too much information will be suspect. People are savvy, and they can figure out if the information you are asking for is related to your business. If marketers have established the value of personalization in the mind of their customers, then there is only one additional step, which is addressing online customer privacy protection.

Addressing Online Privacy Directly

Jupiter Communications (www.jup.com) had these recommendations for preserving the balance between online privacy and building relationships with consumers:

Online marketers should offer more for less in exchange for their personal information. Online marketers should offer incentives in exchange for accurate information and permission to use it.

Online marketers need to come together to agree on and promote the acceptance and usage of privacy standards. A unified approach will give the industry a better chance to enable self-regulation and minimize negative media reporting.

The privacy issue gives Web marketers a window of opportunity to build deep relationships with consumers. Providing a privacy policy and giving users knowledge of how the information is used will build trust.

Brands that have already established *offline* trust will have an advantage of establishing online trust. Web-based companies can also build new brands and trust if they go above and beyond in addressing their users' trust.

Informed Consent

Since its creation, the Web has had its own culture, which has two important characteristics: freedom of speech and choice. As evidence of the controversy around privacy on the Internet, Web users want more choice over what marketing messages they receive online. With television, magazine, telemarketing, and direct mail, people do not have ultimate control over the marketing messages they receive. In these traditional formats, customers can exert some control and choice. They can change the channel on the television when a commercial is broadcast. People can remove themselves from a direct-mailing list. On the Internet, consumers are seeking a higher degree of control. They want to make the initial choice of whether they receive commercial marketing messages, or at least easily remove themselves from an e-mail list or simply ignore advertising by not clicking on the online ad. At the same time, many people have elected to join free e-mail or Internet services in exchange for viewing and responding to online advertisements. The online audience will do this if they perceive they are receiving more in return for their effort in participating in online advertising. All of this comes down to the basic request of online users: informed consent.

In an interview with WebWeek magazine (June 12, 1997), David Sobel, legal counsel for Electronic Privacy Information Center (EPIC), stated, "Surreptitious collection [of personal information] under any circumstances is reprehensible, and if I had my way, there would be legal restrictions on the ability of sites to do that. But when information is knowingly provided, it's just a question of getting consent of the individual to use it for the purpose it's going to be used for." In its article, "Surfer Beware: Personal Privacy and the Internet," EPIC had these recommendations:

Web sites should make available a privacy policy that is easy to find. Ideally the policy should be accessible from the home page by looking for the word "privacy."

Privacy policies should state clearly how and when personal information is collected. A privacy policy should be written in plain English (not legal speak) so that a customer can easily understand what, how, and why information is being collected, and who may have access to the customer's personal data.

Web sites should make it possible for individuals to get access to their own data. When marketers involve customers in the management of their own personal information, everyone wins—both company and customer. Allowing customers to update information will ensure more accurate customer profiles, therefore more effective one-to-one Web marketing.

Cookie transactions should be more transparent. For example, users should know when cookies are activated.

Web sites should continue to support anonymous access for Internet users.

Many advocates like EPIC would like users to have control over online marketing messages and would like to go as far as letting users actively participate in controlling, accessing, and modifying the type of information that is being collected by Web marketers. Privacy advocates also promote anonymity as the ultimate way to protect privacy, but this may be limiting to most one-to-one Web marketers, even if these marketers never intend to sell their users' information.

Offering Incentives

One common philosophy that is evolving to balance the desires of Web marketers and online users is that there be a fair *value exchange.* One way to achieve an optimum value exchange is to offer incentives that entice online customers to participate in one-to-one Web marketing. FreeRide and HotMail have already established successful advertiser-supported online businesses where they exchange free services in exchange for the user profiles they collect. Incentives can include the following:

Protecting privacy. This can be the strongest incentive for online customers who are very conservative or sensitive about their privacy. If you are collecting information to serve your customers better, and if you have no need to sell their information to third parties, then you can build immediate trust among your customers or users by prominently displaying these types of privacy policies.

Personalized information that is useful. Web sites that have built businesses that primarily focus on delivering customized information can strike a successful balance between privacy and value, as long as the information the user provides does not exceed the perceived value of the information received.

Discounted or free products or services. Software companies have widely used incentives such as free technical support, free upgrades, and discounts on related products or services in exchange for getting customers to fill out product registration forms. This can be an effective tool that provides something that a customer already values: your company and its offerings. In addition to trust, it can build loyalty.

Freebies. People enjoy receiving something for free, as long as it doesn't have too high of an intangible cost. In other words, customers will not give away their personal information just to receive something for free. There is always a cost, even if it is not tangible (e.g., money, time), associated with free services and products.

A couple of recent studies have proven that the use of incentives, discounts, members-only offers, and other promotions can be effective tools to get online customers to personalize a Web site, register as a member, and participate in other one-to-one marketing programs. According to a study by Primary Knowledge and Greenfield Online, the most popular incentives among survey respondents included incentive programs (76 percent), members-only discounts (73 percent), giveaways/sweepstakes (62 percent), and coupons (54 percent). According to *"Freebies" and Privacy: What Net Users Think*, published by Privacy & American Business, 86 percent of Net users believe that individuals should be able to make informed choices of giving their personal information in exchange for free products and services such as personal computers, e-mail, Web pages, discounts, and sweepstakes.

Privacy Policies

Privacy policies are now standard fare on any type of Web site. Privacy policies should be prominently displayed with a link right on a home page, and they should even display as a recurring link throughout a Web site. Here is a checklist of what privacy policies should contain:

Easy-to-read language. Please keep the legalese to a minimum. This will allow customers to easily understand the policy and ensure that they will participate in the data collection process.

Benefits to the customer. This is a perfect opportunity to explain to the customer all of the wonderful benefits of personalization and one-to-one Web marketing. Marketers can let customers know that personalization is a free service to them to make their shopping or site experience unique and that customers will receive relevant offers, information, and recommendations. This will save customers time and will give them highly personal service. 1800Flowers.com outlines its Member Benefits to entice Web users to register as members. The member will have express checkout privileges where he or she doesn't have to reenter his or her information. The member can also set up his or her own personal address book and gift reminders. Other member benefits include personalized recommendations and exclusive offers.

ONE-TO-ONE MARKETING GURUS PROMOTE PRIVACY PRACTICES

In their second book together, *Enterprise One to One: Tools for Competing in the Interactive Age*, Peppers and Rogers make recommendations on how to approach the delicate balance of obtaining customer profile information while protecting the customer's privacy. Here is an excerpt from the book on how to establish a "Privacy Bill of Rights":

"The Interactive Age could easily become the Age of Privacy Invasion. Companies already have problems getting their own customers to send in warranty registration cards for fear that they will be deluged with more mail. How can the 1:1 enterprise ever expect even its best customers to participate willingly in a series of more and more intimate dialogues if it can't assure them that their privacy will be respected? Customers whose privacy is violated—or customers who simply don't feel they have control over their own information—are not likely to become willing participants in any dialogue interactions.

If your firm is going into the business of creating relationships with customers based on individual information, you need to adopt an explicit privacy policy early on—then publicize it, and use it. The Privacy Bill of Rights should spell out:

- **The kind of information generally needed from customers.**
- **Any benefits customers will enjoy from the enterprise's use of this individual information.**
- **The specific things the enterprise will never do with individual information.**
- **An individual's options for directing the enterprise to not use or disclose certain kinds of information.**
- **Any events that might precipitate a notification to the customer by the enterprise.**

Notice. A privacy policy should announce that the Web site is collecting and storing information. It should let online users know what data is being collected and how it is being used.

Opt-out capability. Web customers should be able to opt-out of any communications from the Web site itself and any third-party relationships. Customers should be able to opt-out of e-mail marketing and membership registration at any time.

Security information. The policy should let customers know that their personal information, including credit card information, is secure. The description of security should educate customers on the technology being used to keep the information secure.

Use of cookies. Much of the privacy issue surrounds the use of cookies. A marketer should include educational information about the cookie technology. It should also include what cookies are being used by the Web site and what they are able/not able to do if users turn their cookie capabilities off in their browser. Some policies have even instructed the user how and where to modify cookie settings in the browser.

Security and privacy guarantee. A guarantee increases the customer's confidence in participating in a personal relationship with a company. Many Web sites provide a safe-shopping guarantee to make online customers comfortable with giving their credit card information.

Sharing tracking information with third party ad servers/networks. A privacy policy should disclose any relationships with third-party ad server/networks that collect information via clickstream tracking and anonymous online profiling.

Updating the privacy policy. The policy should communicate that it may be changed in the future. Marketers should notify customers by e-mail if they make a change to policies.

Contact information. Make it easy for customers to contact the Web site if they run into trouble or have additional questions.

Access to customer information. Allow Web customers to view, modify, and add to their personal information that has been collected by the site. A policy should provide instructions to the customer if there is any dispute over the accuracy or completeness of the information.

NOTE **In order to provide access to customer information capability online, a Web site needs to be extremely secure in order not to give access to personal information to someone other than the customer.**

TRUSTe has also developed a model for a privacy policy that is available at www.truste.org/webpublishers/pub_resourceguide.html. In addition to visiting the FTC, DMA, and privacy advocacy groups, visit the Web sites listed here to view their privacy policies, which are accessible from their home pages:

1800Flowers.com	www.1800flowers.com
Dell	www.dell.com
Disney	www.disney.com
drkoop.com	www.drkoop.com

IBM	www.ibm.com
Nordstrom	www.nordstrom.com
SciQuest	www.sciquest.com
United Parcel Service (UPS)	www.ups.com
Wal-Mart	www.wal-mart.com

TIP An easily accessible and easy-to-understand privacy policy is key to establishing your online users' trust. But don't stop there. You will want to be up-front with your Web users as to what you plan to do with the information you receive from them.

Privacy Seals and Certifications

For industry self-regulation purposes and for enhanced customer trust and adoption of the Internet, there are organizations that provide online privacy review and certification. These seals can have a positive effect on the perception of a Web site in the eyes on the online customer. According to the AT&T study, *Beyond Concern: Understanding Net User's Attitudes about Online Privacy*, 58 percent of respondents were more likely to provide personal information if a Web site had both a privacy policy and a privacy seal of approval, versus 28 percent who would be more likely to provide personal data if the site just had a privacy policy alone. Here is a sample of available seal programs:

TRUSTe. TRUSTe (www.truste.org) is a nonprofit organization that was founded by the Electronic Frontier Foundation (www.eff.org) and CommerceNet (www.commerce.net) to promote online privacy. TRUSTe has created a seal program that ensures that Web sites are following fair information practices as approved by the U.S. government and advocacy groups. TRUSTe also has a seal program for children's Web sites.

BBBOnline. The Better Business Bureau (BBB) has taken its traditional watchdog efforts online with BBBOnline (www.bbbonline.org) to make sure that Web sites are safe and secure. BBBOnline has a privacy seal that Web sites can apply for and display if they meet the organization's criteria. BBBOnline also has a seal program for children's sites.

CPA WebTrust. CPA WebTrust (www.cpawebtrust.org) is a seal program being managed by the American Institute of Certified Public Accountants (AICPA).

Resources

As the online privacy issue continues to unfold, marketers should regularly monitor these privacy resources on the Web.

ONLINE PRIVACY RESOURCES AND PROVIDERS	
BBBOnline	www.bbbonline.org
Center for Democracy and Technology	www.cdt.org
Cookie Central	www.cookiecentral.com
CPA WebTrust	www.cpawebtrust.org
Direct Marketing Association	www.the-dma.org
Electronic Frontier Foundation	www.eff.org
Electronic Privacy Information Center	www.epic.org
IETF	www.ietf.org
Federal Trade Commission	www.ftc.gov
Junkbusters	www.junkbusters.com
Online Privacy Alliance	www.privacyalliance.org
Privacy & American Business	www.pandab.org
RespectPrivacy.com	www.respectprivacy.com
TRUSTe	www.truste.org
World Wide Web Consortium	www.w3c.org

The future of privacy will rely on the practice by marketers of self-regulation. Successful online marketing activities will be based on the protection of online user privacy. Online customers will gravitate to those marketers that put protection of customer privacy first.

Up Next

Chapter 10, "The One-to-One Web Marketing Future," outlines the future of one-to-one marketing on the Web. Most of the technologies and techniques already covered in this book are still relatively new, and there is a bright future for highly-targeted and one-to-one communications over the Internet. The future of one-to-one Web marketing will also resonate across traditional marketing methods as well. Marketing in cyberspace is teaching all of us marketers how to take a fresh look at how we market, sell, and service in the real world.

The One-to-One Web Marketing Future

"In the real-time communities of cyberspace, we are dwellers on the threshold between the real and virtual, unsure of our footing, inventing ourselves as we go along."

Sherry Turkle, Life on the Screen: Identity in the Age of the Internet (1997, Touchstone Books)

Marketing is about *markets*—communicating with, selling, and servicing them. One-to-one marketing is about individuals, communicating with, selling, servicing them in a unique and valuable personal experience. We have moved from mass marketing to direct marketing and now to one-to-one marketing. One-to-one marketing is being facilitated by the decreasing cost of applying technology and intelligent data to marketing, enabling us to develop targeted messages, identify target markets and even individuals, and transmit or put that specific message in front of the right person at the right time. Then we can use technology to measure response from the various target markets and even individuals. This is definitely marketing nirvana! The Internet brings a whole world of numerous target markets to our fingertips. Technology allows us to reach out and touch each person on the Web.

The Web is already teaching us a new way to communicate with our markets—interactively. We are now taking what we are experiencing and learning on the Web to the physical world. Marketers are integrating the physical world with the Web and, more importantly, vice versa. Marketers can now apply one-to-one Web marketing to other communications vehicles such as direct mail where customized catalogs are created using user preferences and purchase histories to create a personalized catalog of products and services that are tailored to that particular customer. Not only can one-to-one marketing be applied to a computer hooked up to the Internet, it can now be applied to wireless devices such as cell phones, pagers, and personal digital assistants (PDAs). The Web also allows companies to manage their mass customizations strategies where their customers can use the Web to select and customize products and services. This chapter gives a sneak peek into what is possible in the next generation of marketing on the Web, one-to-one Web marketing, and the future of one-to-one communications on and off the Web.

Web Site Marketing

The Web is full of examples that give marketers so many choices when it comes to marketing and promotions on their Web sites. The difficult choice for marketers is to choose what makes sense now and in the future, and when exactly is the right time to implement Web site personalization technologies. Personalization technologies and virtual retailing can help marketers build an effective online experience. Here are just a few examples of leading-edge one-to-one Web marketing that helps sites build loyal, long-term relationships with customers.

Respond.com. Respond.com is a Web site that matches buyers with sellers. Buyers submit a request by product category that is in their own words. Respond.com sends the request to companies that sell products in the category. The buyer will receive personalized responses from various sellers. Finally, the buyer contacts the seller from which he or she wants to buy the product directly (www.respond.com).

Land's End. Land's End has many personalized shopping and services features on its Web site. Your Personal Model is a 3-D virtual reality model that women can build using their physical measurements. Land's End suggests the best outfits for the body type of the customer based on her model (www.landsend.com).

Kraft Foods. Kraft Interactive Kitchen gives customers handy tools to manage grocery lists, plan meals (personalized Simple Meal Planner), and collect recipes (Your Recipe Box). Kraft will suggest recipes based on what a customer has in his or her pantry and/or refrigerator at that very moment (Dinner on Hand) (www.kraft.com).

Web Customer Care

In addition to personalization applications, Web sites are becoming more "personal," where Web users can interact one-on-one with company sales and service representatives or invite friends and family to shop with them. Web customer care is a highly visible issue; companies are rushing to improve online customer care to increase trust, and therefore repeat purchases and loyalty among customers. Web customer care means personalized shopping lists, virtual retailing, self-service information, and instant contact to customer service reps by e-mail, text chat, voice chat (yes, voice chat), and Web telephone (voice-over-IP, or VoIP). Here's a sampling of effective pre- and post-sale customer care online:

Land's End. Land's End has a feature called Land's End Live that allows customers to contact representatives via online chat or by phone during their Web shopping session (www.landsend.com).

IKEA. IKEA is a furniture company that sells through mail order and retail stores. On the IKEA Web site, customers can find a *very* impressive interactive assembly presentation for some of the IKEA products built in Java and Flash. Gone are the days of the archaic how-to instructions (www.ikea.com)!

OfficeDepot. Office Depot offers Custom Shopping Lists that allow consumers and businesses to create shopping lists where the entire contents of these shopping lists can be quickly added to the shopping cart on subsequent visits for easy office supply replenishment (www.officedepot.com).

IBM Printing Systems. IBM's Printer Services division brought a call center application online that allows IBM business printer customers to request service. The system houses information on more than 1.5 million printers located in almost one-half million customer locations. The Web-based system allows customers to open a trouble ticket and monitor the status of their service request in real time as well as cancel or revise the service ticket. The system matches certified service professionals from a service personnel database with the particular printer at the customer location. The system automatically assigns the service request to the right customer engineer based on the engineer's skills, the customer location, product type, service workload, and other data (www.printers.ibm.com).

Online Advertising

When we wrote the first edition of this book, static and animated banners were the single most predominant form of online advertising. At that time, you could target these ads based on demographics and technographics (i.e., computer, type of computer user). Now online ads are advancing toward behaving like television commercials with audio, moving visuals, and video. As marketers and ad companies collect more Web user profile information over time, targeting is becoming sophisticated; online ad campaigns will be self-targeting and self-optimizing in real-time. Also, instead of marketers creating hundreds or thousands of different ads, online ads will be assembled on-the-fly in real time from many elements, depending on the speed of the Internet connection, computer, demographic targeting, and more. For example, a banner ad displayed to women could contain a different background, marketing message, offer, and picture/graphics than another banner displayed to men. Also, e-mail marketing has moved from a fledgling marketing medium to an effective medium for acquiring new customers and keeping existing customers. E-mail is also a medium that can be a true one-to-one marketing technique in which each e-mail could be tailored to an individual customer based on his or her user profile. Other online ad futures to ponder: voice-enabled or chat-enabled banners, micro-site within a banner, convergence—and many we haven't thought about yet.

Increasing Integration

When the Web arrived on the scene, a Web site was a standalone medium. In fact, many companies had separate divisions or companies created to maintain their Web sites. Now, customers expect a Web site to be integrated with other parts of the organization including the call center, e-mail, and retail locations. Customers who order online do expect to be able to talk to a human being when they need to. JC Penney, a long-time mail order and retail company, has integrated its Web site JCPenney.com with its call center and stores. When you order something on the Web site, you can have it shipped directly to your home or to the nearest JC Penney store. If a customer needs to return an item ordered online, he or she can do so in several ways, including returning it to the catalog department at the local JC Penney store. JC Penney also allows customers to redeem promotional offers online. Currently, many companies are moving in this direction. Cross-media and cross-channel integration will be the mainstay in the future.

Going Wireless

While the Internet opportunity is catching on quickly, a new opportunity has already sprung up. The growth of wireless devices such as cell phones and PDAs is at a lightening fast pace. We have already figured out that wireless devices can be hooked up to the Internet, which allows marketers to get hooked up to another way to reach out to customers and keep pulling them back in the hopes of building customer loyalty. According to Strategis Group, about 30 percent of current mobile phone users are interested in having access to the Internet from their mobile phones. The Yankee Group estimates that by 2003 there will be 1 billion mobile Internet access devices in the United States. Marketers will be able to provide customers with valuable marketing and service programs. For example, a mobile customer may want to be contacted by a company when there is a special promotion on a service or product he or she desires. Mobile customers could also receive reminders for reorders/renewals, receive news and information, among other services. Interactive TV, standalone kiosks, audio/music players (e.g., MP3), e-books, and other alternative access devices also represent another opportunity for marketers in the near future. If you are in desperate need of a triple espresso, you can download a Starbucks store locator to your Palm VII, and you'll never be far from your caffeine fix.

Mass Customization

The increasing use of databases and the flexibility of the Web, the near-perfect one-to-one medium, enable the process of *mass customization*. Mass customization is the creation or manufacturing of service or products based on the unique needs, requests, or preferences of an individual customer. Here are a few examples that show how the Web site can assist with mass customization:

Levi's Original Spin. Men and women can modify Levi jeans to their own specifications. Customers go to a store carrying the Levi's collection, have their measurements taken, and then choose a jean style, fabric, leg opening, fly. Customers can create their own jeans from scratch or modify an existing Levi's style. The jeans are made in two to three weeks. Currently, this service is available in California, Illinois, Massachusetts, Michigan, New York, Texas, Virginia, and Washington (www.levi.com).

Barbie. Mattel allows users to create and purchase their own customized Barbie doll with its My Design Web feature. A Barbie doll can be customized based on look, eye color, lip color, hairstyle, hair color, fashion, and personality characterisitics (www.barbie.com).

fatbrain.com. fatbrain.com has a service that allows corporations to create customized internal bookstores for their employees. FINDitNOW is fatbrain.com's intranet building service that companies use to build their own bookstore with their company logo and a bookstore that contains the books the company needs (www.fatbrain.com).

Acumins. Acumins features custom vitamin packets for men and women. The customer answers about 40 health and lifestyle questions. Once the answers are submitted, Acumins recommends what vitamins, minerals, and supplements would be beneficial to that particular customer (www.acumins.com).

Privacy and Security

Of course, as we discussed throughout the book, the one-to-one marketer cannot accomplish his or her task without properly addressing privacy and security online. Early Web customers had a high degree of fear when they first encountered personalization. With the progress of Web data capture, online customers have an even higher degree of fear than before. Although online customers are becoming more comfortable with the Internet, they will continue to voice their need to have choice and control over their own personal information. The direction we are heading is one where users are informed right up front—not that data is being collected, but that the marketer would like their permission to collect data for specific purposes—and the customer will make the choice to participate or not. Bruce Kasanoff, founder of Accerating 1to1 (www.accerating.com), believes marketers should not be collecting information *about* customers, but they should be collecting information *for* customers. This thought is truly a paradigm shift, from database marketing to customer relationship management. And, as we all are aware, successful relationships are built on trust.

Leading-Edge One-to-One

One-to-one marketing on the Web is not simply a possibility; it is a reality. Throughout this book you have seen many examples of how one-to-one marketing and communications are occurring. The Internet is no longer just for the PC; interconnection with information appliances and home appliances is on the horizon. Just for fun, we have put together a few examples of the one-to-one computing future on the Internet.

Smart Homes. Imagine a refrigerator that knows when you are running low on milk, eggs, and rocky road ice cream. What if this refrigerator can add items to a grocery list? What if it then sends your personal grocery list to an online grocery service by e-mail or over the Internet? And finally, what if the order is automatically placed and the online grocery store delivers the items to your door at your regularly scheduled time of 5:30 p.m.? Well, this isn't that far fetched. In fact, many companies are developing smart home technologies (e.g., Sun Microsystems' Jini) and interconnections to enable this dream to become a reality (www.sun.com, www.whirlpool.com, www.qubit.net).

Assistance on the Web. Webhelp.com is a specialized search engine service that has people behind the Web site helping Web users find what they need on the Internet. When you send your initial search request, their search engine presents results just like other search engines. After a few moments, a "Web Wizard" will chat with you and ask you if you need help finding other results. Then, the wizard will take over the search from that point, continuing to push results and Web pages to you (www.webhelp.com).

Convergence. In a keynote speech at Internet World Summer 1997, Eric Schmidt, CEO of Novell, predicted that networks would be designed for mobility, servers would be self-configuring, and all telephones will have IP addresses. We are seeing the convergence of voice, data, video, and wireless communications on the Internet and the creation of personal devices that give users access to the Internet via phones, personal digital assistants (PDAs), set-top boxes, cable boxes, Web television, Internet call center integration, and more. Nortel has created a Java phone that allows customers to make phone calls and access the Internet (www.nortel.com).

Digital signatures. Digital signatures are an *electronic simulation* of a handwritten signature. It is not a handwritten signature scanned into a computer, but a digital identification that is attached to messages being sent over the Internet. It allows one person to send a highly secure message to a recipient, who will be assured that the message is not a forgery. Digital signatures are made when a message is encrypted incorporating a private and unique digital key (www.w3.org/Security/DSig/).

Personal Area Network (PAN). IBM is working on a Personal Area Network technology that allows two people to exchange information simply by shaking hands. Each person has a personally identified PAN card, containing a transmitter and receiver, and their handshake completes the circuit. The information is then transferred to each person's computer. Because the human body has a natural ability to conduct electrical current, PAN can use the body to transmit the information. IBM is exploring other applications, including the ability for people to interact with household appliances and other digital products using their PAN cards. Household appliances such as stereos and toaster ovens can respond to personal preferences stored in the PAN card (www.research.ibm.com/topics/popups/smart/mobile/html/pan.html).

Shopping agents. Using user profiles and intelligent agents (a.k.a. bots), there is a growing service on the Internet of shopping agents that will scour Web sites to find products and services on behalf of users. Check out these shopping agents: MySimon.com, Roboshopper.com, CNET Shopper (www.shopper.com), and Lycos Shop (shop.lycos.com).

Smart cards. Imagine carrying one smart card for all of those cards bulking up your wallet—ATM card, credit cards, phone cards, library card, driver's license, and so forth. It might seem scary, but it could also be extremely convenient to carry your personal information on a single card.

Wearable personal computers. The Massachusetts Institute of Technology's Media Lab is creating wearable computers. Imagine reading your e-mail while you are strolling down the street or in the cab on your way to the airport. MIT has been doing research on creating wearable computers and integrating computing within clothing. Wearable computers contain batteries, digital cellular modem and Internet access, and the Twiddler, which is a one-handed keyboard and mouse. *Wearables* can store information such as phone numbers and notes and allow real-time messaging (www.media.mit.edu/projects/wearables/).

In a simple sense, this one-to-one service is enabled by technology—databases and specialized manufacturing or delivery systems. The magic comes with the imagination of the marketer and customer service experts. We are very excited to see this kind of personalization come to the Web and be facilitated by the Web. When contemplating your one-to-one strategy, think of these words from David Packard, cofounder of Hewlett-Packard:

> The first principle of management is that the driving force for the development of new products is not technology, not money, but the imagination of people.

The Internet has been an exciting phenomenon to watch and experience so far, and it has an exciting future. We hope that you have found our book to be a useful one-to-one Web marketing tool. Please come visit our Web site, *One-to-One Web Marketing Online*, at www.1to1web.com, to see the Web marketing discipline evolve. We wish you success in your Web marketing efforts. Good luck!

WEB SITE **Visit www.1to1web.com for additional information and resources.**

Index

D

J

K

L

O

P

W

X

Y

CUSTOMER NOTE: IF THIS BOOK IS ACCOMPANIED BY SOFTWARE, PLEASE READ THE FOLLOWING BEFORE OPENING THE PACKAGE.

To use this CD-ROM, your system must meet the following requirements:

Platform/Processor/Operating System. PC, Macintosh, Unix/Linux computers with software that can read files created in Microsoft Word, Microsoft Excel, and Adobe Acrobat from a CD-ROM.

RAM. Sufficient RAM to run programs that can read files created in Microsoft Word, Microsoft Excel, and Adobe Acrobat.

Peripherals. CD-ROM reader.